Ontario

Task Force on Access to
Professions and Trades
in Ontario

Groupe d'étude sur l'accès aux
professions et aux métiers en
Ontario

180 Dundas Street West
22nd Floor
Toronto, Ontario
M5G 1Z8

22ᵉ étage
180, rue Dundas ouest
Toronto (Ontario)
M5G 1Z8

416 965-0561

October 1989

The Honourable Bob Wong
Minister of Citizenship
and Minister Responsible for Race
Relations, Multiculturalism
and the Human Rights Commission
77 Bloor Street West
5th Floor
Toronto, Ontario
M7A 2R9

Dear Minister:

We are very pleased to submit to you the Report of the
Task Force on Access to Professions and Trades in
Ontario.

We are confident that our research efforts and
recommendations will be useful to the Province in
addressing the issues set forth in our terms of
reference.

Yours sincerely,

Peter A. Cumming
Chair

Enid L.D. Lee
Commissioner

Dimitrios G. Oreopoulos
Commissioner

TASK FORCE ON ACCESS TO PROFESSIONS AND TRADES IN ONTARIO

Ontario

Peter A. Cumming
CHAIR

Enid L. D. Lee
Commissioner

Dimitrios G. Oreopoulos
Commissioner

1989

Published by
Ontario Ministry of Citizenship

© Queen's Printer for Ontario, 1989

ISBN 0-7729-6120-4

Additional copies of this and other
Ontario Government Publications
are available from:

Publications Ontario, 880 Bay Street, Toronto, Ontario, for personal
shopping. Out-of-town customers write to: Publications Ontario, 5th floor,
880 Bay Street, Toronto, Ontario, M7A 1N8. Telephone (416) 326-5300 or
toll free in Ontario, 1-800-668-9938. Hearing impaired call: (416) 965-5130
or toll free in Ontario, 1-800-268-7095. Master Card and Visa accepted.
Cheques and money orders payable to the Treasurer of Ontario. Prepayment
required.

CONTENTS

APPENDICES *369*

Executive Summary and Recommendations

Executive Summary

As the Terms of Reference indicate, this Task Force was charged with reviewing ''all rules and practices affecting entry to professions and trades to determine whether they have an actual or potential discriminatory effect on persons with training or experience from outside of Canada.'' With this mandate in mind, the Task Force undertook a detailed review of the organizational structures of regulated occupations in Ontario, with a view to determining not only if such structures are giving rise to discriminatory practices but also whether they have the potential to do so, depending upon their use and application. We also selected for review a small number of unregulated occupational groups.

The Task Force contacted, and in most cases met with, representatives of the governing bodies of the occupational groups to be reviewed, as well as with representatives from related voluntary associations and educational institutions. We also heard from and met with community groups, individuals who had had contact with the occupational bodies, representatives of various government departments, and educators and others interested in our subject.

Regulated occupations include those regulated under public statute, such as law, medicine, and engineering; those regulated under private statute, such as chartered accountancy; those regulated directly by government, such as real estate brokerage, and the trades as a whole, which come under the aegis of the Ministry of Skills Development.

The regulatory format determines the degree of public accountability within the occupational body, from minimal to significant. The range extends from private regulatory structures and purely voluntary groups functioning essentially independently of government-imposed structural and procedural controls through to regimes of government licensure and public regulation in which there is substantial accountability. Although only those groups that are publicly regulated, either through a self-regulatory body or a government licensure regime, have the power to grant licences (exclusive entitlements to practise the profession or trade), privately regulated as well as unregulated bodies have the authority to certify their members. This authority involves granting those who meet standards for membership a credential that may have significant value in employment, in some cases a value almost as great as licensure itself. Because concerns relating to these unregulated groups and concerns over this phenomenon of "credentialism" or "reserved titles" were raised repeatedly, we concluded that such bodies should be brought within the scope of our review and our general recommendations.

The primary obligation of occupational bodies, whether they have the authority to grant licences or merely perform the function of certifying practitioners as competent, is to protect the public interest with respect to health, safety, and welfare. In fulfilling this first obligation, however, these bodies must consider a second one: the duty to respect the individual's right to equality of opportunity and to equal treatment without unreasonable or unfair discrimination. These two interests should be complementary, not competing, but the fact is, as our study discloses, fixing a balance between them is a difficult task.

The assessment of competence is a multifaceted process, and the sometimes divergent interests must be reconciled at each step, from a person's first inquiry about a certification procedure to the last stage of any available appeal process. In the course of our study we attempted to identify the points in the process at which conflicts occur and inequities can result. We call these points "barriers to entry," but they also become the pathways to our proposed solutions.

THE BARRIERS

Prior Learning Assessment

Difficulty obtaining an accurate, consistent assessment of prior learning for purposes of certification or licensure is the problem cited most frequently by foreign-trained people, community organizations, and ethno-cultural associations submitting briefs to the Task Force. Our review of the certifying bodies, meanwhile, led us to agree that there is cause for concern that the prior learning of foreign-trained applicants is not always being adequately and fairly assessed.

The purpose of an assessment of prior learning is to determine the equivalency of an individual's qualifications or competencies to educational requirements in Ontario. It is typically used as a preliminary screen to determine who should be permitted to write a licensing examination, if there is one. Although some prior learning assessment is currently being performed in Ontario by occupational bodies, we found, in many cases, significant weaknesses in the methods of assessing the background of the applicants. Sometimes no credit at all is given for training outside an accredited program. Some occupational bodies rely heavily on the personal information provided by the registrar and on other informal sources. Even where a structure for assessment does exist, the information-gathering often tends to be unsystematic and the standards imposed subjective and ad hoc. In addition, there is, with some exceptions, a general reluctance to give credit for any learning obtained outside a formal program of education, no matter how relevant and well documented that learning may be.

The reasons behind the failure of many occupational bodies to make appropriate assessments of prior learning do not necessarily reflect an intent to discriminate. However, considerable expertise in comparative education, significant physical resource materials, and a familiarity and ongoing contact with international educational systems are all necessary to validate documents properly and make an accurate assessment of an individual's prior training. Inadequacies in each of these areas is frequently cited by licensing bodies as their reason for not evaluating prior learning either at all or in anything more than a cursory manner. The reality is that, from a situation some 20 years ago in which immigration patterns to Ontario were relatively consistent and predictable and therefore easier to respond to, occupational bodies now find themselves confronted with the task of assessing the background of candidates from a far broader and more diverse selection of countries, with little in the way of resources or facilities to assist them. Some professions or trades may have only one or two applicants from a particular country in a five-year period; furthermore, the licensing bodies cannot predict the countries from which applicants will arrive and therefore must, in some cases, act in response to a specific situation. All of these obstacles make it difficult to have a coherent approach.

Our concern here not only is that the assessment procedures in some professions are showing evidence of unfair or unequal treatment of some candidates; it is also that current procedures have the potential to be applied in a way that results in unfair or unequal treatment — and that is the broader issue. Much appears to depend upon the personal information received by the assessors, upon the inclinations of the assessors, and upon the human resources needs of the occupation. These factors can, and do, change. The standard of competence required for entry, however, should not.

The failure to assess prior learning appropriately can virtually negate an individual's previous accomplishments and can result in the individual's having to repeat an entire training program or, at best, to complete partial retraining in Ontario. Additional examinations, required only of foreign-trained individuals, are another common response to a lack of mechanisms for assessing prior learning. The result can be not only frustration for the applicant but a waste of resources. The outcome in some cases is the complete loss of the skills that the individual brought to Canada.

It also became clear from submissions to the Task Force and from meetings with individuals that candidates find this early stage of the process most confusing. Initial inquiries can result in a simple rejection on the basis of the applicant's inadequate training. In the absence of objective criteria against which the candidate can compare and assess his or her training needs, coupled with the general lack of appropriate counselling or guidance, it is difficult for the candidate to know whether the assessment is fair and how best to proceed.

Licensure Testing

Where a foreign-trained candidate is required to write some tests in addition to those required of an Ontario-trained candidate, the process can be very demanding and very expensive. It may be possible, in rare cases, to justify these additional requirements on the grounds that, in the absence of other means of assessing skill, they are needed to ensure competence. Such a defence, however, to a large extent hinges on the current identified lack of a systematic approach to the assessment of prior learning.

Where the same examinations are required of all candidates, these tests in many cases have not been subjected to objective test development and analysis procedures reflecting recognized professional standards. Such procedures ensure that the tests are culturally sensitive and administratively fair, that the standard set reflects the required level of competence, and that the level of fluency needed for the examination is appropriate to the occupation.

Language Training

Acquiring a new language is one of the greatest problems facing a foreign-trained individual who arrives in Ontario without speaking English or French. Some level of fluency is required for certification or licensure in most professions and trades, and a significant level is needed in a number of occupations. Yet, although this skill is essential for integration into the workplace, and although there are available numerous programs, it appears that language training is not meeting the need. Among the common problems conveyed to the Task Force were the long delays in gaining admission to programs; the shortage of training allowances and support; the emphasis on training in general fluency rather than on occupation-specific proficiency development; and the difficulty that some categories of immigrants have qualifying for language training.

Language Testing

In many occupations language is not specifically tested at all, because the occupational bodies assume that the licensure or certification examination will function as an adequate language screen. There is, however, often little evidence that such language screens have been scrutinized to ensure, first, that the level of proficiency required reflects the level appropriate to the occupation, and, second, that fluency in language essential to practise is being adequately assessed. The main problem is that very few occupations formally assess language, either English or French, by means of a test designed to determine the level of linguistic proficiency as it applies to the particular occupation. Several occupations rely exclusively on the Test of English as a Foreign Language (TOEFL), the Test of Spoken English (TSE), or the Michigan Test Battery (MTB) in spite of the fact that such standardized tests are weak predictors of performance and do not test occupation-specific language.

Retraining

In the many cases in which a comprehensive assessment of prior learning, based on both academic background and previous experience, is not available to candidates, retraining needs are often not clearly identified. The result of this weakness in the system can be a training requirement that is more onerous than necessary. The scarcity of programs and facilities for retraining is also a significant problem.

Review of Decisions

Mechanisms for reviewing an occupational body's decision to refuse a licence or certificate or to attach conditions or limitations to it are, in some occupations, altogether lacking or severely limited. Some occupations, notably the health professions, are subject to legislative provisions establishing an independent tribunal to review registration decisions. Some provide for an internal review with or without a statutory appeal to the courts. Others have no intermediate appeal mechanism and may or may not provide for an appeal to the courts. The scope of the appeal also varies; for one group of professions, for example, questions of academic and experiential equivalency are expressly excluded.

In addition, a review of complaints lodged with the Human Rights Commission and based on discrimination related to place of training reveals a record of consistent failure for claimants. The primary reason for their lack of success does not appear to be related to the inability of complainants to make a case of discriminatory practice; rather, it appears related to the assertion by the occupational bodies of a defence that involves, and indeed capitalizes on, the fact that a systematic and reliable means to assess prior learning is not available.

THE PROPOSED SOLUTIONS

Prior Learning Assessment

As this summary indicates, the fundamental problem facing occupational bodies and foreign-trained candidates alike is the necessity of determining, fairly and accurately, what the candidate knows. Yet, making that seemingly simple determination is far from straightforward; indeed, to state the need in such simple terms is to trivialize it.

The Task Force is certain that both real and perceived access to professions and trades in Ontario can be improved through the creation of a mechanism specifically designed to assess the prior learning of people seeking to apply for entry to those occupations. Such a mechanism could consolidate and systematize current Ontario-based assessments of the level and type of learning completed by foreign-trained individuals to determine whether or not their education is equivalent to that required of Ontario-trained individuals. This mechanism could capitalize on other Canadian, U.S., and British experience to improve significantly the current provisions in Ontario for assessment of what an individual has learned both formally and through experience. Current developments in the European Community offer other models of leadership in this area.

We support the principle that occupational associations bear the ultimate responsibility of ensuring the competence of members for the protection of the public. For this reason, we take the position that the preparation and administration of all licensure examinations should remain under the control of the appropriate occupational associations and that these bodies should direct the development and/or articulation of a prescribed standard of performance for competence against which all candidates must be measured. We are also of the view that, as a general rule, clinical assessments are best conducted by the relevant occupational association.

Our research shows, however, as the discussion above discloses, that the initial screening of applicants — the assessment of equivalency — is the stage in the process that is least standardized, most difficult, and most open to abuse. Although we recognize that some prior learning assessment is already being carried out by educational institutions and occupational certification agencies, we believe that people throughout Ontario should have access to a more systematic mechanism for assessing their training. This mechanism should consider not only formal education — courses, degrees, diplomas, and certificates — but also knowledge gained through experiential learning. Such experiential learning would be subject to close scrutiny and would need to meet the same criteria as academic learning: it must be relevant and well documented; it must meet the same standard of competence required of Ontario-trained candidates as specified by the occupational bodies and/or relevant educational institutions; and it must assess what the candidate has learned and not merely represent the duration or contents of the experience.

A "PLAN" for Access

Our proposal is the creation of a Prior Learning Assessment Network (PLAN), to be an independent agency operating under the aegis of one or more ministries.

Equipped with the necessary physical resources, linked into the international network of comparative education information, staffed by specialists in comparative education and assessment, and assisted and instructed by advisory bodies representing the various occupations and ethnocultural groups, this agency would be in a position to provide detailed, accurate assessments of the prior learning of individuals for use in their applications for certification or licensure to occupational organizations. If the candidates were considered to have training equivalent to the Ontario standard, such assessments would entitle them to attempt any licensure or certification examination that the occupational body requires for admission. If the candidates' training were assessed as less than equivalent, the comprehensive nature of the assessments would enable them to determine precisely the retraining required.

Beneficiaries of such a scheme would of course include the occupational bodies themselves, who would be relieved of the expense and difficulty of assessing each individual applicant in a way that not only is but must appear even-handed. At the same time, through the mechanism of occupational advisory committees operating through PLAN, through the articulation of standards, and through the administration of licensure examinations, the relevant occupational bodies would retain control over the standards of competence required of each entering practitioner. The relationship between PLAN and each occupational group would be a close one, formalized through the advisory committees, with a significant transfer of information and expertise going on in both directions. Furthermore, PLAN would have the option, at the agency's discretion and subject to revocation if necessary, of delegating some or all of the assessment procedures to an occupational body.

Educational institutions would also be served by such a mechanism. Although most universities and colleges, as well as the Ministry of Education, already have some means for assessing prior education of applicants from countries having high and sustained rates of immigration to Canada, many institutions appear to have no means for systematically assessing prior experiential learning and little capacity for assessing the educational credentials of individuals who may lack complete documentation or have arrived from countries having low or irregular rates of immigration to Canada.

Individuals would benefit, particularly those who wish to apply for certification or licensure in an occupation and need to have their prior learning assessed. We believe that those who currently are the most poorly served are people entering Canada with insufficient formal documentation, people who have left countries with relatively low rates of immigration to Canada, or who come from Third World or eastern bloc countries with only recent significant rates of immigration to Canada, and people who have relevant and useful competencies that were gained through experience rather than formal education.

Although these are our principal target groups, we are confident that the value of our recommendations will extend beyond them. People entering the marketplace directly would also benefit, as would their employers. Also benefiting would be people wishing to re-enter the workplace after an absence, a situation in which women often find themselves. The potential for discrimination in employment is likely to be significantly reduced as employers, presented with comprehensive and credible assessments, would no longer feel compelled or entitled to reject candidates with foreign or otherwise unfamiliar training or experience simply because their level of training could not be determined.

The structure of this mechanism should derive from several principles that underpin other successful prior learning assessment systems. Not only must this mechanism be expert in assessment and in the training of assessors so that its work be valid and reliable, it must also be systematic if it is to be perceived to adhere to high standards.

The following characteristics, which are essential to the success of such a network, are evident in the model we propose:

- It is public.
- It is accessible.
- It is comprehensive in its assessment strategies.
- It is credible to those who use its services — educators, certifying bodies, employers, and individuals.
- It minimizes cost.

We are confident that the specialization and economies of scale inherent in the prior learning assessment mechanism will mean greater overall efficiency than exists at present. The cost of such a system need not be substantial. A review of comparable models discloses that limited staffing should be adequate, and the physical facilities and purchase of other resources need not be expansive. The cost benefits to be gained have the potential, meanwhile, to be substantial. Some examples of such benefits include:

- the elimination or coordination of the now frequently duplicated effort evident among the occupational bodies themselves, the educational institutions, and assessment programs that currently offer limited services;

- the efficient gathering of information and the speedier re-integration of skilled individuals into the workplace;

- the accurate allocation of limited retraining resources to the candidates who require them and in response to their more precisely identified needs; and

- the enhanced mobility among related occupations for optimal use of human resources.

Although the primary function of PLAN is to be the assessment of prior learning, we also anticipate it will play a significant role in the validation of documents, in the dispersal of information, in counselling, and in directing candidates to appropriate retraining — functions closely linked to the assessment process itself, but currently not always conducted in a systematic manner.

Language Testing and Licensure Testing

Although licensure tests and language assessments should remain entirely within the professional bodies themselves, our review of practices currently in place has led us to conclude that the introduction of some new procedures would benefit both the occupational bodies and the applicants themselves.

First, we are of the view that the same licensure examinations should be required of all candidates qualified to write them. An exception to this procedure might be made upon the presentation of a careful case setting out the particular equivalency that cannot be assessed by means other than an additional examination. It would also be necessary to demonstrate that it would be inappropriate to impose such an additional examination on domestically trained candidates. Availability of comprehensive assessments of prior learning should minimize the need for requiring additional examinations of foreign-trained candidates and, correspondingly, limit the grounds available to justify them. This procedure should be monitored and published through PLAN.

Second, to the extent this practice is not being followed, we are of the view that procedures of licensure test development should be more standardized. The occupational body administering an examination as a prerequisite to licensure or certification should be obligated to demonstrate that the test has been developed and analyzed according to recognized professional standards. Such an analysis would ensure, to the extent possible, that the standard on any examination is fair, that its format and administration are appropriate, that the level of fluency required on it is appropriate to the occupation, and that the examination is culturally appropriate. PLAN would play a role in the publication of such standards and would also be available to provide advice and referrals.

Third, although most occupational bodies rely on their licensure examination for language proficiency screening, this use is appropriate only if the examination has been scrutinized to ensure that the level of language proficiency required corresponds with that necessary to perform competently in that occupation, and that occupation-specific language is tested. Ideally, a specific language test would assess such proficiencies, and we are of the view that the use of such tests should be expanded, although licensure examinations that have been developed according to the procedure outlined above should be acceptable. The use of standardized tests, such as the TOEFL, TSE, and MTB, should be phased out where they are relied upon as prerequisites to occupational licensure or certification.

Language Training and Occupational Retraining

Although some language training and occupational retraining are available through the numerous programs operating throughout the province, reductions in federal funding, as well as limited facilities and questionable eligibility criteria, mean that the training is not available to all who need it. Our recommendations, although respecting these realities, reflect a conviction that these services are essential to the integration of foreign-trained individuals into the workforce, with the result that their lack of availability itself carries a large cost to Ontario society. The use of more flexible, focused, and innovative delivery systems coupled with the recognition that learning can be acquired in more than one context is among the methods we suggest for dealing with these difficulties. In addition, we support the targeting, in appropriate cases, of retraining facilities to candidates representing ethno-cultural groups that are in particular need of services. With respect to language training specifically, we identify a need for programs geared to occupational qualifications and including occupation-specific language at an appropriate level.

Review of Decisions

It is essential that candidates know the grounds upon which they are to be refused licensure or certification, that they have an opportunity to make the case against a refusal at an early stage in the process, and that they have a statutory right to obtain a review of a negative decision. Such a responsive appeal structure should be available to candidates in all occupational groups.

Rights under the *Human Rights Code, 1981*, for individuals who encounter discrimination on the basis of their place of education or training, must also be clarified, and claims must be facilitated. The objective, however, is not to bring people to courts and tribunals but to minimize the need for such remedies: to build bridges over the barriers. In our view, the creation of an independent agency to coordinate and oversee the most difficult and contentious aspects of licensure and certification will accomplish that most desirable end.

A Structural Solution

Although the barriers to entry that we encountered in our study do not apply universally to all occupations in Ontario, it is fair to say that they apply generally. There are occupations in which detailed and comprehensive assessments of prior learning are being undertaken; there are occupations that are currently taking steps through formal test development and validation to ensure that their licensure or certification examinations reflect recognized standards of fairness; and there are a number of occupations in which are reflected adequate and comprehensive appeal rights. There are, however, few occupations in which it can be said that none of the barriers we have identified is operating.

It is in the light of this widespread and generalized evidence of practices which are discriminatory, albeit unintentionally, that we propose a broad structural solution rather than a patchwork of lesser remedies to meet individual problems. The number of applicants with foreign training is in some occupations very large, in others quite small. Yet the need of the latter group for direction in the assessment of such candidates is also clear; indeed, because it lacks the opportunity to develop any expertise in such assessment, this group stands to benefit significantly. The solution also recognizes, we suggest, the changing demographics of modern times, in which mobility both among jurisdictions and among occupations is on the rise. Programs being introduced in the European Community and bordering states, for example, will result in greatly enhanced freedom of movement between jurisdictions. The changes we propose have the potential for bringing Ontario into an ever-increasing network of jurisdictions throughout the world in which this demographic reality, rather than being denied or discouraged, is enjoyed to full advantage and for the benefit of all.

It is essential, however, that the introduction of the institution should be seen as evolutionary rather than revolutionary: it will take time for occupational groups and individuals to adapt to its presence and accept as credible its decisions. Although we have formally suggested a phase-in period of three years before full operation, in some cases, for some functions, even that may not be enough. Ideally the idea and institution should grow, with the cooperation and support of the populations they are meant to serve; too early or too rigid an imposition of the scheme is more likely to hinder than help the process.

RECOMMENDATIONS

Chapter 3 — Issues Facing the Trades

We have examined the certification and licensure process and the training program in the Ontario apprenticeship system from several perspectives: historical development; legislative and regulatory basis, and the congruence between legislation and practice; accessibility of the system to foreign-trained tradespeople; and ways in which the system compares with other training and qualification models.

Our principal recommendation is for a fundamental restructuring of the way in which the Province of Ontario delivers training and certifies competence in the trades. We recommend conversion to a competency-based, modular training system that makes significant provision for portability of training and that ties licensure to public health and safety requirements. We recognize that similar recommendations have been made by previous commissions and consultants. Having examined the system from the point of view of the foreign-trained tradesperson seeking entry, we urge the Government of Ontario to address the fundamental problems of the apprenticeship system through implementation of structural changes.

We believe that our recommendations are in step with the important innovations being introduced in other jurisdictions. We also believe that our conclusions are supported by the work to date of the Premier's Council (1988), which establishes the need for a comprehensive review of the "various shortcomings" of the apprenticeship system. We are confident that the structural changes proposed for the apprenticeship system will increase accessibility and fairness for both foreign- and domestically trained tradespeople. Further, the impact on Ontario's economic competitive position will be positive, producing a more responsive and dynamic training system and speeding the entry of skilled foreign-trained people into the workforce.

Although our principal recommendations would involve a basic restructuring of the apprenticeship system in Ontario, a number of our subsidiary recommendations can be implemented immediately while the Government designs a blueprint for large-scale change. We believe that decisive action on such matters as improved access to information and the development of guidelines for the assessment of prior training — essential elements of any restructured system — will enhance the system that currently exists.

    3.1   *We recommend that licensing as a prerequisite to practice be limited to those trades that require such a restriction in the interests of public health and safety. Licensure requirements have to date been applied with little reference to health and safety requirements and in some cases may also constitute an undue restriction on access to employment in the trades for both foreign- and domestically trained tradespeople. An analysis of public health and safety requirements should identify areas of trades practice where licensure is appropriate. Certification of skill should of course remain an integral part of the training system in the trades.*

    3.2   *We recommend the introduction of greater flexibility into the current training system. Accordingly, we recommend a basic change in the structure of apprenticeship training from a time-*

based system to a modular, competency-based training system, and the development of a variety of more accessible delivery models. Such models would include cooperative programs and programs with the in-school portion of training delivered at the outset without a requirement that the trainee obtain employment prior to commencing training. New program development in the trades during the last several years has used a competency-based format, so that movement to a purely competency-based apprentice training system should be technically straightforward. The term "modular" is used throughout this report to refer to training programs with content organized into sets of skills to be mastered progressively.

3.3   *We recommend that training programs for the trades include modules of core competencies that may be learned for credit in more than one trade, as applicable. Core competencies, which we regard as those used in the work performance of more than one trade and transferable from one trade to another, include:*

- *academic competencies, such as communication, arithmetic operations, and science and technology concepts;*

- *reasoning competencies, such as planning and problem solving;*

- *interpersonal competencies, such as teamwork and leadership; and*

- *manipulative competencies, such as careful and safe behaviour (lifting, carrying, storing materials) and hand-eye coordination.*

3.4   *We recommend that the Ministry of Skills Development package informational materials about apprenticeship training, certification, and licensure in a wide variety of formats, to be available in various governmental offices and community resource centres. The information that should be made accessible through one or more formats includes:*

- *a brief description of training programs in the regulated trades, including prerequisites, the duration of apprenticeship and in-school training, and the competencies to be acquired;*

- *an outline of particular certification and licensure procedures applicable to foreign-trained applicants and others with prior experience or training;*

- *referral information, including a directory of offices from which additional information and assistance can be obtained.*

3.5   *We recommend that, in addition to extensive written materials in pamphlet and booklet form, a computer-based information system be established with a more comprehensive, detailed level of information about certification procedures and training opportunities. Further, the trades-training telephone hotline service should be expanded with summary and referral information available on tapes and through live interaction. We also recommend that the Ministry make use of multicultural television broadcasting and multicultural newspapers to deliver information on its training programs to the multicultural community.*

3.6   *We recommend that the Ministry of Skills Development provide written and telephone information in appropriate languages, in addition to English and French. A translation request form should be available if a member of the public seeks information in a language for which it is not available.*

3.7   *We recommend that our proposed Prior Learning Assessment Network (PLAN) be given responsibility to ensure that a systematic process for the assessment of vocational competencies and academic attainment is established and maintained in Ontario. We further recommend that this task be carried out in conjunction with the Ministry of Skills Development and with input from the major stakeholders, and that it include:*

- *the creation of a shared information base on trade certification and licensure processes and on apprenticeship training programs in other jurisdictions for use in the assessment of the credentials of foreign-trained tradespeople;*

- *the development of a readily accessible central registry of assessment decisions in Ontario to provide a public record of precedents and to facilitate consistency of assessments from assessor to assessor;*

- *the development of publicly accessible guidelines to circumscribe the discretionary power of the industrial training consultants and delineate assessment criteria, and the development of a set of procedural rights afforded the applicant. For example, guidelines should require that the applicant be informed of the availability of demonstration of skills tests and of his or her right to appeal the assessment decision or to pursue a remedy before the Human Rights Commission;*

- *the assessment by the Prior Learning Assessment Network (PLAN) of the academic equivalency of foreign-trained tradespeople, with no age restriction or requirement of having been out of school for a given time, and the replacement of the Progressive Achievement Test with other, more appropriate, assessment means; and*

- *the development and maintenance of standards of validity, reliability, fairness, and cultural sensitivity for demonstration of skills tests, licensure and certification examinations, and other assessments of competencies in the trades.*

3.8   *We recommend that Ministry decisions in relation to the assessment of prior training and experience be considered to be binding on the employer. When a foreign-trained individual enters the apprenticeship system with advanced standing, the employer will no longer be permitted to downgrade training and experience below the level suggested by the industrial training consultant. The Task Force recommendations on amendments to the* Human Rights Code *provide, in effect, that in cases in which an employer refuses to accept an assessment by the Ministry, the applicant apprentice would have a remedy before the Human Rights Commission.*

3.9   *We recommend that the Government amend the* Apprenticeship and Tradesmen's Qualification Act *to provide that an applicant for a certificate of qualification and an entrant to the apprenticeship training system be granted a right to appeal registration decisions. An applicant seeking recognition of non-Ontario training and experience should be able to appeal negative decisions to a provincial apprenticeship board that includes members of the public who are not tradespeople. In addition, a right of appeal in respect of the assessment of prior training experience should lie to the appeal body to be established as part of our proposed Prior Learning Assessment Network.*

3.10   *We recommend that practical tests which permit applicants to demonstrate their acquired skills be developed in all regulated trades. We recommend that the written instructions for these tests be available in a wide variety of languages. Requests by candidates for translation should be recorded provincewide and a threshold number set by the Ministry, whereupon a translation would be provided.*

3.11   *We recommend that the Ministry develop skills training programs which recognize both the need for and the needs of foreign-trained tradespeople. Industrial training consultants should be given responsibility to make appropriate training referrals when the results of an assessment or demonstration of skills test indicate that additional training is required.*

3.12   *Specifically, as an initial measure, we recommend the expansion of the admissions criteria of two Ministry of Skills Development training programs to facilitate the entry of foreign-trained tradespeople: the Transitions Program, and the Trades Updating Program. (Transitions provides up to $5,000 of work-related training credits to older permanently laid-off workers. Trades Updating provides qualified tradespeople with access to full- and part-time courses to update their skills.) An alternative approach would be to develop parallel programs for foreign-trained tradespeople who require limited retraining to become fully qualified in Ontario. As discussed in Chapter 9 ("Retraining"), it will be less of a public expense to provide retraining programs than to require the completion of a full training program.*

3.13   *We recommend that the Government identify clearly those elements of trade practice which, for reasons of public health* and safety, require a working proficiency in English or French, and that the Government introduce the use of a valid and reliable test of language proficiency referenced to this requirement. Although we support the current provision for the use of an interpreter in certificate of qualification examinations, we believe it essential that in a trade with a public health and safety impact, the language proficiency of a licensed or certified journeyman be at a level that ensures public safety.

3.14   We recommend that a federally funded and provincially administered apprenticeship training allowance program be established to provide income support at increased levels and be administratively designed to fit the particularities of the apprenticeship program. We also recommend that a program of loans for retraining purposes be established.

3.15   We recommend that the Government allocate funding to establish a computer-based data collection system capable of creating a sufficient statistical base to allow both the monitoring of the operation of the apprenticeship system and the development of a labour-planning function within the Ministry. With respect to the questions under consideration by the Task Force, it is important that the following kinds of information be available to the Government:

  • annual number of applications for recognition of foreign training and experience, broken down by country of training;

  • annual number of foreign-trained candidates writing the certificate of qualification examination, broken down by country of training, and applicable success rates;

  • annual number of provisional certificates issued and renewed, broken down by country of training;

  • annual number of demonstration of skills tests undertaken, broken down by country of training, and applicable success rates.

3.16   We recommend that all employers of apprentices registered under the ATQA be required to sign an undertaking that all hiring will be in accordance with Government-established *employment-equity principles, and that recruitment advertising will so specify.*

Chapter 4 — Issues Facing the Professions

4.1   *We recommend that professional bodies may, if they wish, retain the right to waive any requirements for licensure and certification, subject to the requirement that, in all cases, the instance of the exercise of the discretion and the grounds therefor shall be part of the public record and be made available to any interested parties through the information dispersal mechanism of the Prior Learning Assessment Network.*

4.2   *We recommend that occupational associations which are not publicly regulated and which grant reserved titles, membership, or other credentials to practitioners considered to meet specified criteria, be specifically named and included in the ambit of legislative provisions creating and implementing the Prior Learning Assessment Network; and that these associations be bound by such provisions to the same extent as regulated occupational bodies.*

4.3   *We recommend that all occupational bodies be required to maintain detailed records of all applications and inquiries, such records to include the place of training of candidates, information required of and provided by them, information provided to them, and the disposition of the inquiry or application.*

Chapter 5 — Prior Learning Assessment

Our focus is on assessment of prior foreign education and experiential learning, but the benefit of our recommendations will accrue to all residents of Ontario.

5.1   *We recommend that the Government of Ontario make provision for the systematic assessment of the prior education and experiential learning of individuals through the creation of the Prior Learning Assessment Network (PLAN). Prior learning* assessment is the assessment of (1) education (secondary, postsecondary, and vocational training, including courses, certificates, diplomas, and degrees) and (2) experience that an individual has obtained. It includes assessment of what the individual has learned through structured education and training delivered by employers, associations, and trade unions, and through personal experience, on-the-job training, volunteer work, and independent study.

5.2   We recommend that, in order to ensure consistency and universality of access to its services, PLAN be publicly funded and accountable to a ministry of Government within a framework of provincial legislation and regulations. Legislative implementation should include amendments to the governing Act and/or regulations of all privately and publicly regulated occupations. These amendments should specify that candidates are entitled to equivalency assessments, that they shall be provided with a report of the results of such assessments, and that they shall be entitled to apply for licensure of certification if the report shows equivalency to Ontario standards, provided all other criteria for entry are met, including satisfaction of any examination or work experience requirements. Legislated training requirements should be amended, where necessary, to eliminate references both to formal training in any particular program or discipline and to requirements specifying registration in another jurisdiction. With regard to unregulated occupations, we recommend that the legislation creating and implementing PLAN specifically name and include within the ambit of its provisions any occupational body that grants credentials or "reserved titles" to qualified individuals.

5.3   We recommend that, in designing, implementing, and maintaining PLAN, the Government establish a board of directors to direct the design and ongoing operations of PLAN, with representation from educational institutions, bodies that administer occupational certification and licensure, ethno-cultural groups, and individuals seeking access to occupations or postsecondary education.

5.4   We recommend that the Government allocate funding to enable PLAN (1) to assess prior education to determine its equivalency to formal education in Ontario, and (2) to assess prior *experiential learning that was not previously attested to by a formal educational institution, to determine its equivalency to formal education in Ontario. To these ends, we recommend that PLAN develop:*

- *an advisory infrastructure, made up of occupation-specific occupational advisory committees, for the purpose of ensuring that individual occupations be involved directly in the articulation of standards of competence and the designation of the equivalency of prior education and experience.*

- *staff expertise in research and comparative education, for the purposes of authenticating documents; identifying and validating the content, duration, and required level of mastery of Canadian and foreign education and training programs; and creating a reliable information base that includes descriptions of these programs and a record of equivalency decisions rendered by PLAN.*

- *staff expertise in curriculum development and evaluation, for the purposes of identification and assessment of the objectives of structured education and training programs provided outside of formal educational institutions.*

- *staff expertise in the construction and validation of examinations of theoretical and applied knowledge, including expertise in (1) the subject matter of the examination, (2) the actual design and validation of examinations, and (3) the identification and elimination of ethno-cultural bias in assessments, all for the purposes of developing, administering, and building a bank of assessment instruments and procedures.*

- *staff expertise in the preparation and assessment of portfolios of prior learning, for the purposes of (1) training those who help applicants design and complete their portfolio, (2) training subject specialists who assess the portfolios for credit purposes, and (3) training and advising administrators and decision makers in the client groups in order that their commitment to prior learning assessment be well-informed and ongoing.*

- *translation services that are available to clients as required, with free translation service to newcomers to Ontario during the first two years of their permanent residence in Canada.*

5.5   *We recommend that there be a three-year phase-in period for PLAN, during which period assessments by PLAN of the equivalency of an individual's prior education and experience to Ontario standards not be binding on occupational certification and licensure bodies. We recommend that all assessments conducted by PLAN after this three-year phase-in period be binding, subject to the appeal procedure set out in Recommendation 5.11. In this regard, we recommend that PLAN be responsible for assessing whether or not individuals have the training prerequisites to apply for licensure or certification, and that the actual licensure or certification processes, particularly those relating to examinations and work experience requirements, continue to be the responsibility of occupational licensure and certification bodies.*

5.6   *We recommend that PLAN have the authority to delegate responsibility for prior learning assessment to individual occupations; to monitor the quality of those assessments to ensure that they are carried out efficiently, fairly, and in the interests of public safety; and to rescind such delegation of responsibility for cause.*

5.7   *We recommend that PLAN launch a public education and promotion program about the nature of prior learning assessment and the services that PLAN offers. This program should be made available to Canadians, including newcomers to Canada, and — through Canadian government offices abroad — people seeking to immigrate to Canada.*

5.8   *We recommend that PLAN enter into an agreement with the Skills Bank of the Ontario Training Corporation for the inclusion in its data base of (1) summary information about certification and licensure processes for regulated professions and trades in Ontario, and (2) a description of PLAN's services and means of access to them.*

5.9   *We recommend that in those cases where the assessment of prior learning indicates that the individual does not fully meet the relevant Ontario standards, PLAN provide specific advice about the additional training required to achieve equivalency to Ontario standards, and that PLAN facilitate the provision of information and counselling by other agencies, regarding retraining programs in Ontario. On successful completion of such additional specified training, candidates may reapply to PLAN and will be given due credit for this training and a statement attesting to their equivalency.*

5.10 *We recommend that each assessment of prior learning be prepared by a PLAN staff member who has expertise in comparative education, and that the determination of equivalency be made by the staff member under the general advice of the relevant occupational advisory committee.*

5.11 *We recommend the provision of a right of appeal, to an individual or to an affected occupational body, of PLAN's assessment of an individual's academic equivalency. In this context we further recommend:*

- *that before any formal appeal, the appellant be encouraged to discuss the decision with the research staff member who carried out the assessment.*

- *that a formal appeal should be heard by a Decision Review Committee made up of a pool of eight or nine experts in the area of prior learning assessment, three of whom will be chosen to sit on each appeal. The committee could include university and college registrars, Canadian assessors from national and international bodies such as the AUCC and UNESCO, and faculty from schools of comparative education.*

- *that the Decision Review Committee have access to counsel to clarify legal and administrative procedural issues.*

- *that candidates be permitted to make written and oral submissions to the Decision Review Committee, that expert evidence be admitted, and that the committee have the power to reverse the assessment decision.*

5.12   *We recommend that, at the end of its three-year phase-in period, PLAN be assigned responsibility for affirming that standards of validity, reliability, and cultural sensitivity for certification and licensure examinations are adhered to by occupational licensure and certification bodies in their examination of applicants, and responsibility for publishing such standards. We further recommend that such bodies be required to obtain approval from PLAN for the introduction or continuation of any certification and licensure examination requirements that apply to foreign-trained as opposed to Ontario-trained individuals.*

5.13   *We recommend that the Government appropriate monies for the design, creation, and operation of PLAN at the beginning of the fiscal year that follows the tabling of this Report.*

Chapter 6 — Licensure Testing

A licensure test assesses the competency, knowledge, and proficiency of a candidate for licensure or certification based on standards established by the licensing body. The test must be able to differentiate between those candidates who have the competency required to practise the occupation without compromising the public's health, welfare, and safety, and those who do not.

Any licensure test offered by a professional body must meet required standards of fairness. In order to ensure that any such test is fair to candidates and measures consistently what it is intended to measure, the test developer should follow accepted standards of test development. The test developer must determine precisely what is "competence" for the occupation under consideration, not necessarily only according to what is taught in academic programs relating to the occupation but according to actual practices carried out within the occupation as reflected in identifiable competencies. The questions selected and the formats used should reflect this standard. The test developer must also bear in mind questions of language, cultural responses, and fair use and administration of the test, and the test must be responsive to candidates by being capable of providing them with the feedback they require to improve their skills. Clear guidelines for the use of the test and the setting of scores must be provided for test takers.

The development of a valid test requires specific expertise. In order to ensure that development of licensure tests in Ontario is in accordance with the general principles outlined and that the resulting tests are fair to all candidates:

6.1   *We recommend that licensure tests be developed according to recognized standards and methods of test development, including a consideration of what a licensed individual needs to know for practice, and taking into account the issues of language, culture, administrative fairness, and the availability of comprehensive information to the candidate on the standard being required and on his or her performance.*

6.2   *We recommend that all candidates for testing be directed to preparatory courses or be given detailed preparatory material.*

6.3   *We recommend that the policies and procedures of test development and administration, as they apply to any given occupation, be published and made available to any candidate or interested party, through PLAN.*

6.4   *We recommend that where so requested by the occupational organization, PLAN may provide assistance and referrals.*

The question of universality of testing is a difficult one. (See Chapter 13 of this Report for a discussion of the implications raised by the *Canadian Charter of Rights and Freedoms* as it applies to this issue.) The Task Force is of the view that it is desirable and preferable that, in any specific occupation, all candidates for licensure who have been assessed as qualified to attempt the licensure examination be required to write the same examination. In addition, we are of the view that with the benefit of comprehensive and objective equivalency assessments provided through PLAN, the need for additional assessments through examination will be greatly diminished. We accept the position, however, that in the view of some occupations additional clinical testing may be needed and that the high cost of some clinical and oral examinations may make it undesirable to examine every candidate for licensure; in addition, Ontario training programs in disciplines with a significant clinical component subject Ontario students to rigorous clinical examination that, in a licensure examination, may be duplicated. We have therefore concluded that it is inappropriate to rule out entirely any additional examination of foreign-trained candidates where it is not required of Ontario-trained candidates, provided development of the test is in keeping with the standards referred to in Recommendation 6.1. This practice, however, should be permitted only where the profession can demonstrate that all candidates are being examined on the same content and to the same standard, regardless of the specific examination being taken; that the examination is needed in order to make an assessment of competence that cannot be otherwise determined; that it would be inappropriate to require the examination of all candidates; and that the examination will not impose an unreasonable burden in terms of time or cost on the candidate.

> 6.5 *We recommend that every candidate for licensure be required on examination to master the same content and meet the same standard of competence, and that this be achieved by uniformly requiring all candidates to write the same licensure examination. Should an occupational body wish to require additional licensure examinations of foreign-trained candidates, it should advise PLAN, setting out evidence that the examination is essential to the assessment of competence; that the examination will test the same content at the same standard as for Ontario-trained candidates; that it is inappropriate to require the examination of Ontario-trained candidates; and that the examination will not impose an unreasonable burden in terms of cost or time on the candidates of whom it is required.*

Although we do not consider it appropriate or necessary to impose rigid requirements as to access both to examinations and to retries of examinations, it is essential that the professional bodies recognize the importance of these issues.

> 6.6. *We recommend that professional bodies make every effort to provide candidates with reasonable access to examinations, in terms of both time and location; and that all candidates who are not successful on an examination have the automatic right to at least one retry, with or without retraining.*

Chapter 7 — Language Testing

The Task Force is of the view that language assessment is valid and desirable as a means both of ensuring public safety and of providing assistance to foreign-trained individuals in determining the strengths and weaknesses of their language skills.

7.1 *We therefore recommend that a program of language assessment to an adequate level of competence be carried out by all occupational organizations where it is in the interests of public safety to do so.*

As with all testing, language assessments are acceptable only if they are demonstrably fair. We are concerned that the standardized tests currently being employed by some occupational bodies are deficient both because they are limited as measures of performance and because they are not being used in accordance with the guidelines provided.

7.2 *We therefore recommend that:*

- *The assessment of the fluency of candidates reflect the particular linguistic needs of the relevant occupational groups. This assessment should be made through the use of testing methods intended to test the level of fluency, technical language, and vocabulary relevant to those particular groups. Such tests should be developed with the assistance of language proficiency and testing experts and may take the form of structured interviews, essays, or written assessments. In the alternative or in addition, such language assessments may be conducted through the administration of licensure or certification tests, administered by the occupational body, provided those tests have been developed and validated according to recognized standards of test development and that they take into consideration the level of fluency and the particular linguistic demands appropriate to the occupation. The use of standardized tests such as the TOEFL, the TSE, and the MTB should be discontinued.*

- *The fixing of a required score by any body or organization using a fluency test must be justifiable as accurately reflecting the language proficiency necessary to carry out occupational duties without jeopardizing the health, safety, or welfare of the public.*

- *Interpretation of scores should be clearly specified to the test user and the test taker if the result of the test is to be relied upon.*

- *The use of such language proficiency tests and the elimination of the reliance on standardized tests within occupational bodies should be phased in over the same three-year period as applies to the introduction of the Prior Learning Assessment Network.*

7.3   *To assist the administrators of language tests in meeting Recommendation 7.2, we recommend that the development and validation of occupation-specific language tests, although the responsibility of the occupational bodies themselves, be coordinated through the Prior Learning Assessment Network in the same manner as licensure test development and administration.*

7.4   *We recommend that educational institutions endeavour to introduce additional fluency testing methods as a supplement to, or even as a substitute for, standardized tests currently in use, and that, where appropriate, flexibility be introduced into the interpretation of test scores.*

7.5   *We recommend that in all cases the results of tests be made available and explained to candidates and that candidates be directed, if necessary, to appropriate English or French as a Second Language courses.*

7.6   *We recommend that all candidates for language testing be directed to preparatory courses or be given detailed preparatory material.*

7.7   *We recommend that all the above apply equally to French-language testing.*

Chapter 8 — Language Training

In recognition of the fact that policy changes at the federal level cannot be assured, it is important that this Report acknowledge that significant changes in language training delivery in Ontario would likely necessitate substantial provincial expenditures, particularly in view of Ontario's role as province of choice for 40 to 50 per cent of immigrants arriving annually in Canada. (If people who move to Ontario within the first one or two years of arriving in Canada are included, the percentage increases significantly.) Such an expenditure of public funds must, and inevitably will, be balanced against other spending demands of competing public value. Nevertheless, the Task Force urges the Government, in setting priorities, to recognize the very significant contribution of immigrants to the economic life and the social fabric of Ontario. English/French language capability is an essential prerequisite to full participation. Accordingly, we urge the Government to give a high priority to language training programs.

8.1 *We recommend that the Government of Ontario proceed as soon as possible to the second stage of its review of language training in Ontario. In relation to Phase II of the review, we make the following recommendations:*

- *The results of the survey of ESL/FSL programs by the Ministry of Education and the Ministry of Colleges and Universities should be made available to the public in a form readily accessible both in its presentation and its cost.*

- *The Ministry of Citizenship should establish an advisory committee of representatives from immigrant organizations, organizations of ESL/FSL teachers (for example, TESL Ontario), ethno-cultural organizations, and others. This committee would review the survey and assist in identifying program deficiencies. The mandate of the advisory committee should include the responsibility to report to the Ministry on its findings with respect to appropriate priorities for government action.*

- *In addition, the interministerial committee considering the survey results and the report of the advisory committee should invite written submissions from interested individuals and organizations on appropriate initiatives that the Government could take to improve language programs in Ontario.*

8.2 *We recommend that the interministerial committee reviewing ESL/FSL implement changes to training programs to incorporate the findings of this Task Force. Specifically, we recommend that language training incorporate the following characteristics designed to facilitate the entry of foreign-trained individuals into occupations that match education and experience obtained in their countries of origin:*

- *The function and proficiency level of written and oral language taught should reflect the language skills required for entry to and practice of the occupation for which the individual has been trained in his or her country of origin. The language proficiency requirements of the relevant occupation should be considered in assessing the duration and content of language training appropriate for each student.*

- *Courses should be flexible in duration and level of intensity, with full-time, part-time, evening, and day courses available. This flexibility will allow candidates with various levels of proficiency at entry to develop to the described skill level at their own pace, and it will allow access by people with various scheduling needs.*

- *Language training should, where possible, be integrated with occupational retraining courses, if such retraining is required to prepare the individual for practice in Ontario. Technical terminology and occupation-specific language functions should be included in the curriculum.*

- *Basic language training, with income support, should be available to all immigrants without limitations based on immigration categories, on intended labour force affiliation and employment prospects, on level of skill, or on training.*

- *Specialized language instruction geared to occupational sectors should be available with income support to bring language skills up to the level required for entry to the occupational field for which the individual is qualified on the basis of foreign training, education, or experience.*

8.3 *We recommend that the interministerial committee reviewing language training consider and respond to each of the criticisms at the end of the discussion that precedes these Recommendations. Although many of the comments relate to federal programs, it is important that the provincial review assess the validity of those criticisms so that Ontario can establish programs to minimize, where possible, the impact of shortcomings in federal programs.*

8.4 *We recommend that the Government of Ontario establish a provincial directorate with overall responsibility for language training for immigrants to Ontario. This directorate should work in conjunction with or as part of the proposed Prior Learning Assessment Network (PLAN). The directorate would be responsible for:*

- *compiling in a publicly accessible form a description of the various ESL/FSL courses provided throughout the province;*

- *assisting occupational groups in identifying the necessary level of proficiency required for entry to practice, this level to be reflected in the qualifying examination;*

- *making available to any immigrant to Ontario (including those caught in the backlog of people previously unable to access language training) an assessment of language training needs to determine appropriate entry and exit levels for training, these levels to be matched with the individual's educational and occupational background as evaluated by PLAN;*

- *referring immigrants to appropriate language training as indicated by language training assessments;*

- *developing and implementing a publicity strategy to bring the availability of the assessment and referral services to the attention of immigrants;*

- *compiling statistical information on the language training needs of the immigrant population, including the need for occupationally focused English/French for Special Purposes courses; and*

- *exploring alternative delivery methods for language training, such as those discussed in Chapter 9 of this Report, "Retraining."*

8.5 *We recommend that the Government of Ontario continue to negotiate with the federal Government for a return to 1985 funding levels for training programs under the Canadian Jobs Strategy. Further, we recommend that the Ministry of Skills*

Development, in renegotiating the Canada/Ontario Agreement on Training, explore all options that might afford Ontario increased language training dollars and/or greater autonomy with respect to program delivery.

8.6   *In recognition of the unfairness of federally imposed eligibility restrictions on language training and on subsidies, which impact particularly on immigrant women, we recommend that the Ministry of Skills Development continue to discuss this inequity in negotiations with the federal Government in respect of the Canada/Ontario Agreement on Training. Language training should be recognized to be part of the settlement process for all immigrants, regardless of immediate employment opportunities or intended labour force affiliation.*

Chapter 9 — Retraining

The Task Force is aware of the increasing overall need to retrain people affected by job obsolescence and to update the knowledge of practitioners in an occupation to keep them at the "leading edge." We are also aware that the numbers of foreign-trained professional people and tradespeople are likely to rise in Ontario in the coming years as our more traditional sources grow smaller. Our recommendations regarding training recognize that the Government currently addresses the specific training needs of some populations, including youth, women, and visible minorities. We observe, however, that foreign-trained people are an emerging group whose training needs are not adequately met.

The information that we have gathered indicates that there are great discrepancies in the availability of training opportunities to foreign-trained people — discrepancies from occupation to occupation and from one educational institution to the next. We note the considerable amount of effort and funding being put into these programs, and we are troubled that, in spite of the demographic trends in Ontario, the needs of foreign-trained people do not appear in the planning statements of the major program funders.

We look to the Government of Ontario to set the example for providers of education and training in the province by explicitly including the training needs of foreign-trained people as an important element of its funding and operating plans. Only then, we believe, can we turn to Ontario's educational institutions and certification and licensure bodies for concrete provisions for the efficient and fair reception of foreign-trained professional people and tradespeople.

We do not advocate the creation of an agency for training foreign-trained people. Instead, we advise the Government and the many providers of education and training that the availability of such training makes economic and social sense and that in most cases, through cooperative planning and with adjustments in their existing policies and delivery systems, appropriate provision can be made.

9.1 *We recommend that the Ministry of Colleges and Universities and the Ministry of Citizenship be assigned joint responsibility for encouraging, advising, and assisting colleges, universities, and occupational certification bodies in providing access to retraining, upgrading, and updating by foreign-trained people. We believe that in providing this leadership, these ministries should consult with the Council of Ontario Universities, the Ontario Council of Regents for Colleges of Applied Arts and Technology, the Ministry of Skills Development, and the occupational committees of the proposed Prior Learning Assessment Network.*

We recommend that the Ministry of Colleges and Universities and the Ministry of Citizenship address the following matters:

- *the accessibility of training by foreign-trained people who are partially qualified to apply for certification or licensure in an occupation;*

- *the funding needs of colleges, universities, and professional bodies related to the provision of training;*

- *the funding needs of foreign-trained individuals seeking to take training; and*

- *the accessibility of information about training opportunities.*

9.2 *We recommend that the colleges and universities of Ontario collaborate in the design and execution of a detailed review of each postsecondary educational institution, to ensure that each is providing fair and flexible access to retraining by foreign-*

trained people. We believe that this review should include an audit of the measures that each institution has in place to address institutional, dispositional, and situational barriers to training, and that each institution undertake to file with the Ministry of Colleges and Universities a plan for addressing and removing barriers that are found to exist.

9.3   *We recommend that the Government of Ontario establish financial support structures for the training of partially qualified foreign-trained professional people and tradespeople, and that these structures be designed to:*

- *encourage and assist occupational bodies and educational institutions to develop modules of instruction that foreign-trained individuals can assemble to meet certification and licensure requirements;*

- *encourage and assist occupational bodies to develop additional means, if appropriate, for candidates to meet retraining requirements, with a view to lessening the strain on traditional university- or college-based delivery systems, options to include use of alternate physical facilities, development of mentor training, and recognition of alternate delivery mechanisms such as radio, video, computer, and correspondence;*

- *provide responsive funding to individuals (at the minimum, a loan program referenced to the needs of those seeking training); and*

- *assist employers in providing training, through the extension of such existing funding mechanisms as the trades and technologists updating programs funded by the Ministry of Skills Development.*

9.4   *We recommend that, in order to better ensure the quality, responsiveness, and continuity of community-based programming, a foundation grant program be established to create a more stable planning and operating base for proven community-based agencies that provide programming for foreign-trained people.*

9.5   *We recommend that the occupational bodies and the provincial Government work together, along with the community-based agencies referred to in the above recommendation, to identify particular service requirements in the ethno-cultural communities, especially in the areas of medicine, social work, and psychology, and that such identified needs be taken into account in the allocation of retraining resources to candidates for certification or licensure.*

9.6   *We recommend that the Ontario Training Corporation ensure that any information bases and information services which it is establishing be designed to serve the full range of professions and trades in Ontario, and that it respond to issues of accessibility and accuracy, as set out in Recommendations 3.4, 3.5, and 3.6 in Chapter 3, "Issues Facing the Trades."*

9.7   *We recommend that the Government of Ontario continue to work with other provinces and the federal Government towards the establishment of a Canada Training Allowance.*

9.8   *We recommend that, through the assessment of academic equivalency carried out by the proposed Prior Learning Assessment Network, any partially qualified foreign-trained person who needs additional training be provided with specific information about the nature and duration of training required to fulfil the prerequisites for certification or licensure.*

9.9   *We recommend that for those occupations for which Canadian or Ontario experience is a prerequisite to certification or licensure, professional bodies, colleges, and universities endeavour to design training programs in such a way that this experience can be obtained. Determinations of the amount of such experience to be required should be based on an individual assessment giving full credit for all actual relevant experience of the candidate.*

Chapter 10 — Issues Facing the Medical Profession

Assessment of Prior Learning

It is our view that all graduates of unaccredited medical schools should be entitled to a comprehensive assessment of their training to determine if they meet the Ontario standard of competence. All candidates who meet the standard of competence should be entitled to receive educational licences and, by virtue of these licences, be entitled to apply for internship. The Pre-Internship Program as it now exists should not continue to be required of such candidates.

In any profession such an assessment is difficult and requires sophisticated and well-developed expertise. We have recommended in Chapter 5 of this Report, "Prior Learning Assessment," the creation of an agency, named the Prior Learning Assessment Network (PLAN), to be a resource to professional bodies in performing assessments of prior learning of candidates trained outside of Ontario. We are of the view that it should be made available to the medical profession. Unlike most professions in which a clinical assessment forms part of the final licensing examination, however, in this profession it is clearly important that a clinical assessment take place prior to internship.

We have indicated in our discussion of prior learning assessment that clinical assessments are best conducted by the professional body itself. The testing should, of course, reflect the Ontario standard of competence and be in compliance with recognized standards of test development as discussed in Chapter 6 of this Report, "Licensure Testing."

While we are of the view that candidates capable of demonstrating training equivalent to the Ontario standard should be entitled to proceed to internship, we recognize that a period of acclimatization to the Ontario hospital environment is desirable. For such candidates, however, such a period need not be lengthy. By keeping such a program brief, costs will remain at a reasonable level; at the same time, candidates will benefit as they acquire, with greater expediency, a necessary awareness of Ontario practice.

> *10.1   We recommend that the requirement that all graduates of unaccredited foreign medical schools complete a pre-internship*

program as it is now defined be eliminated from the regulations.

10.2　We recommend that evaluations of equivalency be available to all graduates of unaccredited medical schools. Because of the considerable clinical component in medical training which must be assessed before internship, it is appropriate that such assessments be conducted by the professional body itself. The tests should be developed in accordance with recognized standards of test development.

10.3　We recommend that every such candidate assessed as having training equivalent to the standard required of Ontario-trained candidates be granted the status of a clinical clerk in an Ontario teaching hospital for a brief period of no more than eight weeks, the length required depending upon the needs of the candidate as determined by the candidate and his or her supervisor. During this time the candidate shall observe the practice of medicine in an Ontario hospital; shall practise, under close supervision, his or her clinical skills; and shall be observed by a group supervisor. The purpose of this segment of preparation for internship is to permit the candidate a period of time to acclimatize to the Ontario hospital environment; it is not for further assessment and evaluation.

10.4　We recommend that all candidates who have met the above requirements be eligible to receive educational licences.

Internship

We have concluded that the current allocation of funded internship spots should be retained but that any candidate eligible for an educational licence should be permitted to apply for any of those spots. All positions should be filled through the Canadian Internship Matching Service (CIMS), and there should be no policy or practice that graduates of Ontario schools must all be placed before graduates from schools elsewhere. We acknowledge that in some years there may be more applicants than there are places and that some of those without places may be graduates of Ontario schools. While this is unfortunate, it is unavoidable in the absence of an increase in the number of funded spots. Any problems that exist relating to the cost of health care in this province must be shared among all Ontario residents, whether they have domestic or foreign training. We are also of the view that the introduction of this element of competition and challenge into the system of medical education in this province will not be detrimental. Such a system is more likely to raise than to lower standards, and it should encourage excellence within the profession. The public benefit is enhanced through a selection process that results in the very best physicians qualifying for practice.

The criteria to be considered in the allocation of internship positions to qualified candidates should, to ensure fairness, be clearly articulated and made public. In addition, such criteria should take into account the health-care needs of the community, so that the particular needs of some immigrant groups or of northern communities lacking specific services are more likely to be met.

> *10.5*   *We recommend that any candidate with an educational licence be entitled to apply for and obtain an internship in Ontario on an equal basis with any other candidate, regardless of place of training. The applications of all candidates for internship should be assessed against clearly articulated criteria, which may from time to time reflect particular needs for medical services in the community.*

Language

The TOEFL and TSE tests are relied on in the medical profession to assess fluency. We discuss the use of such tests in Chapter 7, "Language Testing," and reference should be made to that chapter for a full review of the issues. Suffice to say at this point that we endorse the view of analysts that the TOEFL and the TSE are inadequate and inappropriate means of assessing fluency within the context of professional certification. If the profession is of the view that a specific language screen is desirable, we suggest the development of a limited, profession-specific fluency test, to be developed with the assistance of English/French as a Second Language experts, to assess the linguistic level of the candidate as it is relevant to professional practice. In the alternative, the qualifying examination or any other written or oral test administered as part of an equivalency assessment may function as a language screen, provided the level of fluency required is reviewed to ensure that it is appropriate to the profession and that profession- and discipline-specific language is assessed.

10.6   *We recommend that the use of the TOEFL and TSE tests be discontinued. Any other test used to assess language, whether it be a particular test developed for that purpose or the qualifying examinations themselves, should reflect our general recommendations on the use and development of such tests in our chapters "Licensure Testing" (Chapter 6) and "Language Testing" (Chapter 7).*

Chapter 11 — Review of Registration Decisions

Listed below are recommendations that set out a model review and appeal structure for occupational legislation. In considering the appeal rights of applicants to occupational organizations, the Task Force reviewed the position of applicants to non-statutory bodies, but, in view of our mandate, we did not make recommendations in relation to such occupations. Included are references to specific amendments to be made to the various statutes in order to bring appeal mechanisms into keeping with our general recommendations. In addition, we have chosen to include a more detailed discussion of those occupations and professions with a current or proposed right of appeal to the Health Disciplines Board or to the Commercial Registration Appeals Tribunal (CRAT), because these two bodies together are expected to hear appeals from registration decisions in respect of more than 30 professional and occupational groups, assuming recommendations currently before the Government (most notably those contained in the Report of the Health Professions Legislation Review) are implemented.

General Recommendations

11.1   *The Task Force recommends that all occupational statutes be amended to provide that applicants who are refused registration be entitled to a right of appeal, which would incorporate the stages and the procedural protections described below. Judicial review alone is not sufficient to deal with registration denials.*

The Initial Decision

11.2   *Applicants to occupational bodies should have the right to be fully informed of eligibility requirements and standards, of the necessary documentation to be submitted, and of the procedures for obtaining review of a decision to refuse registration. We recommend that occupational legislation be amended to provide that the registrar be required to make appropriate written information available to applicants. An improvement in the flow of information from occupational bodies to all applicants would, in our view, be very helpful in reducing the likelihood of an unnecessarily adversarial relationship between the applicant and the occupational organization.*

11.3 *We recommend that occupational legislation provide the applicant with the right to review his or her admissions file before an initial decision is made. Many difficulties may be resolved quickly if the applicant is given an opportunity to examine his or her file at an early stage.*

11.4 *Where an applicant is facing a proposed negative decision that has been referred to a registration committee, we recommend that the legislation provide the applicant with the right to make written submissions with supporting documentation and evidence to the registration committee. (This documentation could include an equivalency assessment given by our proposed Prior Learning Assessment Network.) This right will increase the fairness of the proceedings without adding undue delay or complication; and, it is hoped, it will minimize the need for a costly and lengthy appeal.*

11.5 *Where occupational legislation provides that a registrar must refer proposed registration refusals to a registration committee, as is the case, for example, for all the professions established by the* Health Disciplines Act, *we recommend that the legislation should provide applicants with the right to be notified in writing of the grounds for the registrar's negative recommendation.*

11.6 *Where registration decisions are reviewed by a registration committee, we recommend that the committee have full rights of review, including the power to substitute its own opinion about the equivalency of the applicant's education and experience. (This recommendation will have particular impact on the professions of engineering, architecture, and surveying. Currently, a final equivalency assessment is made by two internal committees in each of the professional organizations:*

the academic requirements committee and the experience requirements committee. The equivalency assessment is, accordingly, not subject to any right of appeal under the present legislation for these three professions.)

11.7   *We recommend that occupational legislation be amended to afford the applicant the right to be provided with written reasons for a negative initial decision.*

11.8   *Where statutory procedure requires that a registrar refer an application to a registration committee, we recommend that the committee be required to make a decision within 30 days of that referral.*

Appellate Tribunal

Recommendations 11.9-11.14 apply only to occupations established by legislation. The Task Force has given limited consideration to the position of applicants to unregulated voluntary occupational associations that grant a credential or a reserved title. (See our discussion in Chapter 4, "Issues Facing the Professions.")

11.9   *Where the initial decision maker has determined that registration should be denied or that conditions or limitations should be attached to the registration, we recommend that the applicant have the right to a review of the decision by a specialty tribunal composed in whole or in part of members of the public, independent of the occupation, appointed to represent the public interest.*

11.10   *Professions that currently have no mechanism for review by an independent tribunal include engineering, architecture, surveying, accounting, and law. We recommend that the Government enter into discussions with these professions to determine whether one appellate tribunal should be established to hear appeals in respect of registration refusals from all these professional bodies, or whether instead tribunals should be established for each specific profession.*

11.11   *Several occupational groups regulated under private legislation do not provide applicants with a right of appeal to an independent tribunal. A new tribunal could be established to provide an appeal forum for applicants to these groups. Alternatively, the government could consider expanding the jurisdiction of an existing tribunal such as the Commercial Registration Appeal Tribunal. (See Recommendation 11.36.)*

11.12 *We recommend that the applicant should have the choice of applying either for an oral hearing or for a review based on evidence and written submissions. The* Health Disciplines Act *currently provides applicants with such a choice. It is our view that the proposed optional review mechanism is cost-effective and more convenient for applicants who may wish to avoid the time and expense of preparing for and attending an oral hearing, with or without counsel. Given that much of the evidence to be considered consists of documentation, a review based on written submissions may in many cases be more appropriate than an oral hearing. The applicant would still have the option of selecting an oral hearing and calling witnesses on his or her behalf.*

11.13 *We recommend that the appellate tribunal be granted full powers of review by statute and, specifically, be able to exercise all the powers of the decision maker of first instance, including, where applicable, the power to exempt applicants from the usual requirements for registration; the power to review the merits of the application, including the equivalency assessment; and the power to consider the procedural and substantive fairness of the process, including the validity of any assessment or licensing examinations.*

11.14 *Procedural protections must be afforded the applicant at the stage of a review by an independent tribunal. We recommend that professional legislation provide the following:*

- *The applicant should have the opportunity to examine, no later than 10 days before the hearing, any written or documentary evidence that will be produced or any report or written summary of the evidence that will be given by each expert witness. (The tribunal should, however, be granted the power to admit evidence even if the time limit has not been strictly observed.)*

- *Hearings should be required to be held in public unless (1) involving matters of public security, (2) involving intimate financial or personal matters of such a nature that the desirability of avoiding public disclosure outweighs the principle that hearings be conducted in public, (3) prejudicing anyone in an actual criminal or civil proceeding, or (4) jeopardizing the safety of any person. The appeal tribunal should be empowered to ban publication of identifying information as well as to prohibit publication of the identity of witnesses testifying as to allegations of sexual impropriety.*

- *No member of the tribunal should be permitted to participate in the decision unless he or she was present throughout the hearing.*

- *A party to the hearing before a tribunal should be granted the right to be represented by counsel or agent, if so desired.*

- *A party to the hearing before a tribunal should have the right to call, examine, and cross-examine witnesses.*

- *The tribunal should be required to give written reasons for its decision.*

Appeal to Court

11.15   *We recommend that the applicant have a final right of appeal to the Divisional Court on questions of law, fact, or mixed law and fact. (This recommendation will require amendments to several professional statutes, including the* Chartered Accountants Act, 1956, *the* Certified General Accountants Association of Ontario Act, 1983, *the* Society of Management Accountants of Ontario Act, *the* Law Society Act, *the* Chiropody Act, *and the* Drugless Practitioners Act, *if the professions covered by that Act are not brought under the* Health Disciplines Act. *Also requiring amendment will be several private statutes establishing occupational organizations.)*

11.16   *We recommend that occupational legislation should expressly grant the Court the power to affirm or rescind the decision under appeal, to exercise all the powers of the tribunal, and to direct the tribunal to take any action that the Court considers proper; the Court should be empowered to substitute its opinion for that of the tribunal or to refer the matter back for a rehearing with such directions as the Court considers proper.*

Professions Under the Health Disciplines Act

11.17   *We recommend that the* Health Disciplines Act *be amended to provide that the registrar for each profession be required to inform applicants in writing of the standards and requirements to be met, of the documentation to be submitted, and of the procedure for review and appeal of negative decisions.*

11.18   *We recommend that the* Health Disciplines Act *be amended to provide that if the registrar should propose to refuse registration and refer the proposal to the registration committee, the applicant would have the right to notification in writing of the grounds for the negative recommendation of the registrar.*

11.19   *We recommend that the* Health Disciplines Act *be amended to grant applicants the right to submit written evidence, documentation, and argument at the registration committee stage.*

11.20   *We recommend that the* Health Disciplines Act *be amended to provide that all applicants have a right to access to their application files before an initial decision is made.*

11.21   *We recommend that the* Health Disciplines Act *be amended to provide that the registration committees be required to make a decision and give written reasons for it within 30 days of referral of the application by the registrar.*

11.22   *We recommend that the Health Disciplines Board, or its successor, continue to afford applicants denied registration a right to either an oral hearing or a review on the basis of written submissions, at the option of the applicant.*

*11.23   We support the recommendation of the Health Professions
          Legislation Review that applicants be afforded an opportunity
          to examine the evidence no less than 10 days before the
          hearing and that summaries of the evidence of each expert
          witness be provided. We also agree with the suggested
          amendment reversing the current presumption in the* Health
          Disciplines Act *that hearings be conducted in camera. It is
          recommended that hearings be conducted in public unless other
          interests will be prejudiced.*

*11.24   We recommend that the Health Disciplines Board have full
          powers of review. The Health Professions Legislation Review
          has also concluded that the powers of the Health Disciplines
          Board should be broadened and has recommended that the
          board be able to direct registration if it finds that the applicant
          substantially meets the requirements. We concur with this
          recommendation, but would also recommend deletion of the
          current requirement that the board find the committee has
          "acted improperly." Further, it is our recommendation that the
          board be given the power to grant exemptions. We have
          reviewed several decisions of the board, and we note that its
          members have expressed frustration that the board is unable to
          exempt applicants from registration requirements. The board is
          able to make strong recommendations only and must refer the
          matter back to the registration committee. We are of the view
          that giving the board the power to exempt applicants from
          statutory requirements would expedite the appeal process and
          avoid further costs and delays.*

*11.25   There should continue to be a right of appeal to the Divisional
          Court on questions of law, fact, or mixed law and fact. We
          agree with the suggestions made by the Health Professions
          Legislation Review and recommend that the legislation detailing
          the nature and extent of the powers be clarified so that it is
          clear that the Court has all the powers of the registration
          committees and the Health Disciplines Board, including the
          power to grant exemptions.*

*11.26   We recommend that dental hygienists be given full status under
          the* Health Disciplines Act, *thereby entitling applicants to the
          full package of procedural protections in the* Act.

11.27   *In accordance with the Report of the Health Professions
         Legislation Review, it is our recommendation that the following
         health professions be brought under the* Health Disciplines Act:
         *audiology and speech language pathology; chiropody;
         chiropractic; dental hygiene; dental technology; denture
         therapy; dietetics; massage therapy; medical laboratory
         technology; medical radiation technology; midwifery;
         occupational therapy; ophthalmic dispensing; physiotherapy;
         psychology; and respiratory therapy. Applicants to these
         professions would then be afforded a full review before the
         Health Disciplines Board and the Divisional Court.*

11.28   *For those health professions which remain outside the scope of
         the* Health Disciplines Act *but are currently regulated by
         statute (for example, naturopathy), we recommend that the
         enabling legislation be amended to reflect the procedural
         recommendations of this chapter. More particularly, we would
         recommend that the legislation provide for a review of negative
         decisions by the Health Disciplines Board and a full right of
         appeal to the Divisional Court on questions of law, fact, and
         mixed law and fact.*

Professions with a Right of Review by the Commercial Registration Appeal Tribunal

11.29   *The enabling legislation for each of the professional and
         occupational groups with a right of appeal to the Commercial
         Registration Appeal Tribunal (CRAT) should be amended to
         provide applicants with the appropriate procedural protections
         recommended in this chapter, including the right to be informed
         of requirements and standards, the right to see their application
         files, and the right to receive written reasons for a negative
         decision.*

11.30   *Section 7(7) of the* Ministry of Consumer and Commercial
         Relations Act *currently provides that one member of a three-
         person appeal panel be a representative of the occupational
         group that is the subject of the appeal. Given our
         recommendations below to expand the jurisdiction of CRAT, it
         is recommended that the panel be expanded to include*

representatives of the new occupational groups being considered in appeals before CRAT.

11.31   *We recommend that the* Act *be amended to provide that the applicant have the option of applying to CRAT for either an oral hearing or a review based on written evidence and submissions.*

11.32   *We recommend that the* Act *be amended to incorporate the right to see written or documentary evidence and a summary of expert evidence at least 10 days before the hearing.*

11.33   *We recommend that the* Registered Insurance Brokers Act *be amended to provide a right of appeal to CRAT, which would replace the current statutory scheme that requires the qualification and registration committee to sit in review of its own decision.*

11.34   *We recommend that applicants for registration as insurance agents under the* Insurance Act *be granted a statutory right of appeal to CRAT. There is currently no provision for review before an independent body.*

11.35   *We recommend that in keeping with the proposed new* Funeral Directors and Establishments Act, *applicants for registration in the death-care sector be granted a right of appeal to CRAT, and that the Funeral Services Review Board no longer serve this function.*

11.36   *Finally, we recommend that consideration be given to expanding the jurisdiction of CRAT. The tribunal could hear appeals from registration refusals by occupations currently regulated under private "reserved title" legislation, as discussed in Chapter 4, "Issues Facing the Professions." With respect to the accounting professions, we have recommended above (11.11) that a new appellate tribunal be established to hear appeals from registration refusals.*

Chapter 12 — Human Rights Legislation

12.1   *We recommend that the* Human Rights Code, 1981, *be amended to prohibit discrimination because of "place of education or training" as an additional ground of discrimination in respect of services (section 1 of the* Code*), employment (section 4 of the* Code*), and membership in occupational associations and self-governing professions (section 5 of the* Code*), subject to the reasonable and* bona fide *qualification defence (section 23(1)(b) of the* Code*), provided such defence is not maintainable unless it is established that there cannot be accommodation without undue hardship considering the cost, outside sources of funding, if any, and health and safety requirements, if any (section 23(2) of the* Code*).**

12.2   *We recommend that the* Human Rights Code, 1981, *section 9, be amended to include a definition for "occupational association," as follows: " 'occupational association' includes an association in which membership provides a reserved title in the carrying on of a trade, occupation or profession."*

Chapter 13 — Application of the Canadian Charter of Rights and Freedoms

13.1   *The Task Force is of the view and recommends that legislation and regulations governing entry to a profession or providing for a reserved title, with a "good character" stipulation, be worded to provide that registration is denied only where the evidence relied upon as demonstrating a lack of good character is rationally related to the applicant's competence or ability to practise.*

---

*This recommendation apparently constitutes a novel approach to providing remedies in addressing the problems of individuals trained in one country attempting to gain access to professions or trades in another country. No Canadian jurisdiction has "place of education or training" as a prohibited ground of discrimination in human rights legislation. Nor does "place of education or training" appear as a prohibited ground of discrimination under human rights legislation in the United Kingdom, Australia, or the United States (federal legislation or in the individual states).

ACKNOWLEDGMENTS

Throughout the work of this Task Force it has been the Commissioners' good fortune to have had the invaluable assistance and support of many highly qualified people. The mandate involved analysis of multifaceted, complex, and subtle issues, and breaking new ground in making recommendations and proposing solutions. On behalf of the Commissioners, I want to thank everyone most sincerely for their contributions.

First and foremost, Ann Wilson, as Project Coordinator, deserves immense credit, especially for accepting the task of revising and completing the writing of much of the Report and the background studies on specific professions. Ann's tremendous dedication, coupled with her analytical, researching, and writing abilities, deserves the very highest recognition.

Patti Bregman, Project Director until February 16, 1989, provided imagination and a far-ranging perspective during the research phase of the work of the Task Force. Her selection of topics formed a solid base for the Report.

The Assistant Project Director, Kathy Laird, provided excellent work as a researcher and writer and capably coordinated the research staff. She brought to the Task Force an overview of the issues and an eye for detail, and throughout the project she contributed significantly to all facets of the development of the Report.

Inge Sardy, as Administrator, brought sound management skills and judgment, and a good sense of humour to her task. She provided valued guidance on all matters and frequently took on added responsibilities. Her input was much appreciated by the Commissioners and the staff. She is an excellent administrator. Vincenza DeMedicis assisted very efficiently in the financial aspects of the Task Force work. We also very much appreciated the excellent advice and assistance in respect of logistical and budget matters which we received from Roland d'Abadie of the Ministry of the Attorney General.

Researchers who provided valued expertise in a wide variety of topics were Shona Bradley, Susan Charendoff, Carlota Ferrier, Catherine Frid, Wenona Giles, Shireen Jeejeebhoy, Winnie Lem, Winston Mattis, and Kaan Yigit. Ruby Barber, Martha Campbell, Lisa Douglas, Azmina Karim,

Kenneth Marley, and Odida Quamina also assisted ably in respect of research on specific topics.

The Task Force was fortunate in obtaining the assistance of many highly qualified consultants. In particular, Phil Schalm's broad perspective, immense knowledge of the subject, research skills, and writing ability were invaluable contributions. Other consultants who also contributed excellent research material and advice were Hugh Ashford, Dr. Barbara Burnaby, Dr. Betty Chan, Graham Debling, Nancy Goodman, Dr. Frances Henry, Dr. Peter Hogg, Bjorn Johansson, Dr. Les McLean, Christopher Reed, Dr. Alan Thomas, and Dr. Sharon Williams.

Linda McClenaghan, as senior secretary, masterfully kept track of the myriad of documents and research papers, and organized and managed the files and record keeping. She directed and supervised staff with sensitivity and diplomacy, and her management skills, secretarial skills, and unfailing good humour were much appreciated.

It would be impossible to prepare a report such as ours without highly skilled word-processing operators, and we wish to thank Kay Coghlan, Marilyn Harris, Peak-Choo Hew, and Helen Warburton for their endless energy and patience. Thanks also go to Elizabeth Sinclair for lending her technical expertise when necessary.

Carol Brown, Peter Melnychuk, Sharon Miller, Cherilyn Roosen-Runge, and Samer Tabar were able and congenial receptionists.

Excellent editing and direction on the style of the Report were provided by Dan Liebman and his assistant, Duncan McKenzie.

Constructive criticisms were given to aspects of developing papers and chapters by a great many people, some of whom are listed in Appendix D. Particular thanks must be given to Ted Kerzner, Q.C., Elaine Zinman-Madoff, and Jean-Claude Letourneau. They gave extremely able advice and valuable insights, and provided generously of their time.

We appreciated the very willing and able contributions of the immigrant and community groups, professional bodies, and government officials interviewed. The list of names in Appendix D represents but a fraction of the assistance that the Task Force received from many sources, for which we are indeed grateful.

Finally, I must say that the contributions of my colleagues as Commissioners, Enid Lee and Dimitrios Oreopoulos, in every facet of the Report, were conscientiously and ably provided. Above all, no matter how difficult the problem, they gave immediate and sound direction and guidance throughout, while always maintaining both good sense and good humour.

Peter A. Cumming

PART I

Introduction and Background

CHAPTER 1
Introduction

As a citizen of Canada, I should not have to fight so hard to be allowed to learn and work and contribute to the country I had, until now, always regarded as being fair and truly multicultural.

— from a Brief submitted to the
Task Force by an individual

In the fall of 1987, the Task Force on Access to Professions and Trades in Ontario was created by Order-in-Council. The Terms of Reference for our study were as follows:

1) Review all rules and practices affecting entry to professions and trades to determine whether they have an actual or potential discriminatory effect on persons with training or experience from outside of Canada.

2) Determine whether the identified rules or practices can be justified as necessary to maintain professional or trade standards.

3) Investigate actual or potential barriers beyond the control of the professions and trades, such as lack of support services during re-training periods; and

4) Recommend changes to rules and practices which cannot be justified as necessary for the maintenance of professional or trade standards, and recommend how foreign qualified persons can be assisted to meet those rules which can be justified.

The creation of the Task Force represented the commencement of the second phase of a study that had begun earlier that year. In May 1987, Abt Associates of Canada, social research consultants, reported its preliminary findings on completion of its exploratory study on the issue. Abt's three general and tentative findings were:

- Systemic barriers are administrative, economic, and cultural in origin.

- Entry requirements rest largely with certifying bodies.

- Requirements have a disproportionately negative impact on members of minority and ethnic groups.

In order to consider and examine these early findings, the report recommended that the Phase II study look at these issues: information exchange and cultural sensitization; language proficiency; credit for work experience; and academic equivalency. It also recommended that a detailed assessment be made of the nature and extent of the barriers.

Keeping these recommendations in mind, this Task Force began its work by undertaking a detailed occupation-by-occupation review of all requirements for entry into the professions and trades in Ontario. This process involved a detailed review of legislation and regulations, discussions with representatives of the various occupations to determine actual practice, and, in many cases, formal meetings with representatives of the various arms of the occupations — the certifying body, the educational institution, and any voluntary association — with a view to clarifying procedures and identifying barriers that we perceived to exist. At the same time, we made a public appeal through newspaper advertisements and mailings to ethno-cultural organizations for submissions from affected individuals and others with information or views on the subject.

The response to our solicitation for opinion on the subject made it clear that significant numbers of individuals are affected. We received well over 200 written briefs, the majority from foreign-trained individuals who had encountered significant difficulties obtaining the required credentials to work in Ontario. These difficulties went beyond the problems that one expects to be associated with an assessment of credentials. They extended to situations in which the individuals felt the procedures were distinctly unfair. Nearly one-quarter of the submissions were from community bodies and organizations, many of them serving ethno-cultural groups in the province. In making their submissions and presenting their views at meetings with Task Force staff, the chair, and the commissioners, such groups were often in a position to represent the views of considerable numbers of their members. Repeatedly we heard of individuals who felt frustrated in finding themselves unable to work, productively and with a sense of self-satisfaction, in the province they had chosen as their new home. Sometimes there was bitterness; more often, profound disappointment.

We received considerable statistical data from the occupational bodies, which were highly cooperative and in some cases went to great lengths to provide us with the most comprehensive data available to them. Much of the data were useful and informative, but in a number of cases the statistics provided to us by the occupational bodies were, as is discussed in more detail in Chapter 4 of this Report, "Issues Facing the Professions," lacking on some key issues. For example, many occupational organizations do not keep records of inquiries that are not followed up with formal applications; yet our discussions with the community groups, some foreign-trained individuals, and even some of the occupational organizations themselves disclose that this is the stage when many foreign-trained individuals are rejected on the grounds that they lack the necessary qualifications. Typical of this situation is the case of the candidate who, before making an application, is advised by the registrar of the occupational body that he or she has less than the necessary academic requirements. Often in such cases there will be no record anywhere of an inquiry or of the advice given. Statistical evidence from the occupational groups is likely therefore to understate significantly the extent of the problems encountered by foreign-trained people, particularly because these problems relate to determinations of academic equivalency, which are made at a very early point in the entry process.

During the early stages of our study we concentrated on listening, gathering information, and identifying barriers through an occupation-by-occupation review. Our focus was on the particular deficiencies we could identify within the procedures of any given occupation, based on our review of specific regulations and practices and of information received from affected individuals and groups. As our research progressed, however, it soon became evident that the barriers being encountered by foreign-trained individuals in obtaining entitlement to work in their specialized fields were not, by and large, particular to any occupation. Rather, they were reflected, to greater and lesser degrees, in the entry requirements imposed by each of the occupational groups. There were, of course, some barriers that had very limited application: the rigid limitations put on the number of foreign-trained physicians who may qualify for educational licences in Ontario are peculiar to the medical profession and can be profitably studied only in the context of the structure of that profession. Generally, however, recurring patterns emerged.

We therefore shifted our focus from the particular to the general, reviewing these identified generic difficulties and seeking broader solutions to them. As academic equivalency and the assessment of prior learning at a very early stage identified itself as the most consistently problematic area, we turned our attention to studies and literature on the subject and to models and structures currently in place in jurisdictions attempting to cope with the problem. Our inquiries led us, for example, to a review of the European Community and its comprehensive plans for 1992; to the United Kingdom and the United States, where schemes for the assessment not only of academic but also of experiential learning are already in place; and to British Columbia, Alberta, and Quebec, which offer three distinct examples of steps that can be taken to address the issue.

Other identified barriers did not require so much comparative study. Our review of the problems that arise in language testing and licensure testing led us to consult with experts on the proper development of testing mechanisms and on English/French as a Second Language instruction and evaluation. In devising an appropriate appeals structure, we consulted with members of the Ontario legal community. In considering the problems raised by the needs of foreign-trained individuals for retraining, both in occupational skill and in language, we consulted leading educators in the province.

Although precisely the same difficulties apply to the trades as to the professions, the organizational structures surrounding the entry process to the trades required that we treat them as a unit distinct from other occupational groups. For this subject, which covers myriad employment functions, we consulted with the Ontario Ministry of Skills Development and with employers and labour unions, and studied comparable structures in other provinces.

Although the barriers to entry that we encountered in our study cannot be said to apply universally in Ontario to all occupations, it is fair to say that they apply generally. There are, and these are referred to in our Report, examples of professions in which detailed and comprehensive assessments of prior learning are being undertaken; professions that are taking steps, through formal test development and validation, to ensure that their licensure or certification examinations reflect recognized standards of fairness; and professions in which are reflected adequate and comprehensive appeal rights. However, there are few professions in which it can be said that none of the barriers which we have identified is operating, and it is in the light of this widespread and generalized evidence of practices which are discriminatory, albeit unintentionally so, that we have proposed a broad structural solution rather than a patchwork of lesser remedies to meet individual problems. The number of applicants with foreign training is, in some occupations, very large; in others it is quite small. Yet the need of the latter group for direction in the assessment of such candidates is also clear; indeed, lacking the opportunity to develop any expertise in such assessment, this group stands to benefit significantly.

Background studies relating to the individual occupational structures reviewed and our commentary on any identified barriers were prepared and are available on request. Brief summaries of the structures and entry mechanisms for each of the occupations studied appear in Appendix H. Our discussion of the medical profession and the issues we see arising out of its entry structure is, however, included in full in the Report. We singled it out for review because it alone among all the occupations reviewed posed unique questions on the subject, making it necessary to respond directly with particular comments and recommendations. In contrast, the broad solution which we propose, the Prior Learning Assessment Network, and our other general recommendations, should respond to weaknesses identified in the procedures of the other occupations reviewed. The benefits of this broad-based approach will accrue not only to individual applicants, who will be assured that the assessment of their abilities meets a standard of fairness, both real and perceived, but also to the occupational bodies themselves, who will be relieved of the expense and difficulty of assessing each individual applicant — each with a unique set of qualifications. Implementation of the proposed Prior Learning Assessment Network (PLAN) will enhance both equity and efficiency. The solution also recognizes, we suggest, the changing demographics of modern times, in which mobility both between jurisdictions and, perhaps to a lesser extent, between occupations, is on the rise. PLAN will bring Ontario into an ever-increasing network of jurisdictions throughout the world in which this reality, rather than being denied or discouraged, is taken full advantage of, for the benefit of all.

CHAPTER 2

Foreign-Trained Individuals in Ontario

Canadians gain when persons with valuable training and education immigrate to Canada. Over the post-war period, the education and skills levels of immigrants have enriched our society and improved the performance of our economy.

— Royal Commission on the Economic Union
and Development Prospects for Canada[1]

As the Terms of Reference indicate, our mandate is to review conditions for entry to occupations facing individuals "with training or experience from outside of Canada." Our study therefore is not formally limited to immigrants to Canada, although they compose our principal target group. This chapter includes a review of the policies and patterns relevant to the entry of immigrants to Canada and Ontario. As well, there is a brief discussion of Canadians trained outside Ontario.

IMMIGRANTS TO CANADA

Canada's immigration policy is conducted under the legislative authority of the 1976 *Immigration Act*,[2] the objectives of which are to define the rights and obligations of visitors to this country; to modernize the means by which persons seeking to enter Canada are examined and dealt with; to reaffirm the Government's commitment to family reunification and to the alleviation of the plight of refugees and other displaced persons; and to provide the provinces with a greater opportunity for participation in the determination of quotas more closely tied to specific Canadian labour force needs.[3] The *Act* provides a framework for the federal Government to shape Canada's immigration policy based on the country's best interests, and among other things the immigration program is responsible for recruiting and selecting individuals as future residents and citizens, admitting refugees and other special groups, and helping immigrants adapt to the social, economic, and cultural life of Canada through services provided by federal, provincial, and municipal governments and by voluntary agencies.[4]

Canada's immigration policy has demographic, social and humanitarian, and economic objectives. The demographic objectives relate to the federal Government's determining of the size, the rate of growth, and the age structure of the Canadian population. Social and humanitarian objectives focus on the admission of refugees and on family reunification. Economic objectives foster the development of a strong and viable economy.[5]

Immigration has always played an important role in Canadian population growth. With lower fertility rates in Canada, the demographic contribution of immigration is very likely to be even higher in the future.[6] The 1987 *Annual Report to Parliament on Future Immigration Levels* noted that both the fertility rate and net immigration have been relatively low in recent years. Further, the report suggested,

> If fertility were to continue below the replacement level and if low net immigration had been permitted to continue, the Canadian population would begin to decline shortly after the turn of the century. There is no evidence that a decline in the Canadian population would be beneficial to this country.

Noting that the Canadian population is aging, the report went on to state:

> If current trends [in fertility and net immigration] continue, there will be relatively fewer people of working age to support a relatively greater number of people.[7]

Social and humanitarian objectives encompass family unification, admission of refugees, and promotion of social harmony. Through immigration, Canada is able to fulfil its continuing humanitarian obligation to protect and resettle people who have fled their countries for fear of persecution.[8]

Immigration continues to have a net positive economic impact, playing an integral part in labour force growth and, as a result of increased aggregate levels of consumption, assisting in job creation. Larger domestic markets stimulate investment, and population expansion through immigration also helps Canadian industry to achieve economies of scale, thereby lowering production costs. As well, consumption expenditures of immigrants boost demand and cause expansion in related industries.

Immigration Patterns: Canada and Ontario

Immigration to Canada since 1970 reached its high point of 218,465 in 1974, while the number of immigrants admitted under all immigration categories declined steadily between 1980 and 1985. Since 1985, the immigration levels have shown an increase, reaching 152,098 people in 1987 (see Table 2-1). The 1987-88 *Annual Report to Parliament on Future Immigration Levels* announced a continuing policy of moderate, controlled growth in immigration levels.[9]

Table 2-1 Immigration by Calendar Year, 1978-1987

Year	Canada Total	Ontario Total	Ontario % of Canada Total
1978	86,313	42,397	49
1979	112,096	51,947	46
1980	143,117	62,257	44
1981	128,618	54,890	43
1982	121,147	53,031	44
1983	89,157	40,036	45
1984	88,239	41,527	47
1985	84,302	40,730	48
1986	99,219	49,630	50
1987	152,098	84,807	56

Source: Ontario Ministry of Citizenship, Ethnocultural Data Base.

The profile of the immigrant population is changing (see Table 2-2). Although traditional sources of immigration, such as England and the United States, still rank high on the list, their overall share of immigration continues to decline as new sources, such as Hong Kong, Guyana, Vietnam, and El Salvador, rise to prominence.

Table 2-3 highlights changes in immigration patterns. Immigration from European countries showed a dramatic decline during the past two decades, while the percentage of immigrants coming to Ontario from Asia, South America, Central America, the Caribbean, and Africa quadrupled. (The shift reflects the one occurring in Canada as a whole. More than 60 per cent of all immigrants living in Canada in 1986 were born in Europe, but of those who arrived between 1981 and 1986, more than 70 per cent were born in non-European countries.[10])

Table 2-2 Major Sources of Immigrant Landings to Ontario

Rank	1967	1987
1	England	Hong Kong
2	Italy	Guyana
3	United States	Portugal
4	Scotland	India
5	Germany	Jamaica
6	Greece	Poland
7	France	England
8	Portugal	United States
9	West Indies	Philippines
0	China	Vietnam
11	Australia	El Salvador

Source: Employment and Immigration Canada statistics.

Table 2-3 Immigrants to Ontario by Area of Last Permanent Residence (ALPR), 1967 and 1987

ALPR	1967		1987	
Europe	89,979	77.0%	23,781	28.0%
United States	7,011	6.0%	3,804	4.5%
Asia	8,957	7.7%	33,135	39.1%
South and Central America (includes Caribbean)	7,027	6.0%	18,714	22.1%
Africa	1,660	1.4%	4,668	5.5%
Other	2,216	2.9%	705	0.8%
Total	116,850	(100.0%)	84,807	(100.0%)

Source: Ontario Ministry of Citizenship, Ethnocultural Data Base.

Ontario's share of immigration to Canada has been traditionally high and relatively stable, and it continues to climb. During the 10-year period 1978-87, as Table 2-1 shows, 47 per cent of all immigrants to Canada designated Ontario as their intended destination (averaging more than 50,000 people annually), reaching 55.7 per cent in 1987. Actual immigration to Ontario averaged slightly higher, at 49.6 per cent during the five-year period 1983-87. The primary destination of the newcomers who settle in Ontario is Toronto and its vicinity. In 1987, 65 per cent of all immigrants to Ontario designated Toronto as their intended destination. The five-year average over 1983-87 was 60.6 per cent.

Table 2-4 Profile of Immigrants to Ontario, 1985-1986

	1985	1986
	Per Cent	
Male	47.18	48.66
Female	52.82	51.34
Age		
Under 5	4.78	4.55
5-14	12.60	12.93
15-21	15.15	14.11
22-44	45.77	49.70
45-64	15.11	13.08
65 and over	6.59	5.63
Language ability		
English	51.13	56.29
French	1.11	1.02
Both	2.01	2.25
Neither	45.74	40.45
Years of schooling		
Under 9	28.61	25.82
9-12	40.98	42.35
13+	30.35	31.75
Destined for the workforce (of those age 15+)	74.43	61.40
Intended occupation (of those destined for the workforce)		
Professional and technical	11.69	15.1
Manufacturing, mechanical, and operating	13.68	19.6
Service-related	11.71	13.4

Source: Ontario Ministry of Citizenship, Ethnocultural Data Base materials, compiled from 1985 and 1986 figures.

According to 1986 figures (see Table 2-4), 56 per cent of immigrants to Ontario had some facility in English, 1 per cent had some in French, 40 per cent did not have facility in either language, and 2 per cent spoke both. Approximately 32 per cent of immigrants over 15 years of age had a minimum of 13 years of education. More than 48 per cent of immigrants to Ontario destined for the workforce designated the "professional and technical," the "manufacturing, mechanical, and operating," and the "service-related" categories as their intended occupations.[11]

These various sets of statistics translate into a number of realities. First, immigration, which as recently as 20 years ago was from a limited number of primarily European countries and therefore somewhat familiar locales, has very rapidly expanded to include significant numbers from a large number of different countries, about which generally less information is available to Canadians on the subject of their educational systems. The need for facilities and expertise to gather comprehensive information across such a wide spectrum of training systems is therefore much greater, both to assist occupational groups in determining whether candidates may be qualified and to ensure, from the candidates' point of view, that their qualifications are not ignored. Second, with the traditional sources of employable workers diminishing in Canada, the need to supplement this pool with foreign-trained individuals to support and enhance economic growth becomes imperative, and the easy and equitable integration of these individuals into their fields in the workplace becomes a necessary function of occupational bodies. Third, the mix of cultures in Ontario represents a culturally diverse market for services. A number of groups representing various cultural communities pointed to the difficulties immigrants to Canada can face in obtaining services in their language, especially where the services required relate to medicine, psychology, social work, and other areas that demand clear and culturally appropriate communication.

The thrust of the work of this Task Force has been to make recommendations to assist in ensuring that foreign-trained people facing certification procedures are treated fairly, that their level of skill is fully and accurately assessed, and that the steps they need to take to supplement their training are clearly indicated. Our approach has reflected the point of view of the foreign-trained individuals and that of the occupations they are entering, rather than that of the communities which may be served. We are, however, impressed by the level of concern that many groups have expressed on this issue. We heard of hospital patients unable to communicate their symptoms to physicians and of hospital cleaning staff being called upon to perform translation services; we heard of immigrants with severe psychological problems being unable to obtain treatment because there was no one qualified to help with whom they could communicate. Although we are of the view that clearing barriers from the path of entry will help alleviate this problem, other steps may also be needed. Increased access to retraining, where it is required, both through a basic increase in retraining facilities and through giving priority in the allocation of retraining spots to candidates particularly qualified to meet these identified needs, has been considered by the Task Force as a way of increasing the likelihood that cultural communities will be served by their own members. We discuss this issue in Chapter 9, "Retraining," and make a particular recommendation there on this problem.

Immigration Classification System

The *Immigration Act* defines the word "immigrant" as a person who seeks landing or lawful permission to come to Canada to establish permanent residence.[12]

The *Immigration Act* currently specifies three broad classes of immigrants: family class, Convention refugees, and independent applicants.[13] The planning of immigration levels, a joint consultative process between the federal and the provincial governments, results from an independent analysis of each of these main program components.[14]

The point system to assess the admissibility of immigrants to Canada was introduced in 1967, following the introduction of the federal White Paper on Immigration in 1966. The point system is a selection system based on education, specific vocational preparation, occupational experience, occupational demand, arranged employment, demographic factors, age, language ability, and personal suitability. The maximum points awarded for each category range from five to fifteen. The 1967 regulations officially eliminated all references to racial and ethnic characteristics as criteria for admission.[15]

"Family class" immigrants are those sponsored by certain close relatives and may, depending upon actual circumstances, include the sponsor's: spouse, son/daughter (unmarried), father/mother, grandfather/ grandmother. The sponsor must be a Canadian citizen or permanent resident at least 18 years of age and residing in Canada. Individuals in this class are not assessed under the point system; the sponsors must sign undertakings of assistance for them, which may be required for up to 10 years.

The definition of "Convention refugees" is based on the United Nations Convention and Protocol Relating to the Status of Refugees. Refugees seeking resettlement in Canada are assessed against factors relating to their adaptability to Canadian life and on the amount of settlement assistance available to them in Canada, or they are admitted on humanitarian grounds in times of crisis.

The "independent and other" category is composed of independent applicants, including assisted relatives, as well as business class immigrants and retired individuals. People in this class, apart from retirees, are assessed and selected according to the point system, with various applications (depending upon category of applicant).

"Assisted relatives" are those who do not fit within the definition of family class and are unable to qualify under the normal selection criteria, but who have a relative in Canada able and willing to sponsor them. Assisted relatives are assessed for permanent residence status in the same way as independent applicants with no relatives in Canada, except that they are not required to have the same number of units of assessment (points). In addition, they must have training and experience in an occupation identified as in demand; must have an employment offer that could not have been filled by a Canadian; or must be qualified in an occupation designated as in demand in a particular geographic area. Sponsors of assisted relatives may be required to provide undertakings for up to five years.

"Business class" immigrants include entrepreneurs, investors, and self-employed individuals. An entrepreneur is an immigrant who intends to and has the ability to establish or purchase a substantial interest in the ownership of a business or commercial venture in Canada whereby employment opportunities will be created or maintained for more than one Canadian citizen or permanent resident. An investor must have a proven track record in business, a personal net worth of $500,000 or more, and agree to invest capital in a Canadian business venture which will bring a significant economic benefit to the province in which it is located. A self-employed immigrant must intend to and have the ability to establish a business in Canada that will create an employment opportunity for himself/herself and will make a significant contribution to the country's economy or its cultural and artistic life. The usual occupational and employment-related factors are not applied to business class immigrants.

A "retiree" is an immigrant who is financially secure, at least 55 years old, and does not intend to seek or accept employment in Canada.

There are also separate provisions for the entry of foreign domestics, applicants essential to a family business, and applications based on humanitarian and compassionate grounds.

We encountered in our studies different attitudes towards different categories of immigrants. The suggestion was frequently made that immigrants coming to Ontario who are not refugees should be viewed as arriving with the knowledge that their opportunities for licensure or certification in their occupation might well be limited. Some applicants, it was said, were presented with documents for signature that advised them of the limited opportunities here, and therefore these candidates entered Ontario with full knowledge of restrictions on opportunities for licensure. From immigrants themselves, among others, we heard of very limited counselling and of documents being presented in English or French only — if presented at all — with little or no explanation.

We have considered the question of this immigrant "waiver" in more detail in our study of the medical profession (in Chapter 10), where the issue arises most often. Our conclusion, which is based on consideration of the written and oral submissions of foreign-trained individuals and representatives of organizations serving the immigrant communities, is that counselling in general is sporadic, and that the presentation of these waiver documents is sufficiently irregular and so often accompanied by such an inadequate explanation that they cannot be relied on. Even if such were not the case, we have further taken the position throughout our study that all foreign-trained individuals legally present and entitled to employment in Ontario should be viewed as having equal status for purposes of professional registration. We do not endorse any notion of "qualified citizenship" through the placing of such limitations on basic human rights from the moment of entry. The determinations made about entry to this country, however, are matters of immigration policy and regulation beyond the jurisdiction of this Task Force. We do not question those judgments here; but we insist on the principle that all Ontario residents, once admitted, must be treated equally.

CANADIANS TRAINED OUTSIDE ONTARIO

Although foreign training is most often associated with immigrants to Canada, it is not in fact limited to that group. There are numerous instances of Canadians training abroad and returning to Canada to practise their profession. It is clear that Canadians who train abroad cannot be given any more, or any less, credit for the training they have received than any other candidate with similar training, and we have encountered no profession that varies its standards this way. Apart from the linguistic and cultural advantages they have, foreign-trained Canadians in general apply on a basis equal to that of other foreign-trained individuals. If, however, entry to Ontario academic programs becomes increasingly difficult, the numbers of Canadians training offshore can become significant (medicine is a prime example), giving rise to a concern that these candidates for licensure may be finding an easier route to professional status than those who stay and train at home. This might be the case, for example, if the foreign program were shorter than that offered in Ontario, or if the admission standard or the demands of the program were lower. Although we endorse the view that it should not be easier for an out-of-province-trained candidate to qualify for registration or licensure, the situation is unlikely to arise because comprehensive assessments of equivalency should take into account each of these factors. The structure of assessment that we propose (Chapter 5, "Prior Learning Assessment") is, in our view, responsive to this issue.

As a final note here, although our study is formally restricted to candidates who received training or experience outside of Canada, we have also considered the situation faced by individuals trained in other provinces. In some cases, their situation highlights and puts into perspective the kind of treatment afforded candidates trained outside of the country.

The degree of interprovincial mobility in Canada varies from profession to profession. On the one hand, where there exists a national body or board that conducts assessments or examinations of candidates (for example, the National Dental Examining Board, the Pharmacy Examining Board of Canada), mobility is high, and even where such a system is not in place, accreditation procedures and reciprocity schemes may exist to aid in mobility. On the other hand, a transfer from one province to another can in some cases entail assessment and re-examination.

It should be noted that for some immigrant Canadians, problems remain regardless of the fact that they may have domestic training. It was brought to our attention that in spite of the advantages Canadian training may give them in the credentialing process, their visible minority status is sometimes an impediment to full and rewarding acceptance and employment. Our study is limited to candidates with foreign training and therefore we did not consider the plight of this group, but their concerns merit further attention.

MULTICULTURALISM

Canadians see their country as multicultural, multilingual, and multiracial. In first announcing a policy of "multiculturalism" in 1971, Prime Minister Pierre Trudeau emphasized as a primary objective the breaking down of discriminatory attitudes by overcoming barriers to full participation in Canadian society. The Canadian value expressed in "multiculturalism" thus embraces an interest in equality and amicability among racial and ethnic groups, as well as an interest in cultural maintenance and enhancement. It is a value that emphasizes respect for the different backgrounds of all who come to Canada. Indeed, the *Canadian Charter of Rights and Freedoms* includes section 27, which provides that "This Charter shall be interpreted in a manner consistent with the preservation and enhancement of the multicultural heritage of Canadians."

The *Canadian Multiculturalism Act*,[16] enacted in July 1988, sets forth the Multiculturalism Policy of Canada, which reads in part:

3. (1) It is hereby declared to be the policy of the Government of Canada to

. . .

(c) promote the full and equitable participation of individuals and communities of all origins in the continuing evolution and shaping of all aspects of Canadian society and assist them in the elimination of any barrier to such participation;

. . .

(e) ensure that all individuals receive equal treatment and equal protection under the law, while respecting and valuing their diversity;

(f) encourage and assist the social, cultural, economic and political institutions of Canada to be both respectful and inclusive of Canada's multicultural character;

. . .

(2) It is further declared to be the policy of the Government of Canada that all federal institutions shall:

(a) ensure that Canadians of all origins have an equal opportunity to obtain employment and advancement in those institutions; [and]

(b) promote policies, programs and practices that enhance the ability of individuals and communities of all origins to contribute to the continuing evolution of Canada;

The Canadian Government takes pride in referring to this legislation as unique in the world. These declarations represent a codification of core Canadian values. Although Canada is a federal state, and the articulated formal policy is that seen at the federal level, the provincial governments subscribe to these policy values as well.

In June 1987 the Ontario Government articulated its Policy on Multiculturalism, which states:

I   The Government of Ontario acknowledges and welcomes the diversity of cultures in this province.

II   Our varied cultural backgrounds are a source of enrichment and strength.

III The government is committed to ensuring that people of all cultures and races live as equal and responsible citizens in the province.

IV   Every person in Ontario is entitled to equal access and participation, and each person may choose to preserve or share aspects of his or her culture.

V   The goal of the government's multiculturalism policy is to ensure that individuals of all cultural heritages have equal opportunity to develop their individual potential.

- To that end, the government will promote greater knowledge, understanding, acceptance and celebration of our cultural diversity.

- An extensive, systematic program of public education will encourage the people of Ontario to become more aware of the province's many cultures.

VI   Government policies, appointments and programs will reflect the spirit of this policy.

- The government will actively seek out the ideas, views and concerns of individuals and cultural communities.

- All government ministries will review and revise all current and future policies to ensure they reflect our policy on multiculturalism.

- The government will reflect the spirit of this policy in its hiring practices and in its appointments to agencies, boards, commissions and similar groups.

VII General public services provided by the government will be sensitive to cultural values and traditions.

- All government ministries, agencies, boards and commissions will plan, design and deliver programs, services and initiatives which are accessible to all Ontarians.

- The government will encourage other levels of government, as well as non-government committees, groups and organizations, to offer programs and services which are accessible to everyone.

Ontario's Policy on Multiculturalism, as expressed by the Government's declaration, encourages "all people to celebrate and share their history, while participating fully in the economic and social life of the province." The policy seeks to utilize the strengths of our rich, cultural heritage "to prosper and live in harmony" and to "provide an opportunity for equal and responsible citizenship for all."

The Government of Ontario's Policy on Race Relations, announced in May 1986, provides in part that:

The Government of Ontario recognizes that the diversity of our community has brought cultural, social and economic enrichment to the province and its residents.

The government also recognizes that racial minorities often encounter barriers to their full participation in society. The government is committed to equality of treatment and opportunity for all Ontario residents and recognizes that a harmonious racial climate is essential to the future prosperity and social well-being of this province.

Therefore the government declares that:

I   Every person in Ontario has the right to a life free from racial discrimination and prejudice.

II   The government will take an active role in the elimination of all racial discrimination, including those policies and practices which, while not intentionally discriminatory, have a discriminatory effect. To this end, the government is committed to:

    (a) Employment equity policies and practices within the public service and throughout Ontario that ensure equality of treatment and opportunity through affirmative strategies.

    (b) Government services to the public that reflect the particular needs and perspectives of racial minorities.

    . . .

    (d) Appointments to agencies, boards and commissions that ensure these bodies fully reflect the racial diversity of Ontario.

    (e) The elimination of racial prejudice and negative stereotyping and their effects.

Hence, multiculturalism should be seen as "one of a bundle of related policies, including those concerning immigration, citizenship and human rights."[17] Ontario's policies on multiculturalism, race relations, and human rights mean that systemic discrimination towards immigrants in respect of access to the professions and trades is contrary to expressly stated public policies. Such discrimination must be effectively addressed and remedied to achieve the objectives of these policies.

PART II

Issues Facing the Trades and Professions

CHAPTER 3

Issues Facing the Trades

The participants ... come from many different cultural, educational, economic and professional (and non-professional) backgrounds. At least half, however, have a trade or profession acquired from the country of origin. Despite this apparent advantage to enter the Canadian workforce, we have found they are (at least in the first three years) just as employment disadvantaged as an immigrant with no marketable skills.

— from a Brief submitted to the
Task Force by an organization

SCOPE OF REVIEW

There is no uniformly accepted definition of a trade. The most common approach to defining the trades as a category is to describe the type of work performed, such as carpentry, plumbing, or masonry, or to use a requirement of manual skill gained through on-the-job training to distinguish trades from occupations requiring academic training. Such descriptions are not wholly satisfactory, however. Not only do a wide range of occupations include on-the-job training or experience as a prerequisite to qualification, but, as the amount of technological skill required for all occupations increases, the traditional distinction between trades and professions based on educational achievement diminishes.

In this Report, "trades" is used to refer to those 70 occupations that, in Ontario, use apprenticeship[1] as the primary means of training and are regulated under the *Apprenticeship and Tradesmen's Qualification Act (ATQA)*.[2] The decision to restrict our review to the trades regulated under the *ATQA* is consistent with the Task Force's focus on occupations that require licensure as a legal prerequisite to practise or for which certification confers a title or elevated employment status. A list of these 70 trades appears in the Appendix at the end of this chapter.

CURRENT CONTEXT

The review by the Task Force of the policies and procedures used in the regulated trades to evaluate foreign-trained tradespeople comes at a critical time in Ontario, given shortages in the labour force and the rapid development of highly technical trades. An ever-increasing demand for skilled labour has resulted from both an increase in construction and manufacturing activity and the trend in goods-production and service-production industries to use increasingly complex technology.[3] The shortage of domestic labour, however, is expected to continue to be most evident in the high-skilled technical occupations.[4]

At the same time there has been a decrease in the number of immigrants who designate high-skilled technical occupations as their intended occupation in Canada.[5] A high and increasing proportion of immigrants is coming to Canada from countries with dissimilar technological development and skills training. The result is that Ontario can no longer rely on immigration to remedy its shortfall in the supply of trained labour. It has therefore become increasingly important to ensure that appropriate retraining opportunities are available to both foreign-trained and Ontario-trained workers who have partial training and need to master only a limited number of additional competencies to move into a highly technical trade.

The position of the foreign-trained tradesperson parallels that of the domestically trained tradesperson working in a skills area in declining demand because of changes in technology: he or she will require retraining but should be able to use competencies already acquired to build towards certification in another trade. In this way, accuracy in assessing prior training is as important as establishing the appropriate training programs.

Immigration, particularly of partially and fully skilled tradespeople, will be essential to the continued economic growth of Ontario, and an increasing percentage of immigrant tradespeople will require a degree of skills training. The province's education and training system cannot avoid being put under stress as it attempts to assimilate the immigrant with partial skills into Ontario's high-technology manufacturing, construction, and service industries. Unless the system is adjusted to serve this vital new client group effectively, a principal source of skilled labour will be lost to the province. Moreover, adjustment is equally important to meet the needs of Ontario-trained tradespeople displaced by technology or, in the years ahead, by the impact of the *Free Trade Agreement* with the United States. Such adjustment should include, above all, the creation of an education and training system that can accurately and fairly assess prior training and experience and provide training opportunities to match identified gaps in skill. Such a training model must be able to function within a medium-range planning framework and not simply respond to the vagaries of economic cycles and the marketplace.[6]

TRADE REGULATION IN ONTARIO

The first government-sponsored apprenticeship program in Canada was established by the *Ontario Apprenticeship Act, 1928.*[7] The *Act* was of limited scope, making provision for the registration of minors in the six construction trades (bricklaying, masonry, carpentry, painting, decorating, and plastering) that suffered from chronic labour shortages in the 1920s.[8] The *Act* went through two major revisions before the present form was established.

The first major revision of the legislation was enacted in 1962, pursuant to the recommendations of a Select Committee of the House under the chairmanship of J.R. Simonett, MPP. In an effort to deal with shortages of skilled labour resulting from technological advances, the Simonett Report recommended compulsory licensure[9] of tradespeople, which was introduced in the new legislation. The amendments sought to promote apprenticeship training, raise the status of the trades, and attract more apprentices. Prior to 1963, only motor vehicle mechanics and hairdressers were required to be licensed. By 1966, six other trades were designated as licensed,[10] with the number eventually reaching a total of nineteen.

In 1972 a further comprehensive review of apprenticeship was undertaken by a provincial task force under the chairmanship of W.R. Dymond. The Dymond Report recommended moving away from licensing, arguing that public health and safety did not require licensing in any trade other than motor vehicle repair. Opposition from employers and trade unions persuaded the Government not to eliminate the requirement that tradespeople be licensed in order to work in those trades already so designated, but the Government did create another category of trades: the "voluntary" certified trades. Any trades that have become regulated since 1969 do not require licensing as a condition of practice,[11] but regulations provide that certification may be obtained on a voluntary basis. (Exceptions were hairstylists, who gained compulsory certification as a branch of the hairdressers trade, which already had compulsory certification; and hoisting engineers, whose compulsory certification status was maintained when the trade was transferred from the Ministry of Consumer and Commercial Relations.)

In 1985 responsibility for administration of the *Apprenticeship and Tradesmen's Qualification Act* was shifted to the newly created Ministry of Skills Development.

THE REGULATORY SYSTEM

The apprenticeship training system in Ontario is established under the *ATQA*. The director of apprenticeship, under the authority of the Minister of Skills Development, is responsible for the administration of the *Act*.

Two principal categories of trades are covered by the *ATQA*: the regulated trades and the non-regulated, or employer-sponsored, trades.

Regulated Trades

The regulated trades, which are the primary focus of this chapter, are those for which the *ATQA* prescribes an apprenticeship training program through regulations. There are 70 trades in this category, including branches of trades (see Appendix at the end of this chapter). The regulations set out the general terms of the apprenticeship contract, a detailed description of the competencies to be learned, and the duration of each portion of the training program. In each of the regulated trades an apprentice may earn a certificate of qualification and become a fully qualified journeyman[12] by successfully completing the apprenticeship program.

Licensed Trades

The regulated trades are in turn subdivided into two groups. The first group consists of those designated in the *ATQA* as certified,[13] meaning that in order to work in the trade, a practitioner must possess a certificate of qualification in the trade or be registered as an apprentice. There are 19 trades or branches of trades in this category, commonly referred to as the "compulsory trades." (The branch trades within a trade area, such as construction lineman and power lineman, which are the two branches of the lineman trade area, have a common core curriculum plus a specialized training component. They also have differentiated training periods of 6,500 hours and 8,000 hours, respectively, which are designed to reflect the levels of competency required.) Certification is a legal prerequisite to practice of the trade, and so the certification process for the compulsory trades is actually a licensing process. Our Report refers to these 19 trades as the licensed trades.

Voluntary Trades

The second subgroup of regulated trades are commonly referred to as the "voluntary trades." The regulations for the voluntary trades mirror those for the compulsory trades, except that there is no legal requirement that a person hold a certificate of qualification or be registered as an apprentice in order to work in the trade. An employer or union may, however, make certification in a voluntary trade a prerequisite for obtaining employment. There are 51 voluntary trades, including branches of trades, which in our Report are referred to as non-licensed regulated trades. Although certification operates as proof of completion of apprenticeship training, it is not a prerequisite to practice of the trade.

Finally, it should be noted that categorization of a particular regulated trade as compulsory (licensed) or voluntary (unlicensed) is not based on inherent considerations of public health and safety. As noted in our historical overview, categorization is primarily a question of timing: trades that became regulated after the Dymond Report in 1973 have, with two exceptions, all been regulated as voluntary or non-licensed trades.

Non-Regulated Trades

The non-regulated, or employer-sponsored, trades are not the focus of this Report. These are trades for which particularized training programs have been established at the instigation of an employer who wishes to upgrade the skills of his or her current workforce. The employer, in consultation with the apprenticeship branch of the Ministry of Skills Development, determines the nature and scope of an apprenticeship training program suited to the training needs of the workplace and registers the program with the director of apprenticeship. The apprenticeships in the employer-sponsored trades may not for the most part include any classroom training. There is no curriculum set by regulation, and there is no provincewide final examination. Completion of the apprenticeship leads to a certificate of apprenticeship but does not allow the participant to attain full journeyman's status and a certificate of qualification as in the regulated trades.

Because access to employment is not limited by a licensing or certification requirement imposed by law, the approximately 450 trades in the non-regulated category are not discussed further in this Report.

CERTIFICATION AND LICENSURE PROCESS — THREE ROUTES

The ultimate goal of someone participating in a regulated apprenticeship training program is to obtain a certificate of qualification. As we have noted, this certificate is available only for regulated trades and is a prerequisite for only the 19 compulsory trades. To obtain a certificate of qualification one must complete an apprenticeship training program in Ontario; demonstrate an acceptable level of training or experience; or hold an interprovincial red seal certificate. We look at each of these three routes in turn.

Route 1 — Apprenticeship Training

The training route is followed by an Ontario resident who either does not have any training in the particular trade or may have received partial training, in or out of Canada, but does not have sufficient competency to qualify for a certificate of qualification without further training.

Entrance Requirements

Applicants wanting to enter an apprenticeship training program must satisfy requirements of employment, age, education, and language.

Employment. A primary condition of entry into apprenticeship training is the obtaining of employment as an apprentice. In the present system, apprenticeship training is delivered pursuant to a contract between an employee and an employer: the employer provides training, and the apprentice delivers progressively more skilled labour. (It is important to note that employers in the apprenticeship system may include union hiring halls, local apprenticeship committees, the Ontario Industrial Training Institute in rare instances, and private businesses, such as construction contractors or automobile service stations.) The employer sets the employment criteria, which may exceed those required by legislation; the Ministry of Skills Development does not monitor or intervene in the setting of these standards.

Age. All applicants must be age 16 or over.

Education. A minimum Grade 10 standing is required by the General Regulations under the *ATQA*, unless otherwise provided in the trade-specific regulation.[14]

Academic credentials from out of province are evaluated by an industrial training consultant (ITC) employed by the Ministry of Skills Development in one of the 27 apprenticeship field offices. (The primary responsibility of the industrial training consultant is to administer the apprentice training program on behalf of the director of apprenticeship within a particular geographic region. Responsibilities may include program promotion; employer liaison; assessment of credentials and competencies of prospective apprentices, and of those seeking to challenge for a certificate of qualification; and co-ordinating of in-school training in cooperation with the colleges.)

If an applicant's documents are not in English or French, they are first sent to the Ministry of Education for translation.

Foreign-trained applicants who cannot demonstrate attainment of a Grade 10 education or who have not been educated in English or French are asked to write an entrance examination, called the Progressive Achievement Test (PAT).[15] The PAT includes the Gates-MacGinitie test of language proficiency, as well as a mathematics and science component. Although the legislation makes no reference to an entrance examination, Ministry policy is to require that the PAT be written and that candidates be at least 18 years old and out of school for at least one year.

Language. All applicants not educated in English or French are required to demonstrate, through the Gates-MacGinitie language test, the ability to read and speak English at a Grade 8 level. This requirement is not set out in the *Act* or regulations.

Training Program

An individual seeking to be a tradesperson enters an apprentice training contract with an employer and, over a period of two to five years, as specified in the trade-specific regulation, learns the trade through a combination of on-the-job training, supervised by a journeyman (approximately 90 per cent of total hours), and classroom training, usually provided by a community college. (The hairdressing trades are an exception in that the in-school portion of training can be offered through licensed trade schools. In rare instances, unions deliver the in-school portion based on a provincially developed curriculum.) At the end of the apprenticeship period the apprentice writes examinations set by the director.

In-school training typically consists of two or three blocks of full-time instruction ("block release"), each six to ten weeks, during which the skills of the trade are covered cyclically at progressively more sophisticated levels. Some colleges schedule the classroom training one day per week for the duration of the apprenticeship, ("day release"). Other variations in program delivery include the Modified Apprenticeship Program (MAP). MAP 40, for example, provides all the classroom training for a motor vehicle mechanic apprentice up-front in a 40-week block. MAP 1-2-3 schedules alternating eight-week periods of classroom instruction and on-the-job training; instruction is not cyclical but covers one set of skills completely before moving to the next.

The minimum wages earned by an apprentice while on the job are set by regulation at a percentage of the average rate of pay for the employer's journeymen in the trade.[16] The pay rate increases at each training period in the apprenticeship and, unless otherwise specified by regulation, begins at a minimum of 40 per cent of the journeyman rate for the first period, progressing at 10 per cent intervals to 80 per cent for apprentices in their fifth period of training.

Apprentices, although generally not paid by the employer for classroom days, may qualify for benefits under the *Unemployment Insurance Act*[17] or for a federal training allowance pursuant to the *National Training Act*.[18] In modified apprenticeship programs, the apprentice receives a provincial training allowance during the initial 40 weeks of classroom instruction.

Advanced Standing

People entering the apprenticeship training program with prior trade-related training or experience, whether gained in Ontario or elsewhere, may be able to obtain advanced standing as an apprentice.

The General Regulations[19] provide that the director may grant hourly credits according to a review of documentary evidence on relevant training or experience. The applicant's skill may be tested, as required by the director. In practice the applicant submits documentation to an industrial training consultant who, under the guidance of the director, evaluates the relevance and completeness of the training or experience. If advanced standing is warranted, the consultant may recommend to the apprentice's prospective employer that hourly credits be granted to reduce the length of apprenticeship. There are no written guidelines outlining the circumstances under which advanced standing is given. Moreover, the assessment by the consultant is not binding on a prospective employer; the level at which the apprentice is hired will depend on the balance of bargaining power between the employer and the applicant apprentice. In a market characterized by labour shortages, the apprentice may be hired with the degree of advanced standing recommended by the consultant. The only option for the prospective apprentice not content with a credit assessment is to try to find an employer willing to give greater recognition to the prior training or experience.

Route 2 — Demonstration of Competence

The second route to certification is based on the provisions in the General Regulations that allow a tradesperson who can demonstrate prior training and/or experience to receive a provisional certificate of qualification and write the certificate of qualification examinations on a challenge basis.

A foreign-trained applicant who wishes to obtain a certificate of qualification without entering the apprenticeship training program must first arrange to be interviewed by an industrial training consultant, who assesses the applicant's background and skill. If documentation demonstrates prior employment as a journeyman for a period equal to or longer than the required apprenticeship period, the applicant may be granted a provisional certificate and be permitted to write the qualifying examinations.[20] Work experience as a journeyman outside Ontario may be documented through time sheets, letters from employers, or the applicant's affidavit.

The completion of a formal training program in another jurisdiction may also be considered by the industrial training consultant[21] and qualify the applicant to receive a provisional certificate and write the final examination.

If the consultant does not feel the documentation of experience or training provided by the applicant demonstrates the necessary competencies, the applicant may be given an opportunity to take a demonstration of skills test (DOST). This practical test, available in only five compulsory trades (for electrician, motor vehicle mechanic, plumber, steamfitter, and sheet metal worker) is developed and administered by faculty at the colleges of applied arts and technology who teach the classroom component of the apprenticeship training courses. The written instructions for the test are available in 15-20 languages, depending upon the trade.

Applicants who satisfy the industrial training consultant of their competence on the basis of documentation of experience and/or training, or on the basis of a demonstration of skills test, will be permitted to write the qualifying examination at the next scheduled sitting. If the DOST results indicate that the person needs time to learn additional material, such as Ontario-specific procedures (for example, the *Ontario Building Code*), a provisional certificate may be issued for 90 days and renewed as necessary until the applicant is ready to write the qualifying examination.

If an applicant does not pass the demonstration of skills test, or if a test is not available and the industrial training consultant does not think that the applicant has the qualifications necessary to write the certificate of qualification examination, the applicant must enter an apprentice training program. The industrial training consultant may recommend that the applicant be given some credit for prior training and experience, but this recommendation, as mentioned above, is not binding on the employer.

If the applicant is permitted to write the certificate of qualification examination an interpreter may assist, provided the interpreter is not a practitioner of the trade and has not served as one during the preceding 12 months.

Route 3 — Interprovincial Transfers

Interprovincial mobility for tradespeople is accomplished through a pan-Canadian certification agreement administered by the interprovincial standards program co-ordinating committee in cooperation with the provincial, territorial, and federal governments. The interprovincial standards' "red seal" certificate may be earned in 21 of the regulated trades by writing the prescribed interprovincial standards examination (an interpreter is not permitted) and earning a minimum score of 70 per cent. The holder of a red seal certificate may practise the trade throughout Canada without further training or examination.

TRAINING AND SKILL CERTIFICATION: OTHER MODELS

Although apprenticeship as a method of vocational training is common to many jurisdictions, other models exist in Ontario and elsewhere and are useful as examples of ways in which programs may be more responsive to the particular needs of people who enter or re-enter the workforce having experience or training behind them. The Task Force reviewed programs in Ontario, Sweden, and Great Britain. A summary of some aspects of other models in Ontario and Great Britain is included below. The Swedish vocational education system and the program for the evaluation of foreign training are discussed in Chapters 5 ("Prior Learning Assessment") and 9 ("Retraining") of this Report.

Ontario

Two non-apprenticeship approaches to training developed in Ontario were examined: the cooperative education model used in high schools, colleges, and universities to provide on-the-job training to students through placements arranged by the educational institution; and the competency-based training program developed in the hard- and soft-mining sector, which is based on the development of specific skills organized in sets or modules.

Cooperative Education

The term "cooperative education" is used to describe a program of classroom-based course work into which related work experience, as arranged by the educational institution, is formally rotated. The type and length of the work experience component depend upon the program. The educational body supervises both the student and the placement, ensuring that the training goals of the placement are met.

Since 1985 funds for cooperative education programs have been a cost-sharing option within the job entry program of the Canadian Jobs Strategy, under which the federal Government will match up to $200,000 over a four-year period to cover start-up or improvement costs. The funding contract is with the educational institution delivering the cooperative education program.[22]

The Ministry of Skills Development does not at present deliver any cooperative programs but is developing a cooperative apprenticeship training project in conjunction with school boards. The format under discussion involves three days of on-the-job training followed by two days in school, with a summer in-school component added. The school board would assist the apprentice in obtaining appropriate employment. This program will constitute a form of modified apprenticeship programming.

The *Report of the Premier's Council* (1988) has applauded the move by the Ministry towards use of a cooperative education model, noting that it allows flexibility in the timing of in-school and on-the-job training.[23] The Task Force also noted a particular advantage from the point of view of ensuring equal accessibility to foreign-trained tradespeople, who could enter an apprenticeship training program at a community college and not be required to secure employment independently as a prerequisite to the training.

Competency-Based Learning

A competency-based (also called performance-based) training system has standards of learner performance explicitly built into its description of learning objectives. Mastery of learning is demonstrated by the learner performing at the standard set out in the objective. Competency-based learning is particularly useful in skill-oriented areas where, once skill mastery can be demonstrated, the learner is able to move on. Traditionally, learning programs have been time-based, requiring the learner to spend predetermined periods in learning; although there is some opportunity for repeating the period on failure, there is not the flexibility that allows the learner to shorten or lengthen the time spent according to how quickly he or she demonstrates mastery of the skill.

The training program for the hard- and soft-rock mining trades in Ontario, established by regulations under the *Occupational Health and Safety Act*,[24] follows a competency-based model that differs substantially from the time-based apprenticeship model described earlier in this chapter. There is no classroom component, and the worker must master a core curriculum and a number of specialized sets of skills organized in groups that are referred to as training or skill modules.

A person is required to take only those modules for which he or she cannot otherwise demonstrate competency through the challenge examinations. A miner coming to Ontario may complete the program, by successfully writing a battery of challenge examinations, in as little as one week. If the person requires further training, it must be provided by the employer as specified in the regulations.

The organization of learning into modules and the option of completing skill modules by demonstrating performance ability struck the Task Force as particularly attractive aspects of the training program's structure.

Great Britain

The Report of the Premier's Council (1988) has noted the absence in Canada of a single institution with responsibility for advocating and developing training priorities and programs on a national level, in cooperation with all levels of government and industry. The Manpower Services Commission in Great Britain is cited as an example of such an institution.[25]

The Task Force reviewed four training initiatives recently developed by the Manpower Services Commission,[26] which is responsible for administering public employment and training services in Scotland, England, and Wales.

In the first initiative, introduced in Scotland in 1983, the Scottish Action Plan set out to convert the vocational education curricula to a modular, competency-based system and introduced a single, cumulative certificate, the Scottish National Certificate.

The cumulative certificate allows students to change specialization without loss of credit, to accumulate nationally recognized programs suited to the employment needs of the locale, and to receive credit for prior related learning.

The second initiative introduced by the Manpower Services Commission in the area of vocational training is the Standards Programme, a developing system of employment-related performance standards targeted to cover all occupations by 1991.

The new standards, which are competency-based, are stated in a standardized format in order to facilitate credit accumulation and transfer. The commission anticipates the adoption of these standards by different industries and businesses, as well as by the public sector.

The third vocational training initiative in Great Britain is directed at unemployed adults. The New Job Training Scheme, launched in 1988, offers up to six months' training based on the Standards Programme, thereby guaranteeing relevance to employment criteria. Portability of training is a key element. A participant who leaves the program to take employment can obtain credit for the completed portion of training.

The fourth major initiative is the National Record of Vocational Achievement, introduced in 1988 as a national vocation certification available to all people in England and Wales, which provides an individual record of successful completion of a recognized unit of training, independent of the awarding educational body. Unlike the Scottish National Certificate, which is administered by a single awarding body, the National Record of Vocational Achievement records credits for programs delivered by other awarding bodies.

These four initiatives in skills-training — the Scottish National Certificate, the Standards Programme, the New Job Training Scheme, and the National Record for Vocational Achievement — appear to be having a significant impact on the quality and relevance of occupational training. The four initiatives have created a training system that is receptive to adults and facilitates both the transferability of skills and the recognition of prior learning. In this respect, the Task Force believes that developments in vocational education in Great Britain produce a useful model for consideration in Ontario.

ISSUES RELATED TO ACCESS

The Task Force, in examining the apprenticeship system in Ontario, reviewed each step in the entry process and, where appropriate, compared programs in other jurisdictions in an effort to identify specific policies or procedures that may put people with foreign training at a disadvantage.

The Task Force concluded that the following specific aspects of the entry and qualification process may be disadvantageous to foreign-trained applicants:

• the unavailability of information about how to become certified or licensed, including information about the evaluation of prior education and experience and the alternative types of training programs available;

• the integration of employment into the qualification, certification, and licensure process, and the resulting ability of the employer to control access to government-sponsored training programs;

• the absence of a reliable and publicly accountable system for evaluating foreign training and experience; in matters of such assessment, the delegation of the decision-making power of the director of apprenticeship to employers; and the absence of an appeal mechanism to afford applicants the right to an independent review of decisions concerning the equivalency of non-Ontario training and experience;

• the unavailability of retraining opportunities for people who have completed part of their training outside Canada;

- the invalidity and inappropriateness of examinations and tests used in the certification and licensure process;

- the unavailability and inadequacy of the financial support provided to apprentices;

- the level of language proficiency required and the inappropriateness of the examinations currently used in assessing language proficiency; and

- the absence of statistical data on both the apprenticeship training program and the population of registered journeymen.

We now discuss each of these issues in detail.

Availability and Nature of Information

The unavailability of information about the apprenticeship program and the requirements for obtaining a certificate of qualification in the regulated trades is a serious problem. There is virtually no material available to a foreign-trained person before or after coming to Ontario that explains in simple, clear language how to become certified or licensed in a trade and sets out the specific requirements involved in the evaluation process.

The type of information that is essential goes beyond a simple explanation of the system and the listing of the name and address of the office where application forms are available. It must describe the process and requirements for licensure or certification sufficiently to allow a candidate to prepare for an interview or examinations and assess whether further training would be appropriate prior to attempting an examination.

Information about the apprenticeship system in Canada is distributed to immigration offices around the world through an annual report prepared by Employment and Immigration Canada. The section on trades training in Ontario is reviewed annually for accuracy by the Ministry of Skills Development. A copy of the report provided to the Task Force was found to be sparse in detail. It did not include any information covering the requirements that a person with partial foreign training would have to meet to complete his or her training in Ontario.

A newly arrived immigrant will find general information on apprenticeship and other trades- training programs available through a number of provincial and federal government offices. There is no material available in languages other than English and French, however, nor is there a specific booklet or pamphlet written in easily understood language and geared to the information needs of immigrant tradespeople seeking recognition of prior training.

In addition to a paucity of information about the licensure and certification process, there is no written information made available by the Ministry of Skills Development on how to obtain a job as an apprentice. (The Ministry does not currently assume any responsibility for assisting applicants in this area, despite the fact that employment is an entry requirement to apprenticeship training.)

Role of Employer

Employers[27] are gatekeepers to entry into an apprenticeship training program: an apprentice may be registered by the Ministry of Skills Development only after obtaining employment as an apprentice. There are currently no programs that would allow an individual to complete the in-school portion of training prior to seeking employment as an apprentice. Entry to the training system is therefore disproportionately more difficult for people who may be disadvantaged in the employment market, including people from cultural or racial backgrounds that differ from those predominant in the trade, people with imperfect language fluency, and women generally.

The second area in which the role of the employer may create accessibility problems is the assessment of prior learning and experience. The employer has final decision-making power over the degree of credit that a foreign-trained tradesperson registering as an apprentice should receive. As we noted, this authority is not in keeping with section 9 of the General Regulations, which gives the director of apprenticeship the power and responsibility to assess the prior training and experience of apprentices and grant hourly credits where appropriate.

Evaluation of Non-Ontario Training and Experience

A foreign-trained tradesperson seeking recognition of his or her skills in Ontario is subject to the General Regulations that govern the evaluation of training and experience.

Section 9 of the General Regulations is applicable to partially skilled people and gives the director of apprenticeship the power to assess training and experience for advanced standing in the apprenticeship program. Sections 20 and 21, which apply to fully skilled people, give the director authority to recognize foreign trade *experience*, rather than *training,* as the basis for granting a provisional certificate and allowing an applicant to write the certificate of qualification examination on a challenge basis. Section 17, however, applies to people with or without experience who have completed alternative training. The director may grant a provisional certificate and allow the candidate to write the certificate of qualification examination if the training program is sufficiently long.

The Task Force makes the following observations on the process of evaluation of foreign training and experience:

- There is a consistent pattern of delegation of the director's decision-making power to employers of apprentices in the granting of credit for foreign training and experience. A Ministry of Skills Development industrial training consultant recommends a credit to be given by the employer; however, the employer is not bound by the recommendation. The actual degree of credit that a foreign-trained person is granted will depend on the balance of bargaining power between the employer and the applicant apprentice. The employer may ignore the recommendation and offer the applicant employment at a less advanced level. It should be noted that the more credit granted for prior training, the higher the starting wage that the employer must pay the apprentice.

- There is no comprehensive information base that an industrial training consultant making an assessment recommendation can draw upon to evaluate non-Ontario experience and training. Industrial training consultants may confer with the provincial program coordinators in the Program Standards office in Toronto, but there is no resource library on vocational training in other jurisdictions available even to the coordinators.

- The practice of assessing foreign training and experience lacks clarity and is not necessarily in accordance with the regulations. For example, we were advised that the director does not "approve" alternative training programs pursuant to section 17 of the General Regulations, although the section clearly requires such approval.

- In the evaluation of foreign credentials and experience, there is a very wide margin of unstructured discretion in the decision-making process. Putting aside for the moment the fact that the Ministry, in effect, gives final decision-making power to the employer, it should be noted that there apparently are no current comprehensive written guidelines to assist the industrial training consultant in making a recommendation concerning foreign training or to ensure consistency in credit recommendations from one consultant to another.[28] Further, there is no reporting system in place to promote consistency in evaluation by keeping industrial training consultants up to date on assessments being made across the province.

- Finally, there is no right of appeal or right of review in relation to evaluations of foreign training and experience. The *ATQA* provides a right to appeal only a decision to cancel an apprenticeship contract, a refusal to renew a certificate of qualification, and a decision to suspend or revoke a certificate of qualification.[29] By contrast, provisions in the apprenticeship legislation in Saskatchewan, Alberta, and British Columbia afford a wider right of appeal to a provincial apprenticeship board.

Retraining

In 1963 the *Report of the Select Committee on Manpower Training*[30] (the Simonett Report) recommended that special programs, including upgrading opportunities, be developed to assist immigrant tradespeople to prepare for the workforce and to obtain exposure to components of the Ontario training program not matched in their country of origin. As we discuss in Chapter 9 ("Retraining"), because both the demand for and the sources of skilled labour in Ontario are changing, the need identified in 1963 is increasingly urgent.

The design of training systems should aim to minimize the "down time" of people seeking entry to Ontario's labour force. An essential part of this design would include an effective and systematic means for assessing foreign training and experience and for identifying and delivering the training required to enable such individuals to be productive members of the labour force. The 1986 touchstone document of the Ministry, *Breaking New Ground*,[31] does not, however, make reference to the needs of or the need for foreign-trained tradespeople. Further, the province has yet to act on the recommendations on retraining set forth in the Simonett Report.

Testing

There are three types of testing featured in the apprenticeship system:

1) licensure and certification examinations (the certificate of qualification examination);
2) demonstration of skills tests (DOSTs); and
3) tests of educational equivalency and language proficiency (the Progressive Achievement Test (PAT), which incorporates the Gates-MacGinitie test of language proficiency).

Certificate of Qualification Examination

The absence of validity studies on the certificate of qualification examination is a cause for concern (see Chapter 6, "Licensure Testing"). There may be a cultural bias in the language of the examination; for example, the use of colloquialisms can put a candidate with foreign training at a disadvantage. Further, the level of language of the examination itself has not been assessed to determine if it is in keeping with the level required for practice in the trade.

Demonstration of Skills Tests (DOSTs)

From the point of view of the foreign-trained tradesperson, the availability of demonstration of skills tests can be extremely helpful: the tests provide an opportunity to prove competence in the field and are particularly useful when documentation of training cannot be provided. Demonstration of skills tests, however, have as noted been developed for only five of the compulsory trades. The five tests are available in 15-20 languages. But when is it appropriate to provide translations? There does not appear to be any consistent policy in this area.

Tests of Educational Equivalency and Language Proficiency

The Task Force is concerned that the Progressive Achievement Test (PAT), which is used to establish the educational level that has been attained by the test taker, may not be an appropriate measure of educational equivalency for the apprenticeship system. We understand that the Progressive Achievement Test, despite the name, examines intelligence and aptitude, not achievement or adult competence, as would be appropriate given its use in assessing educational equivalency.

Further, eligibility to write the Progressive Achievement Test is unduly restricted by an administrative policy that requires candidates to be at least 18 years old and out of school for no less than one year. This restriction, which was designed to discourage Ontario youth from leaving school early, is certainly inappropriate for foreign-trained applicants who wish to pursue their trade in Ontario.

The Task Force is also concerned that the Gates-MacGinitie test is not an appropriate measure of adult language performance. It was developed for use in the regular school system to test knowledge of language but is being used by the Ministry of Skills Development to test the language performance of adults. In other words, it appears that the test is inappropriate for use in testing the language skills of foreign-trained adults seeking entry to the apprenticeship training system.

Financial Hardship

The federal Government is responsible for providing income support for apprentices. Two principal vehicles deliver income support: the *Unemployment Insurance Act*[32] and the *National Training Act*[33]. From our perspective both are limited in terms of scope, adequacy, and efficiency.[34]

Section 39 of the *Unemployment Insurance Act* authorizes the payment of extended unemployment insurance benefits to apprentices receiving in-school training without subjecting them to employment search and availability requirements. An apprentice will qualify, however, only if he or she is otherwise eligible to receive unemployment insurance benefits. Some apprentices may not be eligible, either because they lack the required number of insured weeks of employment or because employment has not been terminated within the meaning of the *Act*. Further, apprentices in a day-release program do not qualify because they are not considered to be unemployed for the one day of training a week.

Somewhat problematic is the level of support received under the *Unemployment Insurance Act.* The current maximum weekly allowable benefit is $363 before taxes, but, because the level of unemployment insurance benefits is calculated as 60 per cent of insurable earnings during the 20-week period prior to layoff, the wage levels of first- and second-year apprentices, which are generally 40 per cent to 50 per cent of the journeyman's wage, mean that unemployment insurance is received at considerably less than the maximum allowable level.

Finally, apprentices face an administrative problem when they apply for unemployment insurance as an income support mechanism during in-school training. Because of delays in the processing of claims, the first payment is often not received until after the eight- or nine-week training period is over and the apprentice is back at work.[35]

Although apprentices who do not qualify for unemployment insurance benefits may be eligible for a training allowance under the *National Training Act,*[36] this allowance does not provide adequate income.[37] The current hourly rate for a trainee living independently and without dependants is $3.50 to a maximum of 40 hours weekly.[38]

A significant factor contributing to the unwillingness of adults to participate in long-term training, including apprenticeship, is the absence of appropriate income support. Indeed, the 1988 *Report of the Premier's Council* emphasized that inadequate income support contributes to the significant drop-out rate in the apprenticeship program.[39]

The lack of a properly funded training allowance program has a particularly strong impact on recently immigrated foreign-trained tradespeople who require some retraining; if they have dependants and have not brought with them a reserve of capital or had the opportunity to accumulate reserve financial resources in their new country, they will be unable to make use of appropriate training opportunities.

Language Proficiency

Although language testing is dealt with as a separate chapter (Chapter 7) of this Report, the absence of consistent, validated standards of language proficiency in the regulated trades raises particular concerns that merit consideration here.

The Ministry of Skills Development allows candidates writing the certificate of qualification examination to bring an interpreter to the examination. (The only exception is with respect to the interprovincial red seal examinations, for which an interpreter is not allowed.) Further, if a foreign-trained applicant is required to take a demonstration of skills test, written instruction, if available, is provided in his or her own language. Accordingly, for a fully qualified tradesperson seeking licensure or certification in Ontario, on a challenge basis, the language barriers to certification have been all but eliminated.

For a partially trained individual seeking to enter the apprenticeship system to complete his or her training, however, the requirements are quite different. If the candidate's formal education was in a language other than English, the individual is required to demonstrate at least a Grade 8 level of English proficiency on the Gates-MacGinitie language test. (Even if our earlier discussion of the inappropriateness of the language test being used is disregarded, the rationale for requiring Grade 8 proficiency seems displaced. If this level is required in order to ensure that the individual is able to benefit from classroom instruction in English, it would be more appropriate to transfer responsibility for language testing to the community colleges, along with responsibility for the provision of language training, as required. The test should be an assessment tool, not a barrier to entry to the training program.)

The problem, however, is more fundamental than a lack of consistency in language standards: it is the absence of validated language proficiency standards referenced to the requirement of public health and safety. Standards of language proficiency, related to public welfare concerns, should be developed for each regulated trade and should be applied equally to all applicants, whether entry is by taking the certificate of qualification examination on a challenge basis or by completing the apprenticeship program. This concern, in fact, was raised in a submission to the Task Force by the International Brotherhood of Electrical Workers, Local Union 105: "We believe that in the Spirit of Safety in the Construction Industry, everyone in the workplace has to be able to speak, read signs, and take directions in English to insure his own safety as well as the safety of his or her fellow employee.''

Statistical Data

The Ministry of Skills Development has no ongoing method of data collection to monitor participation in the apprenticeship system of people with foreign training or who are members of cultural or visible minority groups. The only data regularly collected by the Ministry are on age and sex of apprentices. Such data indicate that an average participation rate of women is 4.5 per cent, dropping to less than 1 per cent when the hairdressing/hairstyling, cook, and baker trades are removed from the calculation.

In 1988 the Ministry commissioned a survey of visible minority participation levels in the apprenticeship program. For the purposes of the survey, visible minorities were defined as Canadian-born or immigrant Ontario residents whose ethnic or racial background may act as a real or perceived barrier to full participation in training. These groups were specified to include:

Black:	Caribbean
	Other
Asian:	Chinese
	East Indian/Pakistani
	Japanese
	Korean
	Vietnamese/Cambodian/
	Laotian
	Filipino/Malaysian/
	Indonesian
	Other
Native:	Status Indian
	Non-Status Indian
	Métis
	Inuit

The survey results showed a 5 per cent participation rate of the specified visible minorities in the apprenticeship system. Findings also demonstrated that visible minorities earn less than other apprentices and are concentrated in the industrial and service sectors, which have relatively lower pay scales than construction and motive power.[40]

Although the 1988 survey revealed valuable information on the accessibility of apprenticeship training to cultural and visible minorities, there is a need for ongoing data collection if the Ministry is to monitor improvement in participation rates. Nevertheless, the Ministry has expressed a reluctance to burden the employer with the requirement of compiling statistics. Moreover, the Ministry itself, perhaps because of funding restrictions, does not compile statistics within its own information base. (An example is the failure to keep statistics on the annual number of provisional certificates issued and renewed, with a breakdown indicating the places of training.) Yet such an undertaking should not be especially expensive or administratively difficult. It would also be relatively easy to keep information on the number of people writing the certificate of qualification examinations who have received their training outside Ontario; and on the number of demonstration of skills tests taken annually, broken down by trade, by language of test, and by number of foreign-trained versus Canadian-trained candidates.

RECOMMENDATIONS

We have examined the certification and licensure process and the training program in the Ontario apprenticeship system from several perspectives: historical development; legislative and regulatory basis, and the congruence between legislation and practice; accessibility of the system to foreign-trained tradespeople; and ways in which the system compares with other training and qualification models.

Our principal recommendation is for a fundamental restructuring of the way in which the Province of Ontario delivers training and certifies competence in the trades. We recommend conversion to a competency-based, modular training system that makes significant provision for portability of training and that ties licensure to public health and safety requirements. We recognize that similar recommendations have been made by previous commissions and consultants. Having examined the system from the point of view of the foreign-trained tradesperson seeking entry, we urge the Government of Ontario to address the fundamental problems of the apprenticeship system through implementation of structural changes.

We believe that our recommendations are in step with the important innovations being introduced in other jurisdictions. We also believe that our conclusions are supported by the work to date of the Premier's Council (1988), which establishes the need for a comprehensive review of the "various shortcomings" of the apprenticeship system. We are confident that the structural changes proposed for the apprenticeship system will increase accessibility and fairness for both foreign- and domestically trained tradespeople. Further, the impact on Ontario's economic competitive position will be positive, producing a more responsive and dynamic training system and speeding the entry of skilled foreign-trained people into the workforce.

Although our principal recommendations would involve a basic restructuring of the apprenticeship system in Ontario, a number of our subsidiary recommendations can be implemented immediately while the Government designs a blueprint for large-scale change. We believe that decisive action on such matters as improved access to information and the development of guidelines for the assessment of prior training — essential elements of any restructured system — will enhance the system that currently exists.

3.1   *We recommend that licensing as a prerequisite to practice be limited to those trades that require such a restriction in the interests of public health and safety. Licensure requirements have to date been applied with little reference to health and safety requirements and in some cases may also constitute an undue restriction on access to employment in the trades for both foreign- and domestically trained tradespeople. An analysis of public health and safety requirements should identify areas of trades practice where licensure is appropriate. Certification of skill should of course remain an integral part of the training system in the trades.*

3.2   *We recommend the introduction of greater flexibility into the current training system. Accordingly, we recommend a basic change in the structure of apprenticeship training from a time-based system to a modular, competency-based training system, and the development of a variety of more accessible delivery models. Such models would include cooperative programs and programs with the in-school portion of training delivered at the outset without a requirement that the trainee obtain employment prior to commencing training. New program development in the trades during the last several years has used a competency-based format, so that movement to a purely competency-based apprentice training system should be technically straightforward. The term "modular" is used throughout this Report to refer to training programs with content organized into sets of skills to be mastered progressively.*

3.3   *We recommend that training programs for the trades include modules of core competencies that may be learned for credit in more than one trade, as applicable. Core competencies, which we regard as those used in the work performance of more than one trade and transferable from one trade to another, include:*

   • *academic competencies, such as communication, arithmetic operations, and science and technology concepts;*

   • *reasoning competencies, such as planning and problem solving;*

   • *interpersonal competencies, such as teamwork and leadership; and*

   • *manipulative competencies, such as careful and safe behaviour (lifting, carrying, storing materials) and hand-eye coordination.*

3.4   *We recommend that the Ministry of Skills Development package informational materials about apprenticeship training, certification, and licensure in a wide variety of formats, to be available in various governmental offices and community resource centres. The information that should be made accessible through one or more formats includes:*

   • *a brief description of training programs in the regulated trades, including prerequisites, the duration of apprenticeship and in-school training, and the competencies to be acquired;*

   • *an outline of particular certification and licensure procedures applicable to foreign-trained applicants and others with prior experience or training;*

- *referral information, including a directory of offices from which additional information and assistance can be obtained.*

3.5 *We recommend that, in addition to extensive written materials in pamphlet and booklet form, a computer-based information system be established with a more comprehensive, detailed level of information about certification procedures and training opportunities. Further, the trades-training telephone hotline service should be expanded with summary and referral information available on tapes and through live interaction. We also recommend that the Ministry make use of multicultural television broadcasting and multicultural newspapers to deliver information on its training programs to the multicultural community.*

3.6 *We recommend that the Ministry of Skills Development provide written and telephone information in appropriate languages, in addition to English and French. A translation request form should be available if a member of the public seeks information in a language for which it is not available.*

3.7 *We recommend that our proposed Prior Learning Assessment Network (PLAN) be given responsibility to ensure that a systematic process for the assessment of vocational competencies and academic attainment is established and maintained in Ontario. We further recommend that this task be carried out in conjunction with the Ministry of Skills Development and with input from the major stakeholders, and that it include:*

- *the creation of a shared information base on trade certification and licensure processes and on apprenticeship training programs in other jurisdictions for use in the assessment of the credentials of foreign-trained tradespeople;*

- *the development of a readily accessible central registry of assessment decisions in Ontario to provide a public record of precedents and to facilitate consistency of assessments from assessor to assessor;*

- *the development of publicly accessible guidelines to circumscribe the discretionary power of the industrial training consultants and delineate assessment criteria, and the development of a set of procedural rights afforded the applicant. For example, guidelines should require that the applicant be informed of the availability of demonstration of skills tests and of his or her right to appeal the assessment decision or to pursue a remedy before the Human Rights Commission;*

- *the assessment by the Prior Learning Assessment Network (PLAN) of the academic equivalency of foreign-trained tradespeople, with no age restriction or requirement of having been out of school for a given time, and the replacement of the Progressive Achievement Test with other, more appropriate, assessment means; and*

- *the development and maintenance of standards of validity, reliability, fairness, and cultural sensitivity for demonstration of skills tests, licensure and certification examinations, and other assessments of competencies in the trades.*

3.8   *We recommend that Ministry decisions in relation to the assessment of prior training and experience be considered to be binding on the employer. When a foreign-trained individual enters the apprenticeship system with advanced standing, the employer will no longer be permitted to downgrade training and experience below the level suggested by the industrial training consultant. The Task Force recommendations on amendments to the* Human Rights Code *provide, in effect, that in cases in which an employer refuses to accept an assessment by the Ministry, the applicant apprentice would have a remedy before the Human Rights Commission.*

3.9   *We recommend that the Government amend the* Apprenticeship and Tradesmen's Qualification Act *to provide that an applicant for a certificate of qualification and an entrant to the apprenticeship training system be granted a right to appeal registration decisions. An applicant seeking recognition of non-Ontario training and experience should be able to appeal negative decisions to a provincial apprenticeship board that includes members of the public who are not tradespeople. In addition, a right of appeal in respect of the assessment of prior training experience should lie to the appeal body to be established as part of our proposed Prior Learning Assessment Network.*

3.10   *We recommend that practical tests which permit applicants to demonstrate their acquired skills be developed in all regulated trades. We recommend that the written instructions for these tests be available in a wide variety of languages. Requests by candidates for translation should be recorded provincewide and a threshold number set by the Ministry, whereupon a translation would be provided.*

3.11   *We recommend that the Ministry develop skills training programs which recognize both the need for and the needs of foreign-trained tradespeople. Industrial training consultants should be given responsibility to make appropriate training referrals when the results of an assessment or demonstration of skills test indicate that additional training is required.*

3.12   *Specifically, as an initial measure, we recommend the expansion of the admissions criteria of two Ministry of Skills Development training programs to facilitate the entry of foreign-trained tradespeople: the Transitions Program, and the Trades Updating Program. (Transitions provides up to $5,000 of work-related training credits to older permanently laid-off workers. Trades Updating provides qualified tradespeople with access to full- and part-time courses to update their skills.) An alternative approach would be to develop parallel programs for foreign-trained tradespeople who require limited retraining to become fully qualified in Ontario. As discussed in Chapter 9 ("Retraining"), it will be less of a public expense to provide retraining programs than to require the completion of a full training program.*

3.13   *We recommend that the Government identify clearly those elements of trade practice which, for reasons of public health and safety, require a working proficiency in English or French, and that the Government introduce the use of a valid and reliable test of language proficiency referenced to this requirement. Although we support the current provision for the use of an interpreter in certificate of qualification examinations, we believe it essential that in a trade with a public health and safety impact, the language proficiency of a licensed or certified journeyman be at a level that ensures public safety.*

3.14 *We recommend that a federally funded and provincially administered apprenticeship training allowance program be established to provide income support at increased levels and be administratively designed to fit the particularities of the apprenticeship program. We also recommend that a program of loans for retraining purposes be established.*

3.15 *We recommend that the Government allocate funding to establish a computer-based data collection system capable of creating a sufficient statistical base to allow both the monitoring of the operation of the apprenticeship system and the development of a labour-planning function within the Ministry. With respect to the questions under consideration by the Task Force, it is important that the following kinds of information be available to the Government:*

- *annual number of applications for recognition of foreign training and experience, broken down by country of training;*

- *annual number of foreign-trained candidates writing the certificate of qualification examination, broken down by country of training, and applicable success rates;*

- *annual number of provisional certificates issued and renewed, broken down by country of training;*

- *annual number of demonstration of skills tests undertaken, broken down by country of training, and applicable success rates.*

3.16 *We recommend that all employers of apprentices registered under the ATQA be required to sign an undertaking that all hiring will be in accordance with Government-established employment-equity principles, and that recruitment advertising will so specify.*

APPENDIX

Table 3-A1   Apprenticeship Programs in Ontario Registered Trades

Sector	Trade	Certified or Voluntary
Motive Power	Air cooled & marine engine mechanic:	
	Small engine mechanic	V
	Marine & small powered equipment mechanic	V
	Small engine mechanic (construction)	V
	Boat motor mechanic	V
	Alignment & brakes mechanics	C
	Autobody repairer	C
	Automotive machinist	V
	Automotive painter	V
	Farm equipment mechanic	V
	Fuel & electrical systems mechanic	C
	Heavy duty equipment mechanic	V
	Motorcycle mechanic	C
	Motor vehicle mechanic	C
	Service station attendant	V
	Transmission mechanic	C
	Truck trailer repairer	C
Service	Baker	V
	Junior baker	V
	Baker patissier	V
	Cook	V
	Assistant cook	V
	Dry cleaner	V
	Hairstylist	C
	Hairdresser	C
	Barber	C
	Horticulturist — nursery/greenhouse worker	V
	Horticulturist — landscaper/greenskeeper	V
	Radio & television service technician	V
	Watch repairer	C
Construction	Brick & stone mason	V
	Cement mason	V
	Construction boilermaker	V
	Construction millwright	V
	Electrician — construction & maintenance	C
	Electrician — domestic & rural	C
	Fitter (structural steel/platework)	V
	General carpenter	V

Sector	Trade	Certified or Voluntary
Construction (cont'd.)	Glazier & metal mechanic	V
	Hoisting engineer:	
	Mobile crane operator	C
	Tower crane operator	C
	Ironworker	V
	Lather	V
	Lineman — power	V
	Lineman — construction	V
	Painter — commercial & residential	V
	Painter — industrial	V
	Painter & decorator — commercial & residential	V
	Painter & decorator — industrial	V
	Plasterer	V
	Plumber	C
	Refrigeration & air conditioning mechanic	C
	Sheet metal worker	C
	Sprinkler & fire protection installer	V
	Steamfitter	C
Industrial	Automatic machinist	V
	General machinist (a)	V
	General machinist (b)	V
	Industrial electrician	V
	Industrial mechanic (millwright)	V
	Industrial wood worker	V
	Mould maker	V
	Tool & die maker	V
	Printer:	
	Printer — letter press (job shop)	V
	Printer — lithography (job shop)	V
	Offset pressman (plant)	V
	Linotype operator	V
	Compositor:	V
	Pressman — letter press	V
	Compositor — photo typesetting	V
	Compositor & camera technician	V

Source: Ministry of Skills Development, apprenticeship branch. *Summary, Apprenticeship Programs: Regulated Trades*, 87-09-14.

CHAPTER 4

Issues Facing the Professions

It must be recognized that the interests of the association of members of one profession might not always coincide with the interests of the community. While the community would aim for ampler, safer, and lower costs of services, the professionals might be looking for loss [of] competition and higher fees for themselves, thus being tempted to oppose, block, or diminish the presence of foreign professionals in Canada.

— from a Brief submitted to the
Task Force by an individual

As the Terms of Reference indicate, this Task Force has been charged with reviewing "all rules and practices affecting entry to professions and trades to determine whether they have an actual or potential discriminatory effect on persons with training or experience from outside of Canada." Before beginning this review it was necessary that the Task Force determine what constitutes a "profession" within the meaning of the Terms of Reference. For purposes of our analysis, we have broken down the notion of occupations, referring to all forms of employment, into two groups: trades and professions. Issues facing the trades specifically are dealt with in Chapter 3 of the Report.

The very broad definition of "profession" that we have adopted as our starting point is: "an occupational or vocational group organized for purposes of employment and subject to some form of regulation." This category may then be broken down into two groups: the self-regulating professions, which may be either privately regulated (such as chartered accountancy) or those regulated under public statute (such as law); and government-regulated professions (for example, educators and real estate brokers).

We have attempted to canvass fully the self-regulating professions that fall under provincial jurisdiction and operate within the Province of Ontario, reviewing the publicly regulated professions and a selection of the larger or more prominent of the 25 or so privately regulated professions. We have as well selected a small number of professions regulated directly through government, and the basis of our selection will be indicated below. Finally, and again for reasons that will become apparent in the course of our discussion, we elected to go slightly beyond our definition and also reviewed a few professions that are currently unregulated but are organized through voluntary associations.

PROFESSIONALISM AND THE PRINCIPLES OF SELF-GOVERNANCE

The authority and power inherent in self-regulation carry with them responsibilities which, over the years, have been characterized in studies on the concept. The *Report of the Royal Commission of Inquiry into Civil Rights* under Mr. Justice McRuer (The McRuer Report), although now some 20 years old, deals in a broad and comprehensive way with the self-governing professions. The report states with clarity that it is the obligation of the professional bodies to protect the public interest:

> The right to control admission to a profession or occupation, and to issue licences authorizing persons to engage in the practice of a profession or occupation, confers a power to control the number who may be admitted to it, as well as to ensure competence of its members. The power to set educational standards and prescribe training includes the power to exclude persons even though they may qualify to meet reasonable standards. Excessively high standards may produce specialists but leave a vacuum with respect to areas of a profession where the services of a specialist are not required . . .

> The traditional justification for giving powers of self-regulation to any body is that the members of the body are best qualified to ensure that proper standards of competence and ethics are set and maintained. There is a clear public interest in the creation and observance of such standards. This public interest may have been well served by the respective bodies which have brought to their task an awareness of their responsibility to

the public they serve, but there is a real risk that the power may be exercised in the interests of the profession or occupation rather than in that of the public. This risk requires adequate safeguards to ensure that injury to the public interest does not arise.[1]

For its part, the Professional Organizations Committee is somewhat more equivocal in its consideration of the responsibilities of self-governance.[2] In considering regulatory policy regarding the professions, the committee's 1980 report adopts four fundamental principles: protection of vulnerable interests, fairness of regulation, feasibility of implementation, and public accountability. Each of these, with the exception of feasibility of implementation, recognizes the dimension of public responsibility inherent in professional self-regulation; in addition, two of the three "vulnerable interests" identified by the committee are the general public (third-party interests) and clients of the services (second-party interests). The committee, however, specifically acknowledges the right to protection of the first-party interests — the professionals and paraprofessionals themselves — stating that such protection is essential to the overall scheme "if professionalism in the best sense of the term is to prevail."[3] The committee's report refers to the cost of government supervision as well as to the benefits of self-regulation and autonomy.

This balancing of the rights of the professional body with the rights of those it is bound to protect — namely, the public — is a delicate task. But because protection of the public and the maintenance of standards to that end are the reasons for the self-regulating bodies' existence, the protection of interests must, in the view of this Task Force, prevail. We therefore endorse the view expressed by the Committee on the Healing Arts in its 1970 report:

> Again we emphasize the importance of the realization of the true nature of the grant of licensing and regulating powers to a self-governing profession. It is a grant by the sovereign legislative authority, representing society, to a licensing body, owing its existence to an Act of the Legislature, to permit it to exercise its powers, conferred for the protection of the public against incompetent or dishonest practitioners. These powers must be exercised by the licensing body as a trustee, not for the practitioner, but for the public.[4]

How that interest is best protected is, of course, not always easy to determine. Even deciding on a fair standard to ensure a candidate's competence without unduly restricting entry is, as McRuer noted, problematic.

That the standard set must be equal for all is clear, and our recommendations relating to assessment of prior learning and to licensure testing evolve from that starting position. The setting of the standards themselves must, however, be determined not according to the whim or preference of those bodies but in response to the notion of a recognized level of competence required to practise the profession. What this task must involve is the development by the professions, where they have not already done so, of a set of what are commonly referred to as "competencies" or functions that must be mastered by any competent practitioner. The standard set by these competencies should, and inevitably will, be reflected both in Ontario academic programs designed to train professionals and in licensure or certification examinations. The power to develop these standards lies with the professional bodies themselves; however, these standards must be justifiable *in the public interest* as necessary for practising the profession competently.

As emphasized repeatedly to the professional bodies, we are not suggesting that standards should be altered to accommodate foreign-trained individuals. On the contrary, our suggestion reflects the need to ensure that standards do not fluctuate — up *or* down — to accommodate any group, but, rather, that they remain constant, reasoned, and appropriate. The comment of the Committee on the Healing Arts is apt:

> The Committee has discerned an interesting contrast between the normally rigid attitude towards the foreign-trained practitioner and relative flexibility when the restrictive licensing practices are under the public spotlight. When the public has become aroused the reflex action that it would be unthinkable to license physicians from some parts of the world has changed to an attitude that on humanitarian grounds, for example, practitioners who have fled from a politically oppressive society might be licensed. If the restrictions against foreign practitioners were valid in the first place, the only acceptable criterion being the public interest, we are unable to see why exceptions should be made for refugees from totalitarian countries. The reasonable suspicion which arises in the mind of the public is that the restrictive regulations were dictated more by professional concern than by concern for the safety of the foreign practitioners' potential patients.[5]

When a standard is set inappropriately high in any field, it is foreign-trained professionals who are most affected, since they will almost inevitably be unable to meet that standard. At the same time, the broader public interest is also at stake if professional access is unreasonably withheld. Where the standard is used simply to limit the professional pool, it can rarely be said that such controls operate in the public interest. The case for such controls is made most strongly in the medical profession, where it is argued that an overly large physician pool can lead to enhanced health care costs and/or lowered health care standards. We have considered this issue in the individual professions as it has arisen, but we have concluded that from the perspective of this Task Force, which is focused on foreign-trained individuals, control of the workforce cannot justify or explain limited access. Even if it were considered a valid exercise of authority in the public interest to control access to a profession for all applicants, it would not be valid or in the public interest if such control limited the access of one group as compared to another, namely foreign-trained in comparison to domestically trained individuals.

When we consider the balance between interests of the regulatory bodies and those of the public they are protecting, the guiding principles of fairness must be those articulated in the *Ontario Human Rights Code, 1981*,[6] the *Canadian Charter of Rights and Freedoms*,[7] and the principles of natural justice. By virtue of these legal requirements, all candidates are protected from practices that, intentionally or otherwise, discriminate against them or deprive them of procedural protection, whether the discrimination is on the face of legislation or in the way the legislation is applied; whether it is direct or systemic.

Professions Regulated Under Public Statute

Professional regulation under public statute is the most direct and common method of regulation. Governing bodies are created by statute to control essentially every aspect of the governance of the profession, and in most cases the Government, through the Lieutenant Governor in Council, has a say in the composition of the governing bodies or their councils. Such bodies are given the power to grant licences, which are entitlements to practise the profession in Ontario (occasionally, publicly regulated professions have only the authority to control the use of a title, not full power of licensure), and, typically, regulation is through regulations passed by the governing bodies but subject to the approval of the Lieutenant Governor in Council. As well, the Minister may be empowered to direct the professional body to pass such regulations as he or she directs and may also be required to give prior review to regulations. In most cases, members or candidates for membership have avenues of appeal outside the professional body itself. By virtue of the statutory structure and the veto and directive power of the Government over the regulation-making authority, the responsibility of these professions to the public interest is presumed to be assured.

Of the professions reviewed by the Task Force, those regulated under public statute are listed below:

Profession	*Statute*
Architects	— *Architects Act, 1984*, S.O. 1984, c. 12, as amended
Chiropodists	— *Chiropodists Act*, R.S.O. 1980, c. 72
Dental technicians	— *Dental Technicians Act*, R.S.O. 1980, c. 114
Denture therapists	— *Denture Therapists Act*, R.S.O. 1980, c. 115
Engineers	— *Professional Engineers Act, 1984*, S.O. 1984, c. 13
Funeral services directors	— *Funeral Services Act*, R.S.O. 1980, c. 180, as amended
Registered insurance brokers	— *Registered Insurance Brokers Act*, R.S.O. 1980, c. 444
Land surveyors	— *Surveyors Act*, S.O. 1987, c. 6
Lawyers	— *Law Society Act*, R.S.O. 1980, c. 233, as amended
Ophthalmic dispensers	— *Ophthalmic Dispensers Act*, R.S.O. 1980, c. 364, as amended
Psychologists	— *Psychologists Registration Act*, R.S.O. 1980, c. 404

Profession	Statute
Radiological technicians	— *Radiological Technicians Act*, R.S.O. 1980, c. 430
Veterinarians	— *Veterinarians Act*, R.S.O. 1980, c. 522
Chiropractors Masseurs Naturopaths Osteopaths Physio- therapists	— All regulated under the *Drugless Practitioners Act*, R.S.O. 1980, c. 127
Dental hygienists Dentists Doctors Nurses Nursing assistants Optometrists Pharmacists	— All regulated under the *Health Disciplines Act*, R.S.O. 1980, c. 196, as amended

The regulatory structures of the publicly regulated professions are similar but not identical. The composition of the councils or governing bodies varies somewhat from profession to profession as do the levels of involvement available to the Lieutenant Governor in Council in the making, review, and approval of regulations. Rights of review and appeal vary considerably from profession to profession (see Chapter 11, "Review of Registration Decisions").

One exceptional statute in this context, and one that is worth noting, is the *Veterinarians Act*. Although the *Veterinarians Act* is a public statute, the structure of regulation lacks many of the basic indicia of public regulation. For example, the Council of the association, which is the management body of the profession, consists entirely of elected members and has no lay representation and no appointees of the Lieutenant Governor in Council.[8] The Council has authority to pass bylaws, and there is no provision for regulations. These bylaws, although dealing with the fundamental powers of self-governance, including admission and registration of members, are not subject to approval or review by the Minister or the Lieutenant Governor in Council. New legislation relating to veterinarians has been drafted by the profession but has not received first reading. This proposed legislation would bring the structure more in line with other publicly regulated professions. The current structure follows the private-regulation model, which will be discussed below.

The *Health Disciplines Act*, the *Drugless Practitioners Act*, and the health disciplines in general are currently under review. New legislation governing the health disciplines is in preparation. Under the proposed legislation, the structure outlined above will undergo significant changes.[9]

Most significantly, members of the professions currently regulated under the *Health Disciplines Act*, including dental hygienists, will be joined by chiropractors, masseurs, osteopaths and physiotherapists, currently regulated under the *Drugless Practitioners Act*. The naturopaths (or drugless therapists) will not be included and may be deregulated. In addition, chiropodists, dental technicians, denture therapists, ophthalmic dispensers, psychologists, and radiological technicians, currently regulated under their own statutes, will be included. Finally, speech-language pathologists and audiologists, dietitians, midwives, medical laboratory technologists, occupational therapists, and respiratory technologists, none of which are currently publicly regulated, will enter the regulatory scheme.

The effect of this new legislation will be to create an entirely new regulatory structure for some professions and a significantly altered one for others. For members of professions already within the health disciplines structure, and for those with similar procedures already in place, such as the denture therapists, there will be some structural and procedural changes. For others, such as psychologists and dental technicians, the introduction of specific and detailed certification procedures and appeal mechanisms will have a significant impact. The newly regulated professions, currently operating through voluntary associations, will feel the greatest impact. We shall discuss some of these groups later in this chapter, in our section on credentialism.

The format of the new legislation will consist of a general act setting out the basic procedural protections, accompanied by individual acts for each of the included professions. Each of the individual acts will detail the scope of practice and particular regulatory structure of the relevant profession. The particulars of standards for entry and mechanisms for admission will, as is generally the case now, appear in regulations.

Professions Regulated Under Private Statute

The concept of public accountability is, as we noted above, considered by many to be inherent in the nature of professionalism. A great deal of our study has therefore been directed towards the professions described above, which are governed under authority of public statute and are, by a variety of means, made accountable to the public. A number of groups, however, are self-regulatory professions but governed through private statutes. Of the professions that fall within this category, the following were selected for review:[10]

Profession	*Statute*
Accountants	
Certified general accountants	— *Certified General Accountants Association of Ontario Act, 1983*, S.O. 1983, c. Pr6
Certified management accountants	— *Society of Management Accountants of Ontario Act*, S.O. 1981, c. 100
Chartered accountants	— *Chartered Accountants Act, 1956*, S.O. 1956, c. 7
Agrologists	— *Ontario Professional Agrologists Act, 1960*, S.O. 1960, c. 158
Foresters	— *Ontario Professional Foresters Association Act, 1957*, S.O. 1957, c. 149
Engineering technicians and technologists	— *Ontario Association of Certified Engineering Technicians and Technologists Act, 1984*, S.O. 1984, c. Pr14
Dietitians	— *Ontario Dietetic Association Act*, S.O. 1958, c. 147

These professions are typically controlled by bodies elected entirely from the membership, without lay members or government appointees. Lacking the statutory authority to license, they do, however, have the power to control use of certified titles and thereby effectively to control employment in the profession. Their regulation is through bylaws, which are not subjected to government review or approval.[11] Appeal mechanisms, if any, are usually, although not always, internal review procedures.

Although privately rather than publicly regulated, these professions operate within the public domain. Members of these professions enjoy the status of self-governing professionals in the community, and this professional status has been specifically acknowledged by the Legislature of Ontario through passage of the governing acts. In addition, there are in many cases linkages between these professional organizations and public acts.

These linkages aside, the Task Force has come to understand that professional bodies, not only through control of entry to licensure (under the public statutes) but also through restricting of entry to certification or membership (under the private professional statutes or through voluntary association), can have a tremendous impact on the employment opportunities of applicants. The restriction on the right to use a protected designation — the concept of the "reserved title" — is an especially significant issue for our study.

CREDENTIALISM AND THE USE OF THE RESERVED TITLE

Publicly Regulated Professions

The use of a "reserved title"[12] is present even in some of the publicly regulated professions, although it is somewhat unusual to encounter it there. For example, only an individual holding a certificate of registration under the *Psychologists Registration Act* may use the designation "psychologist" or hold himself or herself out to the public as offering psychological services for a fee under this title. The *Act* contains some specific exceptions to this policy, but in addition there is opportunity to practise in the field without registration, provided the designation "psychologist" is not used. (Nurses and nursing assistants, too, may practise without registration, but may not use the designation "registered nurse" or "registered nursing assistant" without registration.)

Radiological technicians fall under what could be termed a modified reserved-title regime. Under the governing *Act*,[13] registration is not required for practice but permits an individual to hold himself or herself out as a registered radiological technician; however, registration of certain categories of radiological technician, namely those involved in the operation of X-ray machines, is effectively made compulsory by virtue of the provisions of the *Healing Arts Protection Act (HARP)*.[14] It is also possible to work in the field of dental technology without registration, provided the designation "registered dental technician" is not used. (The status of the professions covered by the *Drugless Practitioners Act* is, in this regard, equivocal. In the regulations, it is stated that chiropractors, masseurs, naturopaths, and physiotherapists cannot hold themselves out as qualified to practise as such unless they are registered. This regulation comes very close to requiring registration but does not go quite that far. Only naturopaths, or drugless therapists, are specifically required to register. Yet, under section 8 of the *Act*, which applies to all these professions, registration is apparently required for practice, although even this statement is subject to interpretation, owing to a significant apparent error of language in the text. Reading the regulations and section 8 together, one can safely say that registration in these professions is mandatory. It is hoped, however, that the ambiguity will be cleared up when the *Act* is restructured pursuant to the health disciplines review.)

The regulated professions can be affected by credentialism when the granting of a title by a voluntary organization exists alongside the regulation of the profession by its governing body. For example, the modified reserved-title regime under the *Radiological Technicians Act* in itself raises no difficulty because of the accountability imposed through public regulation. In spite of the fact that the technicians are in a regulated profession, however, the standards set by the voluntary association continue to be relevant in gaining access to employment. The Canadian Association of Medical Radiation Technologists (CAMRT) certifies members of this profession, and evidence indicates that this credential, which is based on higher standards than those demanded by the governing body, is at least as significant as and perhaps more significant than the governing board registration.

Generally, however, although employment opportunities are clearly affected by the granting of a reserved title, any unfair withholding of access to the title by the governing body can be monitored, by virtue of the accountability of each of these publicly regulated professions, and any necessary amendments can be made. This option may not, however, apply in the case of privately governed professional bodies, where the issue of "credentialism" arises.

Privately Regulated Professions

Public accountancy is a professional field, entry to which is controlled by a privately regulated group with the legislative power to grant a reserved title. It involves the preparation and verification of financial statements that may be relied on by the public, and the profession is regulated under the *Public Accountancy Act*.[15] This *Act* creates the Public Accountants Council, which is responsible, among other things, for issuing licences to accountants who meet the criteria for public accountancy. Under the *Act*, the Institute of Chartered Accountants of Ontario, created under the *Chartered Accountants Act*, is designated as the qualifying body for admission to public accountancy.[16] Membership in this privately regulated reserved-title profession therefore takes on enormous significance in the public sector.[17] In addition, the designation is a meaningful credential and a key to employment generally.

The Institute of Chartered Accountants of Ontario has in place rigorous and comprehensive educational and training requirements that must be met in order to obtain membership privileges (outlined in Appendix H of this Report). At issue here is the enormous impact that a private organization has on both individual applicants and the public through its unfettered control over entry to what in the legislation is specifically designated a public function. These linkages also appear, although to a lesser extent, in forestry, where only foresters registered by the private governing organization can perform certain functions under the *Crown Timber Act*.[18] Furthermore, on a more general level, access to employment is being restricted by private organizations as employers increasingly require such credentials as a prerequisite to employment. "Credentialism," as this phenomenon is called, is apparently on the rise. As a means of screening applicants, employers are looking to credentials that are not authorized by public law or required by public statute.

Voluntary Professional Associations

The concept of credentialism causes greatest concern where it extends beyond the regulated professions. In the course of our study, we reviewed four unregulated professions. Two of these, medical laboratory technology and occupational therapy, are going to be brought in under the *Health Disciplines Act*. One other, social work, has prepared an independent piece of legislation and is in the process of applying for publicly regulated status. The fourth, early childhood education, was of particular interest to us because it currently combines a scheme of government "approval" of qualified workers with an active credentialing system through the voluntary association for the profession; studies are currently under way to clarify and define appropriate entry mechanisms to the profession.

Our initial intention was to review the entry procedures of these professions as they currently exist, with a view to making recommendations regarding procedures that might be continued or amended once the new structures are in place. What we found was evidence of considerable authority being exercised by purely voluntary credentialing organizations, effectively to control entry into their fields of expertise through the use of the reserved title.

It also became apparent that these four bodies are merely representative of many such organizations functioning in Ontario: in the course of its study, the Professional Organizations Committee received submissions from twenty-two occupational groups that fall within the definition of certification or reserved-title regimes, in addition to the four that fell directly within the ambit of its study (the chartered accountants, the certified general accountants, the society of management accountants, and the engineering technicians and technologists). These twenty-six consisted of both privately regulated and unregulated occupations. In conducting our review we gathered information on fourteen privately regulated or unregulated occupational bodies, twelve of which we discuss in this chapter in some detail, the remaining two being the professional translators and the dental nurses and assistants. We do not believe that our survey was in any sense exhaustive.

Those professions that are about to become regulated will of course no longer be an issue; however, the numerous other voluntary associations that carry on this credentialing function will continue to be of concern.

Occupational Therapists

Occupational therapists who are members of the Ontario Society of Occupational Therapists may use the designation "registered occupational therapist." In order to become a member, one must meet the educational and experiential requirements of the Canadian body, the Canadian Association of Occupational Therapists. The advantages of being registered in this profession are significant: most employers designate registration as a job requirement, and it is extremely difficult to obtain malpractice insurance without registration. There are therefore relatively few practising occupational therapists who are not registered.

Social Workers

Social work is currently administered through two bodies, neither of which has legislative status. The Ontario Association of Professional Social Workers was incorporated in 1964 as a voluntary, non-profit organization. The association admits as members only those who meet its academic and experiential requirements. The reserved title, "certified social worker," a term protected by federal trademark legislation, is available to everyone who meets the requirements of the Ontario College of Certified Social Workers, a body created by the association through bylaw. To be eligible for certification, candidates not only must be members of the association and meet its entry requirements but must meet some further experience and examination requirements. Membership in the association is common among social workers and is significant for employment purposes; certification by the college is a new procedure and therefore not yet a requirement for employment. The college is currently working towards full self-regulation and has prepared a draft act that would alter its procedures.

Medical Laboratory Technologists

To refer to the profession of medical laboratory technology as unregulated is slightly inaccurate. The *Laboratory and Specimen Collection Centre Licensing Act*[19] and its regulations specify the academic and experiential requirements needed in order to be approved by the Ministry of Health to work in certain medical laboratories. Compliance with these requirements is verified by representatives of the Ministry of Health. However, the voluntary association, the Canadian Society of Laboratory Technologists (CSLT), plays a large role in employment in the field through control of the designation "registered technologist" (R.T.). This organization, authorized through its incorporating statute, sets standards of competence for the profession and monitors these standards through evaluative procedures. Although certification by the CSLT is purely voluntary, the majority of laboratory technologists in this province are in fact certified because certification dramatically enhances employment opportunities.

Although certification by the CSLT is a ground for approval for employment by the Minister under the *Laboratory and Specimen Collection Centre Licensing Act*, the Minister does retain the right to grant approval on other grounds. It remains to be decided, we understand, which set of entry criteria will prevail once the profession is regulated under the new Health Disciplines legislation.

Early Childhood Educators

It is possible to work in the field of day care without having any form of licensure or certification. Pursuant to regulations under the *Day Nurseries Act*,[20] however, an operator of a day care centre must employ a minimum number of workers who have diplomas in early childhood education from an Ontario college of applied arts and technology, or the equivalent, or are otherwise approved by the Minister. The number of such qualified workers required depends on the age of the children and the specific staff/child ratio that applies under the regulations. The Ministry, through a director, will provide candidates or employers with a statement that the candidate meets with the approval of the director. This assessment is based on a review of the training and credentials of the applicant.

A statement of equivalency, which is considered adequate to meet the regulated requirement, can be obtained from the voluntary professional organization for day-care workers, known as the Association of Early Childhood Education, Ontario (AECEO). The Ministry exercises no control over the procedures or power of this organization. Certification and membership in the AECEO are not legal prerequisites to employment, and the Ministry applies its own standards in determining which candidates meet with its approval. Nonetheless, the voluntary association provides, by one means, the necessary certification to meet the legal requirement; in addition, it provides a credential that makes employment easier to obtain.

The issue of credentialism has a significant impact on our study. Any barriers to entry being erected by publicly regulated professional bodies can be addressed directly by this Task Force through recommendations relating to provisions in the governing acts and regulations. Although in our view caught by the provisions of the *Human Rights Code, 1981*,[21] privately regulated professions (because of the lack of accountability in their rule-making structures) and voluntary occupational associations (because they are not creatures of statute at all) are currently beyond the reach of many of our other substantive recommendations. Voluntary occupational associations are also beyond that of governmental control generally, in spite of their impact on employment opportunities in this province.

Various methods have been suggested to us for dealing with this problem. One is to attempt to curb the rise of reliance on credentials in the workplace by constraining employers' rights to hire purely on the basis of credentials not authorized by law. This position is reflected in the policy position taken by the Province of Ontario, which restricts the use of credentials to a limited number of specific situations: "Where it is required by statute; where it is essential, without equivalent, for satisfactory job performance, or where a credential or an equivalent consideration of education and experience would indicate possession of the knowledge, skills, ability and experience required for satisfactory job performance."[22] It is also reflected in the fact that the Ministry of Colleges and Universities restricts the right of non-publicly regulated professional bodies to carry out accreditation procedures as part of their credentialing procedure, a policy presumably intended to discourage such credentialing, or at the least to take away some of its authority.

These policies in themselves, however, highlight the inherent difficulty in requiring employers to operate without reliance on credentials. In the absence of any readily available and reliable mechanism for determining how qualified an individual may be, the closest substitute, namely a credential, will be looked to.

It is the view of the Task Force that employers cannot and should not be prevented from relying on candidates' credentials as a means of ensuring competence; and that it is essential that the public at large, in attempting to distinguish among various services in order to select those that will appropriately and adequately meet their needs, have the assistance of credentials. Credentialism is not a phenomenon to be discouraged or inhibited but one that should, and inevitably will, flourish in a highly developed, complex, and increasingly technically oriented economy. The point is not how to control credentialism; rather, it is how best to ensure that the credentials accurately convey to the employer or purchaser of the service the skill and level of competence which they purport to attest to. In other words, the problem is not credentialism *per se*, but the reliability of the assessments they are based on.

The Professional Organizations Committee in its 1980 report directly addressed the question of credentialism in the context of the numerous representations made to it from unregulated groups seeking regulated professional status.[23] In recognizing the reality of credentialism, the committee considered one other method of dealing with the issue: public regulation of the bodies in question. As the committee noted, however, regulation is a cumbersome and relatively static mechanism that should not be overutilized. As an alternative, it proposed a statutory certification regime to apply generally to credentialing bodies. Prior government approval of all professional designations would be a requirement, and such approval would be granted only if the certifying or credentialing body's internal structure and processes met certain minimum standards.

We are of the view that this proposal has considerable merit and may ultimately prove necessary to deal with the issue (and we note that Alberta's proposed Professions and Occupational Associations Registration Act would place reserved-title occupational groups under a similar regulatory structure). At this stage, however, and in response to the particular difficulties we have identified relating to foreign-trained individuals, we propose a more moderate solution: making available to any candidate an assessment of prior learning that is credible and reliable and comes directly from a source independent of the occupational association. As is discussed in considerable detail throughout this Report, the Task Force recommends the creation of a Prior Learning Assessment Network (PLAN), an independent body under the aegis of one or more government ministries, which will have the capability to provide such an assessment.

The thrust of our objective in recommending PLAN is to ensure that candidates to the professional bodies and educational institutions have access to accurate and unbiased assessments of their learning. At the same time, a further benefit of such a scheme would accrue to employers generally and to applicant employees, in that a reliable means of assessing the background of potential employees would be made available. It is therefore our view, and we so recommend at the conclusion of this chapter, that certification bodies should be brought within the ambit of PLAN's reach, with respect to both equivalency assessments and other, perhaps less critical, issues, such as the validation of any examinations. This would be accomplished through the legislative structure creating PLAN, in the case of unregulated bodies, or through specific amendments to the relevant acts, in the case of privately regulated occupations. The influence of certification regimes may not completely disappear, but with the alternative of a binding assessment from an unbiased source available to candidates, the quality and credibility of the credentialing process will be significantly enhanced. It is therefore our view that our proposals with regard to PLAN, extended to unregulated and privately regulated credentialing occupational organizations, should be a sufficient answer to the problem of credentialism in Ontario.

The Use of Discretion

One other procedural matter merits mention at this stage: the reservation of the right of the registrar and/or the registration committee (and in some cases of internal and external appeal bodies) to exempt a candidate for licensure and certification from any of the requirements specified in the governing *Act* or regulations. This right is common to most of the professions. The authority to grant exemptions in appropriate circumstances at the discretion of the decision makers is a significant power in the eyes of the professional bodies, and we are not of the view that it necessarily operates contrary to the public interest nor that the professional bodies should be relieved of this exercise of discretion. Its exercise can, however, lead to some startling results. In the medical profession, for example, although only 24 foreign-trained individuals are, under the regulations, entitled to receive educational licences for purposes of admission to internship in any given year, the fact is that in the period April 1987 to February 1988, by virtue of the exercise of the discretion of the registration committee, a total of 79 candidates from unaccredited medical schools and 108 candidates from accredited medical schools were exempted from licensure requirements and thereby granted licences.[24]

The use of discretion can clearly be beneficial to individual candidates by overriding provisions in legislation that may otherwise result in inequities. For example, the regulations governing the profession of funeral services directors state that a candidate shall have completed training in a funeral services program, yet in many jurisdictions such programs do not exist. The registrar is able to waive this requirement in appropriate cases.

Nevertheless, legislative provision for discretion in relation to entry criteria can be justified only if the exercise of such discretion is demonstrably fair and objective. To ensure that discretion is properly exercised, the grounds for its exercise should be subject to public scrutiny.

The Task Force is of the view that the professional bodies should be permitted to retain the right to waive licensure or certification requirements. These bodies, however, should be obliged to publish each case in which the discretion was exercised along with the reasons for its exercise. Such information should be made available to interested parties through the professional bodies directly and through the information dispersal function of PLAN.

GOVERNMENT LICENSURE

A number of professions, including the previously discussed medical laboratory technologists and early childhood educators, receive their authority to practise directly from the Government of Ontario. We selected the following for review here:[25]

Real estate and business brokers

— Licensed under the *Real Estate and Business Brokers Act*, R.S.O. 1980, c. 431

Educators (primary/ secondary)

— Licensed under the *Education Act*, R.S.O. 1980, c. 129, as amended

Real Estate and Business Brokers

The real estate and business brokers group was selected as representative of those commercially oriented professions or occupations whose members must complete a licensure procedure through the relevant ministry before being able to work in the field. In this case, the registration is by the registrar, appointed by the Lieutenant Governor in Council, and under the supervision of the director of the consumer protection division of the Ministry of Consumer and Commercial Relations. No person is permitted to trade in real estate as a broker or seller without being registered. The requirements for entry are set in the regulations by the registrar, the education policy having been determined by a standing committee to the Ministry of Consumer and Commercial Relations and consisting of representatives of the Ministry, the Canadian Real Estate Association, industry, and the Ministry of Colleges and Universities. On a refusal of licensure, an appeal may be taken to the Commercial Registration Appeal Tribunal and from there to Divisional Court.

Educators

We turned our attention to the teaching profession for three reasons:

1) The number of practising members of this profession is so significant that we felt the study would be incomplete without consideration of its procedures.
2) We received a sufficient number of submissions from individuals attempting to enter this profession to warrant investigation of the issues raised.
3) The complexity of the entry system and the system's interaction with other bodies conducting parallel assessments gave us cause for concern.

An Ontario Teachers Certificate (OTC), which is with some exceptions the prerequisite to permanent employment in the primary and secondary publicly funded school system, is granted by the Ministry of Education to qualified candidates. An assessment of training is carried out within the Ministry itself, and candidates either receive the OTC or are referred to an appropriate educational institution. There is no right of appeal from a decision of the Ministry.

PROFESSIONS: BARRIERS TO ENTRY

As our examples indicate, the regulatory structure of a profession in and of itself may raise questions of fairness not only because of a lack of procedural protections available in some of the governing acts, but also because of the very nature of certification procedures that exist outside the more accountable self-regulated professions. The issues of procedural fairness will be dealt with in some detail in Chapter 11 of this Report ("Review of Registration Decisions"). Our recommendations on the issue of the exercise of discretion appear at the end of the present chapter.

These broader issues aside, our study demanded a detailed review of the actual requirements imposed by each professional group as conditions of licensure or certification and of the impact those requirements have on foreign-trained individuals.

In reviewing the professions, we asked ourselves the following five initial questions:

1) Is there anything in the governing legislation of the profession that is or has the potential to be inherently discriminatory?

2) Is there anything in the legislation that can or does discriminate by setting standards that are not related to the skills needed to practise the profession and that cannot be met by some applicants?

3) Is there anything in the legislation that can or does discriminate by requiring a particular method of meeting the established standard which either is inaccessible to foreign-trained people or does not take into account their education or experience?

4) If the statute itself is not discriminatory, is there anything in the way the professional bodies may implement it, in actual practice, that is inherently discriminatory?

5) Are data available to substantiate intentional or systemic discrimination?

In order to answer these questions, we reviewed the applicable legislation, reviewed the actual practice within the professions, and requested specific data on numbers of foreign-trained applicants and the outcome of their applications.

We focused on areas that the affected professions and individuals pinpointed as being the most problematic: availability of information, assessment of prior learning, language training and testing, licensure testing, and availability of retraining programs.

Information

A lack of detailed, clear, and comprehensive information on what is required for licensure or certification, including what training opportunities are available, was cited many times as a source of difficulty for foreign-trained individuals.

Assessment of Prior Learning

This area involves assessments of both prior academic training and prior relevant experience. The method of assessment was highlighted as a source of concern, as was the question of the fairness of the standard required for entry. The position taken by the Task Force, which is discussed in some detail earlier in this chapter, is that the standard set must be that needed to perform competently in the profession.

Language

Our review of language encompassed the need for fluency in each profession, the means of testing for fluency, the importance of profession-specific language skills as opposed to general fluency, and the availability of language training.

Licensure or Certification Examinations

In the area of licensure or certification examinations, the issue of the fairness of the standard was prominent, particularly in occupations that require different examinations of different categories of candidates, along with issues related to examination format, availability, methodology, cost, language, and cultural sensitivity.

Retraining

Candidates arriving from another country may require training for a number of reasons. Even fully qualified individuals may require training to learn particular practices that are common in Ontario but not elsewhere. These individuals may also need preparation for licensing or certification examinations that have an unfamiliar style and format. Those who have considerable training in a field but require some further training here to be considered equivalent would also benefit from retraining. The availability of such programs was reviewed.

Standards of Fairness

Our findings on each of these issues are outlined in the following five chapters: "Prior Learning Assessment," "Licensure Testing," "Language Testing," "Language Training," and "Retraining." Our study has revealed deficiencies in each of these areas among many of the professional bodies.

Almost without exception, the practices that concern us do not appear on the face of the legislation but in regulations, bylaws, rules, and applications.

In many cases, provincial licensing or registration bodies rely on national organizations for competency assessments. This practice may involve conducting nationwide accreditation procedures on behalf of all the provincial bodies, but it may extend further, into the actual assessment of training and examination of candidates. Examples of bodies of the latter type include the National Dental Examining Board, the Pharmacy Examining Board of Canada, and the Canadian Architectural Certification Board. There are undoubtedly advantages to having these bodies perform such functions in terms of interprovincial mobility and standardization of examinations, but their procedures, because they are relied upon by provincial occupational bodies, have been reviewed and commented on in this Report, and our recommendations will affect them as well. Although we recognize the jurisdictional difficulties posed by this, it was essential that we consider the practices of these bodies in order to do a comprehensive survey of barriers to entry in Ontario. We do not presume to instruct these national bodies on how best to conduct their affairs, but it is well within provincial authority to advise the provincial bodies of the appropriateness of assessment mechanisms being adopted by them. Although a national structure may be desirable, its existence cannot be used as a shield to protect all participants from criticism or recommendation. The services being provided to Ontario's professional bodies must be in keeping with standards required in this province.

Although many of the professions provided us with the data available, we were for a number of reasons unable to collect sufficient data to make proper statistical analysis feasible:

- Some professions do not maintain records of ethnic origin or foreign training, thinking it improper to keep and/or release such information.

- The passage of a given candidate through a licensing procedure from first inquiry to licensure can cover several years, several examinations, and possible retries of examinations. Few professions are able to provide statistics that trace the performance of candidates through the process in a manner that presents a meaningful picture.

- Few professions keep records of initial inquiries and some even do not keep records of applications that do not proceed beyond that stage. Yet from interviews with professional representatives and individuals, it appears that large numbers of foreign-trained individuals — probably the majority — are rejected at this early stage in the process.

Where data are available, we have generally reproduced relevant statistics in our background studies relating to each of the professions reviewed. We note, however, the importance of maintaining such detailed records: first, to ensure that candidates and the occupational bodies they are applying to have a clear record of what has transpired between them; and second, to permit a monitoring of the progress of foreign-trained candidates as they attempt to obtain recognition of their skills and entitlements to practise. We appreciate the concern of some occupational bodies that they do not wish to discriminate or appear to discriminate by maintaining records on the background of the candidates, and we recognize that such information should not of course be available to examiners or employers at any late stage of the certification process. However, the failure to maintain records on the place of training does put candidates at a disadvantage, should they feel that discriminatory practices are operating and wish to demonstrate that fact. The duty to maintain such records from the point of initial inquiry should be with all occupational bodies.

In some cases, the practices that we found inherently discriminatory against foreign-trained people are justified by the professional bodies as excusable, and in fact unavoidable, owing to either a lack of comprehensive information about training in other countries or a lack of resources to acquire such information.

To deal with the deficiencies we noted, and in recognition of these concerns of the professional bodies, we have proposed the creation of a new structure, the Prior Learning Assessment Network (PLAN), which is described in Chapter 5, ''Prior Learning Assessment.'' We have also made recommendations, which appear in the relevant chapters, that are intended to provide the professional bodies with guidance and direction in structuring testing mechanisms and procedural protections which meet the standards of fairness we have articulated and which will, we hope, minimize the identified barriers to entry that face foreign-trained professionals.

RECOMMENDATIONS

4.1   *We recommend that professional bodies may, if they wish, retain the right to waive any requirements for licensure and certification, subject to the requirement that, in all cases, the instance of the exercise of the discretion and the grounds therefor shall be part of the public record and be made available to any interested parties through the information dispersal mechanism of the Prior Learning Assessment Network.*

4.2   *We recommend that occupational associations which are not publicly regulated and which grant reserved titles, membership, or other credentials to practitioners considered to meet specified criteria, be specifically named and included in the ambit of legislative provisions creating and implementing the Prior Learning Assessment Network; and that these associations be bound by such provisions to the same extent as regulated occupational bodies.*

4.3   *We recommend that all occupational bodies be required to maintain detailed records of all applications and inquiries, such records to include the place of training of candidates, information required of and provided by them, information provided to them, and the disposition of the inquiry or application.*

PART III

Developing a Prior Learning Assessment Network: PLAN

CHAPTER 5

Prior Learning Assessment

They usually label anything that is not Canadian, American or British as "not accredited."

> — from a Brief submitted to the
> Task Force by an individual

As stated in the last two chapters, the primary obligation of the occupational licensing body is to protect the public's health, safety, and welfare. In carrying out this responsibility, the licensing body must duly respect the general and individual good, justly and without capriciousness. The right of the individual to equality of opportunity and to equal treatment without unreasonable or unfair discrimination must be balanced against the interest of the public to protection. The Ontario Human Rights Commission, in its submission to the Task Force, stated that

> *. . . it is the public policy of the government to provide all persons in Ontario with equal rights and opportunities and to facilitate their full contribution to life in Ontario. Certainly, it is clear public policy in Ontario to assist the newcomer from another country to contribute fully to the development of the province. This commitment is demonstrated through a wide range of services for immigrants, from the funding of information, counselling and legal centres to the instruction of English as a second language. This commitment to equal treatment and equal opportunity is not, however, unqualified. As with many rights within society there are competing values which may have the effect of limiting the extent to which opportunities can be made equally accessible to all. The issue of foreign trained persons gives rise to such a balancing of competing values. The right to equal opportunity must be balanced against the right of members of our society to be confident that the services they receive, particularly in matters which involve their*

physical well-being, are rendered by qualified and capable individuals.[1]

When presented with a candidate for licensure, a professional association or a certifying body must determine whether he or she has mastered the skills necessary to practise the profession or trade. The failure to ensure that the requisite standard of competence has been met would be an abdication by the certifying body of its responsibility to the public, and the failure to give due credit for training completed and learning acquired would be an abdication of responsibility to the applicant. Many people arrive in Canada with valuable assets of prior education and experience. It is essential that any system of licensure or certification recognize such prior learning in order to ensure that individuals who have received all or part of their education or training outside Ontario have the same opportunities as those who have received their education in the province.

The problem cited most frequently by foreign-trained people, community organizations, and ethno-cultural associations submitting briefs to the Task Force was the difficulty in obtaining an accurate, consistent assessment of prior learning for purposes of certification or licensure. (Issues related to educational and experiential equivalency were raised in more than half of the briefs submitted to the Task Force; more than half of these briefs specifically referred to the assessment of educational equivalency.) Our review of the certifying bodies led us to agree that the procedures in place are not always adequate to ensure that the prior learning of foreign-trained applicants is being thoroughly assessed. (For summaries of the methods used by the professional bodies to review credentials, see Appendix H of this Report and the background studies on the professions reviewed.) The concerns expressed by affected groups and individuals relate not only to the quality and consistency of assessments but also to the difficulties that people encounter when trying to find the authoritative source of assessments and trying to obtain clear and reliable information about occupational entrance requirements and procedures. The following five comments exemplify the frustrations felt by many individuals:

The point is that thousands of Filipino professionals who came to this province could not get an entry in their field of expertise for failure of the system to recognize their educational achievements. The present system is downright discriminatory. The institutions are playing the game of volleyball. They pass us from one institution to another.

Degrees from other countries are sometimes validated as equivalent to Grade 13 in [Ontario]. Some evaluations are very subjective.

In conclusion, my bad experiences have formed my outlook and I would like to express my disappointment. It surprises me that a country like Canada when selecting potential immigrants takes education as one of the criteria, but later does not want to use their professional knowledge and experience, but prefers to keep them on unemployment as useless people.

To be where I am now I was required to hide my country, my background, to lie and in general to misrepresent facts. Better than a master's degree obtained after four full time years to say only about an evening course at U of T.

Taking into account all the excuses and justifications, I still claim that general rule of justice "innocent until proven guilty" doesn't apply to immigrants. We are presumed and treated like incompetents, cheaters and dummies unless we can prove otherwise.

In the following discussion, we shall define prior learning assessment, including both academic and experiential learning; outline some of the ways in which prior learning assessment has evolved; and review the current system in Ontario. The section following that one contains a brief description of organizational models followed elsewhere and looks at international trends. Our conclusions follow, along with our proposal for a new direction for the Province of Ontario in its establishment of a mechanism for prior learning assessment. The chapter ends with our specific recommendations for the implementation of our proposal.

PRIOR LEARNING ASSESSMENT: DEFINITIONS AND CURRENT ONTARIO PRACTICE

The purpose of an assessment of prior learning for occupational certification is to determine the equivalency of an individual's qualifications or competencies to educational requirements in Ontario.

The assessment may act as a preliminary standard that entitles the individual to write a licensing or certification examination or enter an educational program. It may also be used to judge whether or not an applicant has the particular competencies needed to be entitled to apply for an occupational certification or licensure (provided all other requirements are met). If the applicant does not, the assessment will specify clearly what additional training is required. Regardless of how the assessment is used, its purpose remains the same: to ensure that anyone licensed or certified in Ontario meets the standards required of all candidates by the profession, the trade, or the educational institution.

ASSESSMENT OF PRIOR ACADEMIC EDUCATION

Prior academic education is that which has been acquired in a formal educational institution and is attested to by the institution through the awarding of course credits, certificates, diplomas, and/or degrees. The assessment of academic equivalency is a sophisticated discipline, built upon an understanding of the nature of curricula and learning and a knowledge of both the common and unique characteristics of the world's many educational systems.

An accurate assessment of prior education can permit an educational institution to place an individual appropriately within the Ontario educational system. It can also assist a licensing or certification body in ensuring that the standards of the profession or trade are maintained without unfairly limiting access. The basis of assessment should be the standard of training required in Ontario for the occupation or profession, as reflected in the educational system here.

Academic Equivalency Assessment in Ontario

Academic equivalency assessment is currently being performed in Ontario by a number of groups and institutions, the primary participants being government departments, educational institutions, and occupational bodies.

Of the government departments involved in assessment, two are involved in a broad and significant way. Ministries that are themselves involved in occupational licensing, such as the Ministry of Community and Social Services, which grants approval for child-care workers, do their own assessments. For purposes of all other occupational assessment, however, the Ministry of Education is the dominant government participant, and so we review its procedures in some detail. The second government department, the Ministry of Skills Development, is responsible for procedures relating to the trades. The role of this Ministry is discussed in Chapter 3 of our Report, "Issues Facing the Trades."

Colleges and universities throughout Ontario assess the educational background of applicants educated elsewhere. A detailed review of all their individual assessment procedures is beyond the scope of our study (the expansion of their procedures into the area of experiential learning assessment is addressed later in this chapter), but we did elect to look closely at the Comparative Education Service at the University of Toronto. This agency has evolved beyond the point of offering advice to its own registrars and department heads and provides assessments for some occupational bodies and employers.

As for the occupational bodies, the vast majority attempt some type of assessment of the academic learning of applicants. Most function independently of other sources of expertise and of each other, performing their own research and data collection.

In the balance of this section on assessment of prior academic education, we review the roles of the Ontario Ministry of Education, the Comparative Education Service of the University of Toronto, and the occupational bodies.

Ontario Ministry of Education's Evaluation Services[2]

The Registrar Services Unit of the Ontario Ministry of Education performs some functions analogous to a university's registrar service, assessing credentials and maintaining records on students and teachers in Ontario. Within the unit, Evaluation Services is responsible for evaluating equivalencies.

One of the responsibilities of Evaluation Services is to assess out-of-province elementary and secondary school credentials, in comparison with the Ontario education system, for employment purposes. The assessments are provided to the individual applicants rather than to prospective employers, although information on foreign training systems is available to employers. A general statement of comparable academic attainment is provided, but there is no detailed statement of equivalency. The quality of the institution attended is not assessed.

Those with foreign education who wish to enrol in an Ontario postsecondary educational institution are generally assessed by the institution itself. Those with foreign education who wish to enrol in an Ontario elementary or secondary school are placed within the school system by the principal of that school or by the school board. Although in such cases Evaluation Services does not prepare an assessment, it makes available summaries of foreign educational systems. The Ministry will respond as it can to requests for further information.

Evaluation Services does not assess trades qualifications. Foreign technical-school training is assessed, but only in terms of how comparable it is to Ontario secondary school technical training.

Professional qualifications are not assessed here, except for those of teachers. Reference is made to information on file relating to the length and content of degree programs and secondary school programs in the jurisdiction in question. Only institutions listed as acceptable in the regulations to the *Education Act* are eligible for consideration. The assessment also considers content in relation to teacher education programs. A detailed review is carried out with reference to criteria reflecting the Ontario standard.

The Ministry's evaluation services are available free to anyone with an official status in Canada (landed immigrants, Canadian citizens, and holders of diplomatic visas, employment authorizations, or refugee status) who received his or her elementary education outside Ontario. The Ministry of Education will also evaluate documents for people who reside outside Canada but have some status here. Refugee claimants are not able to receive an evaluation until they obtain official status in Canada or are granted a work authorization. Original documents are required, along with Ministry of Citizenship translations. Documents are visually inspected for authenticity, and an assessment is refused if a document is found to be invalid. Statutory declarations may be permitted if it is impossible to obtain documentation.

The three evaluators on staff handle about 7,200 applications and inquiries per year and are also responsible for creating and updating summaries of elementary and secondary school systems throughout the world. Credentials are assessed in accordance with these educational summaries and a considerable amount of reference material. Evaluation

Services belongs to a number of educational associations and receives information from them on foreign educational systems.

If a client disputes the assessment, a reassessment by a more senior evaluator is available.

Evaluation Services is listed in the Welcome House handbook, *Newcomers Guide to Services in Ontario.* Availability of the service is also communicated through employers, who refer potential employees to it.

Comparative Education Service[3]

The Comparative Education Service (CES) of the University of Toronto is the only body in Ontario that assesses foreign postsecondary qualifications for employment purposes in a range of occupations. Individuals with foreign trades qualifications are referred to the Ministry of Skills Development.

CES evaluations, which are provided to individuals as well as to institutions, are not binding, although licensing groups and educational institutions may choose to follow CES recommendations. The Ontario Board of Examiners in Psychology, the Canadian Dietetic Association, and the Certified General Accountants Association of Ontario are among those that utilize the CES assessment of foreign academic credentials but, typically, do not rely on CES assessments as evidence of equivalency. The CES assessments are considered preliminary screens and are followed by more detailed assessments by the professional bodies concerned.

The Comparative Education Service evolved out of the University of Toronto's office of admissions, where assessments of documents were already being made, intended primarily to serve companies and government ministries that wished to assess their employees' prior education. The service is staffed by the administrative officer, an assistant, and a clerk/receptionist.

The University of Toronto funds the service under the budget of its office of admissions. The service is available to the public at large. Since May 1989 there has been a charge of $50 for an assessment, with institutional clients, including universities, exempted.

Official Ministry of Citizenship translations of original documents are preferred. The CES does not translate. Although official documents are generally required, a statutory declaration will be accepted. The service is not equipped to detect fraudulent documents. In cases where the documentation is inadequate or unclear, a transcript stating that the candidate graduated will be accepted as a certificate of completion.

The focus of the Comparative Education Service is on finding the level of achievement in the Canadian educational system that the applicant has reached. The CES does not prepare a content analysis of the program completed or of the grading standard in the educational system. The document produced by the CES states that the service considers the client's qualifications to be equivalent to a particular academic level in Canada. Whenever it is appropriate, the grading system is included. The document states:

> This assessment is for general and employment purposes only, and it does not constitute an offer of admission to a university. Neither may it be taken as having a bearing on any evaluation or decision made for professional purposes . . .

Sources of information include standard reference books, accreditation associations, professional associations, and professors at the University of Toronto. Immigrant groups provide the service with information. Occasionally, the CES will contact a foreign institution or a Canadian embassy. If an institution is not listed in one of the international reference books that the service subscribes to, the CES requests further information from the applicant or does further research in order to give the applicant some kind of response.

The CES processes the documentation of 35 to 70 clients per week, and in 1988 it issued 2,609 equivalency letters.

Applicants become aware of the service through the Ministry of Education; by Ontario Welcome House, which includes the service in its booklet for immigrants, *Newcomers Guide to Services in Ontario*; and through employment agencies and employers, who refer applicants.

Assessment by Occupational Bodies

Some academic equivalency assessment is currently being performed in Ontario by the occupational bodies, in certain cases thoroughly and comprehensively. In Appendix H of this Report, "Professional Summaries," we briefly summarize the procedures currently in place in the professions we reviewed. (A more detailed outline appears in the background studies, with reference to each of these groups, where we also comment on some of the strengths and weaknesses we perceive to exist within the professions.) There is, however, considerable variation in the type and comprehensiveness of the methods being employed, which range from carrying out a detailed review of prior training to preparing essentially no review at all. Generalizations are therefore difficult to make, and praise and criticism must be carefully dispersed.

In addition, our study is necessarily constrained by the following reality. Although the structures of assessment, the difficulties encountered by disappointed candidates, and the needs expressed by some occupational groups themselves, all of which we have considered, have led us to conclude that weaknesses and deficiencies in current procedures exist in many cases, the actual rightness or wrongness of decisions being rendered in assessment can be determined absolutely only by those with complete knowledge of the individual case, expertise in the particular discipline, and an awareness of comparative education and of prior learning assessment techniques. Ill-placed to make such judgments, we have not, therefore, ''gone behind'' individual decisions. Finally, although we have attempted a comprehensive survey of occupational structures in Ontario, we did not attempt to analyze the entry procedures for every occupation imposing such requirements.

Although we recognize the efforts being made and the level of expertise being developed within a number of occupational bodies, we nonetheless encountered recurring actual and potential weaknesses in the methods being applied to assess the educational backgrounds of applicants.

Lack of recognition of academic qualifications. In some instances, licensing or certifying bodies or educational institutions have refused to recognize any certification or competencies obtained outside an accredited program. Accreditation is typically limited to Canadian or, at most, North American training programs, and candidates from elsewhere may thus find themselves turned away with no assessment. For example, a candidate for licensure in dental technology must have completed the accredited Ontario training program or have been apprenticed for four years in Ontario; previous training elsewhere is not counted for credit against these requirements. Similarly, in the profession of optometry, graduates of accredited North American schools are considered to have degrees comparable to those of Ontario graduates and are permitted to write the licensure examination. In practice, all others must apply to an accredited school for admission in order to obtain an acceptable degree; although they may be entitled to some credit by the educational institution for their previous work in optometry, they must complete a sufficient portion of the accredited curriculum to entitle them to a degree from that institution. Such substantial retraining may be needed in some cases, but it may in others exceed the actual retraining needs of the candidate necessary to bring him or her to the requisite level of competence. Compounding this problem is the fact that entry into the upper years of academic programs in professional schools is often very difficult. Space is so limited, in fact, that complete retraining in many cases becomes the only available avenue to licensure.

Arbitrariness of standards. Where attempts are made by an occupational body to conduct an assessment, a problem we noted frequently was the application of arbitrary standards. In one case we were told that the awarding of credit on entry to a student from a non-Ontario institution is based on the performance of the most recent applicant or applicants from that institution. This type of follow-up may not be irrelevant, but such reliance on it is inappropriate; the performance of the first student may reflect many factors unrelated to the quality of his or her prior education. In several cases we were told that a positive assessment could depend on whether someone in the administration of the profession had recently been exposed, for one reason or another, to the educational program in the jurisdiction of the applicant. Sometimes assessments are based simply on personal information gathered by the registrar. In other words, the information-gathering is often sporadic, ad hoc, and subjective.

Use of outside evaluators. Some licensing bodies rely on outside evaluators to assist them in their assessments. Typical of these evaluators is the Comparative Education Service of the University of Toronto, described above. Although such services adequately perform a limited function, there is no such service in Ontario with the capacity to perform a detailed, comprehensive assessment. For example, the Comparative Education Service does a general assessment of academic level achieved, but it cannot do a course-by-course content examination. This much more precise and revealing review can be made only if there is available to the assessor comprehensive information on the applicant's program (notably its standards and those of the educational institution); a source of expertise within the particular subject area; and an explicitly defined Ontario standard against which other standards can be measured. The CES is also constrained in its capacity to assess by its very limited physical structure; it is essentially a one-person operation. The best that can be provided, therefore, is a general evaluation.

Use of international accrediting systems. Although some occupational groups look to an accrediting system that extends beyond North America, problems exist here as well. For example, to determine equivalency, occupational therapists rely on a worldwide registry of programs in the discipline; the profession takes the position that a graduate from a program accepted by the international body is adequately equipped to attempt the certification examination. This system poses problems for candidates who have graduated from programs that have not yet been reviewed. Such candidates may apply to have their programs considered for inclusion on the approved list, but the procedure may take years. A further difficulty in relying on an outside accrediting system is that many accreditation systems depend on application for inclusion. Some jurisdictions attempt to limit the mobility of their trained graduates by not applying for accreditation, with the result being that their candidates are unable to gain the recognition for their training that is deserved.

Reciprocity arrangements. Where recognition of foreign programs rests on reciprocity, inequities can result. In one profession we reviewed, reciprocity was broken off by the U.S. professional body. The Ontario professional body responded by denying entry to U.S. candidates to that profession, despite the acknowledgment by those within the profession that the U.S. applicants were adequately qualified.

No assessment of foreign training. Some occupations do not undertake any assessment of foreign training. In dentistry and veterinary medicine, for example, all foreign-trained candidates who have degrees recognized by the World Health Organization (WHO) are granted access to the licensing examinations. The training received in Canadian programs and, to a lesser extent, in U.S. programs, is well known. Because of a lack of information about the programs of candidates from other countries, these professions look to WHO, and as a result require examinations of some candidates that are not required of other candidates. This method of controlling entry has two deficiencies: it fails to recognize the validity of any training outside the WHO-recognized formal training programs, and it imposes on some candidates the requirement to complete costly and demanding examinations that would not be necessary if their true level of skill could be ascertained by other means.

Inconsistencies in external factors. The looseness of the existing assessment structures can result in inconsistency. Ease of entry based on "equivalency" as assessed by the individual occupational bodies has the potential to change over time or show sharp variations among similar structures, more because of the profession's own human resources situation than as a result of an increase or decrease in the number of qualified candidates.

Examinations to confirm equivalency. Candidates for some professions, in spite of having been assessed as equivalent in an internal review of their academic credentials, are required to write examinations not required of Ontario-trained candidates — simply to demonstrate their equivalency of training. The rationale for such a procedure presumably is a reluctance on the part of the occupational body to rely on its own assessment.

Conflict-of-interest situations. In some cases, the body responsible for licensure or certification delegates the job of assessment to the voluntary association for the occupation or to the educational institution responsible for training. Such delegation can create conflict-of-interest situations. Although recruitment of students by an educational organization or protection by an occupational association of the interests of its membership (through limiting numbers entering the occupation) may not be consciously brought into consideration, the risk of such irrelevant factors' having an impact is enhanced in such situations.

Overlapping of disciplines. Significant overlap may exist among disciplines, and applicants trained in one area may be qualified to receive considerable credit for training in another. Nevertheless, some occupations require that the candidate have completed a program in a specific discipline. This somewhat rigid requirement tends to appear in the regulations themselves and is simply applied by the registrar. For example, an ophthalmologist, although not qualified to be an optometrist, might well be entitled to credit for training received; similarly, a dentist or dental technician might well have completed considerable training applicable to denture therapy. However, the wording of the regulations applying to optometry and denture therapy restricts the right of the registrar to recognize these alternate routes. Representatives of the governing body for denture therapists have indicated that they feel a broad interpretation, giving some recognition to such training, is possible within the regulation as it stands, but they acknowledge that current practice does not reflect their position. Such strict drawing of lines between disciplines is common to a number of occupations and indicative of a broader reluctance, on the part of occupational bodies generally, to recognize the potential for transferability of skills from one discipline to another. This transferability would not be for purposes of immediate certification, which generally would be impossible and inappropriate, but for purposes of credit against training requirements.

Registration in previous jurisdiction. On a related point, some professions specify that candidates must be licensed in the particular discipline in their previous jurisdiction before qualifying for licensure here. Not only does this requirement restrict the candidate to precisely the same discipline; it precludes from certification candidates who come from jurisdictions in which the discipline happens not to be regulated.

Rejection because of uncertainty. Representatives of some occupational bodies themselves emphasize the difficulty they face in assessing foreign training, acknowledging that, lacking any adequate assurance about the quality of a candidate's training or in the face of ambiguity on that issue, they feel bound in the public interest to reject the candidate or require him or her to do extensive retraining.

Lack of specificity and guidance in assessments. Assessments often lack detailed information about the precise standards that need to be met. One submitter referred to a letter of rejection which advised that he had graduated from an "unacceptable" program. The use of the word "unacceptable" may have reflected the terminology of the applicable regulations, but it conveyed nothing but insult to the recipient. In some cases candidates who are considered to have inadequate training are given guidance and instruction on what further steps they must take in order to meet the required standard; in other cases they are not. This deficiency may be owing in part to a lack of specificity in the assessment itself.

As several of the above factors indicate, failure to make an appropriate assessment of prior education may not reflect an intention to discriminate but is in many cases simply the result of the licensing body's inexperience with such assessment. The expertise and extensive resources required to make an accurate assessment of an individual's prior education are frequently cited by licensing bodies and academic institutions as reasons for not evaluating in depth, or at all. The licensing body cannot of course predict the countries that applicants will come from, and therefore it must act in response to a request. Indeed, any given profession or trade may have only one or two applicants from a particular country in a five-year period, and so it is difficult to establish a coherent approach.

The failure to assess this education appropriately effectively negates an individual's prior accomplishments and results in either a complete rejection of prior education, by requiring the individual to repeat his or her entire training program here, or a requirement to complete partial retraining that may or may not be necessary. The need to complete additional examinations, not required of other candidates, is another typical response to the lack of adequate assessments. The result is frustration for the applicant and a waste of resources. The applicant may be forced to forgo earning any income during a retraining process that may be unnecessary. In disciplines where no retraining is available or in cases where it is economically impossible for an applicant to undertake retraining while supporting a family, the ultimate result could be the complete loss of the skills brought to Canada.

The proper response to these problems should not be to declare that assessments of prior education cannot be undertaken. Rather, it should be to recognize that they can be done, comprehensively and efficiently, by an expert body whose primary responsibility is this assessment of prior academic and experiential learning and designation of academic equivalency. Not only will a centralized approach be the most economical way to assemble the resources and expertise necessary to evaluate prior learning competently, but it will also ensure the quality of the assessment, whether the applicant is attempting to obtain licensure, further education, or employment.

Assessments that rely only upon a school catalogue with limited course information differ significantly from those performed with reference to detailed material on the relevant educational system, the courses taken, the content of those courses, and the status of the educational institution within its own country. It is this latter form of assessment that operates in the context of a comprehensive equivalency assessment body.

A number of assessment bodies from around the world regularly prepare extensive research documents on particular education qualifications and provide frequently updated material through periodicals; as well, there are large numbers of educational and accreditation journals in circulation. Although such materials cannot reflect the current status of all secondary and postsecondary educational institutions, these publications do represent a significant source of information. It should be emphasized, however, that this information is intended for specialists in comparative education — a distinct discipline with specialized skills. These specialists not only are familiar with the literature available but also have been trained in the application of the information and in the techniques of linking up with the growing international network in comparative education. Without such expertise, these data can be difficult to use, as the following submission to the Task Force emphasized:

One of the problems in the evaluation of foreign credentials is that much of the resource material currently available is not written in the Canadian perspective. The findings and recommendations contained in these publications must be interpreted once again to render them comparable to Canadian or Ontario educational systems.

Given the number of educational institutions that exist around the world, the various levels of education available in Ontario and other jurisdictions, the variety of sources of learning, and the shifts occurring in sources of immigration, effective and economical assessments of academic equivalency require that a central body be established. Not only could this body reduce the current duplication of effort as licensing associations individually attempt to research and assess each applicant's prior education, but it could better ensure a consistency of treatment of individuals throughout trades, professions, and educational institutions.

Although comprehensive information can be gathered and individually updated through a single professional body, it is a time-consuming, difficult, and expensive task. Where these functions are coordinated as part of a general data-collection procedure relating to many disciplines within the same countries and institutions, there is enhanced efficiency in time and cost and a greater assurance that the results, as to content and quality of programs and institutions, will be accurate and up-to-date. The expertise currently in evidence in the professions and trades can be utilized effectively through the advisory boards to the Prior Learning Assessment Network (PLAN) that we recommend be created (see our conclusions and our recommendations at the end of this chapter), while the ongoing process of information collection and program evaluation can be left to the comparative education analysts.

ASSESSMENT OF PRIOR EXPERIENTIAL LEARNING

A great deal of learning goes on outside the aegis of formal educational institutions, and four types of learning contexts are particularly relevant to any discussion of the equivalency of prior experiential learning.

First, learning may be acquired through actual, on-the-job experience, both in the refinement of existing knowledge and skills and in the application of knowledge and skills to situations within the work environment. Such is the case with an autobody repairer who improves efficiency with traditional fabrication materials and learns to deal with new materials and design elements. Likewise, a corporate lawyer adjusts to a business environment dominated by acquisitions and mergers; an office administrator learns computer skills; a teacher learns new skills and knowledge in order to maintain instructional effectiveness in a multicultural community; and a hairstylist learns to manage hair transplants. Often, there is no inherent mechanism for attestation of what has been learned by these means, and traditionally none has been needed; such learning has simply been considered "part of the job."

Second, learning can occur in structured education and training programs, sponsored by employers, professional associations, trade unions, and others, which are not actually a part of the formal educational system. In-house management training, organization-specific development of knowledge and skills, career-path planning, and succession planning are examples of the kinds of learning programs sponsored outside formal education. The Carnegie Foundation reported that, at the beginning of the 1980s, more people in the United States were enrolled in education and training programs outside formal educational institutions than inside them.[4] The Ontario pattern seems similar, as does that in other industrialized locations. These learning opportunities typically have some form of associated attestation mechanism, although there is rarely any carry-over into formal academic credit or recognition for certification or licensure.

Third, people learn through participation in volunteer activities: planning, organizing, communicating, fund-raising, marketing, investing, and many other kinds of knowledge- and skills-enhancing activities. A means for attestation of learning seldom exists in the volunteer sector.

The fourth type of learning is self-instruction, which includes carefully structured independent learning programs. Attestation of learning is not usually a consideration in this context.

Assessing experiential learning is one way to determine the academic equivalency of various kinds of competencies acquired outside of formal educational institutions. This assessment can then be used for credit towards an educational credential or an occupational certificate or licence. It is important, however, to recognize two key points. First, the standard against which the assessment is made must be the same as the one looked to in the assessment of prior academic learning (that is, the standard required of Ontario-trained candidates as specified by the occupational bodies and/or the relevant educational institutions). Such an assessment should not be based on a loose or flexible system of assessment, but rather on a rigorous and detailed evaluation of learning achieved through past, documented experience. Second, although such learning is gained through some form of experience, its assessment must focus on the competencies that the individual has actually acquired and not simply consider the duration or contents of an individual's experience. In other words, it is the quality of learning, not the length of experience, that is relevant.

Gauging experiential learning as an indicator of competence may strike many people as a novel concept, but in fact occupations have historically relied heavily upon assessment of such learning to satisfy certification and licensure requirements.

Indeed, for many occupations a relationship with formal educational institutions is quite recent. For example, most teacher training colleges were established during this century and, with few exceptions, were relocated into universities during the last 25 years. The history of legal training is rooted within law offices and the professional body, and its association with universities is quite recent; the University of Toronto Law School, for example, was established in 1949 as Ontario's first university-based law school. The transition of nursing training from its hospital base to community colleges in Ontario, is even more recent; the profession is endeavouring now to move nursing education into universities. Whatever the reasons for the increasingly academic nature of occupational preparation, the power of certification typically has been retained by the professional association. Through accreditation and other approval procedures used by these bodies, some significant degree of control is retained over the academic programs themselves.

Recognition of experiential learning has not come easily to colleges and universities: our formal educational systems have evolved as bounded systems that do not happily acknowledge or attest learning which they themselves have not initiated and regulated. Nevertheless, several phenomena have stimulated postsecondary educational institutions to begin the assessment of prior experiential learning for credit.

In North America, credit given for military service is an early example of pressure brought to bear on formal education to acknowledge experiential learning. Interest in prior learning assessment emerged after the First World War, when servicemen re-entered civilian life, and the United States — notably the State of New York — looked for means to encourage these young people to resume their schooling. A process was created whereby postsecondary credit could be awarded for military experience.

Following the Second World War, provisions for crediting military experiential learning were made more systematic and comprehensive, although such an extension of credit remained the exception within the formal education system. Because high school retention and graduation rates were slowly climbing, postsecondary educational institutions concentrated on creating a continuity of learning from secondary to postsecondary schooling. The members of the adult population who wished to re-enter formal education typically had to do so on the same terms as their younger counterparts fresh out of high school. Apart from the military example, there was no overall pressure on colleges and universities to make special provision for adults, least of all to establish means to assign credit for what an individual had learned outside the formal educational system.

The late 1970s and early 1980s saw a sharp decline in the number of students graduating from high school. The postwar baby crop had moved into the workforce, and many postsecondary institutions recognized that if they were to retain their enrolment levels, and thereby their funding and faculty, access to postsecondary education would have to be improved and the recruitment net cast more broadly. The strategies used included admissions policies directed to mature students and the growth of part-time programs.

Some universities, such as the University of Regina, adopted a mature-student admission policy that permitted anyone over age 16 to enrol in a trial semester and, if successful, register as a "regular" student. More frequently among Canadian universities, mature-student admission was restricted to people 21 and over. Such measures brought only partial solutions to the problem of decreased enrolment, however, because most universities continued to operate on the assumption that all students should be full-time students.

Gradually, throughout North America, part-time enrolment came to be promoted by many colleges and universities on the premise that many people are more likely to pursue higher education if they do not have to become unemployed in the process. Today it is no longer unusual for an

Ontario community college or university to have two or three times the number of people enrolled in part-time as in full-time programs.

It should be noted that North America has not been alone in this change process. As an example, Sweden has widened adult access to postsecondary education through the introduction of its 25/5 rule. Sweden's educational system is highly centralized, which has permitted the government to implement this rule to increase adult enrolment. The 25/5 rule permits adults 25 or older with at least five years in the workforce to gain general eligibility to higher educational institutions. Work experience is interpreted broadly: military experience and time spent in child care are equally applicable. In 1975-76, 22.5 per cent of new entrants to university faculties of arts, social sciences, and natural sciences were admitted by the 25/5 rule.[5] Concern has been raised that 25/5 students are occupying so many spaces that direct entry from high school is endangered.

It was primarily in this overall context that an important means for improving access, and for attracting more adult students, was implemented by a growing number of North American postsecondary institutions: provision for the assessment and crediting of experiential learning. As some postsecondary institutions sought to attract adult enrolment, they offered to assess not only the formal educational credentials of the recruits but also what had been learned at work, in on-the-job training, and through personal experience. This assessment took a variety of both ad hoc and systematized forms, but the general goal was the same: to increase enrolment by making formal postsecondary education more accessible and more attractive.

Although the introduction of experiential learning assessment is an exciting innovation for postsecondary institutions, for occupational groups served by these institutions the cycle has come full circle. Formal postsecondary education is beginning to recognize what some occupational certification and licensure officials have always known: that valid and useful learning can take place in a variety of settings outside of formal institutions, and that there are efficient means for assessing experiential learning both for academic credit and for occupational certification and licensure.

Methods of Experiential Learning Assessment

In the area of experiential learning, four basic methods of assessment are generally recognized: examination-based courses, challenge examinations, equivalency of non-formal courses, and portfolio development.[6]

Examination-Based Courses

One of the most notable institutions to grant degrees based on examinations exclusively is the University of London. Since its establishment in the 1830s, this university has had a non-teaching program that awards degrees on the basis of examination scores. Students have access to reading lists and course guides, and lectures are scheduled periodically, although mainly for the general edification of the student body. Students are permitted to write their examinations when they feel ready.

In the United States, the College Level Examination Program (CLEP) and the Advanced Placement Program (APP) were developed by the College Board's Educational Testing Service. CLEP sets 50 different examinations, which are written annually by about 140,000 adults, based on typical objectives of credit courses as identified by the Board through surveys and comparative research. Success on the examination earns the individual a course credit that is awarded by the College Board. More than 1,500 universities and colleges recognize student course credits based on CLEP and APP performance.[7]

Challenge Examinations

Challenge examinations gained some degree of popularity as a result of their use with servicemen returning from the Second World War and, subsequently, with refugees from Europe whose transcripts were unavailable.

Unlike examination-based courses, challenge examinations typically are administered by individual institutions or certification bodies to determine if a person who has not taken a regular course has learned that material through some other means. The examination is based on an existing course, and under certain circumstances its successful completion is a permissible way of gaining credit for the course.

In Ontario's community colleges, the challenge exams generally used either are the final examinations written by regular students or are specially created examinations for the challenging student. Depending on the institution, the student pays either the same fee as a regular enrolee or a reduced fee.

Although challenge examinations sometimes are used to assign credit or advanced standing to a student, the university and college registrars contacted by the Task Force indicated that they more often are used to waive entrance requirements or grant course exemptions.

Equivalency of Non-Formal Courses

As noted earlier, military programs have a history of awarding formal academic credit for non-collegiate learning. After the First World War, a mechanism was created to award returning U.S. servicemen one or two years' credit for military experience. In the United States, this initiative evolved through challenge examinations into the present elaborate system of published equivalencies.[8] In Canada, Seneca College in Toronto and College Ahunsic in Montreal provide opportunities for anglophones and francophones, respectively, to gain college credit for experience acquired and courses taken in the armed forces.

The American Council on Education has refined the U.S. system to enable adults to gain credit for their prior learning through military course work, employment or professional activities, and demonstrated proficiency in military occupations. The specific equivalencies to formal academic credit are published in the *Guide to Evaluation of Educational Experiences in the Armed Forces*.[9]

The New York Regents' Program on Noncollegiate Sponsored Instruction publishes an annual *Guide to Educational Programs in Noncollegiate Organizations*,[10] which includes the military along with many corporately sponsored education and training programs. Equivalencies, which are determined through a comparison between these non-formal programs and typical postsecondary course requirements, are published as recommendations for use by colleges and universities, certification and licensure bodies, employers, and others. Those who provide non-formal education and training can approach the New York Regents for inclusion in this assessment program.

Assisted by the American Council for Adult and Experiential Learning, which is universally recognized as the foremost authority on prior learning assessment, the United Kingdom established the Credit Accumulation and Transfer Scheme (CAT Scheme). The CAT Scheme, which is administered by the Council for National Academic Awards for the United Kingdom, provides an experiential assessment service similar to that of the New York Regents and permits individuals to accumulate formal credit for the full range of experiential learning. Such credit subsequently is recognized by universities, polytechnics, and occupations for purposes of certification and licensure. The CAT Scheme is discussed in greater detail later in this chapter.

Through the Open Learning Agency, the Province of British Columbia has begun activity towards these same ends. That agency's Educational Credit Bank is also discussed later in this chapter.

Portfolio Development

A commonly used means for experiential learning assessment is the review of a detailed portfolio of prior learning, assembled by the applicant but with formal assistance provided by the institution. This portfolio features concrete examples of the applicant's work and sometimes includes interviews with faculty members in the areas of study in which credit is being sought. Materials are assessed against program requirements to determine equivalencies.

The Quebec CEGEPs and Loyalist College, each of which makes use of the portfolio method, are discussed in more detail later in this chapter.

Experiential Assessment in Ontario

There is evidence that some of the techniques of experiential assessment described above are being applied in a limited way in institutions in Ontario, specifically in some educational institutions, in the trades organizations, and in some occupational bodies. We discuss each of these in turn.

Educational Institutions

Excluding the affiliated colleges, Canada has 55 degree-granting universities. In a 1984 study on provision for prior learning assessment in these universities, a search of journal articles over several years did not disclose a single reference to prior learning assessment among these bodies.[11] An examination of university calendars, however, revealed that 12 institutions use challenge examinations or some other form of assessment of experiential learning, at least in some departments.

In a current survey on provisions for prior learning assessment to which 60 universities and affiliated colleges and 79 community colleges have replied,[12] the preliminary analysis indicates the following:

- Some 88 per cent of respondents admit students who do not meet normal entrance requirements;

- Some 57 per cent grant advanced standing for prior learning; 38 per cent waive prerequisites; 36 per cent waive course requirements; and 49 per cent award course credit;

- When asked where the influence came from for the development of these procedures, the major influences were cited as presidents (64 per cent), faculty (43 per cent), deans (38 per cent), students (19 per cent), and alumni (7 per cent). External influences included armed services (41 per cent), community (21 per cent), social agencies (18 per cent), trade unions (17 per cent), business (16 per cent), immigrant groups (4 per cent), and women's groups (4 per cent). Notably, government ministries were not perceived to have had any significant influence in the development of these procedures;

- Respondents reported that a broad range of factors were considered in assessing prior learning, including age, community work, courses at work, military experience, domestic experience, work experience, self-directed learning, and volunteer work.

The chief characteristics of prior learning assessment programs that exist in Canadian universities appear to be the relatively ad hoc nature of the assessment strategies and the low profile given these programs.

In general all community colleges in Ontario appear to make some provision for or assessment of prior education, although such assessment programs tend to be low-profile and unsystematic. There is some evidence of case-by-case assessment of prior experiential learning, but there seems to be only rare formal provision for prior learning assessment. The system used by Humber College, which appears characteristic of that in place in Ontario's colleges of applied arts and technology, is explained in some detail below.[13]

Humber College does not have a written policy on assessment and recognition of prior experience, but in any program area in the college an applicant may have prior experiential learning assessed and may gain advanced standing for appropriate prior experiential learning. A student may gain credit for a full year, a semester, or individual courses.

Perhaps because the policy is not published, few students gain credit in this manner. There seems to be no publicized or automatic consideration of experience. The application form asks for academic and experiential background. Where the registrar sees the potential for experiential equivalency, he or she refers the applicant to the appropriate program area for an assessment that includes an interview and, when appropriate, the scrutiny of documents. A written recommendation regarding advanced standing is forwarded from the program area to the registrar.

In some program areas in Humber College, such as funeral services, an applicant might find that he or she has sufficient appropriate experience to bypass college courses and go directly to the association for certification.

The exception we found among Ontario community colleges is the Band Welfare Administration Social Service Diploma program offered by Loyalist College in cooperation with the First Nations Technical Institute. This program systematically uses prior learning assessment to assist each participant in developing an individualized learner plan, and credits and exemptions are granted where earned.

In the Loyalist program, each applicant must also be interviewed by a committee from the Social Service Worker program faculty and must provide oral or written references from a work supervisor, a work colleague, a knowledgeable community member, and one other person.

Trades

In general, the trades in Canada are regulated by the apprenticeship branch of each provincial government. Certification procedures permit the assessment of experiential learning, although the assessment strategies lack clearly defined standards and systematic and consistent application. A discussion of the issues relating to assessment of trades qualifications appears in Chapter 3 of this Report, "Issues Facing the Trades," and key points include the following:

- Throughout the country there typically are some compulsory regulated trades for which the practitioner must obtain certification before being allowed to practise the trade. These trades vary from province to province.

• There typically are voluntary regulated trades for which the practitioner may, but is not required to, obtain certification before practising the trade. These trades also vary from province to province.

• The apprentice training program that leads to the trade credential — a journeyman's certificate — is a combination of (1) structured practical experience, obtained within a business or industry, and (2) structured classroom-based theory, typically obtained at a community college. Both dimensions are set out in an apprenticeship training program registered with the apprenticeship branch.

• Individuals who wish to earn a journeyman's credential in Ontario and do not have an interprovincially recognized certificate but can produce evidence of appropriate training are required to write qualifying examinations. Those who cannot produce evidence of appropriate training generally may present themselves for an interview and, at the judgment of the director of apprenticeship, be permitted to present a sworn affidavit of experience; they may also be required to take a practical demonstration of skills test before being permitted to write the qualifying examinations leading to a journeyman's credential.

Professions

Although the majority of professional bodies in Ontario rely on such established mechanisms as formal accreditation systems and assessments of academic equivalency, some professions accept evidence of learning gained through other means. A few professions attempt detailed case-by-case assessments that have potential for recognizing considerable related experiential learning; others introduce limited elements of experiential learning assessment.

Challenge examinations are offered in a number of professions — including certified general accountancy, certified management accountancy, law, engineering, and forestry — to candidates otherwise assessed as failing to meet the standard of equivalency. Successful results will allow such candidates to bypass some course work requirements.

In funeral services, it is possible for a candidate to become licensed solely on the basis of his or her experience. For example, under the regulations a candidate for licensure as a funeral services director must be a graduate of a program in funeral services, which in Ontario is offered at Humber College.[14] Recognizing that funeral training is obtained in different ways, Humber has developed a program to assess whether the applicants for licensure have the prerequisite knowledge. The procedure consists of an initial interview plus — if the candidate appears to have background sufficient to justify it — a challenge examination. The college prepares and grades the examination, the standard of which is intended to match Humber's own. Those who appear to have training or experience that brings them to a level of competence equal to that achieved by Ontario graduates are permitted to write the licensing examination; those who do not are directed to the portions of the Humber College program that they require. Practical training may also be required. The cost of the assessment is $150. By virtue of this process and of the waiver power available to the Board of Funeral Services,[15] it therefore is possible for a candidate who has not graduated from a funeral services program to be licensed in Ontario. In engineering technology and land surveying also, it is possible to receive a licence based on experience alone, but the likelihood of this is small because the amount of required experience is substantial.

Medicine is another profession that has a comprehensive procedure for assessment of the equivalency of prior learning. Foreign graduates of unaccredited medical schools undergo a rigorous individualized competency assessment. Starting with the Medical Council of Canada Evaluation Examination, which they must pass, and the Test of English as a Foreign Language (TOEFL) test, on which they must score 580, and the Test of Spoken English (TSE), on which they must score 200, candidates are directed through a sophisticated testing procedure to determine who should be entitled to enter the pre-internship program, completion of which is a prerequisite to internship for such candidates. Written examinations, clinical examinations, curricula vitae, and written references are all considered. There are two significant features unique to this profession's assessment mechanisms. The first is that even if a candidate does meet a fixed standard of competence, he or she does not necessarily have the opportunity to enter the profession; only 24 candidates are admitted to the program. The second is that the pre-internship program itself is said to be a program of "assessing and upgrading." The position of the College of Physicians and Surgeons is that the year-long program is a necessary stage in the assessment process.

A number of other professions have introduced elements of prior learning assessment into their evaluations: interviews, portfolios, or, more generally, limited recognition of relevant foreign experience as a credit against academic equivalency. The Toronto Institute of Medical Technology, for example, is introducing a process that will attempt to assess relevant experience. Other professional groups, among them engineering, law, ophthalmic dispensing, massage therapy, and nursing, may take foreign experience into consideration, although the degree of reliance placed on such experience is generally very limited.

This brief survey provides evidence that although awareness of the importance and validity of experience as a means of learning is evident in some quarters, its acceptance in Ontario is far from complete. In part this reluctance is owing to a concern that the assessment of such learning is difficult. We do not deny that is so, but to say something is difficult is not to say it should not be done. The importance of experiential learning is beginning to be recognized around the world, as we shall soon see in this chapter. Ontario cannot afford to be left behind.

The Role of Practical Experience in Formal Education

Before we leave the subject of the assessment of experience, it is important to note the distinction between (1) assessment of experience as equivalent to academic training, and (2) specific Ontario or Canadian experience requirements that exist as part of Ontario training programs and also must be met by foreign-trained candidates. The value of practical experience is well established in education at all levels and in training programs, where it exists in such forms as internship, fieldwork, and apprenticeship. Requirements for practical experience are also found in licensure and certification processes in the professions and trades, including, among a great many others, medicine, education, law, carpentry, and plumbing. Although this experience sometimes may be acquired apart from the academic certification and licensure requirements, it is no less a requirement than academic competency.

The type of experience gained in a formal education setting varies greatly. It includes highly structured, time-based programs such as in medicine, where an intern spends a predetermined number of weeks in the various specialties; and non-structured programs such as in legal clinics, where the student's experience depends on the nature of the cases that arise during this period of training. Practical experience is also gained in competency-based programs, in which an individual able to demonstrate the successful acquisition of specified knowledge and skills is deemed to have sufficient experience, regardless of the time spent acquiring these competencies.

The kind of assessment carried out in these programs also varies widely. In some cases there is no formal summative assessment but rather an expectation that, after a predetermined period, the person will have learned the necessary skills. In others, a formal checklist of skills might be used to structure the learning period. In still others, particularly those that are competency based, a concluding formal examination tests the knowledge and skills required.

Ontario employers, postsecondary institutions' admissions offices, and licensure bodies are generally comfortable recognizing the experience that an individual has had if that experience was a part of a formal educational program; that is, the experience is attested to by the same bodies that attest to the candidate's academic learning. Where experiential learning is not linked directly to a formal academic program, however, or where it has been obtained outside Ontario, there is a reluctance to accept it at face value. Typically, the specific experiential requirements must be met absolutely, as in the case of medicine, or, as in architecture and pharmacy, only limited credit is given for relevant experience obtained elsewhere.

We acknowledge the legitimacy in many disciplines of requiring some Ontario experience. This view reflects the dominant position contained in the submissions received by the Task Force, in which such requirements, although the subject of some comment certainly, were generally accepted as appropriate — provided some credit was given for relevant foreign experience and positions were available and accessible. The reasonableness of such requirements and the fairness of the methods of granting credit against them for foreign experience are responsibilities that the occupational bodies must meet. In addition, as we discuss in Chapter 9, "Retraining," access to adequate opportunities to meet these requirements is essential to overall fairness and is also the responsibility of the occupational groups. Where we have particular concerns about practices in specific occupations, we comment in our background studies.

PRIOR LEARNING ASSESSMENT: AN INTERNATIONAL ISSUE

A variety of structures are used in Canada and elsewhere for the assessment of prior learning. Some of these, such as the Alberta Universities Co-ordinating Council, the Comparative Education Service of the University of Toronto, and the New York State Education Department, focus exclusively on the assessment of prior academic education and the designation of equivalency. Other structures, such as the British Columbia Educational Credit Bank and the Credit Accumulation and Transfer Scheme in the United Kingdom, assess the equivalency of both academic and experiential learning. In the United States about 1,500 colleges and universities use some form of prior learning assessment to grant credit to students. The United States also has well-established national testing programs and a national association, the Council for Adult and Experiential Learning (CAEL), that brokers information and consulting services.

The catalogue of prior learning assessment programs presented here is illustrative, not exhaustive, providing examples drawn from a variety of countries, occupations, and institutions.[16] We discuss the highly centralized and regulatory Office of the Professions in New York State, which is responsible for all aspects of professional certification and licensure, including licensing and the assessment of prior learning. At the other end of the regulatory continuum, the Quebec Government offers a prior learning assessment service that is purely advisory and has no regulatory functions. Between these two are other structures, each with its own purposes and strengths. The following brief descriptions are intended to provide the reader with a view of the context within which this Task Force formulated its proposals for the creation of a Prior Learning Assessment Network in Ontario.

We have also considered, in the context of prior learning assessment, some of the broader international trends, again electing to include only a selection of those we became aware of in the course of our study. In the section on "Globalization," which appears later in this chapter, we look at the European Community (EC), the newly developing Trans Regional Academic Mobility and Credential Evaluation (TRACE), the UNESCO "Convention on the Recognition of Studies, Diplomas and Degrees Concerning Higher Education in the States Belonging to the Europe Region," and the *Canada-United States Free Trade Agreement*.

"Globalization" is the term currently used to describe the trends to freer trade and expanding markets for goods and services. This phenomenon is seen on several fronts: in the continuing multilateral trade negotiations of the *General Agreement on Tariffs and Trade* (GATT) now taking place in the so-called "Uruguay Round"; in the progress of the European Community towards 1992 and the promise of a community-wide free-trade zone for all goods and services; and in the bilateral *Canada-United States Free Trade Agreement* that came into force January 1, 1989. As well, the Eastern bloc of socialist countries is experiencing, in varying degrees, increased economic liberalization.

Accompanying this increasing liberalization in the trade of goods and services is the mobility of professional people and tradespeople. This mobility in turn means a much closer scrutiny of barriers to access in the practising of professions and trades across jurisdictional boundaries.

Such barriers are not seen simply at the national level; interprovincial mobility for professionals within Canada has been a recognized problem for years.[17] The issues that arise over movement in professional services between provinces have increased in intensity, given the general expansion of trade between provinces and given the mobility provision of the *Canadian Charter of Rights and Freedoms.*[18]

Just as modern productive capacities in goods and services, transportation systems, and communications technology have enhanced the expansion of business trade and the accompanying movements of professional people and tradespeople throughout the world, they have fostered new patterns of immigration from the less-developed countries, and from politically repressive regimes, to the democracies of the Western world.

The forces of "globalization" are inexorable; the countries that can better adjust their public policies to turn these forces to their advantage will have a superior chance to flourish and prosper. Pertinent to all these issues is the matter of the access of immigrants to the professions and trades. Ontario, as a trading and immigrant centre of Canada, requires a rethinking of its public policy in this regard.

United States

University of the State of New York[19]

The State of New York has a unique role among all the prior learning assessment agencies identified by the Task Force, being responsible for the education, licensure, and practice of 31 professions that are regulated under Title VIII of the Education Law of that state.

The highly centralized system of professional regulation in New York appears less extreme when placed within the context of the U.S. licensing system. Unlike their Canadian counterparts, the state governments all regulate their professions directly. The states do not have "self-regulating" professional bodies that have been delegated the power to administer their peers. Each profession in a state is regulated by a state board, which is governmentally controlled.

The University of the State of New York (USNY) has centralized the functions of the state boards within the State Education Department, which administers the Office of the Professions. That office is responsible for professional education, licensing, and discipline of the 31 professions. The state boards do not act independently but report through the Office of the Professions to the USNY.

All candidates for professional licensure are required to apply through the New York State Office of the Professions, with three exceptions: law, theology, and teaching. Law is subject to regulation through the judiciary; theology is not regulated by the state; and legislation that would place the teaching profession entirely under the USNY has been tabled recently.

According to the Office of the Professions, "one generally accepted characteristic of a profession is the presence of a body of specialized knowledge that is transmitted through a formal program of education." To ensure that candidates for professional licensure have the required formal education, the New York State Education Department is responsible for evaluating the academic credentials of individual applicants and also for accrediting programs of professional education.

The credentials of licensure candidates who have foreign, non-traditional, or equivalent education in the professions are assessed through the Comparative Education Section of the Division of Professional Licensing Services.

Thirteen staff, eight of whom are research staff, are employed in this division. The researchers attend conferences and professional programs relating to the occupational areas for which they are responsible, regularly updating their knowledge of international education through periodicals and other publications. In addition, the researchers correspond with other groups, including embassies, ministries of education, professional associations, and related organizations in other countries.

The length and content of the programs that the foreign-trained graduates have gone through are assessed to determine whether they are comparable to the accredited New York programs. Foreign-trained candidates are also expected to have completed the equivalent of any prerequisite education required for admission to New York professional training programs. Candidates assessed as equivalent are entitled to write any required licensure examinations.

Under direction of the Regents of the USNY, the state boards are responsible for licensing and disciplining professionals. The boards are wholly responsible for selecting examinations offered by other bodies or preparing examinations, and for determining passing grades; the Division of Professional Licensing Services administers the examinations.

All examinations are in English. For candidates who have not completed their academic instruction in English, the division relies on the professional examination to assess English-language ability.

The office has a Bureau of Professional Career Opportunity Programs, which coordinates the Education Department's efforts to increase minority representation in the licensed professions. This initiative is aimed at enabling minority and disadvantaged students to enter professional training programs.

U.S. Private Equivalency Organizations

The Task Force reviewed the procedures of three private assessment groups in the United States: Educational Credential Evaluators, Inc., of Wisconsin; International Consultants of Delaware, Inc., based in Delaware and California; and World Education Services, Inc., of New York City.[20]

These corporations prepare equivalency statements for individuals, institutions, and professional licensing bodies. Because these accreditation groups are private, their assessments are not binding on any person or group.

International Consultants of Delaware has three evaluators and performs 2,200 evaluations annually; World Education Services, with seven full-time and two part-time evaluators, performs approximately 9,600 evaluations per year.

Although the primary focus is on academic equivalency, two of the three agencies evaluate experiential learning. Two of the three note that they are not-for-profit organizations. For all three, evaluations are entirely paid for by clients. Fees vary from about $55 for a "document by document" assessment to up to $200 for an assessment of experiential learning. Normal processing time is three to four weeks.

An assessment document is issued by the credentialing agency. Educational Credential Evaluators states the direct equivalent of foreign qualifications in terms of a U.S. degree and converts the client's mark to the U.S. grade-point-average scale.

All three of these private agencies assess the validity of the documentation supplied to them. If a document being used in the assessment has been forged or altered, the evaluation will not be performed; the client's fee will not be returned, and those listed as recipients of the assessment (and perhaps other assessment bodies) may be notified.

Assessment of Prior Experiential Learning in Colleges and Universities

In the United States, there is extensive and varied provision for recognizing experiential learning in postsecondary institutions. This information has been summarized by the Council for Adult and Experiential Learning in a 1986 publication, *Opportunities for College Credit: A CAEL Guide to Colleges and Universities*,[21] based on a survey of U.S. colleges and universities. Eight mechanisms for gaining credit are identified. These are:

- national standardized examinations for course credit, such as the College Level Examinations Program (CLEP);

- recommendation by the American Council on Education, as provided in the *Guide to Evaluation of Educational Experiences in the Armed Forces*;

- recommendation by the American Council on Education, as provided in the *Guide to Educational Programs in Non-Collegiate Sponsored Instruction*;

- advanced placement program;

- assessment by portfolio;

- institution-specific faculty-made tests or challenge examinations;

- oral interviews; and

- demonstration of competencies.

Well over 1,000 colleges and universities in the United States responded to the survey with information about their provisions for the assessment of prior experiential learning. In the majority of institutions, more than 25 students had used prior learning assessment to gain college credit. In personal correspondence, Dr. Morris Keeton, executive director of CAEL, estimated that in the United States in 1987 more than 40,000 people earned credit through prior learning assessment of one kind or another. (In Ontario, the certification body for Engineering Technicians and Technologists hopes to introduce an experiential assessment mechanism in the CAEL model.)

In addition to national and statewide examination and equivalency programs, regional consortia have evolved in the United States to support prior learning assessment. One of these is the Compact for Lifelong Educational Opportunities (CLEO), a consortium of 38 colleges and universities in the Delaware Valley region, which includes Philadelphia and southeast Pennsylvania. Many of the institutions in that area are old, prestigious, and conservative:

> Institutions . . . that choose to join CLEO usually have done so because their administrators believe that they must broaden their mission and reach out to new student populations, find new ways to respond to their needs, and cope with new educational imperatives if they are to survive the economic and demographic challenges of the 1980s. CLEO is working with these institutions through the transitional phase, when actual practices and faculty responses can fall short of administrators' visions of change.[22]

CLEO, which is not based within any one institution, makes credit recommendations to participating institutions; offers testing, portfolio assessment, and counselling; attempts to create new markets, particularly in business and industry; and provides faculty training and support, as invited. CLEO does not receive contributions from its participating institutions but relies on "outside" sources, including foundations and contracts.[23] The kind of support that CLEO provides to the change process in its region is, it would seem, provided in the U.K. by government agencies (Further Education Unit, Council for National Academic Awards, Manpower Services Commission); in British Columbia by the Open Learning Agency; and in Quebec by the government-funded Technical Assistance Service. (We will look at these services later in this chapter.)

Prior Experiential Learning Assessment in Occupational Certification

The director of the Office of External Programs for the Vermont State Colleges, whose Assessment of Prior Learning Program claims to be one of the largest in the United States, commented in correspondence on the use of prior learning assessment by U.S. occupational accrediting organizations:

> By and large, as far as I am aware, no consistency whatsoever exists within any trade or profession with regard to policies toward prior experiential learning. If any does exist, it is likely to reflect a negative stance. I do know that such accrediting organizations as the Accreditation Board for Engineering and Technology (ABET) have considered the issue and issued tentative statements leaving themselves open to the "concept" of Prior Learning Assessment but shying away from accepting it.[24]

The director did, however, point to the Program on Noncollegiate-Sponsored Instruction, which works with professional accrediting bodies to integrate the use of prior learning assessment credit gained through industry and business training programs, and to the National Occupational Competency Testing Institute, a testing organization that specializes in technical learning assessment for the trades and occupations.

United Kingdom

In the United Kingdom, assessment of experiential learning has been carried out by several government bodies, including the Further Education Unit, the Manpower Services Commission, and the Council for National Academic Awards. Outside of government, the Learning from Experience Trust (LET), an association supported by its membership and by foundation funds, has established a national network of prior learning assessment institutions and practitioners and serves as an information and consultation clearing house. LET parallels the American Council for Adult and Experiential Learning, although dealing almost exclusively with polytechnics.

Assessment of Prior Experiential Learning in the Colleges and Universities

Evans, in his review of the assessment of experiential learning, summarizes and analyzes the prior learning assessment experience of eight British institutions, one of which is described here to provide some flavour of the British experience.

> In Middlesex Polytechnic interest in the assessment of experiential learning arose from the established practice of granting academic credit in respect of previously acquired knowledge and skills to mature students who were already enroled on the Diploma of Higher Education and Combined Studies degree within the Modular Scheme. Interest quickened when the Polytechnic devised a modular scheme of some 450 units in 30 subject areas, and wanted to find ways of enabling students to complete a part-time degree as rapidly as possible.

> So Middlesex Polytechnic uses the assessment of experiential learning as a means of awarding academic credit retrospectively to mature students enroled on degree-level courses validated by the Council for National Academic Awards. Preparation for assessment is conducted through two or three personal tutorials and two or three group meetings. This process puts on a coherent basis the awarding of credit for uncertificated learning which is equivalent to degree level work.[25]

Overall, Evans concludes, experiential learning is identified and assessed to provide one or more of these functions: guidance and counselling, orientation and access to further study, and, as illustrated in the above example, advanced academic or professional standing.

The CAT Scheme

The Council for National Academic Awards is the validating body responsible for approving the degree courses followed by about half the undergraduates in Great Britain. In 1984, the council established the Credit Accumulation and Transfer Scheme (CAT Scheme), which is a mechanism for allowing people to graduate with course credits assembled from different institutions and credits awarded for experiential learning.

The preface to the 1987 *Regulations for Students Registered Centrally with the CAT Scheme* explains that each course unit and each block of appropriate experiential learning is assigned a credit rating. Awards, including undergraduate and postgraduate degrees, are obtained by accumulating the appropriate credits. Study in an industrial training centre or in a company's in-house education and training program may be considered for academic recognition. Each course unit is graded according to the quality of the performance at assessment; course units passed and grades earned are listed on a transcript.[26]

This centrally administered CAT Scheme has created something very close to a portable cumulative record of learning that brings academic and experiential learning together through a set of common standards and assessment strategies.

Canada

PRIOR ACADEMIC LEARNING

A number of examples exist in Canada of structures that focus on academic equivalency. In the following pages we outline the programs of Alberta's Committee on the Professions, Quebec's Division des équivalences, and the Association of Universities and Colleges of Canada.

Alberta's Committee on the Professions

The assessment of credentials for admission to occupations is organized in Alberta under the Department of Advanced Education. Under a 1978 policy on professions and occupations, the department was given responsibility for setting the standards of education required for admission to occupations and professions.[27]

Because the department controls the funding of new programs, it has the power to approve or deny any proposed changes in academic standards required for admission to a professional body. As an example, the Alberta nursing profession would like to have a "degree for entry requirement" by the year 2000. The professional group attempted to get this requirement inserted into its most recent legislation, but the Department of Advanced Education would not permit the change.

In addition, the department is responsible for the Universities Co-ordinating Council (UCC) and its empowering legislation, the *Universities Act*. The UCC, which is composed of nine representatives from each of the universities in the province,[28] is responsible for overseeing joint university affairs and for professional certification and accreditation. It sets academic standards for Alberta university programs and in this way establishes the standards that foreign-trained as well as domestically trained people must meet.

Assessments of professional academic qualifications are performed through the Committee on the Professions. High school equivalencies are not assessed, except as required for licensure prerequisites. Trades qualifications are handled by the apprenticeship branch.

Some professions currently fall outside the scope of the Committee on the Professions. Medical doctors are exempted. The Association of Professional Engineers, Geologists and Geophysicists of Alberta is the autonomous regulatory body for its members. Teachers, although also outside the scope of the committee, are regulated directly through government, as are occupations regulated under the Professions and Occupations Bureau.

For all other professions, academic assessments, where required, are performed by the Committee on the Professions through professional examination boards. The composition of each board is equally divided between academics in the professional disciplines and practitioners in active practice in the discipline. A representative of the public is also required to sit on each board. The individual professional *Acts* give the UCC responsibility for assessing equivalency of foreign-trained applicants for certification and licensing in the professions. Graduates of approved programs in Alberta institutions can bypass the Committee on the Professions and apply for licensure to the appropriate professional association.

Use of the committee to evaluate foreign-trained candidates is mandatory in Alberta, although the committee may delegate power to professional associations for the assessment of prior learning. Where the committee perceives that the profession is not performing the assessments adequately, or equitably, that authority may be rescinded. Clinical or practical tests are administered by the office only in rare instances and are otherwise left to the professional bodies.

The report on assessment of academic qualifications is issued by the executive of each professional examination board. The assessment may be appealed to the full professional examination board of the profession. There is a right of appeal from a full board decision to a Court, but since the early 1980s there has been only one such challenge, which was unsuccessful.

The Committee on the Professions views the evaluation of academic qualifications as an evolutionary process in which previous assessments are looked to as guidelines, not as precedents, to be relied upon only to the extent that subsequent performances by candidates bear out their accuracy.

The administrative costs of the Committee on the Professions are entirely covered by the assessment fees from candidates for licensure. Because the large professions, such as nursing, generate the most revenue, there is some subsidization of the smaller professions by the larger ones.

Occupational bodies are obliged to advise candidates of their right to an assessment. Candidates not yet in Canada may be advised of the committee through an occupational directory published by Alberta Immigration and Settlement, which is forwarded by the province to Canadian immigration officials abroad.[29]

Applicants must obtain their own translations, these to be accompanied by the original documents.

The Professions and Occupations Bureau, a branch of the Executive Council (Cabinet) of the Province of Alberta,[30] is responsible for the administration of a number of the smaller occupational groups (for example, emergency medical technicians), and in this capacity it initiates legislation, is involved in developing regulations, and serves as the appeal body for decisions made by the government-appointed governing boards of these occupations. The role of the bureau varies from occupation to occupation and may extend to hearing complaints from the public or monitoring and evaluating the administration of the boards.

Quebec's Division des équivalences[31]

The Division des équivalences in the Ministry of Cultural Communities and Immigration is charged with the task of assessing academic qualifications for students who have studied outside the province. It is able to perform detailed assessments of secondary school qualifications and also determines "years of scholarity" for postsecondary education. The division also assesses academic studies leading to professional and trades qualifications. Use of assessments issued by the division is not mandatory, nor are such assessments binding on any licensing bodies.

The assessment service is available to all residents of Quebec who are citizens or landed immigrants, or are refugees who have an official status with the Department of Immigration and Employment Canada. A visa, proof of citizenship, or a ministerial letter is required. The service is entirely government-funded.

The first step in any assessment procedure is the translation and verification of documents. Translation services are provided by the division and the Ministry of Communications. Document verification is carried out through a visual examination (slightly misspelled names or incongruous dates might indicate a false certificate) and through cross-checking against various sources, among these a reference pool that includes:

- lists of "degree mills" and "institutions of doubtful standing" that have been compiled by the Council of Europe;

- lists of the officials who were authorized to sign documents in particular years;

- warnings about irregularities found in some documents; and

- a catalogue of sample documents that have been verified directly with foreign governments, or have been stated by them to be fraudulent.

If a document is determined to be fraudulent, the assessment application is refused.

Although the division has the capacity to produce detailed high-school level equivalency assessments, the assessment of postsecondary academic education is based on in-country recognition of the institution at which the degree was earned, the entry requirements of the program, and a general description of the program. It is not a detailed content analysis. For this reason, the assessment produced by the division will state that a foreign program is equivalent to, for example, "four years of university" rather than "fourth year graduation from university."

All previous decisions are contained in a data bank. If the documents being evaluated parallel a previously decided case, the assessment will reflect the prior decision, although the passage of time, changes in the education systems, and variations in the relationship between foreign and domestic degrees — all taken into consideration — may lead to the modification of a decision. In such case, or if presented with an all-new document for assessment, a full review must be undertaken.

In considering the strength of the candidate's academic training, the entire education system in the jurisdiction, as well as the in-country recognition of the individual institution, is examined. If further information is required, the division proceeds to make independent inquiries of the school or of the educational authority of the jurisdiction. Sometimes intermediate services, such as UNESCO or embassies, provide the necessary information. If ultimately information proves inadequate or unavailable, no assessment is made.

Where no precedent exists, the recommendation from the division must be approved by the Ministry of Education. The recommendations that the division sends to the Ministry are generally accepted.

After a decision has been ratified by the Ministry of Education, the division produces an equivalency statement placing the candidate appropriately within the Quebec education system. Each year the division opens about 8,000 files, makes more than 800 recommendations on new cases, and issues approximately 5,500 equivalencies.

The Division de l'accueil, Quebec's welcome service for immigrants, is instrumental in informing clients of the equivalency service. Information about the service is also provided through multilingual telephone access, airport information services, and the regional offices of the Ministry of Cultural Communities and Immigration throughout the Province of Quebec. In addition, a newspaper for the cultural communities is published by the Ministry, press releases are sent out to cultural and ethnic newspapers and groups, and immigrants may hear about the service through professional organizations, trade groups, and academic institutions.

Association of Universities and Colleges of Canada

The Association of Universities and Colleges of Canada (AUCC) is a national association of degree-granting institutions in Canada. In addition to institutional membership, the association has three other categories of members: regional and provincial members, such as the Council of Ontario Universities; associate members, such as the Association of Canadian Medical Colleges and the Canadian Association of Deans of Education; and honorary associates, such as the Social Sciences and Humanities Research Council of Canada.

This national group has an interest in all matters affecting Canadian degree-granting institutions. Its mandate is "to foster and promote the interests of higher education in Canada."

The AUCC's International Division, which maintains contact with foreign universities, is responsible for information relevant to the evaluation of foreign academic credentials. The Academic Relations section of the International Division is responsible for scholarly exchanges, representation in various international groups, liaison with governments and universities, and information on foreign academic institutions and the credentials that they grant. No assessments of individual credentials are issued from this section. Rather, to enable admissions officers to evaluate a student's file accurately, the AUCC supplies Canadian institutions with information about foreign educational systems and institutions.[32]

This unpublicized information service primarily is used by universities, the Public Service Commission, and granting councils. It does not respond to requests from individuals, but refers them to universities for assistance.

The program is funded by revenue derived from AUCC member fees.

PRIOR EXPERIENTIAL LEARNING

Although other countries have identified existing prior learning assessment programs and services at the postsecondary level, apart from a recent large initiative by the Open Learning Agency of British Columbia and another by Quebec colleges, Canadian provision for assessment of prior education and experiential learning has been neither systematic nor extensive.

To some extent this situation may derive from what might be considered the decentralized decision-making structure of Canadian postsecondary education (although the structure in the United States is even more decentralized). It may also stem from the relatively secure public funding base enjoyed here. As well, innate conservatism and relative stability in traditional sources of students and in the overall economy may have contributed to Canada's colleges' and universities' being cautious about the formal implementation of prior learning assessment.

In any case, British Columbia and Quebec have taken a strong position in this area by entrenching prior experiential learning assessment in the Open Learning Agency and the CEGEPs, respectively. Those initiatives, which might well stimulate similar activity in other provinces, stand as examples of the progress that can be made.

British Columbia Educational Credit Bank

The British Columbia Educational Credit Bank,[33] established by provincial legislation within the British Columbia Open Learning Agency, was designed to allow individuals to take courses from any recognized educational institution and credit them towards an open college diploma or an open university degree or certificate. All requirements for the credential may be completed at other institutions or in conjunction with courses offered through the open college or open university.

The scheme also offers the capability to grant credit towards a degree, diploma, or certificate through prior learning assessment. The student's skills and knowledge may have been gained through a combination of independent study or travel; learning on the job; structured education and training not normally recognized for credit transfer, including education and training sponsored by employers and associations; and community and volunteer work.

The credit bank has been created to administer and coordinate examinations and other assessment procedures within the framework of a detailed statement of principles developed in consultation with the other postsecondary educational institutions in British Columbia. One of these principles states:

> Students will be required to document relevant learning experiences, and
> to differentiate clearly between learning and experience. Learning acquired

should be identified with enough specificity that it can be readily communicated and assessed . . . Credit is awarded for learning which can be readily assessed at the time of application, not for experience, and not for learning which has been forgotten or which is obsolete.[34]

Each participant is required to complete at least 25 per cent of the requirement through B.C. institutions or be a permanent resident of the province.

Quebec's CEGEPs[35]

The development of the provincial implementation model for the program of prior learning assessment in Quebec's CEGEPs (Collèges d'enseignement général et professionnel — colleges of general and vocational education) represents a significant change in the status of prior learning assessment in Canada, in that it is an adequately funded, provincewide initiative at the college level. In 1984, in response to a 1982 report on adult education, the Quebec Government introduced changes to the legislation governing CEGEPs in order to implement a provincewide provision for prior learning assessment. The motives seemed to be to improve general access to life-long learning and, particularly, to make educational institutions more responsive to the education and training needs of business and industry by easing the transition of adults back into formal education.

The implementation structure had three elements:

- A provincial steering committee, with membership from the Ministry of Education, CEGEPs, and private colleges, which had the mandate to define objectives of the program, implementation strategies, organizational models to be employed, financing models for adoption by the Ministry and the CEGEPs, and both policy and finance models for the operation of local projects in the individual colleges. The total provincial start-up grant was $250,000, which was redirected to individual colleges by the committee. The 1988 annual budget was set at $1.5 million.

- A technical assistance service, set up in the provincial federation of CEGEPs for ease of administration, which advises and supports all levels of the prior learning assessment program.

- A local college agents team, which each college was asked to set up, composed of the responsible administrator, the prior learning assessment counsellor, and a faculty member specializing in assessment.

The technical assistance service bridges the partnership between colleges and the Ministry of Education. In this partnership, the Ministry makes overall policy decisions; provides funding to the technical assistance service and, through the steering committee, to the colleges for prior learning assessment programming; and maintains representation on the board. The role of each college is to install prior learning assessment according to its individual capability and operating system, which means that each chooses its own organizational model, financing model, and policy model. The overall operation is by consensus, with each college acting independently but in the context of all. The 49 public and 25 private colleges work together as steering committee members and as members of an information and planning network.

The objectives of the overall prior learning assessment program are to create an accessible, complete, and cost-effective system. The two main problems are ensuring that standards are maintained to the satisfaction of educators and employers, and gaining a cost-effective operation.

The strategies employed were aimed at achieving two top priorities: local training (workshops led by specialists from the Council for Adult and Experiential Learning); and portfolio development (ensuring that the portfolio system of assessment was understood and operational).

A prior learning assessment college fund is administered by a newly created board, assisted by the technical assistance service office. The board is made up of college vice-presidents (four public, two private), a Ministry representative, and the non-voting executive director. The office has two professional staff members and two secretaries. In 1988, 44 public colleges had prior learning assessment activity (86 per cent of CEGEPs). Of the 130 different programs offered by colleges, 40 were affected by prior learning assessment, through 75 distinct projects.

Globalization

The European Community and the Mobility of Professionals

The 12-nation European Community (EC) intends to complete in 1992 the task first begun in 1957 by the *Treaty of Rome* of achieving a fully integrated, single market of 320 million people.[36]

Within the concept of an integrated European economy, freedom of movement among member states is essential. The 1957 *Treaty of Rome* (Part 2) refers to the objective of freedom of movement of goods, capital, services, and persons. The *Single European Act* of 1987[37] provides that the internal market will be completed by December 31, 1992. All member states recognize that they benefit from interdependence and the free movement of persons, as well as of goods, services, and capital. Although freedom to work anywhere within the community is considered one of the basic rights laid down by the *Treaty of Rome*, in many cases member states have refused to recognize professional qualifications obtained in another member state.[38] Accordingly, professionals often have to requalify, in whole or in part, as a prerequisite to pursuing professions in another member state.

The free movement of persons is provided for in the right of establishment, seen in Articles 52 through 58 of the *Treaty of Rome*, being the freedom of professionals[39] to take up and pursue an activity in another member state without discrimination because of nationality. Articles 52 through 56 provide for the gradual removal of restrictions on mobility and also allow for exceptions.

Article 57, which goes further than 52 through 56, calls for directives from the Council of the European Communities on the mutual recognition of diplomas, certificates, and other qualifications, and for the coordination of regulations, legislation, and administration of the different professions. Even in the absence of directives, however, the European Court of Justice has held that national legislation in conflict with the *Treaty* is overruled and that all member states have a duty to adapt their legislation to ensure the right of establishment.[40]

If arbitrary restrictions exist in the qualification requirements of a profession, the Court can act to remove the restrictions. Directives have been issued by the Council for some specific professions. These directives, which coordinate the provisions for taking up a profession in member states and enable individuals to secure recognition of their qualifications and provide services throughout the EC, have the force of law. For example, Directive 75/362 (entered into force December 1976) provides that physicians with credentials from approved institutions of states do not need to take any extra training when moving to other member states. When a Belgian physician with approved training wished to practise medicine in the Netherlands, legislation of the latter state, which required extra training, was overturned by the Court as violating the directive.[41] Other professional groups for which directives have been adopted since 1975 are: nurses responsible for general care (1979), dental practitioners (1980), veterinary surgeons (1980), midwives (1983), architects (1987), and pharmacists (1987). The Council also approved a directive in 1977 to make it easier for lawyers to provide services in other member states.[42]

It is recognized that true freedom of mobility can be achieved only if the member states agree to mutually recognize diplomas and to coordinate training requirements among themselves as stipulated by Article 57. The absence of such agreement makes it difficult for a member state to accept freely a national of another state without scrutinizing the person's qualifications.

Detailed harmonization, profession by profession, has been a very difficult and an extremely slow process. The European Community has decided that it wants the flow of professionals to increase by 1992, when people are supposed to move across borders as freely as goods and services do. Rather than continue the slow process of lifting barriers for individual professions, it has been decided to lift the barriers for all professionals. As well, in order to facilitate mobility of persons and services, it has been found necessary to circumscribe the discretion of member states and their professional organizations, bodies which can sometimes inhibit mobility in their protectionist self-interest. Thus, the EC's current effort is in issuing directives to implement Article 57.[43]

While recognizing the need for the national regulation of professions in the public interest, the European Community members realize that the full advantages of economic integration through a single market cannot be gained without allowing qualified professionals to move freely throughout the Community. Artificial barriers to the mobility of professionals operate like non-tariff barriers to goods and services. They introduce inefficiencies and waste, and they inhibit the maximization of the production of wealth for the benefit of all citizens.[44] As well, economic integration fosters increased specialization, with the more specialized expertise and skills being used throughout the expanded market. With globalization of trading in goods and services, the trend is towards the internationalizing of professions.

In June 1988, the Council of the European Community proposed the "Council Directive on a general system for the recognition of professional education and training of at least three years' duration" (called "the General Directive"),[45] for those professions for which directives have not already been issued. The General Directive was enacted January 1989, for full implementation by member states by January 1991. The objective is to confirm the legal rights of a professional to work in his or her profession within any member state, either self-employed or as an employee. The General Directive covers not only regulated professions but also unregulated professions that confer reserved titles. Some 80 different professions in all will be covered when the General Directive enters into force.

In determining who is a qualified professional, the European Community has abandoned the parochial approach often taken by professions. Rather, each member state has respect for the competent authorities in other member states and the standards they have set for the educating, training, and licensing of professionals. The presumption is that training is of an acceptable standard in every member state. The norm is to grant equivalent status through the mutual recognition of the professional status gained in other member states. This is referred to as the concept of "comparability." If a person is qualified to practise in one member state, he or she should be qualified to work in the other member states. Moreover, the approach to determining equivalency is liberal. As well, where a person does not have substantially equivalent training, a framework is provided for entry through the recognition of experiential equivalency and the allowing of an adaptation period in the host state. Paradoxically, the result is that, for some professions (for example, law), there will be much greater mobility for professionals within the European Community than there is among provinces in Canada.

The General Directive provides that a member state (called the "host member state") cannot refuse to accept a national of another member state (the "state of origin") into a profession if he or she is already qualified for the profession in his or her own country. Under specified circumstances an adaptation period or a test may be required. As well, the host member state may require proof of good character, that the individual has not been declared bankrupt, and that certificates of physical and mental health are provided.

The professions' governing authorities in each state are empowered to take decisions on the implementation of the General Directive and to designate a coordinator to promote the uniform application of the Directive in the state. The coordinators from each state will together form a coordinating group. The General Directive does not require member states to change their present professional training programs; rather, it ensures that professional qualifications issued in any one member state are recognized in the other member states.

Upon the General Directive's coming into force, a professional whose qualifications fall within its ambit has a right to have his or her qualifications recognized throughout the European Community and the right to full membership in the appropriate professional body of any host member state. The essential criterion for recognition of equivalency is that the education and training received in the place of training is substantially the same as that in the host member state to which he or she is going.

Where the professional's education and training differs substantially from what is required for the same profession by the host member state, the professional has the choice either of taking an aptitude test to assess his or her ability to pursue the profession in the host state or of undergoing a period of supervised practice not exceeding three years.[46] However, professionals will not be required to retrain and requalify in subjects they have already studied. The purpose of the aptitude test or period of supervised practice is simply to compensate for the differences between qualifications acquired in different member states. The test is not to be an examination of theory or general knowledge, but rather simply of the local peculiarities of practising in the profession in the host member state. These alternative choices are looked upon as "adaptation mechanisms to compensate for objective differences between the migrant's training or sphere of activity and those of the host state."[47] It is uncertain at this time whether a language test can be a separate, general requirement (even where the education and training of the professional is substantially the same as in the host state, except for language), but it would seem inherent in both the aptitude test and the period of supervised practice routes. The detailed rules governing the adaptation period and its assessment are to be stipulated by the competent authority in the host member state.

Evidence of credentials is through possession of a "diploma." Article 1 of the General Directive defines a "diploma" as any diploma, certificate, or other evidence awarded by a competent authority in a member state establishing the successful completion by the holder of a postsecondary course of at least three years' duration (or of an equivalent duration, part-time) and reflecting the successful completion of any required professional training, such that the holder has met the professional qualifications required to pursue the profession in a member state. If the education and training attested by the diploma was not received "mainly" within the Community, the holder of a third-country diploma must have three years' professional experience certified by the member state that recognized the third-country diploma.

The General Directive provides that the aptitude test be formulated by having the competent authority in the host member state draw up a list of subjects that, "on the basis of a comparison of the education and training required in the member state and that received by the applicant," are not covered by the applicant's diploma. The test may also relate to the rules of the profession applicable in the host member state.

Article 3 provides that, if an applicant comes from a state of origin that does not regulate a profession, the applicant nevertheless has the right to equivalency recognition in a host member state that regulates entry to the profession. He or she must, however, have pursued the profession full-time for at least two years in the previous ten years in the state of origin, and must have a diploma evidencing at least three years' postsecondary education.

Article 4 provides that the host member state may also require the applicant to provide evidence of professional experience where his or her education and training is at least one year less than that required of someone trained in the host state. The article does, however, place finite limits on the length of time of professional experience that can be required in such situations.

Article 6 provides that the host member state must accept the production of documents issued by competent authorities in the member state of origin as sufficient evidence of requirements of proof of good character, of not being declared bankrupt, and of proof of health. If the state of origin does not issue such documents, then the host member state must allow a declaration on oath.

Article 8 provides that an application is to be considered expeditiously by the host member state and a "reasoned decision" provided by the competent authority not later than four months after all documents are presented.

The professions and their professional organizations are now doing the detailed work preparatory to the competent authorities' in each state making decisions on the implementation of the General Directive. In some instances there already exist pan-European professional organizations that have been constituted to facilitate the reciprocal recognition of credentials and freedom of mobility in providing professional services. For example, the Fédération Européene d'Associations Nationales d'Ingénieurs (FEANI) consists of the engineering associations of 20 European countries as members, including all 12 nations of the European Community. FEANI confers the title "European Engineer" ("Eur Ing") and "passports" upon engineers within the 20-nation group who have 4-year university degrees (or a 3-year degree plus one year of approved training) and a further period of professional experience resulting in a total of 7 years from the beginning of their higher education. Undoubtedly, an organization like FEANI can play a significant role in implementing the General Directive as far as engineers are concerned.[48]

Trans Regional Academic Mobility and Credential Evaluation

The need to coordinate the assessment of prior learning throughout the world is being recognized in many forums, one significant one being TRACE, the Trans Regional Academic Mobility and Credential Evaluation project. Formed in order to enhance mobility and employment opportunities throughout the world, it stands both as evidence of the importance of recognizing this issue and as a source of information and expertise in the further development of a prior learning assessment mechanism in Ontario. Its statement of purpose is reproduced below.

> The Trans Regional Academic Mobility and Credential Evaluation (TRACE) project is being created to improve access to and quality of information related to the international mobility of people and the evaluation of academic credentials.

> With the aid of modern technology, TRACE will provide a means of exchanging standardized information on higher education and professional training. It is designed to avoid duplication in the areas of data collection and updating through an international cooperative effort. By linking existing and future educational data bases, agreement on data collection elements and by some modification of current data collection practices, an international data network will be established and made available worldwide. Only hard facts will be gathered; interpretation and evaluation will be left to the specialists in the respective countries. The data link will have additional benefits for research in comparative higher education

and for increasing cooperation among institutions interested in the international exchange process.

TRACE has been conceived by a group of interested international education experts from eight countries who are concerned with questions of student mobility, work in the field of counselling students about studying abroad and are involved in the evaluation of foreign academic, vocational or professional credentials. The long-range goal of TRACE is the establishment of an international data base which will allow for immediate access to information on educational systems and institutions and enable regular updating of the data base by appropriate educational and professional authorities around the world.

Representatives to TRACE have come from the Association of Registrars of Universities and Colleges of Canada, the Association of Universities and Colleges of Canada, the German Academic Exchange Service (DAAD), the Zentralstelle für Ausländisches Bildungswesen, the International Association of Universities, the Netherlands Universities Foundation for International Cooperation (NUFFIC), the National Board of Universities and Colleges of Sweden, Schweizerische Zentralstelle für Hochschulwesen (Central Office of the Swiss Universities), the National Academic Recognition Information Centre of the British Council, the UNESCO Centre for Higher Education in Europe (CEPES), the European Institute for Education and Social Policy (ERASMUS Bureau), and the National Liaison Committee on Foreign Student Admission of the United States, including the Council of Graduate Schools, the College Board, the Institute of International Education, the American Association of Collegiate Registrars and Admissions Officers and the National Association for Foreign Student Affairs.[49]

UNESCO Convention

The "Convention on the Recognition of Studies, Diplomas and Degrees Concerning Higher Education in the States Belonging to the Europe Region" is part of a larger campaign by the United Nations Educational, Scientific and Cultural Organization (UNESCO) to organize cooperation of states in the field of higher education. In the UNESCO context, the "Europe Region" includes Canada, the USSR, and Israel, in addition to the countries of Eastern and Western Europe. Canada is now in the process of considering acceding to this Convention.

The Convention seeks to develop the international mobility of individuals and the exchange of ideas, knowledge, and scientific and technological experience. In order to facilitate cooperation among nations in the fields of education, science, culture, and communications, this UNESCO Convention encourages the recognition of postsecondary education in other countries by providing information about them. This agreement is to be the starting point for concerted action to organize collaboration on the recognition of studies.

The Canada-United States Free Trade Agreement

Chapter 14 of the *Canada-United States Free Trade Agreement* sets forth as a general guideline that "national treatment"[50] shall be extended to the providers of covered services.[51] Otherwise stated, the service provider shall not be discriminated against because of country of origin. The capability of governments to regulate the professions and trades remains unconstrained if regulations are for domestic policy purposes and are not applied in a discriminatory fashion.[52]

The broad rule is subject to three limitations. First, the *Free Trade Agreement* applies only to "covered services."[53] The only professions expressly covered are engineering, architecture, surveying, and agrology, although some other professions and trades are likely brought within other enumerated categories of services.[54]

Second, Article 1402.5 provides that the "national treatment" norm applies only to *new* measures, policies, and practices. (Article 1405.1, however, states that the two countries shall endeavour to eliminate existing measures that are inconsistent with the standard.)

Third, either country may invoke new policies that discriminate, provided "the difference in treatment is no greater than that necessary for prudential, fiduciary, health and safety or consumer protection reasons . . ."[55]

Article 1403, however, states as fundamental principles that the two countries agree that measures governing licensing and certification ". . . should relate principally to competence or the ability . . ." and shall not have the purpose or effect of discrimination in access. The "mutual recognition of licensing and certification requirements . . ." is to be encouraged. Clearly, these are the norms dictated by the forces of globalization.

A "Sectoral Annex," included for architects,[56] states that the Royal Architectural Institute of Canada and the American Institute of Architects, in consultation with professional and regulatory bodies, will develop, before December 31, 1991, mutually acceptable standards regarding such matters as accreditation of schools of architecture, qualifying examinations for licensing, and determination of the experience required for licensing purposes.

Upon receipt, the recommendations of the professional associations will be reviewed by a committee established by both countries, and upon the recommendations' being found to be consistent with Chapter 14 of the *Free Trade Agreement*, the national governments are to encourage their respective provincial and state governments to introduce measures necessary to ensure that licensing authorities "accept the licensing and certification requirements of the other [country] on the same basis as their own."[57]

Article 1405 obligates both parties to endeavour to negotiate further sectoral annexes for other professions.

Chapter 15 of the *Free Trade Agreement* provides for "temporary entry"[58] for business persons to each country. By Annex 1502.1, one category of business persons is "professionals" of those professions listed in Schedule 2. These professions include accounting, architecture, medicine (research and training only), dentistry, nursing (registered nurses only), postsecondary education, law, and dietetics.[59]

With respect to all four categories included within "business persons," Chapter 15 confers entry rights that are only temporary. With respect to the category of "business visitors," those seeking entry must be able to demonstrate that their purpose conforms with one or more of those purposes enumerated in Schedule 1.

As far as "professionals" are concerned, individuals in this category must be able to show they are seeking entry for the purpose of engaging in business activity "at a professional level";[60] that is, doing work which is done by nationals in the same occupational category. Hence, only those who meet the standards and policies of the professional bodies in the country to which they are seeking entry will be able to secure the requisite permission to gain entry.

Undoubtedly, the *Free Trade Agreement* will have a profound influence over time on the question of access to the professions and trades, not only directly, with respect to individuals moving between the two countries, but indirectly, with respect to interprovincial mobility: it is inconceivable that there could be easier access to carrying on the practice of a profession or trade across national borders than across provincial borders.

Finally, Article 1403 states the essential criterion for measures governing licensing and certification: they "should relate principally to competence or the ability to provide . . . services." In short, the inefficiencies and inequities of protectionism and systemic discrimination have no place in a competitive world. Our recommendations at the end of this chapter are consistent with, and supportive of, the economic restructuring consequent upon the *Canada-United States Free Trade Agreement*.

CONCLUSIONS

The Task Force is certain that both real and perceived access to professions and trades in Ontario can be improved through the creation of a mechanism specifically designed to assess the prior academic and experiential learning of people seeking to apply for entry. Such a mechanism could consolidate and systematize current Ontario-based assessment of the level and type of education completed by individuals. It would determine whether or not their academic standing is equivalent to that required of licensure candidates educated in Ontario. This mechanism could capitalize on Canadian, U.S., and British experience to improve the current provisions in Ontario for assessment of what an individual has learned both within and outside academic institutions.

We support the principle that occupational associations bear the ultimate responsibility of ensuring the competence of members for the protection of the public good. (As is discussed in Chapter 4, "Issues Facing the Professions," it is our view that unregulated occupational associations that have the authority to grant credentials or reserved titles must be covered by the structure we are creating for prior learning assessment. All comments and recommendations regarding our proposed Prior Learning Assessment Network should therefore be considered to apply to such organizations.) For this reason, we take the position that the preparation and administration of all licensure examinations should remain under the control of such occupational bodies (see Chapter 6, "Licensure Testing") and that the occupational bodies should be directly responsible for the development and/or articulation of a prescribed standard of performance for competence against which all candidates must be measured. We are also of the view that, as a general rule, clinical assessments are better conducted by the occupational association itself.

Our research has shown, however, as the discussion in this chapter discloses, that the introduction of a systematic structure is called for to assist the occupational bodies in assessing competence. The imposition of such a structure is consistent with similar steps being taken in other jurisdictions.

The initial screen of applicants — the assessment of equivalency — is the stage in the process that is the most problematic, the most difficult, the least standardized, and the most open to abuse. The removal of this function to a specialized, systematized, and independent body is, in our view, necessary.

Therefore, although we recognize that some prior learning assessment is already being carried out by educational institutions and occupational certification agencies, we believe that people throughout Ontario should have access to a more systematic means for the attestation of their learning. This learning includes formal education that they have completed — degree, diploma, and certificate programs, and individual courses — and the current knowledge that they have gained through experience.

We anticipate that the occupational certification and licensing bodies in Ontario will benefit by the creation of a mechanism for prior learning assessment. Structured to assess graduates from Canadian educational and training programs in order to determine whether they have the prerequisites to apply for certification and licensure, many of these bodies do not have the capacity to assess fairly and systematically the credentials of all foreign-trained individuals; nor do most have the know-how to assess experiential learning. A mechanism that will assess individuals to determine whether or not they have the prerequisites for application to become certified or licensed in an occupation will assist these bodies in ensuring that standards of competence are met and that no qualified individuals are turned away or are unnecessarily retrained.

Educational institutions will also be served by such a mechanism. Most colleges and universities, as well as the Ministry of Education, already have some means for assessing prior education of applicants from countries that have high and sustained rates of immigration to Canada. Many institutions, however, appear to have no means for systematically assessing prior experiential learning and little capacity for assessing academic credentials of people lacking complete documentation or coming from countries with low or irregular rates of immigration to Canada.

Individuals will benefit, in particular those wishing to apply for certification or licensure and requiring an assessment of their prior learning. Candidates transferring from other provinces as well as from other countries will be able to take advantage of the mechanism. Individuals who currently are least well-served are, we believe, those entering Canada with insufficient formal documentation, those from countries with relatively low rates of immigration to Canada, and those who have relevant and useful competencies that were gained through experience rather than formal education. These are our principal target groups, but we are confident that the value of our recommendations will extend beyond them.

For example, individuals entering the employment marketplace directly, rather than through a body requiring certification or licensure for entry, will also benefit, as will potential employers, thanks to comprehensive and credible assessments of training. The potential for discrimination in employment will be significantly reduced because employers, when presented with comparative information, will no longer feel compelled to reject candidates with foreign training or experience simply because their level of training or degree of experience cannot be determined.

There will also be potential for substantial benefit to candidates trained in or previously licensed in Ontario who wish to re-enter the workplace after an absence, or to move from one specified field to a related field. Women in particular will be in a position to take greatest advantage of this means for evaluating and demonstrating their competence: they as a group are most affected by these issues. Individuals will benefit not only from the assessments themselves but from the information such assessments will provide about deficiencies in training and means available for completing any required elements.

We believe that the structure of this mechanism should derive from several principles that underpin other successful prior learning assessment systems. This mechanism, in order that its work be valid and reliable, not only must be expert in assessment and in the training of assessors. If it is to be perceived as adhering to such high standards, it must also be systematic.

Systematic prior learning assessment has several characteristics:

It is public. Real or perceived secrecy of assessment policies and procedures will invite skepticism about the quality of assessments. The clients, certification and licensure bodies, and educational institutions must have an active role in policy development and have ready access to policies and procedures.

It is accessible. If services are rendered inaccessible to any clients because of language barriers, high fees, or the length of time required for completion of assessments, efficacy in establishing equity will be hampered. In addition, in order that people throughout the Province of Ontario might be served, prior learning assessment should be accessible on a regionalized basis. Because Ontario already has several such provincewide networks, including the community colleges and offices of the Ministry of Skills Development, the Task Force would anticipate that one of these networks could be designated as the regionalized extension of the prior learning assessment mechanism.

It is comprehensive in its assessment strategies. Strategies should be designed to enable individuals to receive assessment of formal academic credentials, of learning sponsored outside formal education (by associations, business, industry, military, trade unions, government), and of learning gained through work experience, volunteer experience, and independent study.

It minimizes cost. The procedures and centres of activity should be designed to minimize duplication of effort, and should be monitored continually for efficiency and appropriateness. We are confident that the specialization and economies of scale inherent in the prior learning assessment mechanism will mean greater overall efficiency than at present. The cost of such a system need not be substantial. A review of comparable models discloses that, on the one hand, limited staffing would be adequate and physical facilities and purchase of other resources need not be expansive. The cost benefit to be gained in the efficient reintegration of skilled individuals into the workplace has the potential, on the other hand, to be substantial.

It is credible with educators, certifying bodies, employers, and individuals who use its services. We are confident that such credibility can be achieved by maintaining a commitment to participative planning and policy making, by being accessible, and by providing valid and reliable assessments.

In formulating our recommendations regarding prior learning assessment, we have recognized that learning takes place both within and outside formal educational institutions.

We also recognize that comparative education is an established discipline. The assessment of prior learning is a science — albeit a constantly changing one — and not an art.

We believe that people seeking access to postsecondary education and those seeking to apply for certification or licensure in professions and trades should not be required to relearn what they already know. We emphasize that we do not equate simple experience with learning; however, whether an individual has acquired current knowledge and skills through experience or through formal education, we are confident that provision can be made for the demonstration of and attestation to that learning. Such provision is made successfully in other jurisdictions and, to a limited extent, within Ontario. Learning obtained through experience and subject to assessment must be formally and thoroughly demonstrated and must be measured against the same standard of skill or competence established for the assessment of academic equivalency, which, by extension, is the standard required of Ontario-trained individuals.

We believe that, because the mechanism which we propose will serve a broad constituency, and because it must be and must appear to be unbiased in its workings, it should be established under legislation that makes it separate and distinct from individual academic and occupational organizations. Having said that, we are also of the view that a strong association with one or more major educational institutions would, for many reasons, be desirable. Such an association would increase efficiency, because it would result in increased access to specialties in comparative education, language, and examination techniques, as well as to experts in the educational programs in many of the occupational fields. It would enhance and facilitate the linkages between assessments and retraining, and it could build on expertise and resources already in place.

We are confident that the implementation of these recommendations will result in a more efficient process whereby foreign-trained people may obtain certification in professions and trades in Ontario, and confident that benefits will accrue to the affected individuals, to Ontario's educational system, and to its economy.

We are equally confident that our recommendations are in harmony with the provisions for prior learning assessment that are being made in British Columbia, Quebec, the United Kingdom, the United States, and elsewhere. They reflect consistent international trends in the facilitation of mobility among skilled individuals through coordination of training programs and recognition of prior learning.

The model we propose is intended to incorporate many of the elements of existing programs to create a mechanism that is responsive to the needs we have identified in licensure and certification procedures. (The basic structure we propose appears as Appendix 5-A at the end of this chapter.) We propose naming it the Prior Learning Assessment Network (PLAN). We emphasize the very conscious selection of the word "network." Not intended to be an entity unto itself but rather a coordinating agency for the provision of a number of services to assist generally in the preparation of individuals for employment, PLAN would perform certain key functions itself, and delegate, refer, review, and advise on a number of others.

In considering the relationship that should exist between the occupational groups and PLAN, we attempted to arrive at a balance among a number of options. It was apparent that the New York State model, in which there is public involvement in all stages of the credentialing process, is far too great an intrusion on the autonomy of the professional bodies to be acceptable in Ontario. We gave serious consideration, however, to three other options: (1) the model used in the Quebec Government's Division des équivalences, which offers the service of assessment to people educated outside Quebec; (2) a parallel system existing alongside any assessment services operating within the occupations; and (3) a service along the lines of the Alberta model, which would provide individuals with assessments that would be binding on the occupational groups to which they would then be presented, entitling candidates to apply for licensure or certification and, specifically, to write any required examinations and meet any additional requirements.

The Quebec model has much to commend it and appears to be operating with some success in that province. Reliance by the professional occupational groups is not, however, extensive. Having recognized the need for a more systematic and objective system in Ontario, we are concerned that a system which is merely "available" will have little impact on the situation facing foreign-trained individuals in Ontario. Although a number of occupational groups indicated to us that the involvement of such a body would be not only acceptable but useful to them, there is no assurance that bodies with the potential to benefit most would in fact participate.

A model in which PLAN has the capacity to offer parallel and, therefore, possibly different assessments offers a degree of objectivity to candidates but runs the risk of being unworkable in practice. The involvement of the occupations in the assessment process is essential to its success; in an environment of competition, cooperation is unlikely to evolve. In addition, there may be a tendency on the part of PLAN, candidates, and occupations to focus more on demonstrating the superiority of their assessment than on the development and evolution of a comprehensive system for assessment. Appeals and litigation and attendant frustration could result.

We were thus drawn to the third option. As we have stated in this chapter and elsewhere in the Report, the profession's responsibility for determining who is qualified to enter the profession is fundamental to professionalism as we know it in Ontario. This authority is one we respect. Of particular concern to us is the autonomy of the legal profession, owing to the direct links between the bar and the judiciary that must remain insulated from government interference. We have serious concerns also about imposing an external decision on all occupational bodies, because our review has indicated that the structures in place in some occupations are flexible and responsive. Nonetheless, we concluded that the system of prior learning assessment would function most effectively with the employment of this third model. Such a broad-based system would guarantee the involvement of professions currently in need of assistance, including those professions that have not been reviewed in detail in our study. In addition, it would ease the introduction of experiential learning assessments, enhance the efficiencies available in an across-the-board network, and increase opportunities for movement between disciplines.

The authority of the occupational bodies to control entry would remain with these bodies because they would retain control over licensure examinations and all other criteria for entry. Nonetheless, we recognize that the changes we are proposing may cause concerns. We have addressed these by including in our proposal a number of suggested features. By virtue of these suggestions, listed below, any infringement on the autonomy of the occupational bodies will be constrained to the point where, in some cases, there may be no interference whatsoever with the procedures developed by the body for the assessment of prior learning; and, in all other cases, the involvement by the professional body will be such that adherence to its standards for competence will be assured. At the same time, however, the rights of foreign-trained candidates to a fair assessment will be protected.

- PLAN should be given the power to delegate all or part of any assessment procedure to the occupational body concerned, subject to revocation if the procedures fail to or cease to reflect the systematic and objective values that must be evident in them to ensure fairness. A number of occupations have in place procedures that may entitle them to such a delegation; others may wish to develop them.

- PLAN should have specific authority to delegate the administration of any clinical assessments that form a necessary part of an equivalency assessment, and should seek to do so.

- The standards of competence against which all candidates must be measured should be developed and articulated by the occupational representatives themselves, working in conjunction with comparative education specialists in PLAN.

- The occupational bodies should have representation within PLAN through occupation-specific advisory committees, the primary function of which would be to provide advice to assessors conducting evaluations of equivalency.

- Internal rights to review of an assessment should be available not only to individual applicants but also to the occupational bodies.

- In addition to these structural protections, it must be emphasized that it is essential to our vision of the operation of this agency that it be, and be viewed as, independent of government interference. To this end it should be structured as "free standing": under a Crown-appointed board of directors drawn from education, occupations, and the public, thus removing it from direct governmental control.

It is our contention that PLAN should be involved in other aspects of the process of licensure and certification. Here too it may act as much as the fulcrum of an information and advisory network as it would as a central decision maker itself. (Detailed discussion and recommendations appear in Chapter 6, "Licensure Testing," and Chapter 7, "Language Testing.") For example, we shall recommend that it play a role in the development and validation of licensure tests and in the publication of required standards. However, although we recommend that PLAN develop a staff expertise in these areas, and although PLAN should be available to assist in the development of standards of validity and reliability in conjunction with the occupational bodies, the actual development and validation of such tests need not be performed by PLAN itself but by recognized specialists selected by the occupational bodies themselves or with whom PLAN may develop associations and to whom it may make referrals. On this subject, however, we recommend that PLAN have the direct authority to grant or withhold approval when an occupational group proposes imposing additional examinations on foreign-trained candidates. The addition of such a significant burden should, in our view, be permitted only in limited circumstances.

One of the primary functions that we see PLAN performing is to provide information and counselling to candidates. The need for detailed and comprehensive information dispersal and for guidance and direction for applicants as follow-ups to their assessments is discussed not only in this chapter but in Chapter 8, "Language Training," and Chapter 9, "Retraining." In these roles, too, PLAN will function largely as a coordinator of information and referral, relying on existing sources and facilities but providing candidates with easier and more direct access to them. Detailed information available to individuals and occupational bodies alike should include specific requirements for certification, standards to be met, rights of appeal if an application is rejected, and guidance about language training, retraining, and general training programs. Although PLAN will be the central coordinating agency, the dissemination of information can be addressed substantially through existing occupational, cultural, and governmental organizations, including the recently introduced Ontario Training Corporation Skills Bank, which is a remote-access computer data base of education and training available in Ontario. The skills bank is currently focusing exclusively on education and training opportunities, but it does have the capacity to deliver electronically all the information services identified above. Rather than develop a parallel function within PLAN, we propose that PLAN contract with the skills bank for delivery of these services. The Ontario Training Corporation Skills Bank targets being operational in English and French by early 1990.

The model we propose is not intended to provide, and clearly does not provide, a completely detailed picture of how PLAN might operate. Candidates for licensure or certification who are trained outside Ontario must be ensured the fair and equitable treatment to which they are entitled as residents of this province, and the model that we propose sets out the basic functions which this Task Force has concluded must therefore be provided to them. In keeping with this, we consider it essential that the board of directors that we have proposed as part of the PLAN structure have significant ethno-cultural representation to ensure that the interests of foreign-trained individuals have a strong voice in the administration of PLAN.

We have recommended a phase-in period of three years, during which time the PLAN assessments may be issued but need not be obtained and may be considered alternative assessments to those rendered by the occupational bodies themselves. After that time, we recommend that PLAN assessments be binding on occupational organizations.

It is essential, however, that the introduction of the institution should be seen as evolutionary rather than revolutionary: it will take time for occupational groups and individuals to adapt to its presence and accept as credible its decisions. Although we have formally suggested a phase-in period of three years before full operation, in some cases, for some functions, even that may not be enough. Ideally the idea and institution should grow, with the cooperation and support of the populations they are meant to serve; too early or too rigid an imposition of the scheme is more likely to hinder than help the process.

RECOMMENDATIONS

Our focus is on assessment of prior foreign education and experiential learning, but the benefit of our recommendations will accrue to all residents of Ontario.

5.1   *We recommend that the Government of Ontario make provision for the systematic assessment of the prior education and experiential learning of individuals through the creation of the Prior Learning Assessment Network (PLAN). Prior learning assessment is the assessment of (1) education (secondary, postsecondary, and vocational training, including courses,* certificates, diplomas, and degrees) and (2) experience that an individual has obtained. It includes assessment of what the individual has learned through structured education and training delivered by employers, associations, and trade unions, and through personal experience, on-the-job training, volunteer work, and independent study.

5.2　　We recommend that, in order to ensure consistency and universality of access to its services, PLAN be publicly funded and accountable to a ministry of Government within a framework of provincial legislation and regulations. Legislative implementation should include amendments to the governing Act and/or regulations of all privately and publicly regulated occupations. These amendments should specify that candidates are entitled to equivalency assessments, that they shall be provided with a report of the results of such assessments, and that they shall be entitled to apply for licensure of certification if the report shows equivalency to Ontario standards, provided all other criteria for entry are met, including satisfaction of any examination or work experience requirements. Legislated training requirements should be amended, where necessary, to eliminate references both to formal training in any particular program or discipline and to requirements specifying registration in another jurisdiction. With regard to unregulated occupations, we recommend that the legislation creating and implementing PLAN specifically name and include within the ambit of its provisions any occupational body that grants credentials or ''reserved titles'' to qualified individuals.

5.3　　We recommend that, in designing, implementing, and maintaining PLAN, the Government establish a board of directors to direct the design and ongoing operations of PLAN, with representation from educational institutions, bodies that administer occupational certification and licensure, ethno-cultural groups, and individuals seeking access to occupations or postsecondary education.

5.4　　We recommend that the Government allocate funding to enable PLAN (1) to assess prior education to determine its equivalency to formal education in Ontario, and (2) to assess prior experiential learning that was not previously attested to by a formal educational institution, to determine its equivalency to *formal education in Ontario. To these ends, we recommend that PLAN develop:*

- *an advisory infrastructure, made up of occupation-specific occupational advisory committees, for the purpose of ensuring that individual occupations be involved directly in the articulation of standards of competence and the designation of the equivalency of prior education and experience.*

- *staff expertise in research and comparative education, for the purposes of authenticating documents; identifying and validating the content, duration, and required level of mastery of Canadian and foreign education and training programs; and creating a reliable information base that includes descriptions of these programs and a record of equivalency decisions rendered by PLAN.*

- *staff expertise in curriculum development and evaluation, for the purposes of identification and assessment of the objectives of structured education and training programs provided outside of formal educational institutions.*

- *staff expertise in the construction and validation of examinations of theoretical and applied knowledge, including expertise in (1) the subject matter of the examination, (2) the actual design and validation of examinations, and (3) the identification and elimination of ethno-cultural bias in assessments, all for the purposes of developing, administering, and building a bank of assessment instruments and procedures.*

- *staff expertise in the preparation and assessment of portfolios of prior learning, for the purposes of (1) training those who help applicants design and complete their portfolio, (2) training subject specialists who assess the portfolios for credit purposes, and (3) training and advising administrators and decision makers in the client groups in order that their commitment to prior learning assessment be well-informed and ongoing.*

- *translation services that are available to clients as required, with free translation service to newcomers to Ontario during the first two years of their permanent residence in Canada.*

5.5   *We recommend that there be a three-year phase-in period for PLAN, during which period assessments by PLAN of the equivalency of an individual's prior education and experience to Ontario standards not be binding on occupational certification and licensure bodies. We recommend that all assessments conducted by PLAN after this three-year phase-in period be binding, subject to the appeal procedure set out in Recommendation 5.11. In this regard, we recommend that PLAN be responsible for assessing whether or not individuals have the training prerequisites to apply for licensure or certification, and that the actual licensure or certification processes, particularly those relating to examinations and work experience requirements, continue to be the responsibility of occupational licensure and certification bodies.*

5.6   *We recommend that PLAN have the authority to delegate responsibility for prior learning assessment to individual occupations; to monitor the quality of those assessments to ensure that they are carried out efficiently, fairly, and in the interests of public safety; and to rescind such delegation of responsibility for cause.*

5.7   *We recommend that PLAN launch a public education and promotion program about the nature of prior learning assessment and the services that PLAN offers. This program should be made available to Canadians, including newcomers to Canada, and — through Canadian government offices abroad — people seeking to immigrate to Canada.*

5.8   *We recommend that PLAN enter into an agreement with the Skills Bank of the Ontario Training Corporation for the inclusion in its data base of (1) summary information about certification and licensure processes for regulated professions and trades in Ontario, and (2) a description of PLAN's services and means of access to them.*

5.9   *We recommend that in those cases where the assessment of prior learning indicates that the individual does not fully meet the relevant Ontario standards, PLAN provide specific advice about the additional training required to achieve equivalency to Ontario standards, and that PLAN facilitate the provision of information and counselling by other agencies, regarding retraining programs in Ontario. On successful completion of such additional specified training, candidates may reapply to PLAN and will be given due credit for this training and a statement attesting to their equivalency.*

5.10   *We recommend that each assessment of prior learning be prepared by a PLAN staff member who has expertise in comparative education, and that the determination of equivalency be made by the staff member under the general advice of the relevant occupational advisory committee.*

5.11   *We recommend the provision of a right of appeal, to an individual or to an affected occupational body, of PLAN's assessment of an individual's academic equivalency. In this context we further recommend:*

- *that before any formal appeal, the appellant be encouraged to discuss the decision with the research staff member who carried out the assessment.*

- *that a formal appeal should be heard by a Decision Review Committee made up of a pool of eight or nine experts in the area of prior learning assessment, three of whom will be chosen to sit on each appeal. The committee could include university and college registrars, Canadian assessors from national and international bodies such as the AUCC and UNESCO, and faculty from schools of comparative education.*

- *that the Decision Review Committee have access to counsel to clarify legal and administrative procedural issues.*

- *that candidates be permitted to make written and oral submissions to the Decision Review Committee, that expert evidence be admitted, and that the committee have the power to reverse the assessment decision.*

5.12   *We recommend that, at the end of its three-year phase-in period, PLAN be assigned responsibility for affirming that standards of validity, reliability, and cultural sensitivity for certification and licensure examinations are adhered to by occupational licensure and certification bodies in their examination of applicants, and responsibility for publishing such standards. We further recommend that such bodies be required to obtain approval from PLAN for the introduction or continuation of any certification and licensure examination requirements that apply to foreign-trained as opposed to Ontario-trained individuals.*

5.13   *We recommend that the Government appropriate monies for the design, creation, and operation of PLAN at the beginning of the fiscal year that follows the tabling of this Report.*

PLAN (Prior Learning Assessment Network)
Proposed Organizational Structure

Minister

Enabling Legislation

Board of Directors

About 15 members from postsecondary institutions, occupations, and the public (including ethno-cultural representatives). Staggered rotating appointments.

EXECUTIVE DIRECTOR
(Chair of the Board)

Occupational Advisory Committees

One for each of the affected occupations or groups of related occupations; 3-7 members per committee.

FUNCTIONS

Assessment

Design and manage comparative education data base.

Assess equivalency of individuals' prior academic and experiential learning to Ontario prerequisites.

Issue equivalency documents, including precise statement of any additional training required.

Public Education

Promote PLAN roles and functions.

Educate and train public, educational institutions, trade, and professional bodies regarding roles and uses of PLAN.

Administer PLAN's links to the Ontario Training Corporation's Skills Bank with a view to transmitting information on certification and licensure requirements and PLAN services.

Provide translation and counselling.

Standards

Publish standards of assessment design.

Assist in design and validation of licensure and language tests.

Approve any tests imposed on foreign-trained people only.

Administer appeals to **Decision Review Committee.**

Major functions of a prior learning assessment system in Ontario:

- Assessing equivalency. Identifying the additional training required by an individual to fulfil certification and licensure prerequisites. Hearing appeals.

- Promoting the accessibility of equivalency assessments and other services to candidates both within Ontario and abroad. Delivering training on strategies for the assessment of prior learning to: professions and trades, postsecondary institutions, other clients.

- Publishing standards for certification and licensure examinations.

- Assisting certification and licensure bodies in the design of examinations. Approving any additional licensure or certification tests imposed upon foreign-trained candidates.

- Disseminating information about: certification and licensure processes, retraining and upgrading opportunities, language training.

- Collaborating with other national and international bodies involved in the assesment of prior learning and accreditation of foreign-trained individuals.

CHAPTER 6

Licensure Testing

The examination requirements would be onerous for anyone, but particularly so for the newly arrived because they are busy getting settled, having to adapt to new jobs or careers, and for many simply because it has been so long since they have had to study and write examinations. We are sure that most Canadians who have worked as professionals for many years would find it very difficult to study for and write examinations without the additional burdens that an immigrant has.

— from a Brief submitted to the
Task Force by an organization

Examination is an essential component in the process of licensure or certification because it effectively determines who will receive a licence or certification. (We refer to ''licensure tests'' throughout this chapter, a term that should be read to include not only tests for official licensure, but any competency assessment examination administered by an occupational body as a prerequisite to licensure, certification, registration, or membership.) This final step on the road to licensure can be the most demanding for foreign-trained individuals. Struggling to master a new language, confronted with examination formats that are often unfamiliar, intimidated by the ominous implications, both personal and financial, of possible failure, such individuals approach this stage of the process with trepidation. It is, however, virtually an unavoidable requirement. Of the occupations we reviewed, almost all impose a comprehensive examination as a formal part of their certification procedure.

Professional bodies are charged with the task of administering examinations that ''help identify those who possess the knowledge, skills, and abilities to perform critical tasks in a manner that will adequately safeguard the public health, safety, and welfare.''[1] The licensure test makes the final determination between those who have the competency required to practise the occupation without compromising the public's health, welfare, and safety, and those who do not. As we discussed in Chapter 4 ("Issues Facing the Professions"), the right and authority of the professional bodies to set the standard for entry to the profession must reflect this public interest.

THE PROBLEM: HOW TO ENSURE FAIRNESS IN TESTING

Based on the comments and briefs from affected candidates, on our review of the licensure examination procedures of the occupations studied, and on our survey of the literature on the subject of licensure testing, the Task Force has identified several factors that can affect the fairness of the licensure testing encountered by foreign-trained occupational candidates. We emphasize that these are *potential barriers* which *can* arise in the process of licensure testing. The extent to which these factors actually operate varies according to setting, as will be discussed below. What is clear, however, is that licensure testing is a difficult and complex process. Each of these factors has the potential for playing a significant part in the degree of fairness that a test displays.

Factors Affecting Fairness

The factors we have identified are:

1) universality of examination;
2) cultural responses;
3) language;
4) responsiveness or feedback;
5) format and administration;
6) aids to preparation; and
7) selection of the standard to be met.

We deal with each of these in turn.

Universality of Examination

The majority of the occupations we surveyed require the same licensing or certification examinations of all candidates, regardless of where they did their training. (An outline of licensure test requirements for Ontario-trained candidates compared with requirements for candidates trained elsewhere appears as Appendix 6-A1 at the end of this chapter.) In rare cases, all candidates write similar but not identical examinations. For example, in the profession of optometry, the comprehensive examination required of Ontario-trained candidates and offered at the end of the University of Waterloo program is very similar to that offered by the board to other eligible candidates, namely those who trained elsewhere.

Those professions that may require additional certification examinations of some or all foreign-trained candidates include: dietetics, chiropody, veterinary medicine, early childhood education (where the certification being sought is membership in the Association for Early Childhood Education, Ontario), agrology (although the additional examinations may also be required of Ontario-trained candidates who have degrees in a non-agricultural discipline), dentistry, dental hygiene, physiotherapy (which is attempting to institute a national examination that will be required of all candidates), and radiology (the board examination is effectively required only of foreign-trained candidates). In addition, the professional engineers require confirmatory examinations of foreign-trained candidates as a means of affirming a previously assessed equivalency.

Of those professions that require additional licensure examinations of foreign-trained individuals, none has provoked more comment on this subject than the dental profession. The dental licensing examination, administered by the National Dental Examining Board, consists of four parts, one written and three clinical. Graduates of accredited Canadian dental schools are exempted from all four parts; graduates of accredited U.S. dental schools must complete all parts but one — work on a mannequin. All other candidates, including graduates of any other university-based dental program listed in the World Health Organization directory, must complete all four parts. This structure of exemption, coupled with a high failure rate on the examinations which cannot be measured against a Canadian control group, has given rise to speculation from many sources about the standard being set in the examination. A number of practical difficulties which candidates of this examination encounter take on increased significance because the examination is required only of a subgroup. These added difficulties include cost, which is high; access, which is difficult and expensive because candidates have in the past been required to travel to a city outside Ontario, typically Montreal or Vancouver, and stay for several days; and problems of patient-supply, because candidates must supply their own patients. (The actual cost of the examination is currently $4,160; estimates put the total cost, including travel and hotel costs for candidate and patient, at a much higher figure.)

Although the difficulties and potential inequities that can result from the administration of different examinations to different categories of candidates have been noted to us most frequently in regard to the dental profession, they arise, to greater or lesser degrees, in any group in which additional tests are required of a subgroup of candidates. It is the view of the Task Force that candidates trained in jurisdictions other than Ontario should not be required to complete licensure tests that apply different content or set a different standard from tests required of domestically trained candidates. In general, we feel this requirement is best met if the same tests are administered to all candidates.

The justification typically given for the administration of different or additional licensure examinations to foreign-trained candidates is the lack of information available about a candidate's training; such information, if available, would enable the professional bodies to assess a candidate's competence by means other than a special examination. As accurate and comprehensive equivalency assessments become available through our proposed Prior Learning Assessment Network (PLAN), however, this justification for additional examinations will be less compelling (see Chapter 5). Still, the Task Force acknowledges that some clinical testing may remain desirable in certain professions, such as dentistry and veterinary medicine, and that costs and other administrative factors may make the universal administration of the same examination impracticable, particularly when the clinical skills of Ontario-trained candidates are known.

In all cases it must be the responsibility of the occupational body to ensure that any licensure test required can be justified and substantiated as a fair and necessary means of ensuring competence. This fairness can best be demonstrated through administration of the same examination to all candidates. Should the occupational body feel that an additional examination for foreign-trained candidates is merited, however, a careful case must be made for the examination, specifying the equivalency that it deems unable to be established by other means. It would also be necessary to demonstrate the inappropriateness of requiring the examination of Ontario candidates.

We should note that there are a number of ways in which examinations are employed by the different professional bodies. Some professions give credits or exemptions from required examinations to candidates who have trained elsewhere and can demonstrate that they have mastered a required skill. This is the case for certified general accountants, certified management accountants, and real estate and business brokers. In the case of some other professions, there is provision for a series of examinations administered by the professional body for candidates whose training is assessed as less than equivalent. These individuals are given an opportunity to demonstrate their competence in the areas in which they are felt to be deficient. (For example, candidates in forestry may write up to 20 examinations in areas in which they are assessed as deficient; engineers, in addition to writing the Professional Practice Examination required of all candidates, may be required to write up to 21 technical examinations in areas in which they are assessed as less than equivalent.) Such "challenge examinations" can be characterized less as licensure examinations and more as part of the upgrading or assessment of the individual; nonetheless, they are all intended to assess competence and are prerequisites to licensure. Accordingly, they must be subject to the same standards of fairness as licensure examinations. Our comments on the standards to be applied in the development of licensure examinations should be understood to apply to these challenge examinations as well, where they are provided by the occupational body. As such examinations are typically required of a candidate properly assessed as having training that is less than equivalent to Ontario-trained candidates, however, the alternative provided by this option is acceptable and even desirable — provided the assignment of the examinations reflects the deficiencies identified in the equivalency assessment, and provided the examinations can be shown to meet recognized standards of fairness in test development.

Cultural Responses

Cultural responses have been shown to be capable of affecting the outcome of an examination. They can arise in written examinations in which the questions may reflect a cultural background that is not common to all examinees; or they can arise in oral examination situations in which an examiner may be unaware of behavioural characteristics that may lead a candidate to behave in a way that may be "inappropriate" to traditional Ontario culture. Some cultural reactions may alter the treatment or course of action selected by the candidate in a substantive way; these responses, therefore, may appropriately be brought into an assessment of success or failure on an examination. Other reactions may be irrelevant and therefore should be ignored by the examiner. Considerable training and practice are required before an examiner can make these kinds of judgments.

Documentation of the existence of such cultural responses within examinations is scarce as they are often not overt but within the perceptions of the examinees and examiner. The design of an examination totally free of such subtle biases is difficult for all but those expert in test development, and we therefore commend the use of such experts by test administrators.

Language

Because language plays such a major role in the success or failure of foreign-trained individuals, a good deal of our report is devoted to that subject. (See Chapter 7, "Language Testing," and Chapter 8, "Language Training.") In some occupations, fluency is essential to safe practice; failure to attain an adequate level of proficiency, therefore, can and should result in a rejection. At the same time, comprehensive language assessments, particularly in the form of standardized tests, can introduce an artificially high barrier.

It is not inappropriate for a licensure test to function as a screen for fluency. Indeed, focused as they are on the actual tasks to be performed in practice, licensure tests can provide an excellent means of ensuring that candidates are fluent in the technical language and vocabulary of the occupation. These tests, however, are only appropriate for this use if the level of fluency required for the practice of the profession has been directly addressed in their development. A number of professions use their licensure examinations as language screens (among them, optometry, denture therapy, dental technology, forestry, and dentistry); it is essential that the question of the level of language proficiency be directly considered in such cases.

Although a significant level of fluency is appropriately required in the professions generally, care must be taken that the standard required in the examination is not set unnecessarily, and therefore unreasonably, high. The fluency level of a licensure test should not exceed that appropriate to the occupation.[2] If it is determined that the level of fluency appropriate to the occupation is not high, the level of the linguistic requirements, certainly in the questions themselves but also in the instructions and in the very format of the examination, must be set at that level. Experienced editors should be able to help bring the language of the examination close to the required standard.

Responsiveness or Feedback

Many people with foreign training expressed despair over the fact that they failed a test and knew neither the reasons they failed nor the sections in which they did most poorly. More concrete feedback would have helped these candidates prepare for a retry.

We also heard from candidates concerned about limitations on their right to reattempt the examination. Among those occupations reviewed, there are few instances in which no retries are permitted: the confirmatory examinations required as part of the professional engineering certification procedure are one example; in psychology, a retry of the oral portion of the examination is permitted only after a period of retraining. In most professions, the number of retries permitted, either absolutely or before retraining is required, varies from one to three. As an alternative, some professions permit "unlimited retries," provided the requirement is successfully completed within a fixed time frame, such as six years.

The Task Force is of the view that retries as a right, without any retraining prerequisite, should be permitted. Having said that, however, we do not think it appropriate or necessary, in the face of current practices that are for the most part reasonable, to interfere with the decisions made by the professions over the number of retries or the time period within which the requirement must be met.

For candidates who have the opportunity to retry the examination, the availability of information on how they performed is critical. The professional bodies have different practices in this area. In some professions, ophthalmic dispensing for example, there is a personal review of examination results with the candidate; in others, such as engineering, failed candidates receive some guidance on how better to prepare for the examination; and in still others, candidates are given a detailed written explanation of examination results, as happens after the oral psychology examination. But despite the importance of this type of information, in many professions it is not made available to the candidate concerned.

Occupations using tests should be required to reveal both the candidate's score and the minimum passing score to an examinee who fails.

Ideally, even before they attempt a test, candidates should be given a "blueprint" of the examination, showing the various subsections and the scores allocated to each; then, following the examination, the subscores of the segments should be provided to the examinee. In addition, because the score is so significant, an examinee should have available a means of verifying its accuracy.[3] If a test giver cannot release the test or the scoring key, then some other means of verification should be provided; the easiest route would be to include a provision for independent regrading.

In the context of oral and clinical examinations, feedback, for the twin purposes of educating an unsuccessful candidate and maintaining a record of what transpired should a review or appeal be launched, is important. Careful and detailed record keeping and a provision for review are essential.

Videotaping of clinical performances has been introduced in some settings. Medical education researchers have studied the effectiveness of this practice and found it useful for analyzing the reliability of performance tests and subsequently for improving them.[4] Videotaping also provides a record of the examination for use in any appeal of the results. It can, however, be cumbersome in a hands-on multistation clinical setting, and it would add to the already high cost of such examinations.

Format and Administration

A number of questions about the fairness of the examination's administration relate to access: how often is the examination offered? in how many locations? under what conditions? and, at what cost to the candidate? The examination's format is also an issue, having a significant impact on access.

As seen earlier in this chapter, the licensing examinations offered by the National Dental Examining Board impose significant burdens on candidates, and the same is true of other professions. For example, the cost of the clinical proficiency examination required of some candidates for licensure in veterinary medicine is $2,500; the fee for taking the clinical examination in optometry is $1,425; and in those professions that require a number of examinations to demonstrate proficiency, among them forestry and engineering, the cost can be very high indeed.

The issue of frequency or availability of examinations has been noted as a problem in a number of the professions reviewed. Examinations in chiropody, chiropractic, denture therapy, dental technology, funeral services, massage therapy, naturopathy, occupational therapy, ophthalmic dispensing, optometry, social work, and veterinary medicine (clinical) are offered only once annually, generally in only one location. Comprehensive dentistry examinations are available only once annually (although segments are available at other times). Infrequency of sittings means candidates for accreditation face significant delays, during which time employment in the field is either not permitted or, at best, difficult to obtain. Time is a factor in professions that require a number of examinations.

Particularly where the examination is not required of all candidates, high costs, lack of frequency, and limited sites for the examination may be inappropriate. It is the responsibility of each of the professions to offer an examination that meets standards of fairness in every respect, including reasonableness of accessibility and cost.

As noted, the selection of the format of the examination is also critical to fairness. Each of the three standard formats — written, oral, and clinical — presents strengths as well as weaknesses.

Written Examinations

Essay type. Written essay tests, required by some professional bodies, are generally considered excellent assessment mechanisms, despite their built-in subjectivity. The emphasis that some tests place on linguistic ability should be a consideration when selecting this format. The modified essay question, a relatively recent format, suffers less from this defect and may have greater reliability, but more research is needed.[5]

Multiple-choice. The written multiple-choice test is probably the best-known and most widely used format in North America, and it is the type most frequently used by the professional bodies we reviewed. The multiple-choice test is likely the most efficient variety because one can assess a number of areas and in a reasonable time period. This format is relatively inexpensive to administer and score and can therefore be offered more frequently and in more locations. Many acknowledge multiple-choice as the most reliable type of test for assessing the kind of factual knowledge accumulated in the course of professional studies at a university or college.[6]

The multiple-choice examination is familiar to candidates trained in North America, but candidates trained elsewhere may be unfamiliar with the format, a significant disadvantage of this type of test. Clear directions and precise questions help minimize such irrelevant background differences.

Finally, written clinical simulations, which are used typically in the health disciplines setting and are featured in the licensure examination in veterinary medicine, have the potential to be adapted to the multiple-choice format.[7]

Oral Examinations

Oral examinations are used by some professions, although always in conjunction with a written examination.

Oral examinations have several advantages. First, an examiner can observe directly and evaluate a candidate's interactive skills and ongoing problem-solving skills. Second, an examiner can rate the "candidate's ability to apply the knowledge and skills of the profession to concrete situations or scenarios."[8] In other words, the oral test provides the next best method, after direct observation, of seeing the examinee practise his or her profession.[9] Third, the oral test is more flexible than a written test because the candidate can ask the examiner to clarify the questions and the examiner can ask the candidate to clarify his or her answers, especially when the candidate gives seemingly inappropriate responses. Finally, the examiner can tailor the questions to the candidate's background and career interests.

Oral tests do, however, have their disadvantages. First, they are subject to allegations of examiner bias (unless the test developer and examiners take special precautions). Second, "failure to establish and maintain rapport may lead to contamination of examination results if this omission causes undue stress for the candidate."[10] Third, oral examinations are expensive and time-consuming to administer.

Clinical Examinations

Clinical tests are used in many of the professions we reviewed, and are an essential part of an assessment of competence in health disciplines. Typically, as in the dental clinical examination, the test involves one or more examiners watching and evaluating a candidate perform a designated procedure on a patient and then evaluating both the process and the final product. The main weakness of this type of test is that, if the examiners have considerable discretion in how to rate the candidates, and if no rating scales are provided, then the risk of bias or perception of bias is high. As well, clinical examinations are expensive and time-consuming to administer.

In an effort to minimize the subjectivity of the clinical dental examination, the dental examining board in California instituted a procedure whereby examiners rate the finished work once the examinee has left the room, rather than watch and rate the performance of the work. The objective is to prevent factors such as skin colour, accent, race, ethnicity, and social class from affecting the examiner's ratings. Although this method no doubt meets one objective, it rates only the final product, not the process, and thus does not fully address safety.[11] An alternative is to have two independent sets of examiners, one rating the procedure and the other rating the results.

Researchers, primarily in the area of medical education, are studying other methods to minimize the subjectivity of clinical examinations in order to determine their feasibility and applicability to licensure testing. Some of the techniques studied are simulated or standardized patients, chart-stimulated recall (CSR), and objective structured clinical examination (OSCE). Each of these techniques represents a significant development in medical clinical testing. Although still the subject of discussion and research, these methods hold out considerable promise for increased objectivity and predictive validity in clinical testing.[12]

Innovative testing methods, many of them involving computer technology, are emerging. Objective, impersonal, relatively cost-efficient, and flexible regarding time and location, these techniques too show much promise.

Technological Testing Methods

In the area of format, two facts emerge most dramatically from the literature, from commentary from the professional bodies themselves, and from candidates.

First, the use of multiple methods of testing is likely to enhance the validity of the assessments. At the International Conference on Further Developments in Assessing Clinical Competence, Dr. Ian Hart, director of the R.S. McLaughlin Centre for Evaluation of Clinical Competence, discussed "the 5Ms approach" to assessing competence.[13] The 5Ms are "multiple methods, multiple media, and multiple stations." Knowing clearly the objectives of a particular test, a test developer can determine which methods (e.g., oral, written) and which media (e.g., pen and paper, computer) are the most appropriate. By combining more than one of these methods and media, a comprehensive format will evolve that permits a fuller assessment of a particular candidate's competence and performance and, by extension, allows for more comprehensive feedback to the candidate. A number of occupational bodies already use more than one method of assessment in order to better assess their candidates. This approach should be extended to all licensure testing.

The second fact to emerge from our review of examination formats is that the selection of the best and most appropriate method for any given occupation is difficult and requires the application of considerable experience and expertise; the fair administration of a test, once developed, requires detailed attention to current practice in the field of testing and a broad range of knowledge and information about preferred practice. Although the occupational bodies are in many cases attempting to deal with these issues appropriately, they are most likely to obtain the best results if they have access to external expertise.

Aids to Preparation

All candidates for licensure tests, and particularly those unfamiliar with the educational programs and testing mechanisms in Ontario, must be made aware, in advance of a test, of precisely what is expected. They must be told the passing mark, how the examination will be graded, the format to expect, the content that may be covered, and the level of expertise they will be expected to demonstrate. The last is clearly the most significant point, and candidates must be given direction and access to adequate preparatory materials. These materials should include sample test items and, where appropriate, performance tasks. In the absence of such direction, the licensure examination is not a faithful and fair measure of competence.

Most of the professions we reviewed provide candidates with some assistance. For example, before taking the dental hygiene clinical examination, candidates are given an opportunity to view the equipment they will be using and are briefed on examination content and procedure; aspiring dietitians receive a study guide; and candidates for the professional practice examination in engineering are given a list of study materials and invited to take correspondence courses to assist in preparation. There are many other examples of assistance of this kind. In rare cases professions (including architecture and certified management accountancy) release for review a former examination, perhaps the most useful tool to a preparing candidate. Several professions provide materials containing sample questions. It is interesting to note that the candidates for the confirmatory examinations offered by the Association of Professional Engineers are not encouraged to prepare (although they are provided with some preparatory material) on the basis that the examinations are meant to affirm equivalency and therefore should not require preparation. (This is also the rationale behind their not being permitted a retry.)

Efforts are therefore being made to meet this need in many cases. The level of information being supplied, however, is not consistent and not always adequate. In addition, references to study materials are of little value to the candidate if they are not coupled with advice on how to obtain them and an indication of the level of mastery that may be required. Consistent practice, which is what is required in this area, would be accomplished through the information dispersal and counselling functions that would be a part of the proposed Prior Learning Assessment Network (PLAN) mandate. Our recommendations on this subject appear in Chapter 5, ''Prior Learning Assessment.''

Selection of the Standard

Professional examinations, which are tests of competency, should reflect the standard of competence required to perform professional tasks without risk to public safety, health, or welfare. In the past, academic and other training programs have served as a guide in the development of such tests, but there has in recent years been a shift away from this approach to a concentration on what professionals actually need to know in order to practice. This change has come about at least in part as a result of challenges brought against tests devised to test knowledge only, on the grounds that they lack validity as professional examinations.[14] The American Psychological Association's standards for educational and psychological testing,[15] which will be referred to in greater detail later in this chapter, are now being accepted by courts and arbitration panels as criteria for testing.[16]

As discussed in Chapter 5, ''Prior Learning Assessment,'' this shift to competency-based assessments is part of a worldwide trend in occupational accreditation. Inevitably, such a trend is reflected in the development of academic training programs that are structured around identified competencies. Examinations for licensure, as part of the assessment procedure, must focus on skills that are needed for practice. In doing so, these examinations will not be open to challenge that they lack validity on the grounds of testing inappropriate or irrelevant skills, or of testing at a level above that necessary to ensure competent practitioners.

The standard required on licensure examinations of some of the professions under review has been questioned — sometimes strongly, and not only by foreign-trained individuals. An elevated standard is, of course, of greatest concern when the examination in question is one from which all, or essentially all, domestically trained candidates are exempted; yet the mere fact that all candidates write the same examinations does not necessarily ensure that the standard being set is appropriate. In such cases, an unreasonably high standard, and one that is therefore likely to be out of step with that operating in other jurisdictions, affects all candidates, although foreign-trained individuals may suffer the greatest impact because their training would not have been geared to the level of expertise required.

A number of briefs were emphatic on this subject. From two written submissions:

> My lawyer asked over and over again how the pass mark was made up. What was the pass mark? What percentage of candidates passed? All these questions were met with evasions . . . In one letter, the registrar states that between twenty and forty-five percent of candidates pass. Now, I know of examinations where there was a hundred percent failure.

> . . . The results were discouraging for me when only twelve examinees [of about one hundred candidates] were approved, and I found myself among those disapproved. The general impression for the whole group was that there was a predetermined restriction in the number of professionals allowed to practice . . .

In reality, no guidelines exist to guarantee that procedures of test development and evaluation will ensure the examination in question reflects a standard of competence necessary to practise the profession. There are, however, accepted approximations. In the absence of systematic standard-setting procedures, the passing mark is difficult to defend.

THE SOLUTION: TEST DEVELOPMENT AND VALIDATION

As our discussion indicates, there is, within testing procedures, considerable potential for unfairness in all areas reviewed. At the same time, a number of general points should be made. First, the setting of fair examinations is a difficult and complex process — indeed, our recommendations directly reflect our respect for that reality. The professional groups we reviewed consider the licensure test a critical element in their assessment of the competence of individuals and appear to put considerable effort into the testing procedure. In addition, in some cases the efforts being made by the occupational bodies are resulting in testing procedures that reflect the standards of fairness to which we have been referring throughout this chapter.

Nonetheless, we are left with some concern about the testing procedures generally in place. In some cases that concern reflects concrete analysis of a deficiency or a debatable practice. For example, for any given occupation, we were generally able to determine whether the examinations were being required of all candidates or only some, what kind of feedback or preparatory material was being provided to candidates, and how often and at what cost examinations were being offered. Other potential barriers, less easy to define, are difficult to judge without expertise in both the particular profession and, even more importantly, the field of licensure testing generally. Among these potential barriers are the following factors:

* whether the level of fluency required is appropriate,
* whether cultural responses are operating,
* whether the standard reflects the appropriate level of competence,
* whether the examination format is optimal, and
* whether administration of the examination is fair.

In addition, in most cases the examinations used by the occupational bodies were not released for review by the Task Force, their contents being valuable to the examination administrators only so long as they remain private.

With reference to these less concrete factors, it must therefore be made clear that our comments are based on the understanding that, without evidence of the application of appropriate methods of test development in keeping with recognized professional standards, there can be no assurance that these factors are not operating to the detriment of all candidates and, particularly, of those with foreign training. This premise in fact epitomizes the essential challenge of licensure testing: it is only through the application of fixed and recognized standards of test development by experts in the field of testing that strengths and deficiencies can be determined; in the absence of the application of such techniques it is impossible to assess accurately the fairness of a given test.

It is the view of this Task Force, therefore, that many potential deficiencies referred to above can be minimized through the use of test development and analysis methods that meet professional standards. In the following section, we provide a brief outline of a recommended procedure, acknowledging that variations are acceptable. We know that some outside expertise in test development is currently being employed by some professional groups — ophthalmic dispensers, nurses, veterinarians, social workers, to name a few — and, while we do not know precisely to what extent these and other occupations are already conforming to the procedure we outline, we are of the view that the introduction of such procedures in all cases will assist the occupational bodies in offering fair tests.

Developing a Valid Test

Development of a valid test involves a comprehensive review of the competencies that form the basis of practice in the profession. This review begins with a role-delineation study that answers the question, "What are the concepts, knowledge, skills, or abilities that a candidate must have in order to perform competently?"[17] From the information gathered in the study, a table of specifications is created in which the content of practice is cross-referenced to the objectives of the licensure test. Test items drawn from the table of specifications create the "item pool" that forms the basis of the test.

The items themselves are written by committees or groups of professionals who specialize in a particular field of their profession, working under the guidance of experienced test developers. The test developer may also solicit items from individual specialists. The test developer then screens the resulting items for such things as content accuracy, spelling, grammar, ambiguity, and conformity to a workable format. Following this initial screening, other consultants, who have expertise in a particular area, independently review the items for clarity and content accuracy. Finally, committees select items from the resulting item pool in order to draft a proposed test. This draft is sent to the test users, and the committee takes their comments into account when giving final approval to each test item. After each administration of the test, the test developer reviews the statistical performance for each item before including it in the test score.[18]

To ensure that each form of the test is valid and that the test does not remain static, the test developer constructs each test form so that some portion includes old items which have already been empirically validated. The developer then assesses the validity of the new items by comparing them with old items in similar areas.

As a final step, procedures are developed to ensure that the pass-fail mark is set at an appropriate level.

Where clinical skills are being examined through a practical examination, a different methodology applies.[19] Some of the development methods currently employed in this field relate to the use of standardized patients, the objective structured clinical examination (OSCE), and so on; these methods were discussed earlier in the chapter, in the section on clinical examinations. As noted, the choice of the appropriate format and the procedures for administration of the test are essential for fairness.

In *Standards for Educational and Psychological Testing*, a document produced for the American Educational Research Association, the American Psychological Association, and the National Council on Measurement in Education, the test user or developer is provided with a description of general principles of test use and particular principles that govern specific types of tests.[20] Standards to be followed when developing and using a test are presented. The standards particularly pertinent to professional and occupational licensure and certification are:

> The content domain to be covered by a licensure or certification test should be defined clearly and explained in terms of the importance of the content for competent performance in an occupation. A rationale should be provided to support a claim that the knowledge or skills being assessed are required for competent performance in an occupation and are consistent with the purpose for which the licensing or certification program was instituted. (Standard 11.1)

> Any construct interpretations of tests used for licensure and certification should be made explicit, and the evidence and logical analyses supporting these interpretations should be reported. (Standard 11.2)

Estimates of the reliability of licensure or certification decisions should be provided. (Standard 11.3)

Test takers who fail a test should, upon request, be told their score and the minimum score required to pass the test. Test takers should be given information on their performance in parts of the test for which separate scores or reports are produced and used in the decision process. (Standard 11.4)

Rules and procedures used to combine scores or other assessments to determine the overall outcome should be reported to test takers preferably before the test is administered. (Standard 11.5)

In order to ensure that the results of a test can be defended, the test must reflect the application of these and other, more generally applicable, recognized standards.[21] The application of these standards to any given licensure test would constitute the process of evaluation of the examination, which in the view of the Task Force is necessary to ensure fairness. Standards for test construction and evaluation include such items as validity; reliability and errors of measurement; test development and revision; scaling, norming, score comparability, and equating; and the production of technical manuals and user's guides to provide information on the appropriate use to be made of given scores.

In particular, we note that an examinee may perform differently on a test from one occasion to the next or from one form of the same test to another. This discrepancy occurs for a variety of reasons unrelated to the examinee's competence. These so-called "errors of measurement" must be determined. (Test developers and publishers generally conduct and report on studies on reliability and errors of measurement that are expected to be adequate for the test's intended users.) The provision of this information is essential to the test user who intends to rely on the score. In addition, it is essential that test users receive clear information about the appropriate interpretation of test scores.

Test development and evaluation pursuant to recognized standards such as these will ensure, to the degree possible, that the professional examinations attain an adequate level of fairness. We are of the view that all examinations used to control entry to professional organizations should be developed according to such standards. Although the professions themselves should retain control over the development of their examinations, and although we are not of the view that a formalized procedure of compulsory accreditation of examinations is called for at this time, the policies and procedures of test development applicable to any given profession should be part of the public record and available to candidates. Coordination of this function should be through the proposed Prior Learning Assessment Network (PLAN).

RECOMMENDATIONS

A licensure test assesses the competency, knowledge, and proficiency of a candidate for licensure or certification based on standards established by the licensing body. The test must be able to differentiate between those candidates who have the competency required to practise the occupation without compromising the public's health, welfare, and safety, and those who do not.

Any licensure test offered by a professional body must meet required standards of fairness. In order to ensure that any such test is fair to candidates and measures consistently what it is intended to measure, the test developer should follow accepted standards of test development. The test developer must determine precisely what is "competence" for the occupation under consideration, not necessarily only according to what is taught in academic programs relating to the occupation but according to actual practices carried out within the occupation as reflected in identifiable competencies. The questions selected and the formats used should reflect this standard. The test developer must also bear in mind questions of language, cultural responses, and fair use and administration of the test, and the test must be responsive to candidates by being capable of providing them with the feedback they require to improve their skills. Clear guidelines for the use of the test and the setting of scores must be provided for test takers.

The development of a valid test requires specific expertise. In order to ensure that development of licensure tests in Ontario is in accordance with the general principles outlined and that the resulting tests are fair to all candidates:

> *6.1   We recommend that licensure tests be developed according to recognized standards and methods of test development, including a consideration of what a licensed individual needs to know for practice, and taking into account the issues of language, culture,*

administrative fairness, and the availability of comprehensive information to the candidate on the standard being required and on his or her performance.

6.2   *We recommend that all candidates for testing be directed to preparatory courses or be given detailed preparatory material.*

6.3   *We recommend that the policies and procedures of test development and administration, as they apply to any given occupation, be published and made available to any candidate or interested party, through PLAN.*

6.4   *We recommend that where so requested by the occupational organization, PLAN may provide assistance and referrals.*

The question of universality of testing is a difficult one. (See Chapter 13 of this Report for a discussion of the implications raised by the *Canadian Charter of Rights and Freedoms* as it applies to this issue.) The Task Force is of the view that it is desirable and preferable that, in any specific occupation, all candidates for licensure who have been assessed as qualified to attempt the licensure examination be required to write the same examination. In addition, we are of the view that with the benefit of comprehensive and objective equivalency assessments provided through PLAN, the need for additional assessments through examination will be greatly diminished. We accept the position, however, that in the view of some occupations additional clinical testing may be needed and that the high cost of some clinical and oral examinations may make it undesirable to examine every candidate for licensure; in addition, Ontario training programs in disciplines with a significant clinical component subject Ontario students to rigorous clinical examination that, in a licensure examination, may be duplicated. We have therefore concluded that it is inappropriate to rule out entirely any additional examination of foreign-trained candidates where it is not required of Ontario-trained candidates, provided development of the test is in keeping with the standards referred to in Recommendation 6.1. This practice, however, should be permitted only where the profession can demonstrate that all candidates are being examined on the same content and to the same standard, regardless of the specific examination being taken; that the examination is needed in order to make an assessment of competence that cannot be otherwise determined; that it would be inappropriate to require the examination of all candidates; and that the examination will not impose an unreasonable burden in terms of time or cost on the candidate.

6.5   *We recommend that every candidate for licensure be required on examination to master the same content and meet the same standard of competence, and that this be achieved by uniformly requiring all candidates to write the same licensure examination. Should an occupational body wish to require additional licensure examinations of foreign-trained candidates, it should advise PLAN, setting out evidence that the examination is essential to the assessment of competence; that the examination will test the same content at the same standard as for Ontario-trained candidates; that it is inappropriate to require the examination of Ontario-trained candidates; and that the examination will not impose an unreasonable burden in terms of cost or time on the candidates of whom it is required.*

Although we do not consider it appropriate or necessary to impose rigid requirements as to access both to examinations and to retries of examinations, it is essential that the professional bodies recognize the importance of these issues.

6.6   *We recommend that professional bodies make every effort to provide reasonable access of candidates to examinations, in terms of both time and location; and that all candidates who are not successful on an examination have the automatic right to at least one retry, with or without retraining.*

APPENDIX

Table 6-A1   Licensure Tests by Place of Training

	Ontario	Other Provinces/ United States	Elsewhere
Accounting:			
Certified general accounting	4 compulsory examinations; courses with examinations required to satisfy deficiencies in training; business communications course	4 compulsory examinations; courses with examinations required to satisfy deficiencies in training; credits available; business communications course	4 compulsory examinations; courses with examinations required to satisfy deficiencies in training; credits available; business communications course
Certified management accounting	3 compulsory final accreditation examinations; courses with examinations to satisfy deficiencies in training; credits available	3 compulsory final accreditation examinations; courses with examinations required to satisfy deficiencies in training; credits available	3 compulsory final accreditation examinations; courses with examination required to satisfy deficiencies in training; credits available
Chartered accounting	Uniform Final Examinations (UFE)	UFE (designated accounting body members exempt)	UFE (designated accounting body members exempt)
Agrology	Professional examination (waived if candidate holds agricultural degree)	Professional examination	Professional examination

	Ontario	Other Provinces/ United States	Elsewhere
Architecture	Admissions course	Admissions course	Admissions course
Chiropody	None	Registration examination	Registration examination if not from recognized U.K. program
Chiropractic	Canadian Chiropractic Examining Board (CCEB) examinations. 2-day provincial examinations	CCEB examinations. 2-day provincial examinations	CCEB examinations. 2-day provincial examinations
Dental hygiene	Clinical examination	Written and clinical examination	Written and clinical examination
Dental technology	Registration examination	Registration examination	Registration examination
Dentistry	None	Other provinces: none. U.S.: 1 written, 2 clinical examinations	1 written, 3 clinical examinations
Denture therapy	Licensing examination (George Brown final examination)	Licensing examination (George Brown final examination)	Licensing examination (George Brown final examination)
Dietetics	None	None	Qualifying examination

	Ontario	Other Provinces/ United States	Elsewhere
Early childhood education	None	Equivalency examination under Association for Early Childhood Education in Ontario (AECEO); none required by Ministry	Equivalency examination under AECEO; none required by Ministry
Education	None required	None required	None required
Engineering	Professional Practice Examination (PPE)	Other provinces and U.S.-accredited full programs: PPE. Other U.S.: confirmatory examinations; examination program; PPE	Confirmatory examinations; examination program; PPE
Engineering technology	None required; may require confirmatory examinations and examination program	None required; may require confirmatory examinations and examination program	None required; may require confirmatory examinations and examination program
Forestry	Up to 20 examinations if candidate is lacking in any core subject areas or lacking a degree or diploma in forestry	Up to 20 examinations if candidate is lacking in any core subject areas or lacking a degree or diploma in forestry	Up to 20 examinations if candidate is lacking in any core subject areas or lacking a degree or diploma in forestry

	Ontario	Other Provinces/ United States	Elsewhere
Funeral services	Licensing examination	Licensing examination	Licensing examination
Registered insurance brokerage	Basic qualifying examination; advanced level examination	Basic qualifying examination; advanced level examination	Basic qualifying examination; advanced level examination
Land surveying	Professional examination; examination program; credits available	Professional examination; examination program; credits available	Professional examination; examination program; credits available
Law	Bar Admission course with examinations	Bar Admission course with examinations; transfer exams in lieu of BAC if candidate has 3 prescribed years of active practice	Bar Admission course with examinations; transfer exams in lieu of BAC if candidate has 3 prescribed years of active practice
Massage therapy	Oral, practical, and written examinations	Oral, practical, and written examinations	Oral, practical, and written examinations
Medical laboratory technology	Qualifying examination required by Canadian Society of Laboratory Technologists	Qualifying examination required by Canadian Society of Laboratory Technologists	Qualifying examination required by Canadian Society of Laboratory Technologists
Medicine	MCCQE	MCCQE (Americans may substitute NBME)	MCCQE

	Ontario	Other Provinces/ United States	Elsewhere
Naturopathy	Registration examinations	Registration examinations. Other provinces: waivers possible	Registration examinations
Nursing	Registration examinations	Registration examinations	Registration examinations
Occupational therapy	Certification examination	Certification examination	Certification examination
Ophthalmic dispensing	Professional examination	Professional examination	Professional examination
Optometry	University of Waterloo comprehensive examination	Board qualifying examination	n/a
Osteopathy	Written, oral, and practical examinations (but not set since 1952)	Written, oral, and practical examinations (but not set since 1952)	Written, oral, and practical examinations (but not set since 1952)
Pharmacy	Jurisprudence examination (part of standard program); qualifying examination	Jurisprudence examination (part of standard program); qualifying examination	Jurisprudence examination (part of standard program); qualifying examination
Physiotherapy	No examination	Canadian Physiotherapy Association examination for U.S. graduates	Canadian Physiotherapy Association examination, except for certain U.K. graduates

	Ontario	Other Provinces/ United States	Elsewhere
Psychology	Examination for Professional Practice in Psychology (EPPP) and oral examination	EPPP and oral examination	EPPP and oral examination
Radiological technology	Canadian Association of Medical Radiation Technologists (CAMRT) qualifying examination, or Board examination if candidate has not done CAMRT examination	CAMRT qualifying examination, or Board examination if candidate has not done CAMRT examination or is not from reciprocal or acceptable jurisdiction	CAMRT qualifying examination except if from reciprocal country, or Board examination if candidate has not done CAMRT examination or is not from reciprocal or acceptable jurisdiction
Real estate and business brokerage and sales	Examinations as part of required training courses; exemptions available	Examinations as part of required training courses; exemptions available	Examinations as part of required training courses; exemptions available
Social work (OCCSW)	Certification examinations	Certification examinations	Certification examinations

	Ontario	Other Provinces/ United States	Elsewhere
Veterinary medicine	Jurisprudence examination (exempt if applied to OVA within one year of graduation)	Other provinces: jurisprudence examination. U.S.: Jurisprudence examination; National Board Examination (NBE); Clinical Competency Test (CCT)	Jurisprudence examination; NBE; CCT; Clinical Proficiency Examination

CHAPTER 7

Language Testing

While proficiency in English is a very reasonable expectation of anyone who is to have contact with patients in Ontario, the rigidity of the legislated standards is highly questionable. We have encountered numerous candidates who have either completed prior training in English-speaking settings (including other Canadian provinces or the United States), who have trained in countries where English is an almost universal second language (Holland, Sweden, Israel), or who have passed other tests of English proficiency, but who cannot be licensed. Of even greater concern is the fact that the legislated minimum scores may be unrealistically high. We have seen candidates who have been functioning extremely well in English in other Canadian provinces, but who still fail to "make the grade," often because of relatively minor grammatical errors.

— from a Brief submitted to the
Task Force by an Ontario hospital

One of the greatest challenges for an arriving immigrant to Ontario who knows little or no English or French is to learn a new language. Not only is it a necessity of day-to-day life, but the ability to speak and write English or French is effectively, if in some instances informally, a prerequisite of obtaining registration in occupational associations. It is also a significant factor in gaining entry to an educational institution or to the workplace. Time after time, in briefs from foreign-trained individuals, in meetings with the immigrant communities, and in interviews with the professional bodies, the fact of language was raised before the Task Force as posing a significant barrier to the entry of immigrants into the Ontario workplace.

Although the limited availability of language training is the greatest contributor to this difficulty, also of considerable significance is the question of language testing. All professional associations, to some degree, consider fluency essential to safe practice, and thus some assessment is necessary for registration. In the trades, too, fluency can be viewed as essential to public safety, and the level of language proficiency must be ascertained. Because educational institutions play a large role in the retraining of candidates trained outside Canada, their use of language tests is also of interest to our study. In this chapter we consider how testing is already being done and whether the present methods are satisfactory.

The Task Force recognizes and supports the right of professional bodies, ministries, and educational institutions to require an adequate level of language skill. Indeed, we would go further and endorse the use of some form of language assessment for ensuring public safety and providing immigrants with guidance on their linguistic competencies. A language assessment is necessary in order to determine whether a person is sufficiently proficient in English or French to carry out occupational duties effectively. If not, then the test can give the person an indication of the kind of English or French as a Second Language training he or she requires in order to reach the desired level of proficiency. As with all the other licensure requirements discussed in this Report, however, the body administering the assessment and relying on its results must be able to demonstrate both that the level of proficiency required is appropriate and that the instrument used to assess proficiency measures the type of proficiency needed for the specific profession or trade.

A number of submissions emphasized that· in a multilingual environment it is desirable, even necessary, that professional services be available in the language of the client or patient, particularly in areas such as psychology, social work, and medicine. This reality does not, however, alter the fact that registered professionals must be able to provide their services in English or French. The need to service multicultural communities is a very significant issue and may be met in many ways — through recruitment, incentive programs to encourage members of these groups to work within their communities, or supplementary retraining programs — but it cannot be met through a general easing or altering of basic linguistic requirements. (The issue is discussed in Chapter 2, "Foreign-Trained Individuals in Ontario," and in Chapter 9, "Retraining.")

CURRENT PRACTICES

Virtually all the educational institutions in Ontario require formal standardized language testing for entry. (See Table 7-A1 in the appendix at the end of this chapter.) The most commonly used test is the Test of English as a Foreign Language (TOEFL), with the Test of Spoken English (TSE) and the Michigan Test Battery (MTB) also widely used. The professional bodies (see Table 7-A2) and, in the trades, the Ministry of Skills Development,[1] employ a variety of means to ensure fluency. Some employ standardized tests such as the TOEFL (e.g., medicine, pharmacy, nursing); some have developed their own language tests (e.g., pharmacy); others rely on their licensing examination to screen out candidates who lack fluency (e.g., dentistry, medical laboratory technology, funeral services). In some professions, the question of fluency testing has not been addressed directly at all, either because of a limited number of applicants from countries where English or French is not the language of instruction (e.g., denture therapy) or because other standards of entry effectively screen virtually all non-English-speaking candidates (e.g., optometry). In such cases the professional bodies generally hold the view that the licensing or certification examination can act as an effective screen.

Non-Standardized Tests

Of the professional and occupational groups we reviewed, only one has developed its own formal test to assess language. The College of Pharmacy of Ontario administers an oral examination to assess comprehension and communication. This test measures a candidate's ability to take and understand instructions and orders given over the telephone and to discuss a prescription over the counter with a customer. Those who studied in a country where neither English nor French is the official language must demonstrate fluency, as must those who studied pharmacy in a language other than English or French or those whose fluency is in doubt. Sixty per cent is a pass, and three attempts are allowed. There is nearly a 100 per cent success rate on this test, which is administered as part of a language requirement that includes the TOEFL. The TSE may be substituted for the oral test if the candidate wishes.

Other instances of non-standardized tests include the use of interviews. Candidates for licence as professional engineers whose fluency is questioned by a referee may be invited to attend an interview with the assessment committee of the governing body; naturopaths and ophthalmic dispensers also conduct interviews to assess fluency.

Such tests, which have the advantage of measuring how an individual performs when talking and listening to someone, are different from the standardized tests, which place greater emphasis on grammar and syntax. The non-standard tests also permit the testing body to focus in its assessment on the technical language and linguistic skills actually necessary to perform the job. For example, in pharmacy, taking a telephone order and counselling a customer on drug use are the tasks that require careful communication; by means of the interview examination, these two are specifically tested. Although the main drawback to the interview method is, as with all oral examinations, the introduction of subjectivity, this deficiency can be minimized if the test is properly developed and administered.

Standardized Tests

The Task Force's review of the language tests used by the professional bodies indicates that the most commonly used standardized language tests are the TOEFL, the Test of Spoken English (TSE), and the Michigan Test Battery (MTB).[2] These are also the tests used most often by postsecondary institutions to assess applicants for admission purposes. In addition, a group of researchers from several Ontario universities has developed a new standardized English proficiency test: the Ontario Test of English as a Second Language (OTESL). The objectives of this test, which is currently used only by some academic institutions in Ontario, are summarized later in this chapter.

The Test of English as a Foreign Language (TOEFL)

The best-known and most commonly used language test in North America is the TOEFL, which was created in 1963. In literature on the subject, the TOEFL is referred to as a standard against which all other tests of English proficiency are measured. It is used by universities, businesses, and industry. The Educational Testing Service (ETS) administers the test under the direction of a policy council that was established by, and is affiliated with, the College Board and the Graduate Record Examinations Board. Canada maintains representation on the policy council.

ETS "is a private, non-profit corporation devoted to measurement and research primarily in the field of education."[3] Its international office assists in collaborative research and arranges conferences all over the world. ETS teaches educators "how to construct and administer tests, interpret the results, and apply these and other techniques in their own educational systems."[4] The service has the world's largest open library of published assessment instruments and tests and, in addition, houses the Educational Resources Information Centre (ERIC), which collects, catalogues, indexes, and abstracts unpublished material.

Twenty-six years after the TOEFL was initially developed, it has evolved into the form used today: a three-part test composed of listening comprehension, structure and written expression, and vocabulary and reading comprehension. The test is entirely multiple-choice.

The listening comprehension section is intended to measure the examinee's ability to understand both the words spoken and the underlying message given by the speaker. Examinees listen to a tape and answer questions designed to measure if they can determine what written statement is closest in meaning to the spoken statement (Part A), if they can follow a conversation between two speakers (Part B), and if they can answer a series of questions on short talks and conversations (Part C).

An examinee's grasp of formal structure and grammar is measured in the structure and written expression section. The material used is either on standard academic subjects or on information about United States history, culture, or geography. Examinees must complete two parts: in the first, they choose a word or phrase that completes a sentence; in the second, they choose one of four words that is unacceptable in standard written English.

The third section, vocabulary and reading comprehension, contains two parts. In the first part, the examinee chooses a word or phrase that best preserves the meaning of the sentence when substituted for an underlined word or phrase. In the second part, the examinee reads several passages and answers a number of questions about each one. This section measures the examinee's ability to understand the meanings and uses of words in standard written English and the ability to understand reading materials.

All new questions undergo a rigorous review of content and a statistical analysis before they are selected or rejected for the final test forms. ETS looks for cultural and racial bias; for language, content, or symbols that are offensive to major groups of the TOEFL population; and for content appropriateness (does the question ask what it should?). Statistical analyses are done again after the administration of a new test form to verify that the questions are working as expected and to monitor the level of difficulty.

The test results include three section scores and a total score. ETS converts the raw scores of the sections and the total test to standard scores by means of a scale, ensuring that reliability is maintained by relating statistically each test form to all the others.

ETS issues a set of guidelines to all institutions that accept TOEFL scores. These guidelines point out that the standard error of measurement of two-thirds the examinees is 14.1 points, but for 95 per cent it is 28.2 points. These figures indicate that for two-thirds of the people who take the test, a score of 500, for example, is equal to any score between 485.9 to 514.1. For 95 per cent of the examinees, the range equal to 500 extends to between 471.8 and 528.2. Each of the sections also has a standard error of measurement that should be taken into account. Because of this standard error of measurement, ETS strongly discourages the use of rigid cut-off scores and instead advocates ranges. Ranges, ETS suggests, should prevent examinees who achieved a score equivalent to but below the cut-off score from being denied admission.

The guidelines also note that the scores should not be used to predict academic success because research studies have *not* shown a strong positive correlation between grade point average (GPA) and TOEFL scores. The guidelines further suggest that information on the validity of an institution's TOEFL score requirements should be assembled at that institution in order to assess the current standard. They also strongly advocate using other measures, such as interviews, in conjunction with the TOEFL. As well, consideration should be given to the subscores, which can give more detailed information on the proficiency of the test taker.

The Test of Spoken English

ETS administers the Test of Spoken English (TSE) under the direction of the TOEFL policy council. The TSE was designed primarily for academic institutions, but research is currently under way to assess its validity for use by professional associations. The TSE is about 30 minutes long and is administered to examinees who speak their answers into audiotapes.

The TSE consists of seven sections. The first section is an unscored warmup exercise, designed to relax the examinee, that asks basic biographical questions. The second section tests pronunciation and overall clarity of speech. The examinee reads a passage out loud following preliminary silent reading. In the third section the examinee reads a series of 10 partial sentences, which he or she then completes orally, preserving meaning and grammar. The examinee next tells a detailed story based on a series of pictures. The fifth section requires the examinee to answer a series of spoken questions about a single picture. In the sixth section, the examinee answers a series of spoken questions on general topics designed to generate lengthy and detailed responses. This section measures the linguistic quality and adequacy of speech rather than content. Finally, in the seventh section, the examinee reads a printed section and then describes it out loud in his or her own words.

ETS calculates four scores for the TSE: overall comprehensibility, pronunciation, grammar, and fluency. Each score is independent of the others. The latter three are diagnostic and intended to give a more detailed analysis of the examinee's performance. The scores can be referenced to a comparison table, which is based on the scores of examinees tested over a recent period.

The test tapes are rated independently by two trained TSE raters (who are qualified in English, ESL, or linguistics) and by a third if the two raters disagree on any of the sections. If, of the three, two are in agreement, their score is assigned; if all three disagree, an average is taken of the higher two ratings.

Like the TOEFL guidelines, the TSE guidelines advise against rigid cut-off scores, advocate strongly the use of other measures, and recommend looking at the diagnostic sections as well as overall comprehensibility.

The *Manual for Score Users* for the TSE defines the overall comprehensibility scores thus: 0 to 90 means the overall comprehensibility is too low even for simple speech; 100 to 140 means speech is generally incomprehensible because of frequent pauses and/or rephrasing, pronunciation errors, a limited vocabulary, and lack of grammatical control; 150 to 190 means speech is generally comprehensible but with frequent errors in pronunciation, grammar, choice of words, and some pauses and rephrasing; 200 to 240 means speech is generally comprehensible with some errors in pronunciation, grammar, choice of words, or pauses or occasional rephrasing; 250 to 300 means normal speech is completely comprehensible with occasional grammatical or pronunciation errors in very colloquial phrases. The standard error of measurement on the overall comprehensibility score for two-thirds of the examinees is 15 points; and for 95 per cent of the examinees it is 30 points.

The Michigan Test Battery

The University of Michigan developed the Michigan Test Battery (MTB). The skills tested and the purpose of the MTB are the same as for the TOEFL. The MTB is composed of three tests: the Michigan Test of Aural Comprehension, the Michigan Test of English Language Proficiency (MTELP), and the Michigan Composition Test. The MTB takes a total of 130 minutes to complete: 25 minutes for the test of aural comprehension, 75 minutes for the MTELP, and 30 minutes for the composition test.

As can be inferred from the names of the three tests, the test of aural comprehension tests listening skills; the MTELP tests grammar, vocabulary, and reading skills; and the composition test tests writing skills. The University of Michigan grades the tests. Although the MTB tests the same skills as the TOEFL and although the MTELP has concurrent validity with the TOEFL,[5] the MTB differs slightly from the TOEFL in structure and content. Although it has questions similar to those in Part A of the TOEFL's listening comprehension section, the MTB's test of aural comprehension does not have conversations or mini-talks like those in Parts B and C of the listening comprehension section of the TOEFL. The MTELP contains one-paragraph reading passages similar to those from textbooks; the section on vocabulary and reading comprehension in the TOEFL contains one-sentence passages or short passages from newspapers or bulletins. And where the MTB's composition test requires a one-page composition on one of two or three topics, the TOEFL requires the candidate only to identify errors in sentences. The TOEFL requires no writing. (Note that in 1987-88 ETS began offering a Test of Written English to overcome this problem with the TOEFL. This test is given in conjunction with the TOEFL at selected administrations.) The differences between the TOEFL and the MTB can result in an examinee's attaining different scores on the two tests. For example, the greater emphasis in writing skills in the MTB may cause candidates with relative weakness in that area to score lower on the MTB than they would on the TOEFL.

STANDARDIZED TEST DEFICIENCIES

The virtues of standardized tests such as the TOEFL, TSE, and MTB are that they can, if properly administered, be valid, specific, and reliable. At the same time, and in part by virtue of their very nature as standardized tests, they have serious deficiencies. The TOEFL is the most commonly used test in Ontario, and so most of our commentary will be directed at it; generally, however, the suggestions made apply equally to the other standardized tests reviewed.

One suggested defect of the TOEFL is that it may contain a general bias against non-North American test takers for two reasons: first because a significant segment of the content is related to North American (indeed, U.S.) culture and history; and second, because the accent on the tapes is North American.[6] The possibility of cultural bias based on content is acknowledged by some commentators and raises a difficult issue because no test of language can exist entirely isolated from knowledge and information. Whether cultural elements are evident in these standardized language tests to the extent that they distort results is not something we are equipped to decide; we have, however, heard sufficient criticism of the tests on this subject to be convinced that there is some likelihood that such is the case. With regard to the criticism concerning accent, the most common response, and one that we respect, is that as North American English is what the test taker must adapt to in any event, it is not inappropriate that it predominate on the examination. Fairness would require, however, that candidates unfamiliar with the accent have a significant opportunity to practise the tests in order to adapt to it. This opportunity is available through the TOEFL sample test record.

Based on our review of the relevant literature and interviews both with individuals in the field of language testing and with test takers, it appears that the greatest deficiencies of the TOEFL and the other standardized tests may lie in their administration and application.[7] They are as follows:

Setting of Cut-off Scores

As we have discussed, the TOEFL has a standard error of measurement of about 28 points on the total score for 95 per cent of the examinees. In order to reflect this fact, the guidelines from ETS make the recommendation that any pass/fail standard should be set as a range and not as a specified cut-off score. Our review indicates that this recommendation is essentially never followed, although the principle has been formally endorsed in a decision of the Health Disciplines Board.[8]

Although the logic of this position is apparent given the fact of the error of measurement, the practical effect of the application of a range instead of a cut-off is simply the lowering of the cut-off to the low end of the range. The fundamental issue, therefore, is the appropriate setting of the cut-off.

The score set should reflect the language needs of a particular discipline. Our review has disclosed that in most cases the cut-off score is set arbitrarily or according to common practice in other fields and is not formally followed up or validated in any way within the institutions using the test. A comment often made to the Task Force was that the standard required in many cases is high; even someone whose first language is English can have difficulty with parts of the test. One therefore can encounter the situation of a candidate, perhaps in a highly technical discipline in which general fluency does not play a big part, being required to meet a high standard in a test that requires general fluency only.

Interpretation of Scores

Some studies show a significant positive correlation between the TOEFL and academic performance, but most studies show no, or a low, positive correlation.[9] The ETS guidelines point out that the TOEFL is a test of English proficiency and not a predictor of academic success. Put another way, it primarily tests knowledge, not performance.

The TOEFL is generally characterized as a discrete-point rather than an integrative test, although the listening comprehension section is considered to relate closely to integrative tests. In a discrete-point test, all items are independent; on an integrative test there is an interdependence among the items. Integrative tests are considered by many analysts to have higher validity but less reliability owing to greater subjectivity. They are better indicators of performance.

The effect of this characteristic is that candidates are tested against a standard of fluency that bears little relationship to the language needs of the work they plan to undertake. For this reason, criticism of the TOEFL and comparable standardized tests is widespread among test takers and experts in the field. Comments we received in briefs and submissions varied, from expressions of concern that reliance on the tests places too great an emphasis on general language skills to outrage at the unfair burden that these tests place on foreign-trained individuals. Consider this comment from an individual brief submitted to the Task Force:

> *I would have to take the TOEFL to enter the pre-internship program even after having evidence of proficiency in the language, i.e. Canadian degrees, FLEX [Federation Licensing Examination] examination, teaching in Canadian universities, numerous public speaking engagements, writing of grant applications and numerous publications in English. Is the TOEFL examination a better assessment of my proficiency in English than my professional and educational records?*

And this one from a brief submitted by a specialist in the field:

> *. . . the TOEFL and TSE examinations have also been highly criticized as limited and misleading indicators of non-native English speakers' abilities to communicate effectively in English. There is ample anecdotal evidence of fluent, proficient students failing the exams and of students who pass with minimal communicative competence in English. But there are also a number of well-founded reasons for this criticism in the structure and content of the tests themselves . . . the tests are not only misleading, but insidious barriers to non-native speakers' fair admission into Canadian society.*

ALTERNATIVES TO STANDARDIZED TESTS

The deficiencies described are not peculiar to the TOEFL but are likely to be reflected to greater and lesser degrees in any standardized fluency test of such general application. The security that can result from the use of such admittedly reliable tests must be balanced against the far greater relevance (and therefore fairness) of tests designed to measure fluency within a particular discipline. Tests can be specifically developed for this purpose and could include oral or written components, interviews, and essays. The test currently employed in the profession of pharmacy is an example of one type of appropriate language test. It is essential that such tests be properly developed and that the examiners be properly instructed to administer them.

Licensure tests used to assess the general competence of candidates can be employed to assess fluency, as is currently being done in a number of occupational groups. The advantage of this approach is that such tests of necessity incorporate much of the occupation-specific language needed to practise. Using licensure tests as language screens does have the disadvantage of making it somewhat more difficult for a failed candidate to determine whether his or her failure was due to lack of knowledge or lack of language fluency. However, this weakness can to a large extent be corrected through the use of follow-up interviews and careful structuring of the scoring of the test itself.

Licensure tests are *not appropriate* as language screens *if language is not specifically addressed in their development*, and we are concerned that many of the bodies currently relying on them as language screens have not adequately addressed this question in their test development.

In Chapter 6, "Licensure Testing," we raise the need for proper development and validation of tests according to recognized standards and recommend that the application of these techniques be required as part of the development and administration of every licensure test administered by an occupational group. Such a procedure would ensure that the question of language is addressed and that the language of the test and the format chosen reflect the level and type of language fluency necessary for and appropriate to the occupation. As a result, these tests would serve as efficient and relevant measures of fluency. Use of these tests also has the additional benefit of eliminating the need for a preliminary, sometimes problematic, assessment of who needs to be tested for fluency.

We are of the view that such occupation-specific tests, if properly designed, administered, and validated with the assistance of experts in English or French as a Second Language and in testing procedures, display a greater potential for accuracy and fairness in language testing than do the TOEFL, the MTB, and like tests. Not only do occupation-specific tests ensure that candidates are not being required to meet a level of general fluency unnecessary and irrelevant to their work; they also ensure that such candidates *are* fluent in the particular language that is essential to safe and competent performance in the field.

The use of such discipline-specific tests would also assist in the effective teaching of English as a Second Language, which is currently distorted by the necessity to "teach to the TOEFL" instead of being free to emphasize the language skills the individual will need in his or her discipline. Finally, although fluency in French is formally considered an adequate alternative to fluency in English, the imposition of standardized English language tests is inconsistent with this fact. There is, we are told, no comparable French-language test available. The introduction of licensure tests or occupation-specific language tests in the French language would permit fair assessments of fluency in either language.

Our comments and recommendations extend to both the professions and the trades. It is apparent that the educational institutions in Ontario do considerable language proficiency testing, and although they do not fall directly within our mandate their practices have an impact on our study to the extent that they may affect the entry requirements of foreign-trained individuals to training. It is therefore necessary that we comment on their use of the TOEFL and other standardized tests.

The reliance by the educational institutions on the standardized tests for fluency assessment is, as Table 7-A1 (at the end of this chapter) indicates, more widespread than in the occupational groups.

The instituting of interviews, essays, and discipline-specific tests would be desirable, at least as a supplement to the standardized tests. In addition, colleges and universities would benefit from the introduction of flexibility into their interpretation and application of test scores, giving candidates in appropriate disciplines the opportunity to perform in the academic environment, perhaps on a trial basis, rather than denying entry entirely. For example, it is not unusual in the U.K. for students to be admitted with lower scores, given an opportunity to perform (typically with a different course load) and to practise their language skills, and then be retested for fluency. If they have progressed sufficiently, they are given a normal program of courses.[10]

Such a flexible approach would be particularly relevant for candidates attempting to obtain only a few credits to complete equivalency requirements. Following a first assessment of fluency, they might be admitted to the required courses, subject to the further requirement that they satisfactorily complete a language training course and/or perform at an acceptable level on a fluency test before the credits are issued. In disciplines in which discipline-specific terminology is significant, the development of such a vocabulary would ideally be reflected in any required programs and tests. Such a system would permit candidates to move more quickly towards equivalency, and therefore licensure, by allowing them to complete needed prerequisites while, and not only after, meeting language requirements. This approach likely would be more workable within the technological and scientific disciplines; in subject areas with a heavy linguistic component, such as law, a prior finding of significant linguistic competence would be necessary.

Finally, the Ontario Test of English as a Second Language may offer an alternative in the area of language testing for the purpose of academic admissions.

The Ontario Test of English as a Second Language

The Committee on Diagnostic Achievement Testing (CONDAT) of the Council of Ontario Universities requested a procedure for evaluating non-native speakers of English following their admission to Ontario post-secondary institutions. The principal investigators, other ESL educators in Ontario, and CONDAT members spent several years conducting preliminary studies. The result was a proposal for a project that, in the spring of 1983, the Ministry of Colleges and Universities and the Ministry of Education agreed to fund. While the preliminary work was being done, the Ministry of Education requested that the project also take into account ESL testing requirements and academic programs in Ontario colleges.[11]

The objectives of this project are:

The test should provide valid, reliable, feasible evaluation procedures of English language proficiency for Ontario post-secondary institutions, which can be administered locally, and which can serve the following purposes:

a)   determine whether students have the requisite academic English skills to be able to follow given courses of study in these institutions;

b)   identify those areas of English in which students require further tuition, and to provide diagnostic feedback for students and programmes;

c)   provide information for the appropriate placement of students in ESL courses and programmes;

d)   provide information interpretable across institutions for such purposes as facilitation of student transfers and feedback to secondary school programmes.[12]

The OTESL has been developed for use by academic institutions only. Responding to recent developments and trends that emphasize performance-rather than knowledge-based testing, the OTESL focuses on reading, listening, writing, and speaking in a context similar to an academic environment. It differs in another respect from standardized tests such as the TOEFL and the MTB in that it includes sections designed for students in particular disciplines. At the moment two such sections have been developed: social sciences, and science and technology.

The Ontario Test of English as a Second Language (OTESL): A Report on the Research,[13] discusses the theory behind the OTESL and the validity, reliability, and statistical data. Based on these "early returns," the consensus seems to be that the development of the OTESL represents a positive step in language testing because it appears to minimize some of the deficiencies of other standardized tests. Its applicability is, however, limited to academe.

RECOMMENDATIONS

The Task Force is of the view that language assessment is valid and desirable as a means both of ensuring public safety and of providing assistance to foreign-trained individuals in determining the strengths and weaknesses of their language skills.

> 7.1 *We therefore recommend that a program of language assessment to an adequate level of competence be carried out by all occupational organizations where it is in the interests of public safety to do so.*

As with all testing, language assessments are acceptable only if they are demonstrably fair. We are concerned that the standardized tests currently being employed by some occupational bodies are deficient both because they are limited as measures of performance and because they are not being used in accordance with the guidelines provided.

> 7.2 *We therefore recommend that:*
>
> * *The assessment of the fluency of candidates reflect the particular linguistic needs of the relevant occupational groups. This assessment should be made through the use of testing methods intended to test the level of fluency,*

technical language, and vocabulary relevant to those particular groups. Such tests should be developed with the assistance of language proficiency and testing experts and may take the form of structured interviews, essays, or written assessments. In the alternative or in addition, such language assessments may be conducted through the administration of licensure or certification tests, administered by the occupational body, provided those tests have been developed and validated according to recognized standards of test development and that they take into consideration the level of fluency and the particular linguistic demands appropriate to the occupation. The use of standardized tests such as the TOEFL, the TSE, and the MTB should be discontinued.

- *The fixing of a required score by any body or organization using a fluency test must be justifiable as accurately reflecting the language proficiency necessary to carry out occupational duties without jeopardizing the health, safety, or welfare of the public.*

- *Interpretation of scores should be clearly specified to the test user and the test taker if the result of the test is to be relied upon.*

- *The use of such language proficiency tests and the elimination of the reliance on standardized tests within occupational bodies should be phased in over the same three-year period as applies to the introduction of the Prior Learning Assessment Network.*

7.3 *To assist the administrators of language tests in meeting Recommendation 7.2, we recommend that the development and validation of occupation-specific language tests, although the responsibility of the occupational bodies themselves, be coordinated through the Prior Learning Assessment Network in the same manner as licensure test development and administration.*

7.4 *We recommend that educational institutions endeavour to introduce additional fluency testing methods as a supplement to, or even as a substitute for, standardized tests currently in use, and that, where appropriate, flexibility be introduced into the interpretation of test scores.*

7.5 *We recommend that in all cases the results of tests be made available and explained to candidates and that candidates be directed, if necessary, to appropriate English or French as a Second Language courses.*

7.6 *We recommend that all candidates for language testing be directed to preparatory courses or be given detailed preparatory material.*

7.7 *We recommend that all the above apply equally to French-language testing.*

APPENDIX

Table 7-A1 Language Testing in Educational Institutions — Required Scores

Institution	Test of English as a Foreign Language (TOEFL)	Michigan Test Battery (MTB)
Universities:		
Brock	550 (varies according to course of study)	
Carleton	580	
Lakehead	550	
Laurentian	550	85 or 95 (depending upon program)
McMaster	580	85 or 90 (depending upon program)
Queen's	580	90
Trent	550	85
University of Guelph	575	

Institution	Test of English as a Foreign Language (TOEFL)	Michigan Test Battery (MTB)
University of Ottawa	550 (science and engineering), 580 (other faculties). If candidate scores 20 points below the minimum, but provides other evidence of English language competence, he or she may be admitted	
University of Toronto	580	90
University of Waterloo	580 (possible exemptions for those who studied in English)	
University of Western Ontario	550	85 (with no less than 80 in any section)
University of Windsor	550 (science and engineering will consider scores in the range of 500 to 540, if academic score is superior)	
Wilfrid Laurier	560	90

Institution	Test of English as a Foreign Language (TOEFL)	Michigan Test Battery (MTB)
York	580	90
Colleges of Applied Arts and Technology:		
Algonquin	550	
Cambrian	500	
Canadore	550	
Centennial	550	90
Confederation	500	
Durham	520-550 (range)	
Fanshawe	550	85
George Brown	550	90
Georgian	550 (those who score below 550 but not lower than 300 are placed in a suitable ESL program)	
Humber	550	
Loyalist	500 (may administer internal test)	
Mohawk	535	
Niagara	550	

Institution	Test of English as a Foreign Language (TOEFL)	Michigan Test Battery (MTB)
Seneca	550	
Sheridan	550	
Sir Sandford Fleming	520	
St. Lawrence	550	
Ryerson Polytechnical Institute	580	90

Notes:
1. No information available for these colleges of applied arts and technology: Conestoga, Lambton, Northern, Sault, and St. Clair.

2. The scores indicate the general overall requirements for undergradute studies only. Requirements vary according to program of study for most colleges and universities. Most schools offer English as a Second Language classes to upgrade applicants' language skills. In addition, some institutions may administer their own language tests to assess proficiency.

Table 7-A2 Language Testing in Occupational Organizations — Required Scores

Profession	Comments	Test of English as a Foreign Language (TOEFL)	Michigan Test Battery (MTB)	Test of Spoken English (TSE)
Accounting:				
Certified general accounting	No formal testing. Applicants must complete approved business communications course prior to second academic year or sit a challenge examination; language component must be satisfied or applicant required to attend a course to improve language.			
Certified management accounting	No formal testing. Students may take time off from program to study English if necessary.			
Chartered accounting	No formal testing.		Requirement of MTB removed October 1987.	

Profession	Comments	Test of English as a Foreign Language (TOEFL)	Michigan Test Battery (MTB)	Test of Spoken English (TSE)
Agrology	No formal testing, but written and oral examinations are in English; fluency necessary for successful completion.			
Architecture	The Attorney-General of Ontario has created an exception to the English language requirement for those who speak French, although the Ontario Association of Architects feels this practice jeopardizes public interest.		Must be taken if a candidate is from a country where English is not the official language. An average mark of 90 is required although the OAA may accept as low as 85. MTB may be waived if candidate has taken courses in English (spoken and comprehension).	

Profession	Comments	Test of English as a Foreign Language (TOEFL)	Michigan Test Battery (MTB)	Test of Spoken English (TSE)
Chiropody	Currently, all applicants are graduates of English-language training institutions, so specific language testing has not been instituted. For candidates whose training is in another language, the board has discussed the use of TOEFL and TSE assessments.			
Chiropractic	No formal testing. All eligible candidates have graduated from Council in Chiropractic Education-approved institutions, which use English as the language of instruction. Also, the Canadian Memorial Chiropractic College assesses language as part of its academic assessment;			

Profession	Comments	Test of English as a Foreign Language (TOEFL)	Michigan Test Battery (MTB)	Test of Spoken English (TSE)
(Chiropractic, cont'd.)	applicants for whom English is a second language must submit evidence of proficiency.			
Dental hygiene	No formal testing, but the ability to complete licensing examination is considered to be demonstration of fluency.			
Dental technology	No formal testing. A high level of fluency is not considered essential to this profession.			

Profession	Comments	Test of English as a Foreign Language (TOEFL)	Michigan Test Battery (MTB)	Test of Spoken English (TSE)
Dentistry	No formal testing, but a foreign-trained applicant for licensure must satisfy reasonable fluency in English or French requirement. This is accomplished through the licensing examinations.			
Denture therapy	If applicant has not received training in English or French then required to demonstrate "reasonable fluency." (So far, all applicants have been trained in English or French.)			
Dietetics	No formal testing.			

Profession	Comments	Test of English as a Foreign Language (TOEFL)	Michigan Test Battery (MTB)	Test of Spoken English (TSE)
Early childhood education	No formal testing by Ontario Association, but equivalency assessment involves an examination in which fluency is important for successful completion.			
Education (primary/secondary)	No formal testing. Ministry stopped assessing fluency in 1978 because it felt assessments by boards of education would be more appropriate. Local boards, upon hiring the holder of a letter of eligibility to a permanent position, attest to fluency of the teacher by signing letter of eligibility. Assessment process varies from board to board.			

Profession	Comments	Test of English as a Foreign Language (TOEFL)	Michigan Test Battery (MTB)	Test of Spoken English (TSE)
Engineering	No formal testing. Candidate from a non-accredited program must write a professional practice examination, which is informally used to ensure basic comprehension and communication in English. If a referee raises fluency as an issue, an interview may be conducted.			
Engineering technology	No formal testing. Candidates who do not have English as a first language may be assigned a thesis, be required to write the professional practice and ethics examination for assessment of language abilities, or be required to write the TOEFL.	May be required.		

Profession	Comments	Test of English as a Foreign Language (TOEFL)	Michigan Test Battery (MTB)	Test of Spoken English (TSE)
Forestry	No formal testing. Fluency is necessary for successful completion of oral and written examinations.			
Funeral services	No formal testing. Successful examination completion requires comprehension of English or French.			
Insurance brokerage	No formal testing. Examinations serve as language tests.			
Land surveying	No formal testing. Association feels written and spoken English is essential, and ability is assessed through oral and written licensure examinations.			

Profession	Comments	Test of English as a Foreign Language (TOEFL)	Michigan Test Battery (MTB)	Test of Spoken English (TSE)
Law		Written correspondence from a non-English-speaking candidate may indicate that candidate should be required to take the TOEFL.		If candidates have not received training in English then required to achieve a score on the TSE equivalent to 500 on the TOEFL.
Massage therapy	No formal testing. Fluency required to complete qualifying examination.			
Medical laboratory technology				

Profession	Comments	Test of English as a Foreign Language (TOEFL)	Michigan Test Battery (MTB)	Test of Spoken English (TSE)
Medicine	Examinations for non-Ontario graduates are held in English or French; fluency is considered critical for successful completion.	Graduates of a non-English or a non-French program are required to take the TOEFL and achieve a score of 580.		Graduates of a non-English or a non-French program are required to achieve a minimum score of 200 on the TSE or "a comparable score on a comparable French-fluency test" (none exists).
Naturopathy	English ability is assessed through an interview. If skills are not sufficient, then candidate is directed to English as a Second Language course before beginning upgrading.			

Profession	Comments	Test of English as a Foreign Language (TOEFL)	Michigan Test Battery (MTB)	Test of Spoken English (TSE)
Nursing	All candidates for certification must be reasonably fluent in English or French, yet there is no French language test equivalent to the TOEFL to test fluency.	Non-English-speaking nursing and nursing assistant candidates must achieve a score of 500 on the written part of the TOEFL and minimum of 50 in each of the component parts.		Candidates must achieve a score of 200, although candidates may be exempted if they provide proof of fluency through employment or post-graduate study.
Occupational therapy	No formal testing. Certification examination is given in English or French and taken to demonstrate language proficiency.			
Ophthalmic dispensing	No formal testing. Informal language assessment is made by competency committee; recommendation may be made that candidate take English as a Second Language courses.			

Profession	Comments	Test of English as a Foreign Language (TOEFL)	Michigan Test Battery (MTB)	Test of Spoken English (TSE)
Optometry	No formal testing. Regulations require that all applicants for licensure be fluent in English or French. If program is in another language, applicant must present evidence of reasonable fluency.			
Osteopathy	No formal testing; but the only osteopathic training institutions acceptable to board are in the United States, and instruction is in English.			
Pharmacy	Regulations require that applicant's English or French fluency be tested if applicant studied pharmacy in another language or if fluency is in doubt.	Score of 500 must be achieved. French fluency tests in the TOEFL model may also be administered (none exists).	A score of 80 is accepted as an alternative to the TOEFL requirements.	An oral test must be administered by the college; pass score is 60%, and three attempts are allowed. TSE is accepted as an alternative oral test.

Profession	Comments	Test of English as a Foreign Language (TOEFL)	Michigan Test Battery (MTB)	Test of Spoken English (TSE)
Physiotherapy	To be eligible to write examination in English or French and to complete clinical residency, non-English- or non-French-speaking applicants must demonstrate that language of instruction in their program was in English or French *or* pass the TOEFL.	A score of at least 500 on the TOEFL must be achieved if candidate cannot demonstrate that language of instruction was English.		
Psychology	No formal testing. If candidate is able to pass the English or French written examination for Professional Practice in Psychology, which all registered psychologists are required to write, then language ability is judged satisfactory. Extra time is allowed if English or French is a second language.			

Profession	Comments	Test of English as a Foreign Language (TOEFL)	Michigan Test Battery (MTB)	Test of Spoken English (TSE)
Radiological technology		Foreign-trained candidates are required by the Board of Radiological Technicians to achieve a score of 470 in the TOEFL if English is not first language.		
Real estate and business brokerage	No English language requirement.			
Social work	No formal testing. Association requires applicants to be fluent in English or French but assessment of language competency is left to employer.			
Veterinary medicine	No formal testing, although association is contemplating having candidate take the TOEFL or the TSE if his/her fluency is in doubt.			

CHAPTER 8
Language Training

The requirements for English proficiency constitute a tremendous barrier for most non-English speaking immigrants. On the one hand, various professions and trades require a certain level of English proficiency which may or may not be needed in the actual practice; on the other hand, immigrants find it almost impossible to reach that kind of proficiency because the necessary programs and supports are lacking.

— from a Brief submitted to the
Task Force by an organization

Lack of paid English training is probably the largest barrier for immigrant women. It is difficult for immigrants to take the time for proper English training . . . Lack of adequate training allowances are a barrier for all immigrants, especially single parents.

— from a Brief submitted to the
Task Force by an organization

Questions about the accessibility, adequacy, and appropriateness of the language training programs available to immigrants to Ontario were repeatedly raised before the Task Force, in meetings with immigrant service organizations and multicultural groups, in interviews with foreign-trained professionals, and in written submissions. Public input emphasized the tremendous importance of language training to immigrants who come to Ontario with needed skills but are lacking in the level of language proficiency necessary to put to use the training received in their countries of origin.

The Task Force considered language training to be an issue well within the scope of its inquiry. Although the primary mandate of the Task Force was to examine the possible discriminatory effect of the entry rules and practices of the professions and trades, included in the Terms of Reference were two directions that led us to examine language training programs. The Task Force was asked to:

3) Investigate actual or potential barriers beyond the control of the professions and trades, such as lack of support services during retraining periods; and

4) Recommend changes to rules and practices which cannot be justified as necessary for the maintenance of professional or trade standards, and recommend how foreign qualified persons can be assisted to meet those rules which can be justified.

This chapter builds on two questions raised in the preceding chapter, "Language Testing." First, given valid language proficiency standards and assessment methods for entry to the professions and the trades, what barriers impede the meeting of those standards? Second, how can foreign-trained people be assisted in overcoming such barriers?

In raising the question of whether appropriate language training is available to foreign-trained individuals seeking recognition of non-Ontario credentials, the Task Force quickly experienced difficulties in obtaining an overview of the full range of training programs offered in the province. The availability of courses varies from year to year and from community to community. Courses are offered on a non-permanent basis by many different organizations and funded through a variety of federal and provincial programs.

Partly in response to the lack of comprehensive information available, the provincial Government has recently begun a review of English- and French-as-a-Second-Language training (ESL/FSL) in Ontario. The Ministry of Citizenship is coordinating an interministerial review (with the Ministry of Education and the Ministry of Colleges and Universities) as the beginning of a new 20-year planning cycle for ESL/FSL funding and delivery in Ontario. The goal of this review will be to identify priorities for government action, particularly in relation to any deficiencies in the current programs, and there may be opportunity for public input. The first stage of the review is a survey by the Ministry of Education and the Ministry of Colleges and Universities of all programs offered by school boards, community colleges, and universities. The purpose of the survey, which is to be conducted in 1989, is to identify gaps in the range and distribution of programs available.

In the light of the ongoing activity within the provincial Government in relation to language training programs, the Task Force focused its attention on the particular problems of people seeking recognition of foreign training. We undertook to:

- specify those characteristics of a language training program that are essential from the point of view of the individual with foreign training seeking recognition of non-Ontario credentials or education;

- present an overview of the current funding and delivery apparatus, with the expectation that a full cataloguing of courses and programs will be produced in the current government review;

- identify key criticisms of the current system brought to our attention through submissions, meetings, interviews, and a sampling of published and unpublished papers;

- describe programs in other provinces that may be useful models for Ontario; and

- make recommendations regarding the scope of the ongoing government review of ESL/FSL programming and the establishment of programs to assess the language training needs of immigrants.

LANGUAGE TRAINING: A MODEL PROGRAM

The Task Force identified the following characteristics of a language training program designed to facilitate recognition of non-Ontario training and credentials:

- The proficiency level of written and oral language taught should reflect the language skills required for entry to and practice of the occupation for which the individual has been trained in his or her country of origin. The language proficiency requirements of the relevant occupation should be considered in assessing the duration and content of language training appropriate for each particular student.

- Courses should be flexible in duration and intensity, with full-time, part-time, evening, and daytime courses available. This flexibility will allow candidates with various levels of proficiency at entry to develop to the desired skill level at their own pace, and it will allow access by people with various scheduling needs.

- Language training should, where possible, be integrated with prior learning assessment and with any required retraining courses. Technical terminology and profession-specific and trade-specific language functions should be included in the curriculum.

- Basic language training with income support should be available to all immigrants without limitations based on immigration categories, intended labour force affiliation, employment prospects, level of skill, or level of training.

- In addition, specialized language instruction with income support should be available to bring language skills up to the level required for entry to the occupational field for which the individual is qualified on the basis of foreign training, education, or experience.

Terminology

In reviewing current ESL/FSL programming, the Task Force became aware of a number of loosely defined categories of language training that are useful for describing the content or nature of various programs. For ease of reference in discussing the current system, we draw on several key terms.

Basic English/French as a Second Language refers to language training for adults who do not speak English or French as a mother tongue. It is learned for purposes of getting along on an everyday basis in an English or a French community in Canada.

English/French for Special Purposes refers to language training for adults who are not native speakers of English or French. Training focuses on some particular need or interest the learners have in communicating in an English- or French-speaking community in Canada. Examples include learning the language for occupational purposes, for parenting, or for making use of community services.

English/French as a Second Dialect refers to language training for adults who are native speakers of a dialect that differs significantly in vocabulary, syntax, and pronunciation from standard oral and written

English or French in Canada. Language adjustment is required by learners in order to participate in life in Canadian communities.

English/French as Second Language Literacy refers to basic English/French as a Second Language training combined with basic literacy training for adults who are not native speakers of English or French and who are not functionally literate in any other language. In some cases, people who are functionally literate in languages that do not use the Roman alphabet are placed in this category because they need special help learning the writing systems. Adults who have had very limited experience with literacy may need instruction in literacy in their mother tongue as a bridge to literacy in English or French.

English/French for Academic Purposes refers to training of adults who are not native speakers of English or French to assist them in undertaking academic programs, usually at the postsecondary level. Such programs may focus on general academic language and study skills or may relate specifically to the vocabulary and forms of expression used in one field of study (nursing or sociology, for example).

FEDERAL PROGRAMS

Canada Employment and Immigration Commission

The Canada Employment and Immigration Commission (CEIC) is involved in ESL/FSL funding and delivery in three ways: (1) through the Ontario Ministry of Skills Development (MSD), it delivers the Labour Market Entry Language Training Program by purchasing ESL/FSL student places for eligible immigrants from the colleges of applied arts and technology; (2) it directly funds private language schools to offer ESL/FSL courses; and (3) through the Settlement Language Training Program (SLTP), it funds voluntary community organizations to offer language training. Each of these programs is described below.

Labour Market Entry Language Training Program

The Labour Market Entry Language Training Program has been established pursuant to the *National Training Act*,[1] as part of CEIC's "Job Entry" component of the Canadian Jobs Strategy (CJS). Introduced by the federal

Government in September 1985, the CJS provides federal support for labour market adjustment through a number of programs: Job Development, Job Entry, Skill Investment, Community Futures, and Innovations. Job Entry programs are directed to individuals who have difficulty entering or re-entering the labour market. The *Act* states:

> (3) The purpose of this *Act* is to establish a national program to provide occupational training for the labour force and thereby to better meet the need for skills created by a changing economy and to increase the earning employment potential of individual workers.

Officers of the Canada Employment Commission are given broad discretion to determine who is eligible to be enrolled in a course:

> (4) An officer may on the request of an adult, arrange for the enrolment of that adult in a course, if the officer is satisfied,
>
> . . .
>
> b) that the course is suited to the needs of the adult and is likely to increase his earning and employment potential.

According to the CEIC employment manual, language training under CEIC sponsorship consists of language courses specifically designed to remove the employment barrier that stifles the job search efforts of two categories of clients, namely:

> . . . skilled workers who cannot secure employment in their trade or profession or in a suitable related occupation because of a lack of fluency in a second language, and
>
> . . . unskilled workers who cannot be placed in suitable employment because of a lack of fluency in a second language.[2]

The basic criterion for language training under CEIC sponsorship is that the immigrant be "employment-destined."[3] Eligible trainees receive up to 24 weeks of full-time training. Part-time technical language training may be provided in special cases to teach occupational terminology when it is required by trainees to qualify for employment.

There are five types of income support available for participants in CEIC language programs: living allowance ("basic training allowance"), dependant-care allowance, commuting allowance, living away from home allowance, and long distance transportation allowance. The CEIC manual specifies that the basic training allowance is not available for those persons who enter Canada as immigrants in the family class or the assisted relative class, as defined in regulations pursuant to the *Immigration Act*.[4] Such immigrants enter Canada with undertakings of assistance signed by the sponsoring relative for periods of up to ten years in the case of family class applicants, and five years for assisted relative applicants. The sponsor must agree to be financially responsible for the sponsored immigrant.

The Canada/Ontario Agreement on Training, negotiated by CEIC and the Ontario Ministry of Skills Development (MSD) on behalf of Ontario, is the vehicle for the purchase by CEIC of language training places (seats) in community colleges. MSD effects the purchase and is reimbursed in full by CEIC for all the costs of a specified number of seats, including the cost of instruction materials, instructors' salaries, and the per diem costs of renting college facilities. It is CEIC's role to identify the volume of training required, to select the trainees and refer them to the community colleges, and to provide trainees with the training allowances. An annual budget for Ontario, expressed in training dollars and days, is worked out for ESL/FSL training by MSD and the regional CEIC offices jointly. In 1986-87, approximately $17.23 million was spent in Ontario on CEIC-funded ESL/FSL training at community colleges. Funding levels do not meet the demand, however, and it is significant that since 1985 federal funding for the purchase of language and skills training seats at community colleges has been cut across the country by 39.4 per cent. Of the 30,000 immigrants to Ontario in 1988 who spoke neither English nor French, less than one-fifth received any language training from CEIC.[5]

Funding of Private and Voluntary Language Schools

The Canada Employment and Immigration Commission funds a limited number of private and voluntary organizations that deliver language training to immigrants. In Ontario, the organizations that receive funding from CEIC to provide full-time ESL/FSL instruction are the Willis Language School in Ottawa, the Vietnamese Association of Toronto, and, also in Toronto, English as a Living Language. Training allowances to cover child care and transportation are provided directly to the trainees by CEIC.

In 1986-87, CEIC introduced the Settlement Language Training Program (SLTP), a pilot project designed to meet the language needs of immigrants not served under the CEIC Labour Market Entry Program, namely those, typically women, not immediately bound for the workforce. One million dollars was allocated to voluntary community organizations across Canada for the delivery of ESL/FSL training. Funding covered the costs of coordinators' salaries and benefits, curriculum development, teaching aids and supplies, and rent for instruction facilities. Child-care and transportation allowances were provided for trainees. Although $250,000 was designated for Ontario, only $105,000 was spent, owing to administrative difficulties.

The program was delivered by community agencies serving the immigrant population and consisted of approximately 15 to 30 hours of instruction per week over a 10- to 20-week period.[6] In September 1988, the Minister of Employment and Immigration announced new SLTP funding to put the program on a permanent basis. (At the same time, two other new CEIC language programs were announced: an ESL orientation program to be conducted overseas in refugee camps, and a new English in the Workplace program funded under the Canadian Jobs Strategy, exclusively for women.) Under the renewed SLTP, Ontario will receive $639,500 in federal funding for 1988-89.

Secretary of State: CILT Agreements

The Department of the Secretary of State provides ESL/FSL assistance pursuant to two federal-provincial agreements: the Citizenship and Language Instruction Agreement, and the Language Textbook Agreement. These are known together as the CILT agreements.

In contrast to the programs funded by CEIC under the direct purchase plan, which emphasize full-time instruction of people expected to enter the workforce, those funded by the Secretary of State are generally part-time and focus on helping newcomers to achieve Canadian citizenship and integration into Canadian society.

Secretary of State funding is received by the Ontario Treasury and can be used to offset some of the costs incurred by provincial ministries for ESL/FSL programs. Ontario ministries that administer ESL/FSL programs can claim full reimbursement of their ESL/FSL textbook costs and 50 per cent of certain of their teaching and administrative costs. In 1985-86, the Secretary of State spent approximately $2.4 million in Ontario under the CILT agreements, an amount that represents 27 per cent of the $9 million allocation Canada-wide.

Classes subsidized by CILT funding are offered primarily by boards of education and non-governmental settlement agencies, both of which receive the funding through Newcomer Language/Orientation Classes (NLOC) grants from the Ministry of Citizenship.

In Ontario the ministries of Citizenship, Colleges and Universities, and Education all received CILT funds for delivery of various language and citizenship programs.

Citizenship and Language Instruction Agreement

The Citizenship and Language Instruction Agreement was initiated in 1953 to fund programs designed to prepare newcomers to become citizens. Eligible students are defined in the agreement as "newcomers," who "have been granted permanent admission into Canada and have not yet acquired Canadian citizenship, exclusive of young persons in regular attendance at schools." Clients are given "citizenship instruction," which is defined as: "the teaching of the English and French language, and of the elementary facts about Canadian institutions and ways of life, to newcomers, for the purpose of facilitating their adjustment and integration into the Canadian community and of qualifying them for Canadian citizenship."[7]

Under the agreement, the Secretary of State undertakes to pay one-half of eligible teaching costs incurred by provincial governments for such instruction. Eligible costs include salaries and remunerations paid to teachers, program coordinators, and principals. They also include expenditures related to outreach activities.

Language Textbooks Agreement

The Language Textbooks Agreement, which came into effect in 1963, provides reimbursement to the provincial governments for their total expenditures — to a maximum based on the average of the previous five years' contributions — on language textbooks for use by adult immigrants in language instruction programs. Teachers and students are provided with language textbooks free of charge.

PROVINCIAL PROGRAMS: ONTARIO

Ministry of Citizenship

The Ministry of Citizenship funds direct delivery of language programs through its settlement agency, Ontario Welcome House, and non-government delivery of language training through the Newcomer Language/Orientation Classes (NLOC) grants. In addition, the Ministry provides funding for the English in the Workplace program, for a telephone tutoring service, and for the production and distribution of ESL/FSL materials, and it offers training programs for ESL/FSL instructors. Each of these services is described below

Ontario Welcome House

The Ministry of Citizenship funds and delivers language training through Ontario Welcome House (OWH), a service established by the Ministry in 1973 to respond to the needs of immigrants arriving from Uganda at that time. The main office is in downtown Toronto. There are also offices in Mississauga, North York, Scarborough, and Hamilton.

Ontario Welcome House provides a number of services. Upon first contact, usually by referral from the Canadian Employment and Immigration Commission's settlement branch, each client is given orientation information, including a publication entitled Newcomers Guide to Services in Ontario (available in many languages) and information on the different kinds of ESL/FSL classes available through his or her community. Often an immigrant will be given a specific referral to an appropriate language training program offered near his or her home or workplace.

The downtown Toronto OWH office offers five to six levels of ESL, ranging from literacy classes and special needs classes to advanced conversational classes (at the Grade 11 or 12 level). Immigrants who do not meet the eligibility criteria of the CEIC-funded courses or who are on a CEIC waiting list qualify for the OWH program. The registrar administers an oral placement test to anyone considered eligible by the counsellors to determine the level of placement. OWH houses a language laboratory and a resource room offering graded reading materials and tapes. Free day care is provided in the in-house nursery.

Language training at OWH is offered in sessions consisting of six weeks of half-day classes. Student intake is on an ongoing basis. Classes are free. OWH shares the cost of special ESL programs, such as those geared to particular ethno-cultural groups or combining computer skills training, with the Toronto Board of Education; the board pays the instructors' salaries. At the present time, OWH has a backlog of applicants to both the ESL program and the nursery. As an alternative, OWH refers students to local schools for language training.

In 1988-89, Ontario Welcome House and the Toronto Board of Education together served approximately 3,600 students in ESL classes.

Newcomer Language/Orientation Classes[8]

The Ministry of Citizenship, through its citizenship development branch, administers the Newcomer Language/Orientation Classes (NLOC) program, which in 1986-87 provided funding of $1,153,200 to 86 organizations provincewide to operate 355 adult language, orientation, and citizenship programs. Eligible programs include: ESL/FSL training (parent and preschool programs, and bilingual, literacy, workplace, and second dialect classes); citizenship preparation classes; and orientation classes. The sponsored organizations included multicultural centres, boards of education, colleges of applied arts and technology, libraries, ethno-cultural organizations, information centres, settlement houses, YW/YMCAs, and community committees. (The Ministry of Citizenship uses the term "community committees" to describe committees of local residents interested in newcomer integration. Members include representatives from schools, churches, social planning councils, business, and labour.)

The NLOC funding does not cover all the costs of the classes delivered under the program. The costs of outreach activities are included, as well as salaries for program coordinators, supervisors, and preschool instructors. Where programs are co-sponsored by local boards of education, approximately 60 per cent of the total costs are absorbed by the boards through salary payments. The Ministry of Citizenship recovers approximately 35-40 per cent of NLOC costs from the Secretary of State under the CILT agreements.

English in the Workplace Program

The English in the Workplace program is one component of the Multicultural Workplace Program supported by the citizenship development branch. Support includes funding for needs assessment, consultative assistance, and the development of training materials and publications. Financial support for this program, which totalled $660,000 in 1987-88, comes from special community-based grants and coordination grants.

Telephone Tutoring

The Ministry of Citizenship funds the Help a Friend Learn English (HAFLE) program, which uses telephone tutoring as its method of instruction.

The curriculum and tutor guides for this program were developed for use in the Spanish and Chinese communities in Toronto. HAFLE is now coordinated by community groups funded by the NLOC program. Partial funding for the HAFLE program comes from the Secretary of State under the CILT agreements.

Training Materials

Under the CILT agreement and with Secretary of State funding, the Ministry of Citizenship produces ESL/FSL textbooks, periodicals, and instructor-training materials. These are available free to delivery agencies, including school boards and community groups.

Instructor Development

The Ministry of Citizenship offers instructor-development courses to paid and volunteer ESL teachers. Instituted in the mid-1970s, these courses now are frequently co-funded by boards of education. The Ministry also funds "mini-ESL conferences" that are organized by the Teachers of English as a Second Language (TESL) Ontario affiliates, often with the cooperation of a local board of education or college.

Ministry of Skills Development

Ontario Basic Skills in the Workplace

The Ontario Basic Skills in the Workplace (OBSW) program is an integral part of a provincial training policy, the Ontario Training Strategy, announced in October 1986 by the Ministry of Skills Development (MSD). It is designed to help unions, employers, and employer/employee associations provide workplace literacy, numeracy training, and ESL/FSL instruction. The MSD may provide funding for up to 100 per cent of eligible program delivery, instruction, and associated administration costs. (It is preferred that 50 per cent of training costs be contributed by the employer and 50 per cent by the employee.)

The Ontario Federation of Labour in 1988 received a $1-million grant from the MSD under the OBSW program to develop a literacy program that includes ESL instruction. This program, Basic Education for Skills Training (BEST), is to be offered in 43 locations across Ontario. The focus of training is on literacy and ESL/FSL in conjunction with skills development and adult education.[9]

Ministry of Colleges and Universities

Colleges of Applied Arts and Technology

Colleges of applied arts and technology across Ontario deliver ESL/FSL courses at a number of levels on a full-time and part-time basis. ESL/FSL training in these institutions is financed by the Ministry of Colleges and Universities as part of the general funding provided to the community college system. Approximately 90 per cent of the ESL/FSL seats in the community colleges are purchased by the Canada Employment and Immigration Commission as part of the federal Labour Market Entry Language Training program.

Universities

The Ministry of Colleges and Universities, as part of its general funding for universities, provides provincial money for ESL/FSL teacher training in faculties of education. In addition several universities in Ontario offer ESL/FSL courses, either through a continuing education department or through a separate language training department, on an intensive and semi-intensive basis, part-time or full-time. Non-credit courses are offered on a cost recovery basis and often do not require applicants to fulfil university entrance requirements.

Ministry of Education

Boards of education across Ontario offer both full-time and part-time ESL/FSL classes. Full-time ESL/FSL training offered to adults by local boards of education is financed by the Ministry of Education. The Ministry pays a set annual amount ($1,900 in 1987, calculated on the basis of approximately 1,000 hours of instruction) for each full-time student.

Part-time ESL/FSL programs offered by the boards of education are financed by the Ministry of Education with partial reimbursement from the Secretary of State through the CILT cost-sharing agreement. Often courses are co-sponsored by the Ministry of Citizenship through the NLOC program. The boards provide salary payments and, in many cases, free space and supplies. Part-time ESL/FSL classes are usually offered in the evening and are free.

The Ministry of Education also provides the boards with guidance on curriculum, teacher development, and program organization.

OTHER PROVINCES

The Task Force reviewed the delivery and funding of language training in three other provinces: Quebec, Alberta, and Manitoba. Although particular circumstances render it impossible to make direct comparisons with Ontario, the Task Force believes that the examples of programs in other provinces will be useful for consideration by the interministerial committee currently reviewing language training. We recognize that Ontario receives about 50 per cent of all immigrants to Canada, with the result that all language and settlement programs have significant cost ramifications not matched in other provinces.[10] Nevertheless, we present a discussion of those aspects of programs in these three provinces that may be most useful for comparison purposes.

Quebec

Centres d'orientation et de formation des immigrants[11]

Since 1980, Quebec's share of immigrants arriving into Canada has averaged 17 per cent; in 1987, this translated into 26,640 people. Of these immigrants, an average of 39 per cent had no knowledge of English or French, and a further 24 per cent had English language ability only.

The Quebec Government places particular importance on the "Frenchification" of immigrants, because of the special concern for the situation of the French language in the North American context. The primary responsibility of the Ministry of Cultural Communities and Immigration is to ensure that immigrants learn the French language, adapt to Quebec society, and integrate into the labour market.

The language training branch of the Ministry offers a variety of programs aimed at making French language skills accessible to as many people as possible in order to promote their integration into the French linguistic community. Courses are delivered primarily through a system of eight guidance and training centres for immigrants, known as COFIs (Centres d'orientation et de formation des immigrants), five of which are in Montreal, with one each in Quebec City, Hull, and Sherbrooke. These centres are schools with counselling services and a day-care facility.

The Ministry contracts out program delivery to school boards and community organizations, particularly in areas of Quebec not served by the COFI system.

Both full-time and part-time courses are offered. Full-time courses are offered under two programs:

- The National Institutional Training Program (NITP), aimed at adult immigrants of varying immigration classes: refugees, independents, assisted relatives, and immigrants falling into the family class who plan to enter the job market and do not already speak English. About 2,500 adults benefit annually from these full-time courses, with federal financial assistance.

- The New Quebec program, which became effective in September 1988, aimed at adult immigrants already speaking English or not planning to enter the job market. These individuals, about 700 a year, will receive provincial Government grants.

The full-time courses run for 30 weeks, with 25 hours of classtime per week. A program is being developed that will include an evaluation, so that the student will receive a certificate upon completion of the course. Illiterate students (4 per cent of the total clientele) receive special attention.

Part-time courses, which are free, serve from 15,000 to 20,000 students annually. Three kinds of courses are offered on a part-time basis:

- Intensive daytime COFI courses offered in 4-week sessions of 16 hours per week at beginner, intermediate, and advanced levels.

- Tailor-made courses developed for particular clientele at the request of non-government organizations. The Ministry provides teaching staff and materials. Often community groups provide the premises and locate students.

- Evening courses offered at the COFIs in 5-week sessions of 2 or 3 evenings per week at beginner, intermediate, and advanced levels.

Since 1986-87, courses have also been offered to refugee claimants. More than 300 groups of students have been established. Courses last 180 hours.

The New Quebec program was of particular interest to the Task Force. Because it provides full-time training with provincial grants to adults not planning to enter the job market, the program uses provincial funding to meet the needs of adults not well-served by the existing federal language training programs.

Alberta

ESL Assessment and Referral Centres

Approximately 12,000 immigrants arrive in Alberta every year, representing about 11 per cent of Canada's total annual immigration; more than half cannot speak English.[12] In 1984, several government departments, immigrant aid agencies, and community organizations proposed that government-funded assessment and referral centres be established in response to a need for improved services to assist non-English-speaking immigrants in locating appropriate language training among the multitude of delivery and funding agencies.[13] The Alberta Government agreed to pay the cost of delivery, with the service being offered by Edmonton Catholic Social Services and the Calgary Immigrant Aid Society. The centres, which have standing advisory committees with representatives from ESL institutions, settlement agencies, and other interested parties, aim to serve as the link between the immigrant community and language, vocational, and academic upgrading, by helping individuals make education- and career-related decisions and gain access to ESL and other training courses.[14]

Each centre provides a number of specific services to the immigrant clients. Both Edmonton and Calgary employ full-time counsellors and ESL professionals fluent in languages most common to immigrants to Alberta. Both centres also employ speakers of other languages on an as-needed basis. Each client undergoes an assessment process that takes approximately 100 to 180 minutes and includes some or all of the following steps: an interview conducted in the client's own language, an assessment of English language skills, an evaluation of mother tongue proficiency, a discussion of the results with the client, and referral to suitable language or vocational training programs. The centres are finding that "repeat clients" are interested mainly in informal career planning. The client follow-up portion of the assessment involves contacting the individual client approximately three weeks after the first appraisal and determining the appropriateness of the initial referral through questions relating to ESL enrolment, financial assistance (where applicable), and job status. The centres request the return of 20 per cent of the clients for reassessment, three months after the first intake, for a further follow-up.

The two centres provide the province's ESL secretariat with statistical information on the demand for ESL. Demographic information, cultural and language background, and language proficiency are examples of the types of data collected. The statistics show that 3,231 assessments were performed in the 18-month period from June 1985 to December 1986. (The average number of clients processed per month for the two centres is 180.)

ESL Secretariat

In February 1985, the Government of Alberta established an interdepartmental committee to review adult English as a Second Language training. The committee produced a report in June 1985 recommending the establishment of an ESL secretariat, which today is housed and funded within the Department of Career Development and Employment but reports to an interdepartmental coordination committee (the Adult ESL Coordinating Committee).

In 1987, two major objectives were established as the focus of the secretariat's short-term activities:

1)   the development of a pilot project for an ESL student information system; and

2)   the development of a position on options for a provincewide standard system of measuring language competency.

The purpose of the student information system is to provide information about the number of individuals participating in ESL programs across the province. The reason for establishing a standardized system of measuring language competency is to assist in the record keeping of the number of individuals entering and exiting ESL programs at various levels. The system is intended to be a first step in the coordination of ESL curricula throughout the province.

A number of long-term goals for the secretariat, identified by the Government of Alberta, were of interest to the Task Force. These are:

•   to provide a description of the variety and number of ESL programs available throughout Alberta;

•   to provide liaison between the province and both the federal Government and community stakeholders;

•   to establish meaningful general language competency requirements for career entry and training entry;

•   to promote discussion of standardized ranges of language proficiency competencies with a view to promoting greater commonality in curriculum approaches; and

•   to examine the issues around professional development for English as a Second Language teachers, especially teachers of adult students.

Manitoba[15]

Funding of Language Training

Between 1983 and 1986, Manitoba received an annual average of 3,700 immigrants, representing slightly more than 4 per cent of Canada's yearly immigration. More than half these immigrants had no language capability in English or French.

In 1987, in response to the need for language training and to the widespread dissatisfaction with the then-current programs, Manitoba negotiated a unique funding arrangement with the federal Government. The Manitoba Government was concerned that dual funding was creating two uncoordinated language training systems, with a disruptive effect on students, who were often shifted from a provincial program (cost-shared with a Secretary of State program) to a federal program as they moved up the waiting list for CEIC-sponsored training. (See this chapter's earlier section, Federal Programs.)

The Government of Manitoba was also dissatisfied with the level of CEIC language funding in the light of the approximately 40 per cent reduction in CEIC National Training Agreement funds over the period 1985-88. In April 1987, Manitoba advised the federal Government that it would no longer sell community college ESL/FSL seats to the federal Government but would use Secretary of State funding to continue to offer community college language training. This arrangement was made possible by the open-ended nature of Secretary of State funding, with the notable result that the number of federal dollars for ESL/FSL actually increased. The objectives of the Manitoba Government in making this change in funding were identified as follows:

- to maximize the amount of federal dollars available to Manitoba for all types of training; and

- to ensure that decisions of student placement are based on educational grounds rather than purely administrative or funding concerns.

Manitoba completed a comprehensive review of language training in 1984, identifying the following six principles for restructuring the programs then in place:

1) coordination and consolidation of adult ESL training,
2) equality of access,
3) equality of condition,
4) coordination with other settlement services,
5) teacher development and recognition, and
6) input from and accountability to users and deliverers.

Implementation of the identified principles has resulted in the establishment of a number of language programs. Of particular interest to the Task Force is a continuing emphasis on English for Academic Purposes, and English in the Workplace programs. Many of the specific programs developed are small in terms of numbers of students by Ontario standards, but they serve as notable examples of how language training can be combined with skills training and retraining.

Finally, it is worthwhile to note also the position of the Manitoba Government in response to the question, "how much English is enough English?"

> . . . we must increase newcomers' English language competency to a non-discriminatory sufficient level so that the newcomer is able to compete on an equal basis with native English speakers for employment comparable to that which he/she practised or received training for in his/her country of origin, or be to a level which would permit the newcomer to receive appropriate training and/or services available to the mainstream population.[16]

CRITIQUE OF CURRENT PROGRAMS

The Task Force, in reviewing various government and non-government reports prepared in the past several years on language training in Ontario, found there to be a great deal of agreement on the shortcomings of the available programs.[17] We also found many of the same criticisms repeated in the written and oral submissions received. Although the Task Force was not able to assess and evaluate each of the perceived failures addressed in submissions and reports, we have set out the major criticisms that came to our attention. None of the comments listed below will be unfamiliar to government and non-government agencies involved in ESL/FSL delivery. For example, all of the criticisms were raised in the 1984 *Report of the Commission on Equality in Employment.*[18] The Government of Ontario should address each of these cited shortcomings in its current review of language training in the province. We would add that any comprehensive review of ESL/FSL in Ontario should afford the public the opportunity for input and comment. This recommendation is particularly appropriate in the light of the high degree of expertise in this area that exists outside of government in the ESL/FSL teaching community, in immigrant service organizations, in community delivery agencies, and in multicultural organizations.

Major Criticisms: A Summary

1) The dissemination of information regarding ESL/FSL programs is inadequate. There is a need for greater publicity, outreach, counselling, and referral.

2) The CEIC-Labour Market Entry Language Training Program is underfunded, with the result that the waiting list is unreasonably long. In Metropolitan Toronto the waiting period for eligible immigrants averages four to six months.

3) The 24-week program offered through the colleges of applied arts and technology, primarily to CEIC-sponsored students, is not sufficiently varied and flexible. It is not streamed to meet the particular needs of immigrants with differing proficiency levels at entry and differing goals for proficiency levels at exit.

4) Although the CEIC-Labour Market Entry Language Training Program is provided only to people who will be seeking employment, it is not of sufficient duration to allow many students to develop the language proficiency necessary for the practice of the profession or occupation for which they were trained before coming to Canada.

5) The CEIC-Labour Market Entry Language Training Program has unduly limited eligibility. It is available neither to immigrants judged not to be "destined for the labour force" nor to immigrants judged not to need language training to find suitable employment. Immigrant women without advanced training or education are particularly disadvantaged by the

eligibility criteria; the expectation is that they will find unskilled jobs which do not require language training.

6) The ineligibility of immigrants in the family class or assisted relative class under the *Immigration Act* for a basic living allowance while attending classes under the CEIC-Labour Market Entry Language Training Program has an inequitable impact on immigrant women.

7) The basic living allowance, when provided to CEIC-sponsored students, is often insufficient to meet actual living expenses.

8) The CEIC-Labour Market Entry Program fails to recognize a right to basic language training as an essential component of the settlement services that the federal Government should offer, at a basic level, to all new immigrants, regardless of actual or intended labour-market affiliation.

9) The discretion exercised by CEIC counsellors in deciding eligibility for language training needs to be reduced or limited by clear, public guidelines. A right of appeal should be available to applicants denied training.

10) The funding and delivery system lacks coordination at both the federal and provincial level. Too many branches of government are funding and delivering language training in an uncoordinated fashion without having clearly articulated policy goals.

11) There is a need for provincewide standards for ESL/FSL curriculum.

12) No adequate assessment is currently done of the language training needs of immigrants; in particular, entry and exit skills are not matched against occupational status. Prior learning assessment and career counselling should be offered together with language training assessment and referral.

13) Courses are not available to match the occupational goals of immigrants. English for Special Purposes courses geared to occupational goals are needed in areas such as science and technology, trades, and health sciences. Bridging programs should be available to combine skill acquisition with occupation-related language training.

14) ESL/FSL programs are not meeting the needs of the backlog population of immigrants who did not receive language training at the time of entry into Canada. It is estimated that more than 91,000 immigrants entering Canada between 1979 and 1984 had no capability in an official language

and did not receive CEIC-sponsored language training.[19] Of the more than 30,000 immigrants to Ontario in 1988 who spoke neither English nor French, less than one-third received any CEIC-sponsored language training.[20]

RECOMMENDATIONS

In recognition of the fact that policy changes at the federal level cannot be assured, it is important that this Report acknowledge that significant changes in language training delivery in Ontario would likely necessitate substantial provincial expenditures, particularly in view of Ontario's role as province of choice for 40 to 50 per cent of immigrants arriving annually in Canada. (If people who move to Ontario within the first one or two years of arriving in Canada are included, the percentage increases significantly.) Such an expenditure of public funds must, and inevitably will, be balanced against other spending demands of competing public value. Nevertheless, the Task Force urges the Government, in setting priorities, to recognize the very significant contribution of immigrants to the economic life and the social fabric of Ontario. English/French language capability is an essential prerequisite to full participation. Accordingly, we urge the Government to give a high priority to language training programs.

8.1   *We recommend that the Government of Ontario proceed as soon as possible to the second stage of its review of language training in Ontario. In relation to Phase II of the review, we make the following recommendations:*

- *The results of the survey of ESL/FSL programs by the Ministry of Education and the Ministry of Colleges and Universities should be made available to the public in a form readily accessible both in its presentation and its cost.*

- *The Ministry of Citizenship should establish an advisory committee of representatives from immigrant organizations, organizations of ESL/FSL teachers (for example, TESL Ontario), ethno-cultural organizations, and others. This committee would review the survey and assist in identifying program deficiencies. The mandate of the advisory committee should include the responsibility to report to the Ministry on its findings with respect to appropriate priorities for government action.*

- *In addition, the interministerial committee considering the survey results and the report of the advisory committee should invite written submissions from interested individuals and organizations on appropriate initiatives that the Government could take to improve language programs in Ontario.*

8.2 *We recommend that the interministerial committee reviewing ESL/FSL implement changes to training programs to incorporate the findings of this Task Force. Specifically, we recommend that language training incorporate the following characteristics designed to facilitate the entry of foreign-trained individuals into occupations that match education and experience obtained in their countries of origin:*

- *The function and proficiency level of written and oral language taught should reflect the language skills required for entry to and practice of the occupation for which the individual has been trained in his or her country of origin. The language proficiency requirements of the relevant occupation should be considered in assessing the duration and content of language training appropriate for each student.*

- *Courses should be flexible in duration and level of intensity, with full-time, part-time, evening, and day courses available. This flexibility will allow candidates with various levels of proficiency at entry to develop to the described skill level at their own pace, and it will allow access by people with various scheduling needs.*

- *Language training should, where possible, be integrated with occupational retraining courses, if such retraining is required to prepare the individual for practice in Ontario. Technical terminology and occupation-specific language functions should be included in the curriculum.*

- *Basic language training, with income support, should be available to all immigrants without limitations based on immigration categories, on intended labour force affiliation and employment prospects, on level of skill, or on training.*

- *Specialized language instruction geared to occupational sectors should be available with income support to bring language skills up to the level required for entry to the occupational field for which the individual is qualified on the basis of foreign training, education, or experience.*

8.3 *We recommend that the interministerial committee reviewing language training consider and respond to each of the criticisms at the end of the discussion that precedes these Recommendations. Although many of the comments relate to federal programs, it is important that the provincial review assess the validity of those criticisms so that Ontario can establish programs to minimize, where possible, the impact of shortcomings in federal programs.*

8.4 *We recommend that the Government of Ontario establish a provincial directorate with overall responsibility for language training for immigrants to Ontario. This directorate should work in conjunction with or as part of the proposed Prior Learning Assessment Network (PLAN). The directorate would be responsible for:*

- *compiling in a publicly accessible form a description of the various ESL/FSL courses provided throughout the province;*

- *assisting occupational groups in identifying the necessary level of proficiency required for entry to practice, this level to be reflected in the qualifying examination;*

- *making available to any immigrant to Ontario (including those caught in the backlog of people previously unable to access language training) an assessment of language training needs to determine appropriate entry and exit levels for training, these levels to be matched with the individual's educational and occupational background as evaluated by PLAN;*

- *referring immigrants to appropriate language training as indicated by language training assessments;*

- *developing and implementing a publicity strategy to bring the availability of the assessment and referral services to the attention of immigrants;*

- *compiling statistical information on the language training needs of the immigrant population, including the need for occupationally focused English/French for Special Purposes courses; and*

- *exploring alternative delivery methods for language training, such as those discussed in Chapter 9 of this Report, "Retraining."*

8.5   *We recommend that the Government of Ontario continue to negotiate with the federal Government for a return to 1985 funding levels for training programs under the Canadian Jobs Strategy. Further, we recommend that the Ministry of Skills Development, in renegotiating the Canada/Ontario Agreement on Training, explore all options that might afford Ontario increased language training dollars and/or greater autonomy with respect to program delivery.*

8.6   *In recognition of the unfairness of federally imposed eligibility restrictions on language training and on subsidies, which impact particularly on immigrant women, we recommend that the Ministry of Skills Development continue to discuss this inequity in negotiations with the federal Government in respect of the Canada/Ontario Agreement on Training. Language training should be recognized to be part of the settlement process for all immigrants, regardless of immediate employment opportunities or intended labour force affiliation.*

CHAPTER 9

Retraining

Faced with the problem of discounted credentials, immigrants who are determined enough to go through the retraining process in order to re-enter their profession often find themselves in total frustration . . . In many instances, the individual will have to succumb to economic reality, which forces him or her to give up the dream of re-entering the profession.

— from a Brief submitted to the
Task Force by an organization

Foreign-trained people seeking entry to professions and trades in Ontario bring significant assets of skill and expertise but may find themselves only partially qualified to meet the criteria for certification or registration. Our review of the rules and practices affecting occupational certification and licensure indicates that in many professions and trades there is a significant shortage of opportunities for retraining. This phenomenon in itself constitutes a barrier to entry to these individuals.

There are two aspects to the issue of retraining that particularly affect foreign-trained individuals. First, as this chapter's opening quotation indicates, it must be determined with accuracy what the individual's skill level is and what his or her precise retraining needs are; second, structures must be put in place to enable the individual to meet those needs. The first issue, the assessment of prior learning, has been discussed in Chapter 5. Our proposal for the creation of a prior learning assessment agency to oversee and provide learning assessments would offer if not a complete then at least a significant response to that issue. Yet such an assessment will take many candidates only part way to certification or licensure if the second component — access to retraining — is lacking. There is no question that, in many disciplines, retraining needs are not being met. Indeed, this response comes not only from disappointed and frustrated candidates but also from educational institutions and occupational bodies themselves.

Occupational retraining is not a new phenomenon, of course, nor is it relevant only to foreign-trained people who are partially qualified for entry to their chosen occupation. The overall importance of such training to Ontario's and Canada's economies has risen during recent years in conjunction with changes occurring in the world's economies. Any review of the access that foreign-trained people have to retraining opportunities should be referenced to these larger changes.

We are passing rapidly from an economic structure based on a mass economy to a new structure that some call the informative economy.[1] Whereas the mass economy is characterized by manufacturing capability that depends on large-scale extraction and consumption of resources, the informative economy uses a proportionately higher rate of information in the production of goods. The mass economy is characterized by economies of scale, with standardized goods being produced in large quantities by large numbers of workers and consumed by large groups of people. The informative economy is based on a shift to information-enriched goods — in design, engineering, durability, and utility — produced by fewer workers in greater variety to meet more specialized, as compared with mass-market, demands.

This shift has been accompanied by the introduction of increasingly sophisticated technology, human geographical mobility including international migration, and rising female participation rates in the workplace.

Fundamental to this shift in the economy is a changing relation in value among human resources, capital resources, and energy resources. For some businesses, industries, and, increasingly, community service agencies such as hospitals, adult continuing education has become as important a resource investment as equipment, buildings, or a reliable supply of energy. With this higher level of investment in training, the value of human resources has moved towards equivalence with financial capital.

Access to occupational retraining by a foreign-trained person seeking certification or licensure in Ontario should be viewed within this larger context, in which the very nature of work is undergoing redefinition, accompanied by changing demographic patterns related to birth rate, workforce participation rates, and immigration.

Foreign-trained people entering Canada typically must deal with the usual matters of settlement, including language, residence, location of services and facilities, socialization, and occupational certification or licensing procedures. In addition, many also must locate facilities for education and training. However, because the sources of education and training are not confined to formal educational institutions but are being provided increasingly in the workplace, the search can be complicated. As well, for many occupations there simply is a dearth of training possibilities.

In this chapter we outline the nature of the Ontario workplace, the changes occurring within it, and the basic education system. We then discuss provisions for retraining in Ontario and identify some of the barriers that professional people and tradespeople can encounter in their quest for educational retraining. Our recommendations relate to approaches that can be taken to speed the effective entry of foreign-trained people into their chosen occupations in Ontario.

THE ONTARIO WORKPLACE

Changing Nature of Work

Technological change has wrought profound and increasingly rapid changes in the distribution of the workforce. For example, the industrialization of North America resulted in the percentage of the U.S workforce in agriculture-related activities dropping from about 75 per cent of total workforce in 1820 to below 10 per cent in 1945. Occupational dislocation was minimal, because the slowness of the change generally permitted an individual to devote his or her working life to a single occupation, and occupational change generally occurred only from one generation to the next. An occupational choice was perceived to be a choice for a lifetime.

Automation and the introduction of computer-assisted design and manufacturing have produced a similar shift in the workforce, with a concomitant increase in occupational dislocation.[2] In this generation, highly specialized lawyers, teachers, bank and finance workers, government officials, computer operators, media and advertising personnel, and design engineers are among those making up the "information sector," which rose from about 17 per cent of the U.S. labour force in 1950 to nearly 60 per cent in the early 1980s. This current pace of technological innovations creates occupational dislocation, readjustment, and subspecialization on a continuing basis.

Technological change has not only affected the size of the required workforce in different occupational sectors; it has also changed the make-up of job tasks and the nature of their execution. Thus, a second consequence of structural changes in the economy has been the emergence of new kinds of work.

Patterns of rapid change in required knowledge and skills can be found in many long-standing professions and trades, as accountants adjust to desktop data processing, physicians and pharmacists to new diseases and interventions, and engineers and architects to changing environmental sensibilities and new construction materials. The nursing profession in Ontario has paid particularly close attention to knowledge change, and members of the profession who have not practised for five years are required to take upgrading before re-entering practice, a trend likely to be reflected throughout the health disciplines in coming years.

Rapid shifts in the nature of work inevitably result in occupational dislocation. The Canadian Government has stated that in 1984 alone, "more than 100,000 jobs were lost and hundreds of thousands of Canadians were seriously affected by technological change."[3] The implications of the increasing rapidity of change are readily seen. The level of knowledge that an individual has when leaving school cannot be expected to last to retirement, even if the individual stays in the same occupation.

Participants in a 1986 human resources management conference[4] were advised that in the service sector an employee's competencies can be expected to remain relevant for five years or less. The Carnegie Foundation for the Advancement of Teaching documented the boom in education and training within business and industry in response to job change and the failure of formal education to adapt. Business and industry expenditure on education and training, the foundation reported, is approaching that of public education, and slightly more people are obtaining education and training from business and industry than from formal postsecondary educational institutions.[5]

The 1985 Canadian Jobs Strategy (CJS) was designed to address the education and training issues arising from this rapid change, as was the Ontario Government's 1986 Ontario's Training Strategy.[6] Neither of these programs, however, makes explicit reference to, or provision for, the education and training needs of foreign-trained professional people and tradespeople.

Changing Demography of the Workforce

In 1983, Ontario's labour force was 4.096 million people. Net employment growth of more than 610,000 jobs between 1983 and 1987, of which almost 90 per cent were full-time, created an unprecedented strain on labour sources for the province's goods-producing and service-producing sectors. Overall, Ontario's goods-producing industries contributed just under 30 per cent of employment growth, which included manufacturing, construction, primary industries, utilities, and agriculture. The service-producing sector contributed the balance of new jobs.[7]

An important trend has been the increasingly rapid change in workplace competencies; both goods-production and service-production operate within an environment that is expanding the use of high technology. This change includes the automation of processes in design, manufacturing, and quality control; of offices; and of services, among them transportation, communications, health care, and retail. Tradespeople — from motor vehicle and autobody repairers to electricians and lathers — are finding their trades increasingly complex as new fabrication materials and computer-based processes are introduced.

As a result of such changes in the nature of work, dislocation within the labour force has been almost as significant a change as the total labour force growth. In the first half of the 1980s, for example, 7.8 per cent of workers aged 25-64 experienced job-abolition, an average of 73,000 per year; those affected averaged 8.5 years of work experience.[8] The great majority of these displacements were in manufacturing, which nevertheless made a significant contribution to employment growth in the province, accounting for 16.9 per cent of new jobs between 1983 and 1987. Clearly, the manufacturing sector is undergoing significant restructuring. This restructuring can be expected to continue in Ontario, particularly in the light of changes in economic relations between Canada and the United States through the free trade agreement.

The sources of labour are changing. Labour supply can be related to three factors: the birth rate, workforce participation rates, and rates of immigration.

Although the postwar baby boom had a growth impact on the labour force, current birth rates signal this factor's decrease as a source of labour in the coming years. The absolute decline in youth population began in 1980 and is expected to continue; the youth (age 15-24) share of the labour force is projected to decline from 22.3 per cent in 1986 to 17.4 per cent in 1996.[9]

The most significant change in participation rates in recent years has been in the increase of females in the labour force. Today, however, the rate of this change is stabilizing. Female participation rates near those of males, as the female share of the labour force is projected to increase from 43.9 to 46.2 per cent between 1986 and 1996.[10]

As summarized in Chapter 2 of this Report, "Foreign-Trained Individuals in Ontario," immigration continues to be an important, albeit fluctuating, source of professional people and tradespeople. Immigration to Canada since 1970 reached its high point of 218,465 in 1974, with a steady decline in the number of immigrants from 1980 to 1985 and a sharp rise to 152,098 in 1987. Since 1983, there has been an increasing percentage of immigrants designating Ontario as their province of destination, with 84,807 entering Ontario in 1987.

The data presented in Chapter 2 indicate that immigration from a number of capital- and technology-intensive countries has dropped and is being replaced by immigration from countries that are more labour-intensive. Immigration from Great Britain and Italy, for example, has dropped substantially, presumably as their domestic economies have improved. Immigration from Central Europe, Central America, the Caribbean, and some Asian countries has increased significantly.

Many foreign-trained professional people and tradespeople experience a technology gap upon entering Canada, and if efficient occupational entry is to be achieved, retraining programs need to be developed to address the specific gaps that exist.

Thus, traditional sources of labour are no longer readily accessible: the birth rate is falling; female participation rates are likely to level off; and there are few signs of any trend towards delayed retirement. Immigration appears to be of growing importance to the continued economic growth of Ontario, and it seems likely that an increasing percentage of the foreign-trained workforce will require not only language training but also workplace orientation and occupational retraining.

Unless the system — including fiscal commitment from federal and provincial governments and employers — is adjusted to serve this new client group efficiently and effectively, a principal source of human resources may not be utilized fully. The quality and extent of the education and training programs available to immigrants are not only important to their welfare as individuals, but also are essential to the collective welfare of Ontario.

It is necessary to re-examine education and training systems in order to remove barriers to entry and minimize the "down time" of those seeking certification or licensure in professions and trades in Ontario.

ONTARIO'S PUBLIC EDUCATIONAL SYSTEM

Current provisions for retraining are made by occupational groups and associations and by both privately and publicly funded educational institutions — primary/secondary schools, colleges, and universities. The following outline of the structure of publicly funded education in Ontario is intended to provide a base for examining the ways in which foreign-trained people seeking retraining can gain access to the services available.

In brief, a person being educated in Ontario passes through elementary school (eight grades) either into secondary school or into the workforce as an unskilled labourer. From secondary school, the person may enter the unskilled workforce, basic skills programs, apprentice training, or a post-secondary program of studies.

Colleges and universities typically require completion of Grade 12 plus a number of Ontario academic courses (OACs). Most institutions also make some provision for waiving these academic entrance requirements for underqualified adults who perform well in a trial enrolment period. Community colleges may admit a student at age 19 who has not completed high school. In some professions, specific upgrading or retraining courses required for certification or licensure can be obtained (subject to availability of space) from a college or university through a special student status, under which all usual prerequisites may be waived.

Many forms of adult continuing education are available and, depending on age and qualifications, an individual may enter any of them. Some adults might choose to enrol in a program designed purely for personal interest (for example, painting, gardening, personal computing). Others may elect to enter part-time formal education leading to a certificate, diploma, or degree, which typically is delivered by high schools, colleges, and universities, with the same entrance requirements as full-time studies. A third stream is basic education, including literacy and numeracy and the mastery of other skills needed in the workplace and society in general. Basic education is often delivered by community-based agencies as well as by formal educational institutions.

Retraining in preparation for a career change, updating of knowledge and skills in order to remain current, and upgrading for purposes of advanced qualification or promotion make up a fourth area of adult continuing education. Studies may include language acquisition, general employment readiness skills, and specialized occupational knowledge and skills, and they may be available through community colleges and other educational institutions, community agencies, and employers. Not all these offerings are universally accessible. For example, continuing education provided by a union, professional association, or employer frequently cannot be taken by "outsiders" such as non-members or the unemployed.

FUNDING OF RETRAINING OPPORTUNITIES

Funding for retraining in Ontario is provided by several sources, the principal ones being the federal and provincial governments. It is notable that publicly funded retraining, updating, and upgrading programs are aimed primarily at workforce entry skills development and at the skilled and highly skilled occupations. Little specific support is provided for those seeking such training in the professions, other than what is provided by the professions themselves and, as space is available, by postsecondary institutions.

The balance of this section on funding of retraining opportunities, with the exception of the references to the colleges and universities, may be considered to apply essentially to the trades. The particular problems facing the professions in delivery of retraining will be specifically addressed in the section following (Professional Associations).

Federally Funded Training

The principal mechanism that the federal Government uses to support educational delivery systems is through unconditional transfers of money to the provinces. In addition, specific federal training and job creation programs were brought together under the 1985 Canadian Jobs Strategy, which focused on six areas: skill investment, skill shortages, innovations, job entry, job development, and community futures. Each of these strategies

> . . . takes into account the special circumstances of women, Native people, disabled individuals, and members of visible minority groups. Projects with Employment Equity measures, providing opportunities to members of these designated groups, will receive priority attention.[11]

The Canadian Jobs Strategy makes provision for income support for trainees and job entry participants through the payment of unemployment insurance benefits to some job entry participants, and through Unemployment Insurance or an hourly-rate training allowance to those in programs sponsored by Employment and Immigration Canada (EIC). Some trainees may also qualify for other subsidies for dependant care, travel and commuting, and living away from home.

Foreign-trained people, as such, are not a designated target group of any of these six CJS strategies for training and job creation. In fact, they are virtually unaffected by four of the six: innovations, skill investment, job development (except for those deemed to be severely disadvantaged in employment), and community futures. Although foreign-qualified people are served as youth, women, and visible minorities, none of the CJS programs has explicit provisions that would enable these people to obtain specific training to comply with Canadian standards, or to gain Canadian experience that might be required for certification or licensing.

Provincially Funded Training

Provincially funded programs can, for our purposes, be divided into three groups: those funded by the Ministry of Skills Development (MSD), those funded by operating grants through the Ministry of Colleges and Universities, and those that deliver training through electronic systems.

Ministry of Skills Development

The Ministry of Skills Development acts for the Government of Ontario in improving the quality of and access to labour training. It does so through its 49 Ontario skills development offices, which are operated by colleges to provide consultation to firms; its 17 help centres, which provide employment counselling and training information to unemployed workers; its 47 community industrial training committees, which help assess needs and implement programs; its 54 youth employment counselling centres; and its industrial training consultants in 28 apprenticeship field offices.

Through Ontario's Training Strategy, which was announced in 1986, MSD provides conditional support for programming to help workers update and expand their skills. Ontario's Training Strategy has seven components:

- A training consulting service, with more than 160 consultants who provide firms with advice on training objectives, training plans, and ways to gain access to assistance for training.

- Ontario Basic Skills, under which residents of Ontario who are eligible to work may have tuition and some of their child-care and transportation costs paid for three kinds of training: training readiness, when, with a counsellor, they develop a training plan and attitude; academic upgrading, which includes basic skills in literacy, numeracy, technology, and life and work adjustment; and job-search assistance.

- Ontario Skills, which provides financial support to employers, employer associations, and unions for upgrading and training their employees/members. Firms with fewer than 200 employees may have 80 per cent of costs paid, and larger firms are eligible for a 60 per cent payment, to a maximum of $60,000.

- Special support allowances, with priority given to people who traditionally have been underrepresented in training programs — particularly those in the Ontario Basic Skills program and residents of Northern Ontario. Help is provided for child care, transportation, and accommodation.

- A special projects fund that supports innovative community-based ways of providing training and access to training to people who are traditionally underrepresented in training programs.

- Trades Updating, a program targeted at skilled tradespeople, delivered primarily through colleges and designed to help workers respond to technological change, increasing specialization, and shifts in the job market. Courses are being developed in a modular format in order to maximize the program's responsiveness to the needs of tradespeople and the workplace.

- The Ontario Training Corporation, which is a public corporation with a board of directors drawn from government, labour, business, and education. It has four components: (1) the Materials Development Fund, which provides seed money or development money to organizations in a sector (e.g., retail clothing) in order to stimulate sectoral development of training programs and training materials for subsequent sale. (The fund recovers costs through sales of the materials produced.) (2) The Skill Technology Fund, designed to stimulate joint venturing among colleges and the private sector, with an emphasis on improving the technology for teaching and learning skills. (3) A Skills Bank to compile comprehensive, electronically accessible lists of training opportunities and of materials and resources that may be used in training. (4) Training the Trainer courses, which are offered on a fee-for-service basis.

In addition to Ontario's Training Strategy, MSD administers other programs for specifically targeted groups, notably:

- Transitions, under which up to $5,000 of training credits are provided to permanently laid-off workers who are 45 years or older, intended to pay the costs of work-related training for new employment.

- Futures, which utilizes work experience, skills training, and academic upgrading to help disadvantaged, unemployed people, age 15-25 (15-29 for people with disabilities), find and keep permanent jobs.

Operating Grants

In its support for delivery systems, the provincial Government provides operating grants to colleges and universities through the Ministry of Colleges and Universities. The institutions plan and administer these funds within a legislative and policy framework set by the Ministry.

Electronic Delivery

The Province provides funding to three major electronic systems that deliver training: TVOntario, Contact North, and Open College. Foreign-trained individuals who need additional training are not, however, a specified target group of any of these systems.

- TVOntario is known to most Ontario residents as an educational television distribution system that serves elementary school, secondary school, and adult populations. In general, although TVOntario provides some self-contained education and training packages (such as computer literacy), it appears to function principally as a service that complements existing formal institutional programming.

- Contact North, a telephone-based educational network of colleges, universities, and primary/secondary schools providing credit and non-credit programming to remote Northern Ontarians, is undergoing an assessment of its role. The terms of reference for its operation and also for the current assessment do not include reference to immigrants generally or to foreign-trained people specifically.

- The third electronic delivery system is Open College on radio station CJRT-FM in Toronto, which is partly funded by a provincial grant. Open College delivers university credit programming on-air to a clientele within a 160-km radius of Toronto; when combined with its delivery through cable systems, it is accessible to about 90 per cent of the Ontario population. The Province is currently studying the feasibility of a full-time provincewide educational radio network; however, the needs of foreign-trained people were not included in the terms of reference for this study.

School Boards

Although school boards are not principal actors in the funding and delivery of occupation-specific retraining, they do make substantial expenditures in general upgrading, citizenship training, and language training.

School boards receive about half their funding from the provincial Government, with the balance raised through local taxation.[12] Although they operate within legislative and policy guidelines set by the Province, they do have considerable discretionary power in the range and depth of programs offered.

Adult re-entry, student drop-back, and evening courses for credit towards a secondary school graduation diploma are funded through provincial grants and local taxation. A broad range of courses in basic literacy and numeracy, in citizenship for landed immigrants, and in English as a Second Language are available through a delivery system that reaches virtually all communities in Ontario.

Colleges of Applied Arts and Technology

Overall, Ontario's 22 colleges of applied arts and technology offer classroom training for 55 apprentice training programs, 462 diploma specialties, and 304 certificate specialties.[13] In 1987, 111,000 full-time and 715,000 part-time students were enrolled in more than 100 campuses throughout Ontario.

Other factors being equal, students are admitted to any program in this order of preference: permanent Ontario residents, permanent residents of another province or a territory, residents of another Commonwealth country, others.

Although colleges generate some revenue through tuition and contractual activities, their latitude in designing and implementing programs is limited because they have a relatively high preponderance of grant and reimbursement revenue. Discussions with college staff have reaffirmed that the college has to "follow the money" in defining its programs.[14]

Through CJS-sponsored programs brokered through the community industrial training committees, and MSD-sponsored programs brokered primarily through Ontario skills development offices, the colleges offer a number of certificate programs that do provide training needed by recent immigrants, although such programs often are not directed explicitly at them.

In the area of academic improvement, all colleges offer basic training for skills development and English as a Second Language. Several offer an ESL advanced course. Three colleges offer apprenticeship-related English for provisional tradespeople; preparation for certificate of qualification courses are available at four colleges.

Virtually all colleges also offer programs in basic employment training, career planning, introduction to non-traditional occupations, basic job readiness training, people into trades and technologies, and women into trades and technologies. These programs, alongside the academic improvement classes, are potentially valuable to recent immigrants wishing to move into the workforce.

Some of the specialized retraining required by foreign-trained people may be obtained from colleges, although enrolment is normally permitted only if space is available in existing classes. This area will be covered in greater detail later in this chapter, in the section on the professions.

Universities and Ryerson Polytechnical Institute

Universities play a relatively small role in education and training for trades and technologies, but they can provide access to a variety of learning opportunities related to the professions. Generally, access to part-time courses is provided through the continuing education arm of the particular university.

On average, continuing education units obtain 50 per cent of their funding from the university's central budgetary allocation and 44 per cent from tuition fees.[15] The balance is from federal, provincial, and corporate/foundation grants.

Ryerson's Continuing Education Division offers 54 different certificates, which are typically awarded after completion of one year of university-level part-time study made up of courses assembled for a specific occupational need. A number of professional designations can also be prepared for at Ryerson on a part-time basis, in conjunction with the Certified General Accountants Association, the Insurance Institute of Canada, the Ontario Real Estate Association, the Association of Architectural Technologists, the Association of Professional Engineers, the Institute of Canadian Bankers, and others.

Admission to certificate programs, in Ryerson's case, is quite separate from admission to degree programs. The entrance requirement is often Grade 12 or equivalent and/or experience in the certificate area. Some of Ryerson's certificates are cumulative, leading to a degree.

Although 9 per cent of Canadian university continuing education units report use of experiential learning as a criterion for admission,[16] there does not appear to be significant university programming aimed specifically at foreign-trained people. Nor do universities appear to have a general commitment to retraining programs that utilize advanced entry and the waiving of formal undergraduate entrance requirements for practitioners seeking specific retraining courses. A foreign-trained person who has only partial qualifications for taking a certification or licensure examination may, however, sometimes enrol in individual courses for credit as a special student. In these cases, the usual entrance requirements and prerequisites may be waived; access is subject only to space availability in a regularly scheduled course. For example, occupational therapy courses are available on this basis at the University of Toronto.

A unique university-level program development initiative is currently being funded by the Ontario Ministry of Citizenship. Carried out by Ryerson's Continuing Education Division and targeted for 1990 delivery, the Access Action Transitional Education Pilot Program in Human Services seeks to:

1) provide prospective students from ethno-cultural minorities with a basic orientation to the Canadian human services system;

2) raise these students' facility and comfort in acquiring necessary skills for study and practice in a human services school;

3) overcome perceived cultural barriers members of ethno-cultural minorities can encounter in entering human services roles; and

4) adapt curriculum content and approaches in professional educational programs, based on learning from this program.[17]

Other Training Institutions

Community-based training institutions generally regard themselves as responsive — within their frame of reference — to the training needs of recent immigrants who might be considered employment disadvantaged.

One of several such organizations that the Task Force heard from is the Centre for Advancement in Work and Living (CAWL), which operates in Etobicoke in Metropolitan Toronto and provides employment-related services to disadvantaged youth and people with disabilities.

CAWL receives funding from the federal, provincial, and municipal governments and the United Way, and receives contributions from corporations, foundations, and individuals. None of these funding sources provides for general overhead or operating costs, and MSD in particular specifies that its funds are not to go for overhead.

CAWL was established in 1980 and serves Metro Toronto and the surrounding area, offering:

- on-the-job training in marketable skills in the areas of computer clerical, business, welding, and autobody repair;
- vocational and psychological counselling;
- academic upgrading;
- life-management training;
- rehabilitation services;
- job search and readiness training;
- job placement;
- residential and residence-search services; and
- an Independent Living Skills program (funded by Metro Social Services), which provides a five-week exposure to ESL, orientation to the workplace, job search supports, and life skills.

CAWL's programs are aimed at people who do not know how to gain access to work or training. There is a waiting list.

Employers

Employers contribute to education and training in the form of employment skills development, career development, and succession planning. Their participation is essential to cooperative education programs, programs aimed at people already employed, and programs that include an on-the-job component. As noted, employer-sponsored training is of value only to people already employed.

Unions

Trade unions and employers of unionized shops use their local apprenticeship committees to advise on and monitor apprenticeship training in the trades.[18] Unions ensure apprentices get their classroom training and monitor the quality of classroom offerings and performance; in some cases their own inspectors go into colleges. Unions also offer other training; for example, hoist operators have their own school in Toronto.

The Ontario Federation of Labour and its member unions deliver Basic Education for Skills Training, which is free to all employed and unemployed union members who wish to upgrade their skills in reading, writing, mathematics, and communication.

PROFESSIONAL ASSOCIATIONS

Our review of the various professions disclosed that they have a number of ways of dealing with the retraining of candidates viewed as underqualified. There is inevitably a certain overlap in terms of the types of approaches employed. Some categorization, however, is possible.

First, in some professions, candidates assessed as having less than equivalent training are advised that they must obtain an adequate degree or diploma. Particular retraining needs are not determined or articulated. On application to an appropriate educational institution, the candidate may be given some credit for work completed or may formally apply for advanced standing, but he or she must ultimately present to the professional body an acceptable degree or diploma for recognition. Professions falling in this category include agrology, chiropody, dental technology, denture therapy, occupational therapy, optometry, osteopathy, pharmacy, physiotherapy, psychology, and social work.

A second category of professions does not assess credentials beyond documenting their validity, thus enabling candidates who may have less than equivalent training to attempt the licensure examinations. These professions provide very little in the way of retraining, however, which for such candidates limits any likelihood of success. For example, the Royal College of Dental Surgeons for Ontario has no current internal capability for the assessment of educational or experiential equivalency, but instead relies on the accreditation process of the World Health Organization (WHO), and will permit a graduate from an institution on the WHO list to take the licensure examinations. In order to prepare for these examinations, however, candidates have very few training options in dentistry beyond enrolling in the full program at a university and perhaps, space and qualifications permitting, obtaining credit for one year of prior training. The situation in veterinary medicine is similar, although we understand that efforts are under way to institute individualized retraining.

In a third category, specific retraining needs are identified, and training may be provided in one of three basic ways. It may be made available through an examination or training program, usually internally, although sometimes provided in conjunction with a public educational institution. (For example, engineers requiring retraining will be assigned specified examinations. These are internal examinations, but the requirements can be met and prepared for in a variety of ways, including correspondence courses from the University of Toronto, evening classes from several universities, or self-study through old examinations and lists of textbooks provided by the Association of Professional Engineers. Accountants, foresters, land surveyors, and architects can also be said to fall within this category.) It may be through private educational institutions offering specified courses (as is the case for chiropractors, masseurs, and naturopaths). And it may be through public colleges and universities. Professions that rely completely on these institutions include dental hygiene, dietetics, education (primary/secondary), funeral services, law, medicine, nursing, ophthalmic dispensing, and radiological technology.

What this survey demonstrates is that in a number of instances no identification of specific retraining needs is undertaken by the profession, resulting in significant retraining that may exceed what the candidate needs. In such professions, and also in those in which specific retraining needs are identified, there is in the majority of cases almost complete dependence on the educational institution to accommodate candidates within the fixed structures of existing programs. This reliance can in some disciplines severely limit the availability of retraining opportunities.

Ease of Access

The ease with which a foreign-trained person is able to gain access to retraining in a profession appears to be related to several factors. First, does the profession have the means to recognize the equivalency of the foreign training and to determine with precision any retraining needs? Where no direction is given, complete retraining may be the only option. The result can be the duplication of previously completed training, with the candidate bearing the cost, loss of income, and delays. The most serious consequence is that the candidate is unable to complete the requirements, either because of a lack of available training positions or because economic realities make it impossible to forgo any income in order to attend retraining programs. (This issue is dealt with in detail in Chapter 5, "Prior Learning Assessment.")

The second factor to consider is whether the training programs that lead to certification or licensure have sufficient flexibility to accept people at advanced levels. Without some means to provide advanced standing to individuals who can demonstrate related prior learning, all individuals seeking certification in Ontario face the situation of either having full equivalency to Ontario's requirements, and thereby being permitted to take the certification or licensure examination, or being required to enter the professional training program from its very beginning, regardless of how close to full Ontario equivalency the applicant might be. Many programs and institutions make advanced standing an option, but spaces are severely restricted, and in many disciplines ability depends on a vacancy being created through a failure or drop-out.

The third factor concerns the accessibility of retraining opportunities. If an adult breadwinner can find retraining courses only on a distant university campus and as a full-time student, training cannot be considered easily accessible. Scheduling can create a barrier, because an employed person will likely have difficulty taking courses scheduled during working hours.

Certified general accountants, certified management accountants, and chartered accountants recognize the equivalency of specified college and university courses, which may be offered through adult continuing education or regular day classes. As well, these professions offer courses directly. Architectural retraining may be obtained through university studies if classroom space permits, or through part-time correspondence study and internship offered by the professional association. In certain other professions, such as dentistry or optometry, access to required courses is offered only in universities and only as space in classes is available. The result is that required classes may be inaccessible.

Although many professions make provision for retraining of partially qualified applicants, and although some provide comprehensive and accessible programming, the overall picture is one of limited programs and of inconsistency from profession to profession. The Task Force would be the first to assert that some variation is inevitable, and necessary, as a result of the nature of the individual professions. We also recognize the funding restrictions and limited facilities that exist. Nevertheless, we have been able to formulate some recommendations that should improve the overall quality and accessibility of retraining by partially qualified foreign-trained applicants for certification and licensure.

Two other issues relating to professional training requirements should be addressed at this stage. The first is the accessibility to candidates of means to satisfy specific Ontario experience requirements as prerequisites to licensure. Many occupational bodies specifically require candidates to meet a formal "experience" or "in-service training" or "internship" requirement, and in most cases at least part must be completed in Ontario. We have stated in Chapter 5 of this Report ("Prior Learning Assessment") that it is the responsibility of the occupational body to ensure that the requirements are reasonable and that credit is given for relevant foreign experience. In addition, and most significantly in the context of retraining, it is essential that the body imposing the requirement ensure that there are means available to the candidate to meet it. Our primary concern is directed to situations such as the one that exists in medical technology: foreign-trained technologists are not certified without first completing Canadian experience, yet such experience is almost impossible to find because hospitals require certification before employment.[19] A pronounced scarcity of posts can have the same effect. If a situation arises in which an experience prerequisite cannot be met owing to a lack of available posts, then that prerequisite should not be imposed. (We acknowledge an exception in the case of medicine, in which the Government consciously and directly imposes a cap on funded internship positions and does not permit unfunded positions. In our discussion of the medical profession we note this fact, pointing out that if such a cap is to exist, it must apply equally to all candidates. See Chapter 10 of this Report, "Issues Facing the Medical Profession.")

The second issue relates to the allocation of retraining positions as a means of recruiting members of ethno-cultural groups who will service their own populations. Representations have been made to us concerning the need, particularly in such disciplines as medicine, social work, and psychology, for ethno-cultural groups to receive care from professionals of a similar background. One submission to the Task Force put it this way:

> There is need for the provision of more culturally and linguistically sensitive health care to many ethnocultural communities. This need is not only apparent for recent immigrants but is also becoming an increasingly greater issue for the "older" groups which have immigrated to Canada decades ago. As people age there is a tendency to revert to their mother tongue or language of fluency, at times with the accompanying loss of fluency in English. The recognition of cultural needs plays a much greater role in maintaining the well-being of seniors and the treatment of illness for them.

Without altering standards or engaging in the practice, suggested by some, of issuing limited licences, professional bodies could respond to this situation by allocating training spots to representatives of groups in which there is an identified need. We have specifically suggested that such allocations be considered in the medical profession, but the concept should be recognized throughout the professions and by the Government itself, which in some instances would do well to provide guidance and leadership in this area.

OTHER MODELS FOR RETRAINING

Providing foreign-trained people with access to retraining has been addressed in other jurisdictions, and three examples are summarized below to provide some idea of the range of current practice.

Recognition Program in Manitoba

Recognition: Manitoba Work Experience for Professional and Technically Trained Newcomers is a federally funded, provincially administered program designed to give foreign-trained professionals and technologists improved access to Canadian experience.[20] The program provides funding to employers for the creation of new positions for this purpose — up to 70 per cent of the gross wage paid for the first four weeks, 50 per cent for the following 22 weeks, and 30 per cent for the final 26 weeks, for a total of one year.

Under the program, an employer undertakes to create a position of at least 35 hours per week in one or more of the specified functional areas: engineering and scientific activities; product development and design; technology adaptation; international trade; production operation management; human resource management; marketing; and finance.

The potential employee must be an unemployed or underemployed landed immigrant or a recently naturalized Canadian citizen whose post-secondary education has been completed outside Canada and whose credentials are not formally recognized in Manitoba.

Labour Market Training in Sweden

In Sweden, labour market training adapted to meet individual requirements is regarded as one of the most important means of influencing and changing the available labour supply. The Swedish training program is primarily intended to help unemployed individuals, including hard-to-place job seekers who lack occupational skills. Immigrants are one of the target groups of this program. Retraining needs are defined through an assessment program of vocational competencies, and immigrants are provided access to related language training.

Most labour market training assumes the form of specially arranged, vocationally oriented courses, but there are also preparatory courses, including programs at an upper secondary school. The training is free, and participants age 20 or over are eligible to receive training grants ranging from about 50 to 80 per cent of the average daily income of industrial workers. Teenagers without dependants receive about 25 per cent of that average daily income.

To tailor labour market training courses to an individual's specific needs, courses are generally broken down into specific modules. An assessment is then made of the number of modules necessary for an individual to fulfil predetermined standards for qualification in a particular occupation.

Annual follow-up studies have shown that most people who begin labour market training complete it. About 60 to 70 per cent of all students in the specially arranged vocational training courses find jobs on the open labour market within six months of completing their studies.

Vocational and Academic Training in Great Britain

In 1981, the Manpower Services Commission, which is responsible for public employment and training services in England, Scotland, and Wales, released its New Training Initiative, which had three objectives: better skill-training standards; better training for youth; and more adult training opportunities.

The Standards Program was the starting point of the initiative, introduced to develop effective employment-related performance standards for all occupations by 1991. In most occupational sectors, development is spearheaded by industry and business within the sector, with support from the commission.

The new standards are competency-based, criterion-referenced, and stated in a standardized format to facilitate credit accumulation and transfer. This approach is intended to improve transferability of competencies among occupations.

Accompanying the Standards Program is the New Job Training Scheme, directed at the adult unemployed. Offering up to six months' training to unemployed adults, including immigrants, the training is based on the Standards Program, and so guarantees employment relevance. It is designed to allow portability of training; a participant leaving the scheme to take a job can obtain a certificate of credit for the completed portion of the program. A similar program being established in Great Britain, the Credit Accumulation and Transfer Scheme, is discussed in Chapter 5 of this Report, "Prior Learning Assessment."

RETRAINING: BARRIERS TO ACCESS

Barriers to education for adults can be grouped into three categories: dispositional, situational, and institutional.[21]

Institutional barriers are those policies and practices of the education providers that may discourage or prevent participation. These barriers include entrance requirements, tuition fees, prerequisites, and full-time attendance requirements.

Dispositional barriers are related to the adult learner's attitudes that interfere with his or her willingness to seek out education. The individual might feel too old, or too weak in English, or even too inadequate to learn.

Situational barriers arise from situations related to child care, language mastery or ability, scheduling, cost, distance, or physical problems such as poor hearing or sight.

Institutional Barriers

Although a variety of retraining programs exist in Ontario, there is no single, well-publicized source of information covering the nature of programs, the conditions under which they are available, and the support structures available to assist the foreign-trained person complete his or her training.

Concerns were stated that available programs are not promoted adequately within the cultural communities. Word-of-mouth advertising does reach some people, but a systematic promotion of programs is seen to be needed if foreign-trained people are to learn about retraining opportunities.[22]

Prerequisites

Prerequisites form barriers at several levels. First there is the example of specific college or university courses that have course prerequisites. Sometimes these prerequisites are justified because certain knowledge is essential; other times, these requirements are, possibly, directed at gaining more revenue-generating enrolment in entry-level courses.

Some training programs require particular kinds of experience as a prerequisite, including Canadian or even Ontario experience. For some foreign-trained people, this requirement can create a "Catch-22" situation. For example, a foreign-trained individual may require Canadian experience for certification and therefore must find a training program; yet employers may require certification before a person is allowed to work and gain experience. As one solution, the Workers' Educational Association of Canada proposed the establishment of a mandatory "provisional licensing" system that would allow foreign-trained people to gain Canadian experience in a safe and systematic way.[23]

Some retraining has a membership or employment prerequisite. Access to learning programs provided by unions and professional associations is generally available only to members, and membership can in turn have an employment prerequisite.

A fourth kind of prerequisite is unemployment. A number of provincially and federally funded programs are available only to people who are unemployed or on long-term layoff. The federal Job Development

Program and the provincial Transitions Program both have an unemployment prerequisite.

A fifth type of prerequisite is language proficiency. In some cases, as in apprentice training, the Grade 8 language proficiency requirement seems arbitrary. College and university programs often have no in-house capacity to provide language training for students who meet all but the language proficiency requirements.[24]

Financial

In setting their fees for part-time courses, universities must prorate the annual or semester fee for the full-time program. Although this prorating does cap the cost to students, it also serves to restrict access: if the incremental delivery cost of part-time courses cannot be realized under the cap, the course is simply not made available.

Colleges and school boards operate under similar restrictions. Colleges are confined to a regulated maximum hourly fee for continuing education courses,[25] and school boards are not permitted to charge any fee for credit courses, adult basic education, or classes in English or French as a Second Language.[26] However, fees for all other offerings provided by public educational institutions may be set at whatever the market will bear, and continuing education units sometimes are able to make a profit on non-credit courses in order to fund the incremental costs of part-time credit courses.

Shifts in program funding, particularly away from apprenticeship, language-training, and special access programs such as Women into Trades and Technologies, have resulted from priority changes within the Canadian Jobs Strategy. Because the great majority of people enrolled in these courses are federally sponsored, such a shift by the federal Government can place these programs in jeopardy. There are other financial barriers, including costs of materials and books, travel, and in some cases loss of personal income for the time spent in training.

Delivery Systems

A related set of concerns involves delivery systems. Perhaps because many of the individuals who approached the Task Force are active in community-based agencies, strong arguments were brought forward for stable funding structures for retraining that permit responsiveness to individual and community needs in the areas of basic skills, life skills, and preparation for the workplace.

Accountability of Educational Institutions

As a final point on institutional barriers, the Task Force notes the need for reviewing equality of access to education and equality of treatment of those enrolled in educational programs. In his submission to the Task Force the president of Seneca College of Applied Arts and Technology addressed the issue by pressing for such a review:

> *Indeed, it would seem appropriate if the kind of funding provided by the Ministry of Colleges and Universities to the colleges for the purpose of conducting an* employment *equity study was extended further, to support a similar* education *equity review. This would seem to be the missing, final link in the entire question of Access — to Professions, Trades, Education, Training and Retraining Opportunities — for members of minority groups in our province.*[27]

Dispositional Barriers

Perhaps the most significant dispositional barrier identified in interviews and briefs is that the system is structured along advocacy lines, requiring foreign-trained people to be prepared to challenge those responsible for certification and licensure and those who administer admission to training programs. For people whose culture is rooted in different attitudes towards those in authority, our system becomes virtually impregnable. The following remarks typify what the Task Force repeatedly heard on the subject:

> *I worked in the accounting department in a large business in Lima, Peru . . . I contacted the Canada Employment Centre office and spoke with a counsellor. I wanted to take an English course in order to get a job in my profession, but my request was denied because the counsellor felt that I spoke enough English to get a job — but she meant a job in a factory and not in my profession. At that time . . . I lived in the Weston/Lawrence area and I never saw or heard of any community agencies in the area who could have helped me. I never returned to the Canada Employment Centre*

*after that discouraging meeting . . . my academic record was not
assessed for equivalency in Ontario.*[28]

Dispositional barriers to obtaining retraining can be addressed through
education, directed not only towards the foreign-trained people who
encounter the barriers but also to those established Canadians who
inadvertently turn such dispositions into barriers. Educational institutions
generally are not addressing this issue. A review of college diploma and
certificate programs and university degree programs turned up several
programs related to Native Canadians, but very few that appeared to deal
more broadly with multiculturalism.[29]

One program that does address the issue is Ryerson's Continuing
Education, which offers a seven-course certificate in Canadian Cross-Cultural
Studies. "The Politics of Ethnicity and Human Rights in Canada" and
"Managing a Culturally and Racially Diverse Workforce" are two of the
courses in the program. Programs such as this one might be implemented
throughout the province for the benefit of people in public and community
service, business, industry, and education.

Situational Barriers

This category of barriers to retraining is composed of personal situations
that the funders and designers of programs must take into account if fair
and reasonable access to training is to be attained.

Although some foreign-trained people currently have ready access to
retraining programs, many encounter one or more of the following barriers:
(1) the absence of multilingual information about retraining, including
counselling on the kinds of training that should be obtained and the sources
of training; (2) the lack of assessment of the applicant's educational and
language levels; and (3) inadequate financial resources, including child-care
support and training allowances, for those who work and cannot afford to
take leave for retraining. With respect to the last barrier, the provincial
Government has proposed to the First Ministers of Canada that there be a
Canada Training Allowance with six key features:

- straightforward access for people enrolled in or eligible to enter federal
  and provincial training programs;
- prompt income support for trainees in training outside the workplace;

- recognition of the needs of the employed, the recently unemployed, and the long-term unemployed;
- respect of individual choice in training selection;
- ease of access through administrative simplicity; and
- levels of support equal to or exceeding those attained through unemployment insurance.

RECOMMENDATIONS

The Task Force is aware of the increasing overall need to retrain people affected by job obsolescence and to update the knowledge of practitioners in an occupation to keep them at the "leading edge." We are also aware that the numbers of foreign-trained professional people and tradespeople are likely to rise in Ontario in the coming years as our more traditional sources grow smaller. Our recommendations regarding training recognize that the Government currently addresses the specific training needs of some populations, including youth, women, and visible minorities. We observe, however, that foreign-trained people are an emerging group whose training needs are not adequately met.

The information that we have gathered indicates that there are great discrepancies in the availability of training opportunities to foreign-trained people — discrepancies from occupation to occupation and from one educational institution to the nèxt. We note the considerable amount of effort and funding being put into these programs, and we are troubled that, in spite of the demographic trends in Ontario, the needs of foreign-trained people do not appear in the planning statements of the major program funders.

We look to the Government of Ontario to set the example for providers of education and training in the province by explicitly including the training needs of foreign-trained people as an important element of its funding and operating plans. Only then, we believe, can we turn to Ontario's educational institutions and certification and licensure bodies for concrete provisions for the efficient and fair reception of foreign-trained professional people and tradespeople.

We do not advocate the creation of an agency for training foreign-trained people. Instead, we advise the Government and the many providers of education and training that the availability of such training makes economic and social sense and that in most cases, through cooperative planning and with adjustments in their existing policies and delivery systems, appropriate provision can be made.

9.1 *We recommend that the Ministry of Colleges and Universities and the Ministry of Citizenship be assigned joint responsibility for encouraging, advising, and assisting colleges, universities, and occupational certification bodies in providing access to retraining, upgrading, and updating by foreign-trained people. We believe that in providing this leadership, these ministries should consult with the Council of Ontario Universities, the Ontario Council of Regents for Colleges of Applied Arts and Technology, the Ministry of Skills Development, and the occupational committees of the proposed Prior Learning Assessment Network.*

We recommend that the Ministry of Colleges and Universities and the Ministry of Citizenship address the following matters:

- *the accessibility of training by foreign-trained people who are partially qualified to apply for certification or licensure in an occupation;*

- *the funding needs of colleges, universities, and professional bodies related to the provision of training;*

- *the funding needs of foreign-trained individuals seeking to take training; and*

- *the accessibility of information about training opportunities.*

9.2 *We recommend that the colleges and universities of Ontario collaborate in the design and execution of a detailed review of each postsecondary educational institution, to ensure that each is providing fair and flexible access to retraining by foreign-trained people. We believe that this review should include an audit of the measures that each institution has in place to address institutional, dispositional, and situational barriers to training, and that each institution undertake to file with the Ministry of Colleges and Universities a plan for addressing and removing barriers that are found to exist.*

9.3   We recommend that the Government of Ontario establish financial support structures for the training of partially qualified foreign-trained professional people and tradespeople, and that these structures be designed to:

- encourage and assist occupational bodies and educational institutions to develop modules of instruction that foreign-trained individuals can assemble to meet certification and licensure requirements;

- encourage and assist occupational bodies to develop additional means, if appropriate, for candidates to meet retraining requirements, with a view to lessening the strain on traditional university- or college-based delivery systems, options to include use of alternate physical facilities, development of mentor training, and recognition of alternate delivery mechanisms such as radio, video, computer, and correspondence;

- provide responsive funding to individuals (at the minimum, a loan program referenced to the needs of those seeking training); and

- assist employers in providing training, through the extension of such existing funding mechanisms as the trades and technologists updating programs funded by the Ministry of Skills Development.

9.4   We recommend that, in order to better ensure the quality, responsiveness, and continuity of community-based programming, a foundation grant program be established to create a more stable planning and operating base for proven community-based agencies that provide programming for foreign-trained people.

9.5   We recommend that the occupational bodies and the provincial Government work together, along with the community-based agencies referred to in the above recommendation, to identify particular service requirements in the ethno-cultural communities, especially in the areas of medicine, social work, and psychology, and that such identified needs be taken into *account in the allocation of retraining resources to candidates for certification or licensure.*

9.6   *We recommend that the Ontario Training Corporation ensure that any information bases and information services which it is establishing be designed to serve the full range of professions and trades in Ontario, and that it respond to issues of accessibility and accuracy, as set out in Recommendations 3.4, 3.5, and 3.6 in Chapter 3, "Issues Facing the Trades."*

9.7   *We recommend that the Government of Ontario continue to work with other provinces and the federal Government towards the establishment of a Canada Training Allowance.*

9.8   *We recommend that, through the assessment of academic equivalency carried out by the proposed Prior Learning Assessment Network, any partially qualified foreign-trained person who needs additional training be provided with specific information about the nature and duration of training required to fulfil the prerequisites for certification or licensure.*

9.9   *We recommend that for those occupations for which Canadian or Ontario experience is a prerequisite to certification or licensure, professional bodies, colleges, and universities endeavour to design training programs in such a way that this experience can be obtained. Determinations of the amount of such experience to be required should be based on an individual assessment giving full credit for all actual relevant experience of the candidate.*

CHAPTER 10

Issues Facing the Medical Profession

BACKGROUND

In attempting to assess the methodology being employed in Ontario for the admission of foreign-trained candidates to occupational groups, we have reviewed a significant number of occupations. The information gathered and the conclusions reached during this review appear throughout our Report. Although the occupations vary widely in their structure, the issues we addressed were common to many of them. We have presented this information in our general recommendations, which cover all the relevant occupations as a group, rather than treating each as a special case. For ease of reference, occupation-specific information appears in Appendix H at the end of this Report ("Professional Summaries"). For greater clarity, background studies on each of the occupations reviewed have been prepared (see Appendix G). These studies outline in greater detail the entry procedures employed by each group and include commentary concerning the need we perceive for the application of the general recommendations to the specific group.

We concluded, however, that it was necessary to include within this Report a discussion specifically related to the medical profession, the primary reason being that the entry mechanism imposed is particular to medicine. It was therefore necessary to make specific recommendations relating to this profession alone. In addition, the medical profession is the most complex of those reviewed, and has as well, for a number of reasons, raised the most emotions. First, medical care is something that touches every individual in the province, and issues of accessibility and quality of care are of interest to everyone. Second, the number of immigrant professionals currently attempting to enter this profession is significant, and the problems they are encountering are very direct. We received more submissions from physicians than from members of any other profession under review. (Indeed, the issue of entry to this profession carries such a high public profile that we often encountered the public perception that we were reviewing only the medical profession.) Finally, by reason of the Ontario Health Insurance Plan, the provincial Government must concern itself with the important and complex issues in respect of the costs of health services, which, it appears, are increasingly on the rise. Many factors come into play in the study of this issue, and they are in the process of being reviewed and canvassed by many groups in many contexts. Control of the physician pool is, however, seen by some — including, significantly, policy analysts in the Ministry of Health — as crucial to the control of health-care costs. The issue of numbers control necessarily has a significant impact on policies affecting the entry of immigrant physicians into the pool.

In including a detailed review of the medical profession alone, we do not wish to suggest that the issues facing it are in any way more significant than those facing other professions; and we sincerely hope that our specific comments here will not overshadow our more general recommendations, which, being of broad application, have the potential to have greater impact. It is, however, necessary that these particular problems be dealt with in a particular way.

We would raise two cautionary points at the outset. First, it is essential that this chapter be read in the context of the entire Report if misunderstanding is to be avoided. Second, it must be remembered that this Task Force was not created to do an economic analysis of health care in Ontario; there are currently a number of bodies which have been specifically assigned or have taken on that very task,[1] and others which have already considered the matter.[2] Our task is to determine what barriers, if any, exist that prevent those trained outside of Canada from entering their occupations once in this province. Barriers that discriminate against such individuals, overtly or systemically, have been identified and scrutinized. We do not consider as barriers those particular requirements imposed on foreign-trained professionals that are justifiable as needed for the protection of the public and that, to ensure fairness, are subjected to appropriate review. The control of numbers of entrants as justification for such requirements, raised by some, has not in any case been accepted by this Task Force.

We recognize that because of the nature of the funding accorded the medical-care system in Ontario, human resources planning is inevitably going to have a greater impact on this profession than on others, and our discussion acknowledges this reality. But the principles of equity and fairness that we bring to bear in our analysis of barriers as they apply to other professions must apply to medicine as well.

Human Resources

It is difficult to pinpoint precisely how many practising physicians there are in the province. Figures cited by the Ministry of Health range from about 17,000 to more than 19,000. OHIP reports that in 1987 it was billed by 17,245 doctors.

Regulatory Structure

Medicine is one of the professions regulated under the *Health Disciplines Act*.[3] For purposes of the licensing procedure, the structure imposed by the *Act* is as follows. Application is made to the registrar of the Ontario College of Physicians and Surgeons, who considers the application. If the registrar intends to refuse the application or to attach conditions or limitations to it, he or she must refer it to the Registration Committee, which also reviews the case; if the committee intends to reject the application or to attach conditions or limitations to it, the matter is referred to the Health Disciplines Board, where the applicant is entitled to a hearing. An appeal from a decision of the Health Disciplines Board to the Divisional Court is available to an unsuccessful applicant.[4]

THE ADMISSIONS PROCESS

For Ontario Graduates[5]

1. Have a Degree From an Accredited Ontario Medical School

There are five medical schools in Ontario: McMaster University, Queen's University, Ottawa University, the University of Toronto, and the University of Western Ontario. The total enrolment in 1986 was approximately 2,400 undergraduate students and 3,400 postgraduate students, including interns and residents in specialty programs. Approximately 3,900 applicants in 1987-88 applied for the 600 or so available entry positions in medical schools.

The coordinating body for the medical schools is the Council of Ontario Faculties of Medicine (COFM), which consists of the deans of the medical schools and has a mandate to "promote the perceived interest of the medical faculties in Ontario, including representations to and negotiations with the various branches of the government dealing with matters affecting

Ontario universities with faculties of medicine." COFM is the organization that officially participated in the federal/provincial Advisory Committee on Health Manpower Planning, which issued its report in 1984.

The standard medical school curriculum in Ontario takes four years to complete, including the last year, known as a clinical clerkship, which is a 48-week program in which the student spends most of his or her time in the hospital, involved in patient care, under the supervision of residents. The five medical schools vary, to some extent, in their clinical programs, but all meet the basic criterion of a one-year clinical clerkship.

To qualify for admission to medical school at the University of Toronto, the applicant must have completed at least two years of an undergraduate university education, including specific types of chemistry and science classes. The other medical schools have similar requirements of prior academic experience. The non-academic considerations, such as prior experience, references, and interviews, vary from school to school. For candidates accepted into medical school, the failure rate is low.

2. Pass the Qualifying Examination Offered by the Medical Council of Canada

The Medical Council of Canada (MCC) was established in 1912 to develop and promote a qualification in medicine, termed the "Licentiate of The Medical Council of Canada" (LMCC). One of the requirements for obtaining this qualification is to pass the MCC qualifying examination (MCCQE), which is:

> designed to evaluate your medical knowledge and understanding and your ability to apply this to clinical situations. The test questions cover medicine, obstetrics and gynaecology, paediatrics, preventive medicine and community health, psychiatry and surgery. They may include a test of your knowledge of the basic medical sciences.[6]

3. Provide Evidence of "Good Character"

The applicant must show that there have been no findings and that there are no current proceedings relating to professional misconduct, incompetence, or incapacitation.

4. Complete, with Performance Satisfactory to the College, a One-Year Rotating Medical/Surgical Internship in an Accredited Medical School in Canada or the United States

In order to obtain an internship position, a candidate must be granted an educational licence. Such a licence is granted as a matter of course to graduates of accredited medical schools. The procedure in Ontario to obtain an internship position is to apply to the Canadian Internship Matching Service (CIMS). Each applicant and each school lists choices in order of priority; the service matches each student with the highest-rated school that will accept him or her. There are currently about 600 funded internships in Ontario ("funded" meaning that the Ontario Government provides funds to the hospitals for a fixed number of internships to cover the salary and expenses of the interns), this number being equal to the number of graduates from Ontario medical schools each year. Thus, all graduates of Ontario medical schools are guaranteed funded internship positions. Graduates from other provinces apply through CIMS as well, and matches are made across Canada. Graduates of accredited U.S. schools may apply through CIMS. Some Ontario graduates each year seek internships beyond Ontario; hence, there are some positions available each year for graduates from other provinces and from accredited U.S. schools. Graduates of unaccredited foreign medical schools cannot apply through CIMS.

We were told that tasks which interns "routinely" undertake include the writing of orders (these need not be countersigned) relating to patient care and treatment in areas such as the prescription of drugs or therapy, the ordering of further diagnostic testing or investigation, and the ordering of X-rays for diagnostic analysis. Some technical procedures may be undertaken by interns, among these the taking of blood, the draining of fluid from body cavities, the delivering of babies, and suturing. All this work is subject to supervision and dependent on proof of capability. In most cases, the intern functions as part of a health-care team.

For Graduates of Other Accredited Medical Schools[7]

All medical schools in Canada are accredited by the Council on Accreditation of Canadian Medical Schools (CACMS), a body established in association with the Canadian Medical Association. U.S. medical schools are accredited by the Liaison Committee on Medical Education (LCME). The two groups work closely together and have cross-appointments to each association. For the purposes of licensure, an accredited medical school in the United States is equivalent to an accredited medical school in Canada. Therefore, since most U.S. medical schools are accredited, students graduating from a U.S. medical school apply for internship positions and licensing on essentially the same basis as do Canadian students.

Thus, the requirements for graduates of accredited U.S. medical schools and graduates of other Canadian medical schools are the same as those for Ontario graduates, subject to the one qualification that Americans may substitute for the MCCQE the examination given by the National Board of Medical Examiners of the United States.

For Graduates of Unaccredited Foreign Medical Schools[8]

1. Have a Degree from an Acceptable Unaccredited Medical School

To be considered acceptable, foreign institutions must:

- be listed in the World Health Organization (WHO) directory;
- offer a four-year medical program; and
- have been in existence for ten years.[9]

We were told that in the 1986-87 internship year, approximately 565 foreign-trained candidates from 61 countries applied for internship positions in Ontario. (These exclude U.S.-trained candidates from accredited U.S. schools.) It is not known how many actual foreign medical schools these numbers represent, but there are some 700 medical schools in those countries.

2. Be a Canadian Citizen or a Permanent Resident

In addition to meeting the citizenship or residency requirement, graduates of unaccredited foreign medical schools have in recent years been required to reside in Ontario for one year before they enter the Pre-Internship Program (PIP). This requirement does not appear in the regulations. We understand that it will not continue to be a requirement.

3. Complete the Medical Council of Canada Evaluating Examination (MCCEE)

The MCCEE, given by the same body that gives the MCCQE, is available in English and French and is intended to test the candidate's knowledge of the principal fields of medicine. Clinical problems and patient management problems are not specifically assessed. There are approximately 324 multiple-choice questions. The examination is written in two sessions, each of three-and-one-half hours. Scoring is based on the number of correct answers; no penalty is applied for incorrect answers. The MCCEE costs $350 to try the first time and $300 for each subsequent attempt. Study texts are recommended. The examination is held twice yearly, and there is no limit to the number of times a candidate can attempt it.

Although the examination is not written by graduates of Ontario programs, the test is designed with reference to the MCCQE, and questions are drawn from the latter.

4. Have English or French Language Facility[10]

Candidates whose native language is not English or French, or who graduated from programs taught in a language other than English or French, must complete both the written and verbal parts of the TOEFL (with a minimum score of 580) and the TSE (with a minimum score of 200), or comparable French fluency tests. This assessment is completed at a very early stage in the testing procedure for entry to the Pre-Internship Program. Candidates who are not successful in gaining entry to the program are required to redo these fluency tests if they reapply.[11]

5. Provide Evidence of "Good Character"

The applicant must show that there have been no findings and that there are no proceedings relating to professional misconduct, incompetence, or incapacitation.

6. Pass the MCC Qualifying Examination (MCCQE)

The MCCQE is the same examination required of all applicants for a general licence.

7. **Complete, with Performance Satisfactory to the College, Two Approved Internships, or an Approved Internship and an Acceptable Residency**

One of the two internships to be completed must be a rotating internship; and one of the internships or the residency must be taken in Canada (the other may be taken in the United States).

Prior to 1986, graduates of unaccredited medical schools who passed the MCCEE could apply for internships along with all other applicants, although they had to defer to Canadian graduates in priority of placement. Also prior to 1986, when they were eliminated, unfunded internships were often available to candidates who failed to secure funded spots.

In order to qualify for an educational licence to complete an internship, a graduate of an unaccredited foreign medical school must now, in addition to passing the MCCEE, complete a pre-internship program,[12] defined as a program of assessing and upgrading the clinical and language skills of a graduate of an acceptable unaccredited medical school. This program is to be taken at an accredited medical school in Ontario; is to be at least 36 weeks in duration but not exceeding 48 weeks; and is to include assessment and training in internal medicine, obstetrics and gynaecology, paediatrics, psychiatry, and surgery. The stated intention is to model the program after the clinical clerkship year (the fourth year) offered in Ontario medical schools.

There are 24 positions available annually for the Pre-Internship Program (PIP). Some 500-600 individuals applied to the program last year,[13] although we do not know to what extent that figure represents a backlog of candidates for internship positions; the annual figure of new entrants would be significantly lower.

Candidates take a written medical problem-solving examination that includes questions to test knowledge and case-analysis skills in a number of medical disciplines. Candidates with the highest 72 scores move on to the next method of assessment.

This smaller group undertakes a specially structured clinical examination. Several clinical testing formats are utilized to assess communication skills, clinical skills, and clinical management skills.

The written and clinical examination scores, curricula vitae, and written references of the applicants are reviewed. From these 72 candidates, 24 are offered positions in the Pre-Internship Program.

Foreign medical graduates enrolled in the program receive clinical training in a range of areas and special seminars on issues specific to medical practice in Ontario and Canada. These seminars include topics such as medical ethics, medical jurisprudence, available community services, and the role of the coroner and the medical officer of health in Ontario.

At the end of 36 weeks in the program, candidates for internship are assessed to determine whether an additional 12 weeks of remedial instruction and training are required for the pre-intern. If at the end of 48 weeks it is determined that a candidate has not shown an adequate performance level in the program, the program director will decline to provide a letter that the PIP has been successfully completed.

Examinations are given in the twelfth and thirty-third weeks of the Pre-Internship Program.

Those who complete the PIP receive educational licences and are eligible for internship. As indicated, they must complete two years of internship, or one year of internship and one year of residency. These 24 graduates of foreign medical schools cannot compete directly for the 600 funded internship positions through the Canadian Internship Matching Service. The 24 are, however, guaranteed funded spots for each of the required two years.

Assessment of Prior Learning of Candidates for Educational Licences

The requirements for entry into the medical profession for graduates of unaccredited foreign medical schools are substantially different from the requirements for those coming from accredited institutions. Of all the requirements mentioned, three raise questions:

- the one-year Ontario residency requirement;
- the two-year internship requirement; and
- the Pre-Internship Program requirement.

The first of these is not authorized by regulation, and we see no justification for it. We understand that it will no longer be applied, and support this change. The second requirement, we are told, is likely to be expanded to apply to all interns, and on that basis we find it to be acceptable. The third, however, the Pre-Internship Program (PIP) requirement, raises serious issues of analysis and policy, which must be canvassed.

The purpose of any mechanism selected to control entry into a professional body must be to determine whether people are qualified to enter the profession.

What is at issue, therefore, is whether the Pre-Internship Program, including the examination process through which candidates must pass in order to enter it, is both necessary and adequate to meet this end. It is our conclusion that it is not, the fundamental defect with the program being that it does not respond to or give recognition to the actual skills and abilities of the candidates.

Completion of the PIP is required of all candidates from unaccredited medical schools, regardless of their credentials, regardless of their experience, and, most significantly, regardless of how well they perform in the lengthy and comprehensive examination process which they must pass through in order to obtain admission to the program. Candidates who demonstrate a level of skill that would enable them to perform an internship with abilities equal to a graduate of an Ontario medical school are, nonetheless, required to complete the training program.

In addition, the examination process is not performing the function of determining whether candidates are qualified to enter the profession by meeting a satisfactory standard; it is merely being used as a selection technique to choose the best and most qualified candidates. In the result, candidates who are qualified to enter the profession — that is, candidates who can demonstrate a level of competence equal to that of an Ontario graduate — may be completely denied entry to the profession by virtue of the fact of not being among the *most* qualified; at best, they may be delayed a year in their progress towards entry by being required to complete training that they do not require.

Our concern on this issue is supported by the following facts:

- The procedure that has been put in place to examine the candidates from unaccredited medical schools has been developed with great care, is comprehensive, and is showing signs of predictive validity. The results of the examination process can themselves be relied on as a measure of skill necessary to qualify for entry into internship.

- The field of clinical testing of medical practitioners is an area of intense activity and development. While we acknowledge that no test is perfect as an indicator of future performance, our review of current developments in the field of medical testing indicates that it is possible to assess the knowledge and clinical skills of medical practitioners.

- Graduates of unaccredited medical schools have been entering the Ontario health-care system in significant numbers for many years. They have been doing so with significant success, although they have not had the benefit of the PIP. (There are still some graduates being granted licences without completing the requirements being discussed here, by virtue of the waiver power of the College of Physicians and Surgeons, which in 1987-88 affected 79 graduates of unaccredited medical schools.[14] This indirect method of entry will be discussed below.)

- Information concerning unaccredited medical training programs is or should be obtainable.

We acknowledge that there have no doubt been instances in which some individuals were deficient in clinical skills. Specific areas of deficiency cited were language difficulties, lack of familiarity with drug names, and lack of familiarity with the availability of laboratory tests and the speed with which results can be obtained. Representatives of the profession, including those representing other interns, suggested that while graduates of foreign medical schools often displayed adequate academic skill and knowledge of the basic areas of study such as physiology, the testing mechanism in place prior to the PIP, the MCCEE, did not adequately assess the candidates' clinical skills, their individual levels of adaptation to the system of medical practice in Ontario, or their ability to function under stress and deal effectively and sensitively with patients. The result was that the chance existed that patients might receive a lower standard of care from such interns; consequently, other interns and residents on the hospital "team" bore an additional burden in covering the team's cases.[15]

High standards of quality must be maintained. However, several points should be noted. First, the deficiencies in performance of these candidates, as they were described to us, do not represent such a serious or substantial deviation from the standard that extraordinary measures need to be taken to correct them; rather, they appear primarily to indicate a need to adapt existing skills and knowledge to the Ontario medical environment. Second, candidates who entered the profession before 1986 were assessed only through the MCCEE, a mechanism for the assessment of applicants for internship that may not have been sufficiently rigorous to ensure competence. The assessment mechanism now in place for entry into the PIP, or a variation of it, represents a significant improvement over the MCCEE and is capable of determining with a much higher degree of accuracy which candidates are ready to enter internship.[16] Finally, it must be remembered that even these successful candidates are still being permitted only to enter into internship, and it currently extends for two years. During that period they will be supervised and their performances monitored; there remains an opportunity to assess their skills fully.

A program of retraining for physicians from elsewhere whose clinical skills are not adequate to enter internship is desirable, and we applaud the effort; however, we cannot condone its use as an across-the-board requirement of all graduates of unaccredited medical schools who make application to enter the profession. In this position we are consistent with our analysis of other professions. In many professions a period of Ontario experience is required; the compulsory two-year internship meets this need. There is no profession for which we have recommended or permitted compulsory retraining of candidates who can demonstrate a level of skill equal to meet the Ontario standard.

HUMAN RESOURCES AND CONTROL OF THE PHYSICIAN POOL

As discussed above, the provincial Government must concern itself with the important and complex issues related to the costs of health services, which have been linked to the size of the physician pool.

As indicated, this concern must be addressed. However, we repeat that our mandate is not to do a review of health-care costs in Ontario; we leave that task to bodies dedicated to that purpose. A highlighting of the arguments raised on this point relevant to this Task Force is all that has been attempted, and it is our view that that is all that is necessary to address the limited issue facing this Task Force.

The case made by advocates of strict human-resource controls is that statistical demographic analysis leads one to the conclusion that there is now, or will be before the end of the century, a surplus of practising physicians in Ontario. Such a surplus of physicians, it is said, will have a negative impact on health care in the province. It is suggested that this will manifest itself in one of two ways.[17]

First, because doctors — not the patients themselves — are by and large the ones who decide what treatments and other health services are required for the care of their patients, the costs of health care will spiral as an increasing number of physicians expand the quantity of services they each provide to their diminishing number of patients, whether or not those increased services can be justified as essential to the enhanced health of the patient. In other words, doctors will provide more services per patient at increasing cost to the province, without a corresponding increase in actual health benefit to the patient. If costs become too high to fund doctors' services, cutbacks will be required in other areas, such as equipment purchases, hospital beds, and support services, with a resultant lowering of general health-care standards.

The other, quite different, scenario is that the quality of health care will decline as the number of physicians increases. Underemployed doctors, it is suggested, will work less and therefore practise their specialized skills less, with the result that those skills will diminish with lack of use; or the doctors will attempt to obtain enough work by practising in areas outside their specialty when they are not equipped to do so.

The solution, it is said, is to control the physician pool. It has been suggested that the limitation can be imposed at any one of three entry points to the profession: at entry to medical school, where numbers could be reduced; at entry to the profession, where licences could be restricted, salaries imposed, or other means of cost control introduced; or at entry to internship. Advocates of the current policy state that controlling entry to medical school (any more than it now is controlled) is unacceptable for two reasons: first, because young Ontario applicants should not be further prevented from entering the profession; and, second, because reducing the student population base would have a serious detrimental effect on the number and quality of our teaching hospitals that currently fill a valuable role in education, research, and public service. These same advocates also argue that curtailing in any way the right of already licensed physicians to practise would be politically impracticable. Thus, the control of entry to internship is seen as the most viable option.

On this point it is argued that Ontario medical students have completed all of their medical training at great expense to the province (the current estimate is approximately $100,000 per student)[18] and that they should not be limited in their right to complete this final leg of their training; therefore, this control mechanism should be applied only against those attempting to enter the profession from outside Canada. It should be added that another reason given for the preferability of controlling the entry of this group is that, within the province, numbers can be controlled with accuracy and certainty, and controls loosened or tightened as circumstances require; the numbers of graduates of foreign medical schools, meanwhile, fluctuates from year to year and cannot be controlled by Ontario itself. It is inappropriate, it is said, to inject into one's policy such an unreliable variable.

This entire analysis is based on a series of suppositions and hypotheses, and we have serious concerns about a number of them. On the very fundamental question of whether there will be a surplus, we are concerned that factors which would lead to the opposite conclusion may not have been adequately taken into account. For example, an aging population with its increased need for health services may turn a surplus into a shortage. We are also concerned that the need for physicians in underserviced northern areas and the need to service immigrant groups have not been recognized fully. These needs have traditionally been met to a considerable degree by foreign-trained physicians, and a failure to find alternate personnel to service these groups is resulting in inequality of access to adequate medical care for some members of society. In addition, it has been strongly suggested that there are in fact serious shortages in some specialties: psychiatry, ophthalmology, anaesthesiology, and laboratory medicine, to name but a few. We have heard from a number of sources, including health-care institutions, of the difficulties encountered in the recruitment of needed candidates who have been trained outside of Canada. Finally, we note that such projections are not infallible, and that shortages, when they occur, are difficult to respond to quickly and can cause enormous problems. The current shortage of primary and secondary school educators is following close at the heels of surplus projections, and we note as well the current shortage of nursing care in Ontario.

Perhaps most significant was the view presented to us by medical care practitioners themselves: that the increasing costs of health care should not be attributed to numbers but to technological change. The capital costs involved in the purchase of highly sophisticated equipment are themselves enormous; add the cost of administering the new treatments or tests made possible, including the human resources to perform and interpret the procedures, and increases will inevitably result. Yet controlling these costs is difficult: once a procedure is available, doctors and patients alike want it; once equipment can be purchased, there is pressure that it be provided. These decisions are sometimes duplicated and occasionally made before the real benefits of the procedure have been verified. These are not problems related to numbers; they are problems that reflect the enormous advances made in medicine, which all individuals wish to participate in and benefit from.

Finally, each of the scenarios hypothesized presupposes a considerable level of bad faith on the part of medical practitioners in this province, assuming that they will, as a group, act from motives of self-interest above all others. We do not share this view.

Even if one were to concede the concept of a surplus in need of control, we question the analysis which leads to the conclusion that the best way to limit numbers is to restrict the entry of graduates of foreign medical schools. Limiting the entry of foreign graduates does not in our view parallel the existing limitation on entry to Ontario medical schools that faces residents of this province. The immigrants have already faced several such barriers in their careers and are now practising professionals. Ontario-born aspirants to the right to become physicians do not have a superior claim to those who have come here from other countries; nor should a graduate of an Ontario school have a superior entitlement to an internship position over a graduate of any other medical school who is equally qualified and a legitimate member of society in this province.

Other Issues

On the subject of human resources, several further points have been made that do not alter our view of the overall issue but are worthy of merit and recommendation.

Shortage of Physicians in Developing Countries

It has been suggested that the movement of doctors from developing to developed countries represents a "brain drain" which takes from the neediest countries, who have expended large amounts to educate their own doctors, and gives to those countries least in need. Canada does not appear to be a major participant in this equation. The World Health Organization, however, has recommended that all countries work to develop self-sufficiency in physician workforce. Although the argument does lend support to the position that visa trainees and visitors should be discouraged from remaining in Canada after their training is complete, it cannot be used to deny the right of immigrant doctors who have come to Canada to practise their profession; these men and women are entitled to the same basic human rights enjoyed by all Canadians.

Immigrant Waiver

It has been brought to our attention that immigrants to this country who are physicians are in some cases required by federal immigration authorities to sign an acknowledgment that they have been advised that it may not be possible for them to obtain a licence to practise medicine in Canada. It has been suggested that in the face of such an acknowledgment of prior notice of the situation, immigrants cannot in fairness be permitted to insist on their right to licensure. We have discussed this issue in Chapter 2 of this Report, "Foreign-Trained Individuals in Ontario," and concluded there that such conditions on entry cannot be relied upon. Once accepted to this country, a person must come free to work in the field he or she chooses, bringing all the skills he or she has acquired.

Alternate Roles for Medical Personnel

We see considerable merit in study being given to the concept of physicians working in other health disciplines for which they may have partial or full qualificiations. The possibility of membership in such alternative disciplines might prove satisfying to members of the immigrant medical community who are unsuccessful in obtaining licensure as physicians or who are content to work in other roles in the health-care field. The availability of information and training for such individuals might prove beneficial to all concerned. It is also useful to reassess the functions appropriately assigned to physicians and those that can be undertaken by nurse practitioners and by paramedics.

Entry by Other Means

Statistics provided by the College of Physicians and Surgeons of Ontario indicate that between April 1987 and February 1988 as many as 79 graduates of unaccredited medical schools received licences to practise medicine. Some of these were described as having "no acceptable training." Under the *Health Disciplines Act*,[19] the Registration Committee has the authority in its discretion to waive certain entrance requirements; these statistics represent individual cases in which it has elected to do so.

The Task Force has not taken the position, with regard to any profession, that professional bodies should be denied this discretionary power. Prior to 1986, candidates with specialist training approved by the Royal College were entitled to licensure in Ontario; in 1986 that means of entry was closed off, yet it has been effectively retained through the continued use of the waiver power for these candidates. The use of the waiver in such cases has become so common that the Ontario College wishes to have the procedure formally recognized in regulation. The waiver power has, therefore, proved useful. The exercise of the waiver power should, however, be public and publicized and reasons given for each instance of its exercise. We have made recommendations to this effect in Chapter 4, "Issues Facing the Professions."

The recognition by the College of Physicians and Surgeons and by the profession that such numbers of graduates of unaccredited medical schools are qualified to be granted general licences sharply contradicts the position put forward by proponents of the Pre-Internship Program that *all* graduates of unaccredited schools require the pre-internship training in order to be qualified to obtain educational licences for internship. The broad disparity in treatment between the two groups is based, primarily, on the premise that the abilities of one group are known while those of the other are not; as we have indicated above, we are of the view that the abilities of the second group can be determined. Recruitment of physicians needed in a particular discipline might then be possible from the existing pool of physicians already in this province, thus eliminating the need to draw from elsewhere.

SUMMARY OF PUBLIC COMMENTS

We should not leave this subject without reference to the written submissions we received from individuals and ethno-cultural organizations with regard to entry into the medical profession.

The Task Force received a number of written submissions from individuals, agencies serving immigrants, and other community-based organizations regarding the rules and regulations affecting entry into the medical profession in Ontario.

Community organizations and agencies, generally, discussed the limited availability of internships to foreign-trained medical professionals, and considered the Pre-Internship Program (PIP) as posing a significant barrier to entry into the profession. Two of these organizations discussed, at some length, the emerging need for, and the importance of, the provision of more culturally and linguistically sensitive health care to Ontario's many ethno-cultural communities.

Most of the individuals submitting briefs to the Task Force were those who have already passed the required examinations and currently are waiting for internship positions. A recurring theme in these submissions is the somewhat "paradoxical" situation of the apparent lack of adequate health-care services in northern Ontario (in reference to the "underserviced areas program") and the contention that there is an excess supply of medical doctors in Ontario. Suggestion was made time and again that the PIP be abolished and the number of available internship positions be increased. A majority of the submissions considered the evaluation procedures and the examination requirements to be biased and unfair, and they argued that such procedures and requirements placed an emphasis on the location of the training instead of on its quality and equivalence. A number of individuals felt that the abolition of unfunded internships and subsequent changes in entry rules and criteria severely disadvantaged a large number of well-qualified, foreign-trained professionals. Other relevant issues raised in individual submissions are:

- the loss of skills and expertise owing to the potential long wait to obtain an internship position;

- the lack of financial support while upgrading skills;

- the limited accessibility of retraining programs;

- the lack of sufficient, clear guidelines on the accreditation procedure and criteria; and

- the discriminatory nature of the 18-month residency requirement.

RECOMMENDATIONS

Assessment of Prior Learning

It is our view that all graduates of unaccredited medical schools should be entitled to a comprehensive assessment of their training to determine if they meet the Ontario standard of competence. All candidates who meet the standard of competence should be entitled to receive educational licences and, by virtue of these licences, be entitled to apply for internship. The Pre-Internship Program as it now exists should not continue to be required of such candidates.

In any profession such an assessment is difficult and requires sophisticated and well-developed expertise. We have recommended in Chapter 5 of this Report, "Prior Learning Assessment," the creation of an agency, named the Prior Learning Assessment Network (PLAN), to be a resource to professional bodies in performing assessments of prior learning of candidates trained outside of Ontario. We are of the view that it should be made available to the medical profession. Unlike most professions in which a clinical assessment forms part of the final licensing examination, however, in this profession it is clearly important that a clinical assessment take place prior to internship.

We have indicated in our discussion of prior learning assessment that clinical assessments are best conducted by the professional body itself. The testing should, of course, reflect the Ontario standard of competence and be in compliance with recognized standards of test development as discussed in Chapter 6 of this Report, "Licensure Testing."

While we are of the view that candidates capable of demonstrating training equivalent to the Ontario standard should be entitled to proceed to internship, we recognize that a period of acclimatization to the Ontario hospital environment is desirable. For such candidates, however, such a period need not be lengthy. By keeping such a program brief, costs will remain at a reasonable level; at the same time, candidates will benefit as they acquire, with greater expediency, a necessary awareness of Ontario practice.

10.1   *We recommend that the requirement that all graduates of unaccredited foreign medical schools complete a pre-internship program as it is now defined be eliminated from the regulations.*

10.2   *We recommend that evaluations of equivalency be available to all graduates of unaccredited medical schools. Because of the considerable clinical component in medical training which must be assessed before internship, it is appropriate that such assessments be conducted by the professional body itself. The tests should be developed in accordance with recognized standards of test development.*

10.3   *We recommend that every such candidate assessed as having training equivalent to the standard required of Ontario-trained candidates be granted the status of a clinical clerk in an Ontario teaching hospital for a brief period of no more than eight weeks, the length required depending upon the needs of the candidate as determined by the candidate and his or her supervisor. During this time the candidate shall observe the practice of medicine in an Ontario hospital; shall practise, under close supervision, his or her clinical skills; and shall be observed by a group supervisor. The purpose of this segment of preparation for internship is to permit the candidate a period of time to acclimatize to the Ontario hospital environment; it is not for further assessment and evaluation.*

10.4   *We recommend that all candidates who have met the above requirements be eligible to receive educational licences.*

Internship

We have concluded that the current allocation of funded internship spots should be retained but that any candidate eligible for an educational licence should be permitted to apply for any of those spots. All positions should be filled through the Canadian Internship Matching Service (CIMS), and there should be no policy or practice that graduates of Ontario schools must all be placed before graduates from schools elsewhere. We acknowledge that in some years there may be more applicants than there are places and that some of those without places may be graduates of Ontario schools. While this is unfortunate, it is unavoidable in the absence of an increase in the number of funded spots. Any problems that exist relating to the cost of health care in this province must be shared among all Ontario residents, whether they have domestic or foreign training. We are also of the view that the introduction of this element of competition and challenge into the system of medical education in this province will not be detrimental. Such a system is more likely to raise than to lower standards, and it should encourage excellence within the profession. The public benefit is enhanced through a selection process that results in the very best physicians qualifying for practice.

The criteria to be considered in the allocation of internship positions to qualified candidates should, to ensure fairness, be clearly articulated and made public. In addition, such criteria should take into account the health-care needs of the community, so that the particular needs of some immigrant groups or of northern communities lacking specific services are more likely to be met.

> 10.5   We recommend that any candidate with an educational licence be entitled to apply for and obtain an internship in Ontario on an equal basis with any other candidate, regardless of place of training. The applications of all candidates for internship should be assessed against clearly articulated criteria, which may from time to time reflect particular needs for medical services in the community.

Language

The TOEFL and TSE tests are relied on in the medical profession to assess fluency. We discuss the use of such tests in Chapter 7, "Language Testing," and reference should be made to that chapter for a full review of the issues. Suffice to say at this point that we endorse the view of analysts that the TOEFL and the TSE are inadequate and inappropriate means of assessing fluency within the context of professional certification. If the profession is of the view that a specific language screen is desirable, we suggest the development of a limited, profession-specific fluency test, to be developed with the assistance of English/French as a Second Language experts, to assess the linguistic level of the candidate as it is relevant to professional practice. In the alternative, the qualifying examination or any other written or oral test administered as part of an equivalency assessment may function as a language screen, provided the level of fluency required is reviewed to ensure that it is appropriate to the profession and that profession- and discipline-specific language is assessed.

> 10.6   *We recommend that the use of the TOEFL and TSE tests be discontinued. Any other test used to assess language, whether it be a particular test developed for that purpose or the qualifying examinations themselves, should reflect our general recommendations on the use and development of such tests in our chapters "Licensure Testing" (Chapter 6) and "Language Testing" (Chapter 7).*

PART IV

Review and Appeal

CHAPTER 11

Review of Registration Decisions

The decision by an occupational registration body to grant or refuse registration must satisfy the public's right to be assured that practitioners are properly qualified; the applicant's right to use his or her acquired skills; and the occupational organizations' right to set standards of qualification for practice.

As discussed in Chapter 4, "Issues Facing the Professions," applicants may be required by legislation to obtain licensure in order to practise a profession; alternatively, certification may be required in order to use a reserved title (for example, certified general accountant) or as a credential that is in fact a prerequisite for obtaining employment in the occupation. (In this chapter we use the word "registration" to include both licensure and certification, bearing in mind always that a refusal to register in relation to a licensed profession constitutes a legal prohibition on practice, thus making particularly important the right to an effective and independent review of the denial.) Occupational bodies are conferred with the powers to set qualification standards and to register the applicant with or without conditions, or to refuse to register the applicant if he or she fails to meet required standards. This power to set qualifications and determine registration can be justified only if granted and exercised for the purpose of protecting the public interest in ensuring that registrants are qualified and competent.[1]

The validity of the registration decision depends upon conformity with principles of fairness in the decision-making process, principles which are rooted in both the common law and in provincial statutes such as the *Statutory Powers Procedure Act*.[2]

Generally, the principle of fairness in the registration context requires that a decision be based on an unbiased and accurate assessment of the applicant's qualifications, that the applicant be aware of the required standards against which his or her qualifications are to be measured, that the applicant be provided with an opportunity to state his or her case, and that the person reviewing the qualifications properly interpret the entry standards.

This chapter discusses the fairness of the existing decision-making processes of occupational regulatory bodies with a view to these common law and statutory principles. To assist in measuring the existing structures, we have developed five guiding principles that underlie the specific recommendations of this chapter.

1) The various entry requirements established by the occupational bodies, such as academic prerequisites and examinations, should be made known to the applicant and be designed to assist the decision maker to evaluate, objectively and accurately, the applicant's competence to practise. (The question of fairness in testing is discussed at length in Chapter 6, "Licensure Testing.")

2) The applicant should be entitled to present, to the initial decision maker and to the tribunal charged with the power to review negative decisions, all documentation that he or she considers relevant. At the initial stage, the procedure might combine the presentation of documentation such as academic credentials and letters of reference with the opportunity to meet with the decision maker or a delegated representative.

3) The applicant who is denied registration should be given written reasons for the decision, including a reference to documentation or other information upon which that decision has been based, and an opportunity to review the contents of his or her file.

4) The applicant who is denied registration must be granted an opportunity to appeal and challenge that decision before an impartial body that is independent of the initial decision maker. This body must be given comprehensive powers of review, including the power to substitute its own decision for that of the initial decision maker. The tribunal must be able to consider both the merits of the case and the procedural and substantive fairness of the decision, including the validity of the standards and the measures of competence (for example, the licensing examinations).

5) The applicant should be entitled by law to a full review by the Courts of a negative registration decision.

CHALLENGES THROUGH STATUTORY APPEAL OR JUDICIAL REVIEW

The initial registration decision is typically made by one person — a registrar, admissions officer, or superintendent — and is based on the written documentation submitted by the applicant. If that initial decision is negative, an applicant may challenge it in two ways.

First, an opportunity to obtain review of the decision may be found either in the legislation that creates the occupational body or in regulations or bylaws passed pursuant to that enabling legislation. This type of review is referred to as a "statutory appeal." The steps in the appeal route that a licensure applicant is required by statute to follow are not consistent among the various occupations. Commonly, negative decisions of a registrar are referred to a committee, which typically is composed of members of the occupation. If the committee agrees that registration should be refused, the decision may be subject to a right of appeal to an independent tribunal. If the tribunal is prepared to uphold the negative decision, the applicant may be able to appeal the decision to the Courts, generally the Divisional Court of the Supreme Court of Ontario. Alternatively, the legislation may omit one or more stages and may not provide for an internal committee review, an appeal to an independent tribunal, or an appeal to Court.

Where the occupational legislation does not provide applicants with an appeal procedure in respect of negative decisions, the applicant may try the second option, applying to the Divisional Court for "judicial review" pursuant to the *Judicial Review Procedure Act* (*JRPA*).[3] Theoretically, judicial review may provide a narrower remedy than one resulting from a statutory appeal to Court. The scope of judicial review does not allow the Court to substitute its opinion for that of the prior decision maker, and a Court is not empowered to consider the merits or the substance of the decision.

Judicial review is limited to a consideration of whether the regulatory body has committed a technical legal error which is so serious that the Court decides it must intervene.[4] An example would be where a tribunal does something clearly outside the power given by the statute. The Court does not review the merits. The question for the Court is purely technical; for example, whether a serious error in procedure has been made. (Examples of legal errors permitting Court review include the following: reliance on irrelevant considerations, exercising powers in bad faith, exercising powers for an improper purpose, making serious procedural errors that constitute a failure of natural justice or fairness, fettering discretion by applying general rules rather than considering each case on its own merits, making a decision without evidence to support that decision, making an unreasonable decision, and exercising powers in violation of the *Canadian Charter of Rights and Freedoms*.)

Most of the occupational statutes reviewed by the Task Force contain statutory rights of appeal, which will be discussed in detail below. The Task Force has identified several occupations that do not provide for the Courts to review an initial registration decision. The occupational groups with no right of appeal to the Courts range from voluntary associations without legislative basis to self-regulating professions established by statute. The following legislatively regulated occupations currently have no provision for an appeal to the Courts in their statutes: law, chartered accountancy, forestry, agrology, dietetics, dental technology, dental hygiene, radiological technology, chiropractic, osteopathy, massage therapy, physiotherapy, naturopathy, chiropody, veterinary medicine, and ophthalmic dispensing.

An applicant who is refused registration by one of the occupational groups listed above will be able to obtain a Court review of the refusal only by initiating an application for judicial review. In the following sections, we discuss the procedure for obtaining judicial review in Ontario.

Judicial Review Procedure Act

In Ontario, the common law principles that govern judicial review have largely been incorporated into the *JRPA*, which codifies the procedure for obtaining judicial review and gives the Divisional Court jurisdiction to grant relief. In the absence of a right of appeal by statute, an applicant may apply under the *JRPA* for judicial review of a negative registration decision. The *JRPA* also allows an application for judicial review notwithstanding any right of statutory appeal, although where the right of appeal has not been exercised, the Courts will be reluctant to grant judicial review.[5]

The *JRPA* defines two general categories of applications. First, an application for review can be brought by way of an application for an order in the nature of *certiorari*, *mandamus*, or prohibition (see below). Second, an individual may proceed by way of an action or an injunction or a declaration with respect to the exercising of a statutory power (or the refusal to exercise it). All these remedies are discretionary and may or may not be granted, even though a claimant appears to be legally entitled as, for example, in seeking a remedy before the Courts.

The remedy of *certiorari* (literally, "to be informed to a greater extent") permits a Court to quash or set aside a decision when serious legal errors have been committed. *Mandamus* (literally "we command") compels the performance of a statutory duty, but it will not compel the exercising of discretion in a particular manner. An order of prohibition forbids the person against whom it is issued from proceeding with an intended course of action. An injunction requires the person at whom the Court order is directed to do, or to refrain from doing, a particular thing. Declarations are statements of the rights of parties that do not directly require anyone to do anything but are normally adhered to. In the registration context, an applicant would usually rely on the remedies of *mandamus* or *certiorari*.[6]

Natural Justice, Fairness, and the Statutory Powers Procedure Act

As noted above, judicial review may be obtained for serious procedural errors resulting in unfairness or injustice to a party. The Courts will intervene where there has been a violation of a set of basic procedural standards, called the doctrines of natural justice and fairness.

At common law, the doctrine of natural justice has historically had two basic objectives: that the applicant know the case against him or her and be given a chance to answer it; and that the decision be made by an impartial decision maker. To achieve those objectives, the principles of natural justice might require that an oral hearing be granted, that evidence be given under oath, and that the applicant be afforded the right to obtain counsel and the right to cross-examine witnesses.

The doctrine of fairness was developed as an adjunct to the doctrine of natural justice, applicable where the applicant was not entitled to all the protections constituting natural justice. Today, the two doctrines impose an increasingly equal standard of procedural fairness. What is considered to be a "fair" decision-making process, in conformity with the principles of natural justice, however, varies with the circumstances of each case. Neither doctrine has been extensively applied by the Courts to registration decisions of occupational bodies. For example, the Courts have held that the initial granting of a license by a professional body is a privilege, not a right, and that an applicant is therefore not entitled to the full protection of the doctrine of natural justice. The Courts have also been reluctant to apply the doctrine of fairness to decisions such as licensure denials, which are characterized as involving expectancy interests.[7]

Natural justice and fairness are partially codified in Ontario in the *Statutory Powers Procedure Act (SPPA)*,[8] which sets the minimum standard of procedural protection available to applicants in hearings before administrative bodies such as occupational registration committees. The *SPPA*, for example, requires that the parties be given reasonable notice of the hearing; be entitled to representation by counsel; and be able to call, examine, and cross-examine witnesses; and that, if requested by a party, the tribunal give reasons in writing for its decision.[9]

The *SPPA*, however, provides that the procedural protections enumerated apply only to those tribunals that exercise a "statutory power of decision," as defined by the *Act*, and only where a hearing is required by statute or otherwise by law. If the occupational body that has refused to register an applicant is a private organization not established by statute, it will not exercise a "statutory power of decision," and the protections in the *SPPA* will not apply to the applicant's case. Additionally, the legislation establishing the occupational organization must require that a hearing be held; otherwise, the *SPPA* will not apply. (If the enabling legislation of the organization is silent on the question of a hearing, one may look to the common law to determine if a hearing is required by the doctrines of natural justice or fairness. The doctrine of natural justice is not thought to require that licensure applicants be granted a hearing, but it may be through the developing doctrine of fairness that hearings are considered a requirement of the common law.) Neither will the SPPA apply if the occupational legislation specifically excludes its application.

In summary, it should be noted that, in the absence of a statutory right of appeal, applicants to occupational bodies have limited and uncertain remedies in respect of a registration denial. The scope of Court review of registration refusals by occupational bodies is limited not only by the nature of judicial review as a remedy but by a judicial reluctance to apply the doctrines of natural justice and fairness to registration decisions. In addition, if the occupational body is not established by statute or if the applicant is not entitled by law to an oral hearing, the applicant will not be entitled to rely on the protections set out in the *SPPA*.

THE EXISTING STATUTORY APPEAL PROCESSES

As discussed in Chapter 4 ("Issues Facing the Professions"), the range of rights afforded the applicants in the registration process is inconsistent from profession to profession. In the discussion below we summarize and contrast the various statutory appeal routes and outline some of the specific rights afforded applicants to occupational bodies at the various stages of the application process.

The Initial Decision

Occupational legislation may provide that the initial decision over an application for registration may be made by only one person, often called a "registrar," or, when a negative decision is proposed, may require the registrar to refer applications to a registration committee. In either case, the decision is based on documents submitted by the applicant. Currently, no occupation is required by statute to grant the applicant an interview before the registrar or an opportunity to make representations.

The *Health Disciplines Act*[10] is an example of a statute that requires the registrar to refer to a registration committee all applications for which a negative decision is proposed. (A negative decision would include a proposed decision to attach terms, conditions, or limitations on a licence, as well as a proposed refusal to register.) The *Act*, which governs the professions of dentistry, medicine, nursing, optometry, and pharmacy, establishes a registration committee for each profession, composed of members of the profession. Some statutes, for example the *Denture Therapists Act* and the *Funeral Services Act*, incorporate an identical statutory appeal scheme but establish registration committees that include one member who is not a member of the profession, appointed to represent the public interest.[11]

Under each of these statutes, the initial decision of the registrar is not final until the review by the registration committee is complete. The committee has the power to exempt an applicant from licensing requirements, to direct the registrar to issue or refuse to issue a licence, or to issue a licence subject to terms, conditions, and limitations specified by the committee. The committee may also require an applicant to demonstrate competence through the completion of a course of study or a continuing education program.[12]

The *Professional Engineers Act, 1984*,[13] the *Architects Act, 1984*,[14] and the *Surveyors Act, 1987*[15] all have statutory schemes allowing any applications which the registrar proposes to refuse because of insufficient academic or experiential requirements to be referred to an academic requirements committee (ARC) or an experience requirements committee (ERC). In contrast to the *Health Disciplines Act*, the three statutes require these committees to provide applicants with the opportunity to present written submissions of their qualifications. In some cases an applicant will be invited to attend a meeting with the committee, although the committees are not required by statute to grant a hearing or an opportunity for making oral submissions.

The *Denture Therapists Act*,[16] the *Funeral Services Act*,[17] and the *Registered Insurance Brokers Act*[18] are three other occupational statutes that require negative decisions of the registrar to be referred to a registration committee for review. None of these three statutes, however, provides an applicant with the right to make written representations to the reviewing committee.

Review Before a Tribunal or a Board

An applicant facing a refusal of registration may wish to challenge the refusal at a higher level. The next stage in the process is typically a formal review conducted by either an independent tribunal or a tribunal composed of members of the profession or occupation. The statutory review process, however, sometimes omits the committee stage described above and establishes a formal tribunal review as the applicant's first opportunity to challenge a negative decision.

The policies of occupations reviewed by the Task Force vary, depending on whether the applicant is entitled to an appeal hearing before a tribunal, the issues on which the applicant may appeal, the type of hearing to be held, and the appeal body's powers to overturn the initial decision.

Under the *Health Disciplines Act*, if a registration committee proposes to refuse licensure, or proposes to attach terms or limitations to the licence, the applicant is given notice of the proposal together with the reasons. A copy is served on the Health Disciplines Board, which is a government-appointed appeal body composed of individuals who are not members of the profession. Notice to applicants must inform them of their option of the right to an oral hearing or a review of the written evidence and submissions. Applicants must specify which route they prefer — a hearing or a review.[19]

Although the registration committees established under the *Health Disciplines Act* have broad powers, the jurisdiction of the Health Disciplines Board to grant a remedy is more limited. The board can confirm the decision; require qualifying examinations or training; or refer the matter back to the committee for further consideration or direct registration, but only if the board finds that the applicant meets the requirements *and* that the committee exercised its powers improperly. The board has no power to grant exemptions from any of the requirements.

Applicants applying for a hearing before the Health Disciplines Board are afforded procedural rights under the *Act*. For example, applicants must be afforded an opportunity before the proceedings to examine any written or documentary evidence or report that will be produced or given in evidence.[20] The oral evidence taken must be recorded and copies provided to the parties at their own cost.[21] The fairness of the hearing is also ensured by the statutory requirement that board members must be present throughout the hearing before participating in the decision.[22] Currently, hearings before the board are required to be held *in camera* unless the applicant requests a public hearing.[23] Additionally, an applicant who has asked that a hearing be held may rely on the provisions of the *Statutory Powers Procedures Act* (*SPPA*), except where they conflict with the specific provisions of the *Health Disciplines Act*.[24]

Two related professions are also governed by the *Health Disciplines Act*. Nursing assistants are governed by Part IV of the *Act* and are subject to the appeal provisions of Part I. In contrast, dental hygienists, who are mentioned in Part II, are not granted the same right to the appeal process. If refused licensure, they have no right of review by the registration committee for dentistry, nor can an applicant appeal to the Health Disciplines Board. Applicants may seek review only before the Council of the Royal College of Dental Surgeons of Ontario.

A review mechanism identical to that under the *Health Disciplines Act* is found in the *Denture Therapists Act* and the *Funeral Services Act*. Registration committee decisions are reviewed by the Denture Therapists Appeal Board and the Funeral Services Review Board, respectively, both of which are composed of individuals from outside the profession. The procedural protections in the *Health Disciplines Act* are also found in these statutes.

The *Ministry of Consumer and Commercial Relations Act*[25] also provides for a formal review process in respect of registration denials for a number of occupational groups, including real estate and business brokers, motor vehicle dealers, and mortgage brokers. Under this *Act*, proposed negative decisions are not reviewed by a committee; instead, the applicant proceeds directly from an initial decision to an appeal tribunal. The government-appointed Commercial Registration Appeal Tribunal (CRAT) has been established under the *Ministry of Consumer and Commercial Relations Act*, and various occupational statutes require that decisions to refuse registration be referred to this tribunal. For example, the *Real Estate and Business Brokers Act*[26] provides that if the registrar refuses registration, notice of the refusal and the reasons therefor must be served on the applicant. The notice informs the applicant that he or she has a right to a hearing before CRAT.[27]

An applicant appearing before CRAT is granted various procedural rights. The *Ministry of Consumer and Commercial Relations Act* provides that the applicant may examine all evidence before the hearing.[28] Oral evidence before the tribunal is recorded, and transcripts are made available on payment of a fee.[29] Additionally, although the *Act* does not specifically state that the protection of the *SPPA* is available, by law this protection would apply because the tribunal exercises a statutory power of decision and the legislation requires that a hearing be held.

The *Registered Insurance Brokers Act* also provides for a hearing or review before a tribunal. This statutory scheme, however, is different in one key respect from the Health Disciplines legislation: whereas the Health Disciplines Board, the Denture Therapists Appeal Board, and the Funeral Services Review Board perform an independent review, the Qualification and Registration Committee under the *Registered Insurance Brokers Act* does not. The legislation provides that the committee review the proposals of the manager (a registrar) to refuse certification. If the committee proposes to refuse certification, notice and written reasons are served on the applicant, who is informed of his or her right to a hearing before the same committee. The committee at the hearing may confirm its decision or, if the committee finds that the applicant meets the requirements, may require qualifying examinations, additional training, or direct registration.[30]

In our view, whether or not the same members sit on the initial assessment and the review of the initial decision, the legislation can be criticized for allowing the committee to sit in review of itself, a provision that may give rise to a reasonable apprehension of bias.

A formal review of the initial negative decision is also provided for in the bylaws of the Institute of Chartered Accountants of Ontario. The bylaws require that, before reporting its findings of eligibility to the Council of the Institute, the application committee give every applicant prompt written notice of these findings.[31] A dissatisfied applicant may apply for a formal review before the council-appeal committee. The review is conducted as a formal hearing in the nature of an appeal, and the bylaws provide the appellant with a set of specific procedural protections, including the right to notice of hearing, to representation by counsel or agent, to a public hearing, to question witnesses, and to written reasons for the decision. In addition, the bylaws require that the members of the committee be present throughout the hearing.[32] We note, however, that the procedural protections are included in bylaws and not established by statute or regulation and thus may be amended by the profession without approval of the Legislature or the provincial Cabinet.

There are two professions whose enabling legislation, although establishing an appeal tribunal, so limits access to that tribunal as to render the process virtually ineffective. The *Professional Engineers Act, 1984*, and the *Architects Act, 1984*, provide that an applicant must be given notice of the decision of the registrar to refuse licensure and may apply for a hearing before a registration committee. As discussed earlier, decisions related to academic and experience requirements are referred to the profession's academic requirements or experience requirements committee. The decision of these committees is final and binding and may not be reviewed by the registration committee.[33] Essentially, the legislation limits the review of the initial decision to factors other than academic or experience requirements.

The procedural protections found in the *Professional Engineers Act, 1984*, the *Architects Act, 1984*, and the *Surveyors Act, 1987*, parallel those found in the current *Health Disciplines Act*. Prior to the hearing, parties appearing before the registration committee are afforded an opportunity to examine any written or documentary evidence or reports that will be produced or given in evidence.[34] To avoid questions of bias, the legislation provides that members of the committee cannot have participated in any investigation prior to the hearing and cannot participate in the decision unless present for the entire hearing.[35] Unlike the *Health Disciplines Act*, these statutes do not provide that hearings must be conducted *in camera*.

Appeal to Court

A right of appeal to the Courts is the final stage of the review process set out in the occupational legislation discussed in this section on existing statutory appeal processes. The usual course of review takes an applicant before an internal committee of the profession or occupation, then before an appeal tribunal, and finally to the Divisional Court.

The scope of the Court's powers on appeal may be limited by the wording of the statute. Further, even if the actual wording of the appeal provision in the statute grants the Court broad powers of review, the actual scope of the appeal may in practice be limited by a tradition of judicial deference to registration bodies. If there is some evidence to support the decision by the occupational body, the Court may be reticent to substitute its own conclusions for those of the regulatory body.[36]

The *Health Disciplines Act*, the *Denture Therapists Act*, and the *Funeral Services Act* provide that applicants may appeal decisions of the appeal board to the Divisional Court on questions of law, fact, or mixed law and fact.[37] The Court may exercise all of the powers of the registration committee and substitute its opinion for that of the committee. The Court is granted broader jurisdiction than the boards to grant remedies.[38] Notably, the Court is not handicapped in directing registration by having first to find that the registration committee acted improperly. As well, the Court is granted full power to grant exemptions from registration requirements.

Similar appeal provisions are found in the *Ministry of Consumer and Commercial Relations Act* and the *Registered Insurance Brokers Act*. Here, too, applicants may appeal decisions of the Commercial Registration Appeal Tribunal and the Qualifications and Registration Committee, respectively, to the Divisional Court on questions of law, fact, or mixed law and fact. The Court is granted all the powers of the tribunal and may substitute its opinion for that of the tribunal.[39]

A right of appeal is also found in the *Professional Engineers Act, 1984*, the *Architects Act, 1984*, and the *Surveyors Act, 1987*. Decisions of the registration committee may be appealed to the Divisional Court on questions of law, fact, or mixed law and fact, and the Court may substitute its opinion for that of the committee. As we noted earlier, however, decisions related to academic and experiential equivalency are exempt from review by the registration committee and from appeal to the Divisional Court.[40]

A small number of the occupations whose appeal structures were reviewed by the Task Force do not have a formal review process before an internal committee or independent body such as is discussed above, but instead allow an appeal directly to the Divisional Court from the initial decision.

The *Psychologists Registration Act*[41] requires psychologists to obtain a certificate of registration from a government-appointed board in order to practise in Ontario. A hearing is held at this initial stage, and if the board refuses licensure the applicant may appeal the decision directly to the Divisional Court.[42]

The *Insurance Act* gives the superintendent of insurance the power to grant licences to insurance agents. Applications shall be granted where the superintendent is satisfied that the applicant is of good character, has a reasonable educational background, has a satisfactory business or employment record, is a suitable person, will carry on business in good faith, and is not in a position to offer inducement or use coercion to secure business.[43] Applicants may appeal the decision of the superintendent to the Divisional Court.[44]

Neither of the above statutes delineates the grounds of appeal available. Usually, if the merits of the decision are to be reviewed by a Court on appeal, then that fact is specifically set out in the legislation. The grounds of appeal in both the above statutes would likely be limited to questions such as jurisdiction and law.

Most of the accounting professions also provide for an appeal to Court from the initial negative decision of the registration body. For example, the *Public Accountancy Act*[45] provides that applicants refused licensure may appeal the refusal to Divisional Court.

An accountant seeking registration as a certified management accountant must obtain membership in the Society of Management Accountants. This privately legislated organization provides in its bylaws that membership may be refused only after the applicant has been granted the right of an initial

hearing and has been given written reasons. An appeal of this decision lies
to the Court of Appeal.[46]

An accountant seeking registration as a certified general accountant
must obtain membership in the Certified General Accountants Association
of Ontario. Membership eligibility is governed by internal bylaws that do
not provide applicants with a right of review before an internal committee
or independent tribunal. An individual who is qualified for and has been
refused membership may appeal the refusal to the Divisional Court.[47]

Conversely, accountants who seek membership in the Institute of
Chartered Accountants are entitled to a formal hearing, but the decision of
the council-appeal committee is final and binding. Although no appeal to
Court is provided, an application for judicial review could be brought,
provided there has been a serious error of law.

RECOMMENDATIONS

Listed below are recommendations that set out a model review and appeal
structure for occupational legislation. In considering the appeal rights of
applicants to occupational organizations, the Task Force reviewed the
position of applicants to non-statutory bodies, but, in view of our mandate,
we did not make recommendations in relation to such occupations. Included
are references to specific amendments to be made to the various statutes in
order to bring appeal mechanisms into keeping with our general
recommendations. In addition, we have chosen to include a more detailed
discussion of those occupations and professions with a current or proposed
right of appeal to the Health Disciplines Board or to the Commercial
Registration Appeals Tribunal (CRAT), because these two bodies together
are expected to hear appeals from registration decisions in respect of more
than 30 professional and occupational groups, assuming recommendations
currently before the Government (most notably those contained in the Report
of the Health Professions Legislation Review) are implemented.

General Recommendations

11.1   *The Task Force recommends that all occupational statutes be*
        amended to provide that applicants who are refused registration
        be entitled to a right of appeal, which would incorporate the

stages and the procedural protections described below. Judicial review alone is not sufficient to deal with registration denials.

The Initial Decision

11.2   *Applicants to occupational bodies should have the right to be fully informed of eligibility requirements and standards, of the necessary documentation to be submitted, and of the procedures for obtaining review of a decision to refuse registration. We recommend that occupational legislation be amended to provide that the registrar be required to make appropriate written information available to applicants. An improvement in the flow of information from occupational bodies to all applicants would, in our view, be very helpful in reducing the likelihood of an unnecessarily adversarial relationship between the applicant and the occupational organization.*

11.3   *We recommend that occupational legislation provide the applicant with the right to review his or her admissions file before an initial decision is made. Many difficulties may be resolved quickly if the applicant is given an opportunity to examine his or her file at an early stage.*

11.4   *Where an applicant is facing a proposed negative decision that has been referred to a registration committee, we recommend that the legislation provide the applicant with the right to make written submissions with supporting documentation and evidence to the registration committee. (This documentation could include an equivalency assessment given by our proposed Prior Learning Assessment Network.) This right will increase the fairness of the proceedings without adding undue delay or complication; and, it is hoped, it will minimize the need for a costly and lengthy appeal.*

11.5   *Where occupational legislation provides that a registrar must refer proposed registration refusals to a registration committee, as is the case, for example, for all the professions established by the* Health Disciplines Act, *we recommend that the legislation should provide applicants with the right to be notified in writing of the grounds for the registrar's negative recommendation.*

11.6 *Where registration decisions are reviewed by a registration committee, we recommend that the committee have full rights of review, including the power to substitute its own opinion about the equivalency of the applicant's education and experience. (This recommendation will have particular impact on the professions of engineering, architecture, and surveying. Currently, a final equivalency assessment is made by two internal committees in each of the professional organizations: the academic requirements committee and the experience requirements committee. The equivalency assessment is, accordingly, not subject to any right of appeal under the present legislation for these three professions.)*

11.7 *We recommend that occupational legislation be amended to afford the applicant the right to be provided with written reasons for a negative initial decision.*

11.8 *Where statutory procedure requires that a registrar refer an application to a registration committee, we recommend that the committee be required to make a decision within 30 days of that referral.*

Appellate Tribunal

Recommendations 11.9-11.14 apply only to occupations established by legislation. The Task Force has given limited consideration to the position of applicants to unregulated voluntary occupational associations that grant a credential or a reserved title. (See our discussion in Chapter 4, "Issues Facing the Professions.")

11.9 *Where the initial decision maker has determined that registration should be denied or that conditions or limitations should be attached to the registration, we recommend that the applicant have the right to a review of the decision by a specialty tribunal composed in whole or in part of members of the public, independent of the occupation, appointed to represent the public interest.*

11.10 *Professions that currently have no mechanism for review by an independent tribunal include engineering, architecture, surveying, accounting, and law. We recommend that the*

Government enter into discussions with these professions to determine whether one appellate tribunal should be established to hear appeals in respect of registration refusals from all these professional bodies, or whether instead tribunals should be established for each specific profession.

11.11 Several occupational groups regulated under private legislation do not provide applicants with a right of appeal to an independent tribunal. A new tribunal could be established to provide an appeal forum for applicants to these groups. Alternatively, the government could consider expanding the jurisdiction of an existing tribunal such as the Commercial Registration Appeal Tribunal. (See Recommendation 11.36.)

11.12 We recommend that the applicant should have the choice of applying either for an oral hearing or for a review based on evidence and written submissions. The Health Disciplines Act currently provides applicants with such a choice. It is our view that the proposed optional review mechanism is cost-effective and more convenient for applicants who may wish to avoid the time and expense of preparing for and attending an oral hearing, with or without counsel. Given that much of the evidence to be considered consists of documentation, a review based on written submissions may in many cases be more appropriate than an oral hearing. The applicant would still have the option of selecting an oral hearing and calling witnesses on his or her behalf.

11.13 We recommend that the appellate tribunal be granted full powers of review by statute and, specifically, be able to exercise all the powers of the decision maker of first instance, including, where applicable, the power to exempt applicants from the usual requirements for registration; the power to review the merits of the application, including the equivalency assessment; and the power to consider the procedural and substantive fairness of the process, including the validity of any assessment or licensing examinations.

11.14 Procedural protections must be afforded the applicant at the stage of a review by an independent tribunal. We recommend that professional legislation provide the following:

- *The applicant should have the opportunity to examine, no later than 10 days before the hearing, any written or documentary evidence that will be produced or any report or written summary of the evidence that will be given by each expert witness. (The tribunal should, however, be granted the power to admit evidence even if the time limit has not been strictly observed.)*

- *Hearings should be required to be held in public unless (1) involving matters of public security, (2) involving intimate financial or personal matters of such a nature that the desirability of avoiding public disclosure outweighs the principle that hearings be conducted in public, (3) prejudicing anyone in an actual criminal or civil proceeding, or (4) jeopardizing the safety of any person. The appeal tribunal should be empowered to ban publication of identifying information as well as to prohibit publication of the identity of witnesses testifying as to allegations of sexual impropriety.*

- *No member of the tribunal should be permitted to participate in the decision unless he or she was present throughout the hearing.*

- *A party to the hearing before a tribunal should be granted the right to be represented by counsel or agent, if so desired.*

- *A party to the hearing before a tribunal should have the right to call, examine, and cross-examine witnesses.*

- *The tribunal should be required to give written reasons for its decision.*

Appeal to Court

11.15   *We recommend that the applicant have a final right of appeal to the Divisional Court on questions of law, fact, or mixed law and fact. (This recommendation will require amendments to several professional statutes, including the* Chartered Accountants Act, 1956, *the* Certified General Accountants Association of Ontario Act, 1983, *the* Society of Management

Accountants of Ontario Act, *the* Law Society Act, *the* Chiropody Act, *and the* Drugless Practitioners Act, *if the professions covered by that Act are not brought under the* Health Disciplines Act. *Also requiring amendment will be several private statutes establishing occupational organizations.)*

11.16   *We recommend that occupational legislation should expressly grant the Court the power to affirm or rescind the decision under appeal, to exercise all the powers of the tribunal, and to direct the tribunal to take any action that the Court considers proper; the Court should be empowered to substitute its opinion for that of the tribunal or to refer the matter back for a rehearing with such directions as the Court considers proper.*

Professions Under the Health Disciplines Act

11.17   *We recommend that the* Health Disciplines Act *be amended to provide that the registrar for each profession be required to inform applicants in writing of the standards and requirements to be met, of the documentation to be submitted, and of the procedure for review and appeal of negative decisions.*

11.18   *We recommend that the* Health Disciplines Act *be amended to provide that if the registrar should propose to refuse registration and refer the proposal to the registration committee, the applicant would have the right to notification in writing of the grounds for the negative recommendation of the registrar.*

11.19   *We recommend that the* Health Disciplines Act *be amended to grant applicants the right to submit written evidence, documentation, and argument at the registration committee stage.*

11.20   *We recommend that the* Health Disciplines Act *be amended to provide that all applicants have a right to access to their application files before an initial decision is made.*

11.21   *We recommend that the* Health Disciplines Act *be amended to provide that the registration committees be required to make a decision and give written reasons for it within 30 days of referral of the application by the registrar.*

11.22 *We recommend that the Health Disciplines Board, or its successor, continue to afford applicants denied registration a right to either an oral hearing or a review on the basis of written submissions, at the option of the applicant.*

11.23 *We support the recommendation of the Health Professions Legislation Review that applicants be afforded an opportunity to examine the evidence no less than 10 days before the hearing and that summaries of the evidence of each expert witness be provided. We also agree with the suggested amendment reversing the current presumption in the* Health Disciplines Act *that hearings be conducted* in camera. *It is recommended that hearings be conducted in public unless other interests will be prejudiced.*

11.24 *We recommend that the Health Disciplines Board have full powers of review. The Health Professions Legislation Review has also concluded that the powers of the Health Disciplines Board should be broadened and has recommended that the board be able to direct registration if it finds that the applicant substantially meets the requirements. We concur with this recommendation, but would also recommend deletion of the current requirement that the board find the committee has "acted improperly." Further, it is our recommendation that the board be given the power to grant exemptions. We have reviewed several decisions of the board, and we note that its members have expressed frustration that the board is unable to exempt applicants from registration requirements. The board is able to make strong recommendations only and must refer the matter back to the registration committee. We are of the view that giving the board the power to exempt applicants from statutory requirements would expedite the appeal process and avoid further costs and delays.*

11.25 *There should continue to be a right of appeal to the Divisional Court on questions of law, fact, or mixed law and fact. We agree with the suggestions made by the Health Professions Legislation Review and recommend that the legislation detailing the nature and extent of the powers be clarified so that it is* clear that the Court has all the powers of the registration committees and the Health Disciplines Board, including the power to grant exemptions.

11.26   We recommend that dental hygienists be given full status under the Health Disciplines Act, thereby entitling applicants to the full package of procedural protections in the Act.

11.27   In accordance with the Report of the Health Professions Legislation Review, it is our recommendation that the following health professions be brought under the Health Disciplines Act: audiology and speech language pathology; chiropody; chiropractic; dental hygiene; dental technology; denture therapy; dietetics; massage therapy; medical laboratory technology; medical radiation technology; midwifery; occupational therapy; ophthalmic dispensing; physiotherapy; psychology; and respiratory therapy. Applicants to these professions would then be afforded a full review before the Health Disciplines Board and the Divisional Court.

11.28   For those health professions which remain outside the scope of the Health Disciplines Act but are currently regulated by statute (for example, naturopathy), we recommend that the enabling legislation be amended to reflect the procedural recommendations of this chapter. More particularly, we would recommend that the legislation provide for a review of negative decisions by the Health Disciplines Board and a full right of appeal to the Divisional Court on questions of law, fact, and mixed law and fact.

Professions with a Right of Review by the Commercial Registration Appeal Tribunal

11.29   The enabling legislation for each of the professional and occupational groups with a right of appeal to the Commercial Registration Appeal Tribunal (CRAT) should be amended to provide applicants with the appropriate procedural protections recommended in this chapter, including the right to be informed of requirements and standards, the right to see their application files, and the right to receive written reasons for a negative decision.

11.30 *Section 7(7) of the* Ministry of Consumer and Commercial Relations Act *currently provides that one member of a three-person appeal panel be a representative of the occupational group that is the subject of the appeal. Given our recommendations below to expand the jurisdiction of CRAT, it is recommended that the panel be expanded to include representatives of the new occupational groups being considered in appeals before CRAT.*

11.31 *We recommend that the* Act *be amended to provide that the applicant have the option of applying to CRAT for either an oral hearing or a review based on written evidence and submissions.*

11.32 *We recommend that the* Act *be amended to incorporate the right to see written or documentary evidence and a summary of expert evidence at least 10 days before the hearing.*

11.33 *We recommend that the* Registered Insurance Brokers Act *be amended to provide a right of appeal to CRAT, which would replace the current statutory scheme that requires the qualification and registration committee to sit in review of its own decision.*

11.34 *We recommend that applicants for registration as insurance agents under the* Insurance Act *be granted a statutory right of appeal to CRAT. There is currently no provision for review before an independent body.*

11.35 *We recommend that in keeping with the proposed new* Funeral Directors and Establishments Act, *applicants for registration in the death-care sector be granted a right of appeal to CRAT, and that the Funeral Services Review Board no longer serve this function.*

11.36 *Finally, we recommend that consideration be given to expanding the jurisdiction of CRAT. The tribunal could hear appeals from registration refusals by occupations currently regulated under private "reserved title" legislation, as discussed in Chapter 4, "Issues Facing the Professions." With respect to the accounting professions, we have recommended above (11.11) that a new appellate tribunal be established to hear appeals from registration refusals.*

CHAPTER 12

Human Rights Legislation

. . . it is the public policy of the government to provide all persons in Ontario with equal rights and opportunities and to facilitate their full contribution to life in Ontario . . . The right to equal opportunity must be balanced against the right of members of our society to be confident that the services they receive, particularly in matters which involve their physical well-being, are rendered by qualified and capable individuals.

— from the Submission to the Task Force
by the Ontario Human Rights Commission

The *Ontario Human Rights Code, 1981* (the *Code*),[1] plays an essential role in any full consideration of the rights and concerns of individuals trained outside Canada and attempting to gain access to their professions or trades in Ontario. From our perspective, a review of human rights legislation in this province is significant in two ways.

First, some disappointed candidates who seek admission to or certification by a profession or occupational association rely on the *Code*'s provisions for remedies; it is therefore necessary to consider how the *Code* is being applied and whether the mechanism is satisfactory. Second, although the issues raised in relation to foreign-trained professionals and tradespeople attempting to enter the Ontario workforce can be characterized in large part as employment issues, a human rights dimension clearly exists. The Human Rights Commission, created under the *Code*[2] and charged, among other things, with the duty "to forward the policy that the dignity and worth of every person be recognized and that equal rights and opportunities be provided without discrimination that is contrary to law,"[3] is in a position to play a significant role both in protecting the rights of individuals and in implementing and enforcing recommendations made by this Task Force.

HUMAN RIGHTS CODE

History

The predecessor legislation to the *Ontario Human Rights Code, 1981*, was enacted in 1962.[4] The *Ontario Human Rights Code* of that year was designed to address discrimination, to express the community's values regarding equality, and to emphasize the importance of these values. The legislation, which consolidated provincial anti-discrimination legislation passed in the 1940s and 1950s, prohibited racial discrimination in signs and notices, in public accommodation, in services and facilities, in larger housing units, in employment, and in trade union membership.[5]

The Ontario Human Rights Commission was established to assist public understanding of the legislation and to forward the principles of human rights. A full-time staff was hired to investigate complaints of discrimination, to conciliate them, and to conduct public education programs.

Since its enactment, the *Code* has gradually been revised to expand the protection offered. A section was added in 1968 to protect complainants and witnesses from reprisal actions when participating in proceedings under the *Code*. In 1972 the *Code* was amended to consolidate the provisions of the *Women's Equal Employment Act* and the *Age Discrimination Act*.[6] A number of other grounds of protection were added that year, the self-governing professions were brought under the Commission's jurisdiction, and the Commission was given the authority to initiate complaints of discrimination. In 1975 the Commission was reorganized; the commissioners no longer were public employees but became a public body, appointed by the Lieutenant Governor in Council, which reported to the Minister of Labour.

Extensive public meetings were held throughout the province in 1976 as part of a review of the *Code*. Many of the recommendations that came out of the review were incorporated into a new *Human Rights Code, 1981*, that was proclaimed June 15, 1982.[7] The new *Code* expanded the grounds of protection (beyond the then-existing ones of race, ancestry, place of origin, colour, ethnic origin, citizenship, creed, sex, and age) and broadened the Commission's mandate. Newly covered areas of prohibited grounds of discrimination included physical and mental handicap, marital status, family status, the receipt of public assistance, and a record of a provincial or criminal offence for which a pardon has been received. Constructive discrimination (also called indirect discrimination and discussed later in this chapter) is expressly prohibited in the current legislation. Other extensive revisions were made to the *Code* in 1986.[8] The number of prohibited grounds of discrimination increased (to the present 15),[9] and the *Code* was brought into conformity with the requirements of section 15 (the "equality rights" provision) of the *Canadian Charter of Rights and Freedoms*.[10] Still further organizational changes were made in fall 1987, and the Commission now is responsible to a Minister assigned by the Lieutenant Governor in Council. Currently, the Minister of Citizenship has responsibility for the Commission.

The *Human Rights Code, 1981*, applies only within the scope of provincial constitutional authority. The *Canadian Human Rights Act*,[11] and through it the Canadian Human Rights Commission, is responsible for areas constitutionally within the federal jurisdiction.

The *Code* has primacy over other Ontario legislation unless the other acts specifically state differently.[12]

The Complaint Procedure

Part IV of the *Human Rights Code, 1981*, outlines the Commission's procedure for processing a complaint.

First, complainants file cases on their own behalf with the Commission.[13] (The Commission may also institute a complaint on its own initiative or at the request of any person.[14]) The Commission's staff assists complainants in drafting a formal complaint to ensure that they specify the appropriate prohibited grounds of discrimination.

After a complaint is filed, the Commission staff may investigate the allegation.[15] The Commission has the discretion to refuse to deal with complaints outside its jurisdiction; with complaints that are trivial, frivolous or vexatious, or made in bad faith; with complaints based on events that occurred more than six months prior to bringing the matter to the Commission's attention; and with matters more appropriately dealt with under another act.[16]

A copy of the complaint is provided to all parties, and the respondent may be invited to reply in writing to the complainant's allegations.[17] At this point, a "fact-finding conference" may be held whereby the parties meet with a human rights officer to define their positions, provide evidence, and narrow the issues in dispute. Where appropriate, an opportunity is provided to reach a settlement and resolve the case.

Complaints not resolved at this stage are subject to an extended investigation. When the investigation is complete, the investigating officer will, if appropriate, engage the parties in more formal negotiations to conciliate the matter. If a settlement is reached in this conciliation it may still be rejected if the Commission feels the settlement is unfair or not in the public interest. With agreement from the parties, the Commission may at this point also modify a settlement.

The Commission staff recommends a disposition of the case to the commissioners. There are a number of recommended options: dismiss the complaint; ratify a settlement reached in conciliation; accept the complainant's withdrawal of the complaint; or recommend the appointment of a board of inquiry to hold a hearing to determine if a right of the complainant under the Code has been infringed.[18] Apart from a board of inquiry order, all resolutions of complaints must be ratified by the Commission to ensure that the public interest has been served.

Application for Reconsideration

A complainant may apply for a reconsideration of the Commission's decision if the Commission decides not to deal with a complaint or not to appoint a board of inquiry.[19] The respondents are provided with a copy of the application for reconsideration and may make written submissions in response. At this point further investigation may be initiated. The commissioners review all the submissions and determine the disposition of the case, which is final.

If the Commission requests the Minister to appoint a board of inquiry, a panel of one or more members will be appointed to hear the complaint.[20] The board, if it determines the Code has been infringed, may issue an order requiring compliance and providing compensation to the complainant.[21]

Any party to a complaint can appeal the board's decision to the Divisional Court.[22] The Court may reverse or affirm the board's decision or order the board to make any decision that the board is entitled to make, and the Court may substitute its opinion for that of the board.

Complaints Involving Occupational Associations and Self-Governing Professions

The Task Force was allowed to review the Commission's complaint files of allegations by foreign-trained people regarding discrimination in licensing by occupational associations and self-governing professions. No complaints were found that had been initiated by foreign-trained individuals against trade union associations.

The Task Force reviewed 21 relevant complaints relating to six professional groups: architects, dentists, engineers, nurses, physicians, and veterinarians. A breakdown of complaints by primary specific issue cited appears in Table 12-1.

Almost half the complainants alleged that their foreign academic qualifications were not recognized by the professional association. Most of the remaining complaints relate to qualifications that only foreign-trained professionals must complete prior to licensure in Ontario.

There are two sections in the *Code* that can be used by applicants who are denied access to vocational associations or, in order to obtain access, are required to complete additional requirements to those required of Ontario-trained candidates.

Right to Equal Treatment with Respect to Membership in a Vocational Association

Section 5, in Part I of the *Human Rights Code, 1981*, outlines the individual's rights with respect to vocational associations. The language seems broad enough to include, in addition to professional licensing bodies, voluntary professional associations that admit individuals to membership on the basis of professional training or credentials.

> 5. Every person has a right to equal treatment with respect to membership in any trade union, trade or occupational association or self-governing profession without discrimination because of race, ancestry, place of

Table 12-1 Complaints of Discrimination by Foreign-Trained Individuals

COMPLAINT	Architects	Dentists	Engineers	Nurses	Physicians	Veterinarians
Foreign academic qualifications not recognized	x		xxxxxxx		x	x
Failed qualifying examination(s)		xx			xx	
Failed preliminary academic evaluation			x		x	
Inability to get required experience					xxx	
Delay created by requiring original documentation				x		
Unable to obtain Canadian professional education					x	

origin, colour, ethnic origin, citizenship, creed, sex, sexual orientation, age, marital status, family status or handicap.

Unlike the British Columbia *Human Rights Act*,[23] the Ontario *Code* does not offer a definition of "occupational association." Section 9 of British Columbia's *Act* is analogous to section 5 of the Ontario *Code*, but section 1 of the B.C. *Act* defines "occupational association" as:

> an organization, other than a trade union or employers' organization, in which membership is a prerequisite to carrying on a trade, occupation or profession . . .

In *Love Kumar Sharma and Director, Human Rights Code v. Yellow Cab Company Ltd.*,[24] the complainant was not allowed to buy shares in the respondent. The British Columbia board of inquiry found the Yellow Cab Company Ltd. to be an "occupational association" because membership in the cab company was a prerequisite to carrying on the occupation of owner-driver.[25] The narrow definition seen in the B.C. *Act* would not, however, seem to cover an organization that simply confers a "reserved title."

In the Task Force's view, an "occupational association" that provides for a "reserved title" should be brought expressly within the ambit of the Ontario *Code* because the credential afforded by a reserved title may very well be a factual prerequisite to obtaining employment; even if employment is gained without the "reserved title," the credential afforded by a reserved title may well mean at the least that more remuneration is paid in the marketplace for the services of a person with the credential than to one who does not have it. For greater certainty, a definition of "occupational association" should be provided in the Ontario *Code* so that a "reserved title" association is expressly included.

Although under section 5 of the *Code* there is a specific right to equal treatment regarding membership in an occupational association or self-governing profession, this right prohibits discrimination only on the specified enumerated grounds. Place of education or training, the ground on which most of the complainants alleged direct or constructive discrimination, is not among the prohibited grounds. Because of their foreign educational and experiential qualifications, candidates may be required to complete additional academic evaluations, examinations, or experience requirements prior to licensure. If these more onerous licensing requirements are set simply because of the licensing body's concern over the place of education or training, they are therefore not prohibited by the *Code*.

Any occupational association or self-governing profession requiring citizenship as a prerequisite to licensure would be discriminating on a ground covered by the *Code*. (Section 15(1) of the *Code* imposes the limitation that a right to non-discrimination because of citizenship is not infringed where Canadian citizenship is a requirement by law; however, citizenship is not at present a requirement by law in respect of any profession.) Similarly, any candidate, including a foreign-trained person, could allege one of the other prohibited grounds of discrimination listed in section 5. If, however, place of education or training is the only ground for discrimination, then there is no redress under the *Code* on the basis of direct or intentional discrimination — even if the vocational association's requirements are unreasonable.

Constructive Discrimination

Under section 10 of the *Code*, constructive discrimination is also prohibited.

> 10.—(1) A right of a person under Part I is infringed where a requirement, qualification or factor exists that is not discrimination on a prohibited ground but that results in the exclusion, restriction or preference of a group of persons who are identified by a prohibited ground of discrimination and of whom the person is a member, except where,
>
> (a) the requirement, qualification or factor is reasonable and *bona fide* in the circumstances; or
>
> (b) it is declared in this Act . . . that to discriminate because of such ground is not an infringement of a right.
>
> (2) The Commission, a board of inquiry or a court shall not find that a requirement, qualification or factor is reasonable and *bona fide* in the circumstances unless it is satisfied that the needs of the group of which the person is a member cannot be accommodated without undue hardship on the person responsible for accommodating those needs, considering the cost, outside sources of funding, if any, and health and safety requirements, if any.
>
> (3) The Commission, a board of inquiry or a court shall consider any standards prescribed by the regulations for assessing what is undue hardship.

Constructive discrimination, as outlined in section 10(1) of the *Code*, covers a situation in which there is not an intent to discriminate on a prohibited ground but where the practice or requirement results in the restriction, exclusion, or preference of a group of persons who can be identified by a ground prohibited under the *Code*; thus, in the circumstances, the discriminatory requirement is not reasonable and *bona fide*. Although section 10 of the *Code* represents an express statutory basis for constructive discrimination, the pre-existing *Code* was interpreted as rendering constructive discrimination unlawful.[26]

This indirect form of discrimination describes the unequal treatment that foreign-trained people often receive. Ostensibly they are discriminated against on the basis of their foreign qualifications; the effect of the discrimination, however, is the exclusion or unequal treatment of groups or individuals linked according to their place of origin, race, colour, or ethnic origin. Because in most instances people obtain their education or training in their place of origin, place of education or training can generally be used as a proxy for place of origin. Thus, if credentials obtained in a given location are not recognized by the professional body, a candidate who originated in and was educated or trained in that region could claim that he or she is directly or systemically being discriminated against on account of place of origin and that he or she is therefore entitled to relief. This is so regardless of the fact that the occupational association or self-governing profession may be able to show that it had no intent to discriminate on that basis.

For example, a Soviet-born and trained engineer claimed constructive discrimination when he was refused admission to the Association of Professional Engineers of Ontario (APEO). The APEO claimed that he was assessed on the basis of his education; the applicant's position was that although that might be the case, his unfavourable assessment was effectively the result of his being Soviet. Place of education or training is not a prohibited ground of discrimination, yet discrimination on the basis of place of origin contravenes the *Code*.

Nevertheless, neither this complainant nor any other foreign-trained person alleging discrimination in an occupational association or self-governing profession has successfully argued constructive discrimination before the Commission. The primary reason for this failure is the exception contained in section 10(1)(a) of the *Code*: the reasonable requirement exception.

Reasonable Requirement

An exception to section 10 applies where the purported ground of discrimination is "reasonable and *bona fide* in the circumstances." A requirement, qualification, or consideration that could be defined as constructively discriminatory is therefore permitted in some situations.

This "reasonableness" exception has been a major hurdle for foreign-trained people using section 10 to allege discrimination by professional associations.[27] The primary focus of the self-governing professions is protection of the public interest in respect of society's safety, health, and welfare. Professions claim that because they either cannot assess accurately foreign educational training or do not believe the standards to be equivalent, they would be jeopardizing the public interest by licensing foreign-trained people.

This claim is based on an assumption that foreign training is difficult if not impossible to assess accurately within the vocational association. A blanket rejection of such foreign qualifications is therefore asserted as "reasonable . . . in the circumstances." Where the complaint is that foreign-trained applicants are required to undergo testing or assessment not required of other candidates, the argument is made that the particular assessments of foreign-trained people which may be carried out by vocational associations are necessary to ensure these candidates are on a par with Ontario-trained candidates for licensure. This rationale, it is argued, makes the imposition of these requirements "reasonable . . . in the circumstances."[28]

In its brief to the Task Force, the Human Rights Commission stated that it "has not been very successful in dealing with the difficulties experienced by foreign-trained professionals in the past."[29] It attributes this lack of success in part to the fact that the investigations were conducted on a case-by-case basis rather than on a basis of seeking to determine whether systemic discrimination exists. The development of a new systemic unit within the Commission will, it is suggested, help to correct this deficiency.[30]

Duty to Accommodate

A recent amendment to the *Code* has qualified the use of the "reasonable" exception; accordingly, foreign-trained applicants to occupational associations and self-governing professions may have more comprehensive protection from constructive discrimination. By virtue of this amendment, referred to as the "duty to accommodate,"[31] a requirement cannot be found to be "reasonable and *bona fide* in the circumstances" unless the Commission, a board of inquiry or a court "is satisfied that the needs of the group of which the person is a member cannot be accommodated without undue hardship . . . considering the cost, outside sources of funding, if any, and health and safety requirements, if any."[32] The amendment constitutes an express codification of the interpretation given to the meaning of "reasonable and *bona fide* in the circumstances" by boards of inquiry tribunals.[33]

Assuming the maintenance of necessary public standards to be a reasonable and *bona fide* ground for discriminating on the basis of jurisdiction of education or training, it must then be determined whether the foreign-trained person's application for membership can be accommodated without undue hardship to the occupational association or profession. The occupational association or profession will not be able to maintain a "reasonableness" defence unless it can establish that there cannot be accommodation without undue hardship.

In light of this, occupational associations and self-governing professions may be found in some instances to be discriminating against foreign-trained individuals seeking licensure.

The difficult question relates to the balancing of the rights of foreign-trained people against the protection of the public interest in receiving services. The Commission[34] suggests that the following questions be reviewed:

- Is there a disparate impact on the basis of a prohibited ground of the *Code*? If yes, then the threshold standard has been met to allege constructive discrimination under section 10.

- If constructive discrimination is the result, why are the unequal requirements used (in this case, by the occupational association or the self-governing profession)?

- Is there enough information to determine that the more onerous requirements (in this case, imposed upon foreign-trained as opposed to Ontario-trained candidates) are necessary?

- If there is enough information to determine that these requirements are necessary, is there available an alternative, less onerous, procedure that would ensure a reasonable standard is met?

- If there is not enough information to determine that these requirements are necessary, are there other measures to increase access to the vocational association?

The Ontario Human Rights Commission suggests five alternative, less onerous, measures that occupational associations and self-governing professions could use to increase accessibility:

- determine the standard of training in other countries, short of undue hardship in doing so;

- establish a testing mechanism that fairly assesses individual applicants;

- provide access to remedial programs;

- provide financial assistance to those seeking upgrading; and

- establish a mentor system to assist foreign-trained people in becoming familiar with Ontario systems.[35]

It is suggested that, in applying the section, the Commission would look to these factors to determine whether accommodation has been made by the occupational association or self-governing profession sufficient to exempt what would otherwise constitute discriminatory activity.

Difficulties with the Mechanism

The introduction of the accommodation requirement should have the desirable effect of improving employment conditions for immigrants by imposing on occupational associations and self-governing professions the obligation to accommodate — that is, to obtain thorough and unbiased assessments, administer only independently validated evaluation and licensing examinations, assist in retraining, and so on — in order to avoid a finding of discrimination. Gone is the opportunity of citing the lack of availability of assessment mechanisms as a reason for rejecting foreign-trained candidates; furthermore, any additional requirements imposed on such candidates would need to be justified and be demonstrably fair. This step is obviously a very positive one and reflects to a large degree the thrust of many of the recommendations of this Task Force.

There remain, however, two significant deficiencies with the mechanism. First, in order to bring himself or herself within a class of people entitled to the protection of the *Human Rights Code, 1981*, an individual must be able to demonstrate that the requirement, qualification, or factor in question, which in this case is based on place of education or training (not in itself a prohibited ground), has the effect of discriminating against the individual on the basis of a prohibited ground (place of origin). This effect is not easily seen, particularly when the requirement seems to discriminate against foreign-trained individuals generally from all or at least several other countries and even against some residents of Canada.[36] As well, although place of education and place of origin are synonymous in most cases, there will be individuals who trained in a country other than their place of origin; accordingly, they will not fall within the protection of section 10, despite the fact that they face the same unequal requirements for entry. For example, Canadians who train abroad could not effectively allege constructive discrimination; nor apparently could individuals from any country who train in a jurisdiction other than their place of origin. In practical terms, the impact of this deficiency may be minimal because such individuals will as a rule benefit from accommodations made to meet the needs of those who do fall squarely within the section. Still, there remains a potential barrier to enforcement of the rights of these candidates.

The second deficiency we see with the current mechanism is the difficulty and complexity of the systemic discrimination argument.

Unless there are a number of complaints of a similar nature, systemic discrimination is not easily established where foreign education or training is at issue. Although disparate impact can be asserted in the case of a single individual, it is not easily seen as relating to a prohibited ground. As well, any human rights complaint takes considerable time to be dealt with, and because the establishing of systemic discrimination is often dependent upon a number of complaints, the time required to determine the matter is disadvantageous to the complainant who seeks entry to a profession to gain employment quickly.

These deficiencies could be corrected by making discrimination on the basis of "place of education or training" a prohibited ground of discrimination. The prohibition would be qualified by reasonable and *bona fide* qualifications,[37] provided reasonable accommodation[38] is made, as is currently the case in other prohibited grounds.

Moreover, discrimination because of "place of education or training" without reasonable justification is repugnant in unfairly denying equality of opportunity to earn a living, and therefore all Ontario residents (whether immigrants or not) deserve express protection from this form of discrimination.

Elsewhere in this Report, the Task Force has outlined the steps that must be taken and the procedures that must be implemented to remove or at least to minimize the barriers that currently operate to limit entry by foreign-trained individuals into occupational bodies. Some of these proposed steps and procedures, such as language training and equivalency assessment, have been designated as the responsibility of government bodies working in conjunction with vocational associations; others, such as licensure testing, internship, and in-service training programs and appeal procedures, by and large have been left with or assigned to the vocational associations themselves; and still others, such as the compilation and communication of information on rights and procedures, are considered the role and function of both the Government and the vocational associations. Once fully implemented, these changes should substantially diminish the likelihood of discriminatory practices occurring. Nonetheless, the individuals affected by these recommendations must have available to them an enforcement mechanism to ensure compliance.

Subject to our comments above concerning technical difficulties within the provisions of the *Code*, the protective mechanism created under the *Code* stands as a reasonable means of enforcing the rights of foreign-trained individuals. It essentially establishes a standard of fairness which must be met by vocational associations that wish in any way to restrict entry of foreign-trained applicants. The powers of a board of inquiry include the right to order compensation to victims of discrimination,[39] a necessary power where livelihood is at issue, as well as the power to order compliance,[40] which presumably could extend to an order to license the applicant but would in most cases direct that the appropriate steps be taken to assess the individual. Moreover, both the *Code* and the Commission have an educative function for the community, and it is important that the basic human rights of Ontario residents be enhanced through their express recognition and protection in the *Code*. What the occupational associations and self-governing associations must do to meet the duty of reasonable accommodation could be specified, although not exhaustively, in the regulations to the *Code*. There would then be no doubt as to the meaning or breadth of the term "accommodation." The requirements could be drafted to reflect the recommendations of this Task Force.

The issues in question here can be characterized as employment issues. We have found in the course of our research that in most cases the failure of occupational associations and self-governing professions to recognize adequately the rights of foreign-trained applicants was not only unintentional but born of a genuine belief that they did not have the necessary means to make an assessment. In such cases, the suggestion that a human rights complaint is the appropriate remedy for the disappointed candidate is received with considerable consternation because of the strong pejorative connotation of such a complaint. Nevertheless, we characterize as a denial of a basic human right the arbitrary or unreasonable denial of occupational licensing because of place of education or training. Direct discrimination, we emphasize, is intentional discrimination, yet it does not require malice or an evil motive. Discrimination that unreasonably denies equality of opportunity in earning a living should be prohibited as infringing a basic human right, irrespective of the motive underlying the discrimination. Human rights can be abused by the well intentioned, and regardless of intentions, the results are equally harmful. Unlawful discrimination on a prohibited ground depends only upon the intention to discriminate (direct discrimination) or the effect or result of unintentional discrimination (so-called constructive or systemic discrimination). In either case, malice or evil motive is an unnecessary prerequisite to liability; motive is pertinent only to the question of damages awarded. Accordingly, it is our view that a human rights complaint is the appropriate remedy for someone discriminated against because of "place of education or training" without a reasonable and *bona fide* basis in the circumstances.

RECOMMENDATIONS

12.1 *We recommend that the* Human Rights Code, 1981, *be amended to prohibit discrimination because of "place of education or training" as an additional ground of discrimination in respect of services (section 1 of the* Code), *employment (section 4 of the* Code), *and membership in occupational associations and self-governing professions (section 5 of the* Code), *subject to the reasonable and* bona fide *qualification defence (section 23(1)(b) of the* Code), *provided such defence is not maintainable unless it is established that there cannot be accommodation without undue hardship considering the cost, outside sources of funding, if any, and health and safety requirements, if any (section 23(2) of the Code).*

12.2   *We recommend that the* Human Rights Code, 1981, *section 9, be amended to include a definition for "occupational association," as follows: " 'occupational association' includes an association in which membership provides a reserved title in the carrying on of a trade, occupation or profession."*

---

*This recommendation apparently constitutes a novel approach to providing remedies in addressing the problems of individuals trained in one country attempting to gain access to professions or trades in another country. No Canadian jurisdiction has "place of education or training" as a prohibited ground of discrimination in human rights legislation. Nor does "place of education or training" appear as a prohibited ground of discrimination under human rights legislation in the United Kingdom, Australia, or the United States (federal legislation or in the individual states).

CHAPTER 13

Application of the Canadian Charter of Rights and Freedoms

Work is a fundamental aspect of a person's life. Chief Justice Dickson stated in *Reference Re Public Service Employee Relations Act* (Alta.)[1] that "a person's employment is an essential component of his or her sense of identity, self-worth and emotional well-being" in addition to providing a means of financial support. The importance of pursuing a livelihood through a trade or calling may attract constitutional protection through the *Canadian Charter of Rights and Freedoms.*[2]

The right to obtain licensure or certification must, however, be balanced against competing social interests. The self-governing professional or occupational association attempts to protect public health, safety, and general welfare by ensuring, through a registration process, that the incompetent or unqualified applicant is not licensed.

This balancing of interests requires a registration scheme that also addresses in a fair way the applicant's concerns. If the applicant is refused registration, he or she may question whether the application process itself has been fair. For example, a licensure applicant may be denied the opportunity for an oral hearing, the opportunity to review the evidence, or the opportunity to appeal to an independent arbiter the decision to refuse registration.

As well, applicants may challenge the appropriateness of the qualification standards that he or she must meet in Ontario, or the refusal of the Ontario registration body to accept his or her foreign qualifications. The applicant may believe that the mere fact of his or her place of training is the basis for the refusal to license. Further, the applicant may believe that the fact of his or her ethnic or national origin is somehow tied to the refusal to license. Applicants may seek to find redress in respect of these issues through sections 7 or 15 of the *Canadian Charter of Rights and Freedoms*.

The *Charter*, however, lacks precise guidelines as far as who it applies to and how the legal terms and concepts underlying the guaranteed rights are to be interpreted.

Before an aggrieved applicant can rely on the protections of the *Charter*, he or she must demonstrate that the *Charter* applies to the actions of the regulatory body. Section 32 of the *Charter* provides that it is only the actions of "government" to which the *Charter* applies. In the licensure context, some registration bodies are created and regulated by statute (the so-called "self-governing professions"), while others are wholly voluntary organizations (the so-called "occupational associations") whose registration procedure is contained in bylaws. It is not clear which, if any, professional bodies can be considered as "government" within the meaning of section 32.

Although the exact parameters of section 32 are not clearly defined, the Courts have articulated several criteria for determining whether an institution is a "governmental" actor or merely a "private" actor. The Courts examine the extent to which the institution is created and regulated by statute, the relationship between the body and the elected or executive branches of government, and the nature of the role played by the body in public life. The key factor appears to be whether the body maintains control over its core functions without government intervention. In the licensure context, the registration body may not be "government" in that the core power to regulate membership is solely controlled by the professional body albeit, in some cases, within the framework of government-enacted legislation.

If the aggrieved applicant is successful in demonstrating that the registration body is an institution to which the *Charter* may apply, the person must then prove that one of his or her fundamental rights as guaranteed by the *Charter* has been infringed or denied. Two fundamental rights are at issue in the licensure context.

First, section 7 of the *Charter* provides that "everyone has the right to life, liberty and security of the person and the right not to be deprived thereof except in accordance with the principles of fundamental justice." An applicant might argue, for example, that he or she has been denied the right to a licence without the opportunity to present his or her case orally before the registration body, without knowledge of the evidence relied upon by the registration body, or without written reasons for the denial.

It is not clear whether a "right" to a licence is a protected interest within section 7. One point of view suggests that the right to obtain registration, which then enables the applicant to practise his or her profession, is a mere economic right or privilege, unprotected by the *Charter*. Conversely, another view suggests that the practice of a profession is tied to the individual's concept of self-worth and community as an aspect of "liberty," involving more than a mere pecuniary interest.

If the right to practise a profession is a liberty interest protected by section 7, then the applicant has a corresponding right not to be deprived of that right except in accordance with the "the principles of fundamental justice." The Courts have concluded that, at a minimum, fundamental justice ensures a "fair procedure." The procedural protections afforded by section 7 may include protections in addition to those currently required in administrative law by the doctrines of natural justice and fairness. Further, the *Charter* permits review of the substantive fairness of the law, which was not possible at common law.

Secondly, an applicant may argue that the denial of a licence may infringe or deny his or her right to equality without discrimination as protected by section 15, because, for example, the registration body requires the foreign-trained applicant to undergo additional training or to pass onerous examinations not required of domestically trained graduates.

Many laws distinguish between two groups of individuals. The Supreme Court of Canada has, however, affirmed that the act of making a distinction between two groups is not necessarily discrimination for the purposes of section 15. In *Andrews v. Law Society of British Columbia*[3] the Court described "discrimination" as:

> a distinction, whether intentional or not but based on grounds relating to personal characteristics of the individual or group, which has the effect of imposing burdens, obligations, or disadvantages on such individual or group not imposed on others, or withholds or limits access to opportunities, benefits and advantages available to other members of society.[4]

If the individual proves that a fundamental right guaranteed under sections 7 or 15 of the *Charter* has been denied or infringed, then the *Charter* will still not afford protection if the offending party can demonstrate that the denial of a right or freedom can be upheld under section 1, which states that rights and freedoms are subject to "reasonable limits prescribed by law as can be demonstrably justified in a free and democratic society." There may be valid and demonstrable reasons in the licensure context to support a discriminatory distinction. Similarly, the denial of a fundamentally just procedure may in some circumstances be justified.

DOES THE CHARTER APPLY TO LICENSURE BODIES?

Is the Body "Government"?

Although the applicant may wish to rely on the enshrined rights guaranteed by the *Charter*, not all the actions of every institution will attract constitutional scrutiny. Section 32(1) limits the *Charter's* application "to the Parliament and government of Canada in respect of all matters within the authority of Parliament . . . " and "to the legislature and government of each province in respect of all matters within the authority of the legislature of each province." Do the various regulatory bodies of the professions and associated appeal tribunals constitute "government," thus bringing their actions under constitutional scrutiny?

The Courts acknowledge that there is no clear definition of "government." Mr. Justice McIntyre pointed out in *Retail Wholesale and Department Store Union, Local 580 v. Dolphin Delivery Ltd.*[5] that it is difficult to define what degree of governmental intervention is required before a litigant is entitled to rely on *Charter* protections.

For example, in *Re Blainey and Ontario Hockey Association*,[6] a young girl challenged the right of the Ontario Hockey Association to restrict girls from playing in a minor hockey league. The Ontario Court of Appeal found an insufficient nexus between the hockey league and government. The action of the association in refusing Blainey membership on the basis of sex was viewed merely as a dispute between private individuals who could not rely on constitutional protections.[7] The Blainey case suggests that simply receiving government funding provides an insufficient connection with government to render the *Charter* operative.

Recent British Columbia and Ontario Court of Appeal decisions that considered the effect of mandatory retirement policies illustrate the ways in which Courts distinguish between governmental and non-governmental bodies.[8]

In a trilogy of cases, the British Columbia Court of Appeal has suggested that the appropriate connection is established if government maintains control over core functions. The Court looked to the following factors in considering whether the University of British Columbia, Vancouver General Hospital, and Douglas College were governmental actors:

- Is the institution a creature of statute?

- Is management and control over the institution's affairs vested in the governing body of that institution?

- Is provincial control over the membership of the governing body preserved by statute?

- Does the governing legislation require that government not interfere in the forming and adoption of policy or standards with respect to the core functions of that body?

- Do the actions or policies developed by the governing body require ministerial approval by statute?

- Is the governing body a delegate of government in furthering government policy?[9]

The Court also considered the additional argument that a university exercises a delegated public function. In *obiter* the Court remarked that this function could provide the link to government; however, in this specific case, the exercising of mandatory retirement terms in a private employment contract was held not to be a public function.[10]

The Ontario Court of Appeal has also looked to the nature of the statutory entity and control over its core functions. In *Re McKinney and Board of Governors of Guelph*,[11] the Court of Appeal stated that although a body may be a creature of statute, it may not be an emanation of government:

> Those who are subject to the authority of government include those legal entities which are the creation of those governments by Acts of Parliament and the legislatures. Unless it can be said, however, that in a particular case an emanation of government is itself the government or a branch of it, the emanation is not subject to Charter scrutiny. The statute which creates the non-governmental entity is subject to Charter scrutiny because it is a piece of legislation, but the non-governmental entity whose enabling statute survives Charter scrutiny has the status of a private person, and, like any private person, is subject only to the appropriate federal or provincial human rights legislation.[12]

It is not clear whether all institutions exercising statutory authority are bound by the *Charter*.[13] For example, in *Re Klein and the Law Society of Upper Canada*,[14] the High Court concluded that the mandate of the Law Society under the *Law Society Act*[15] is to regulate the affairs of the profession in the public interest. As the Law Society is part of the regulatory scheme established by the Legislature, it is a statutory authority performing a regulatory function within the meaning of "government" in section 32 of the *Charter*.[16]

Similarly, in *Re Lavigne and Ontario Public Service Employees Union*,[17] the trial judge, as affirmed by the Court of Appeal, suggested that the Council of Regents in exercising statutory authority was a governmental actor. The Ontario Court of Appeal in *McKinney* noted these cases but declined to discuss them because several were on appeal.[18]

The Ontario Court of Appeal decision in *Lavigne* illustrates that although a party which exercises statutory authority may be a governmental actor, the act complained of may not be a governmental action. Mr. Lavigne, a teacher at a community college, challenged the use of compulsory dues by the Ontario Public Service Employees Union (OPSEU) for purposes other than collective bargaining. The collective agreement between the Council of Regents of the college and OPSEU provided that a portion of employees' salaries would be automatically deducted for membership dues in the union. The *Colleges Collective Bargaining Act*[19] provides for the entering into of collective agreements and for the payment of compulsory dues. The Court concluded that the Council of Regents, as a Crown agency, exercised statutory authority in the collection of dues and thus was a governmental actor. However, the mere making of funds available to the union, a private organization, could not convert the union's expenditures into a governmental action. Mr. Lavigne had challenged OPSEU's use of the dues and not the validity of the legislation providing the statutory authority to the Council of Regents to collect the dues.[20]

In Ontario, the *Charter* has been applied to school boards established under the *Ontario Education Act*.[21] However, the *Charter* was held not to apply to the internal bylaws of the Ontario Teachers Federation, which regulates membership in that association. The bylaws considered by the Court to be "private law" did not require approval by the Lieutenant Governor in Council and were not thought to have any public dimension.[22]

In summary, to determine whether a body or institution is a governmental actor, the Courts will consider the nature of the institution, the extent to which that institution is created and regulated by statute, the nature of the relationship between the institution and the elected or executive branches of government, and the nature of the role the institution plays in public life.

In the licensure context, some decisions of registration bodies seem clearly to be the actions of government; in other cases, however, relationship is doubtful. On the one hand, the enabling legislation itself may comprise a procedural code that limits the procedural protections to be afforded the applicant. For example, the *Health Disciplines Act*[23] provides an applicant with the right to an oral hearing when the registration committee proposes to refuse licensure or attach terms and conditions to the licence. Conversely, the enabling legislation of architects,[24] professional engineers,[25] and surveyors[26] specifically states that the decisions of the registration committees are final and binding on both the registrar and the applicant, yet neither committee is required to hold a hearing or allow oral submissions. If an applicant for licensure as an engineer, for example, challenges the procedure, which denies the right to an oral hearing, the challenge is in respect of the constitutional validity of the enabling legislation itself. Whether or not the professional governing body is a governmental actor becomes a moot point, as the *Charter* applies to challenges directed at statutory provisions.

On the other hand, the enabling legislation may simply grant the profession the statutory power to register applicants but not provide for specific procedural protections.[27] In this situation, procedural protections to be afforded the applicant could be dealt with in one of two ways.

First, some administrative tribunals have their own internal code of procedure, which may or may not provide adequate procedural protections in the constitutional context. If the internal procedure of the tribunal is perceived to afford inadequate procedural protections, the applicant may challenge the actions of the governing body in failing to provide him or her with adequate procedural protections. A consideration of whether the particular governing body is "government" is crucial to any successful *Charter* argument that the applicant was denied fundamental procedural protections.

Alternatively, the governing legislation or internal bylaws may not provide for specific procedural protections. If, however, the decision maker exercises a *statutory power of decision* and a hearing is required by statute or otherwise by law, the *Statutory Powers Procedure Act (SPPA)*[28] specifically affords procedural protections. The provisions of the *SPPA* as discussed in Chapter 11 of this Report, "Review of Registration Decisions," comprise a comprehensive procedural code; accordingly, a *Charter* challenge in the face of these protections very probably would not succeed. In this context, however, the question of whether the governing body is a governmental actor should not pose a barrier to a Charter action because the litigant really challenges the constitutionality of the *SPPA* legislative provisions.

In any event, whether or not a licensing body exercises a statutory power of decision, as defined by the *SPPA*, if that body exercises statutory authority over licensing it may be subject to the *Charter*, even if operating independently of government, through the section 32 reference to "legislature."[29]

Whether the governing body or its delegate, the registration committee, constitutes a governmental actor will depend on the composition of the body and the degree of control maintained by the government over the core functions. Those governing bodies composed of a majority of government-appointed members and whose mandate and guidelines are government dictated, or whose policies require ministerial sanction, would quite possibly be considered as part of "government" within the meaning of section 32 of the *Charter*. Their actions in granting or refusing a licence would likely be considered a governmental act by virtue of the fact that licensing is exercised in the public interest and, therefore, affects more than private matters.

It is not yet clear whether governing bodies that exercise a delegated function as the agent of the provincial or federal Government are caught by the *Charter. Harrison*[30] seems to suggest that this is the case, but only if the particular function is a public function. A good argument could be made that the licensing function, as part of the regulatory scheme exercised in the public interest, would be considered a public function.

Finally, it seems doubtful that the procedures of wholly voluntary ("contractual") associations are subject to the *Charter*. These associations do not exercise statutory authority, they generally are governed by councils composed of elected association members, and they make and enforce their own policies without governmental control. As management and control over core functions rest solely with the association, it is very unlikely that the *Charter* applies to the actions or policies of these groups.

Sources of Remedial Power

Charter rights are of little use to an aggrieved applicant unless they can be enforced by appropriate remedies. There are two sources of remedial powers within the *Charter*. Section 24(1) confers broad remedial jurisdiction by allowing "[a]nyone whose rights or freedoms . . . have been infringed or denied" to apply to a "court of competent jurisdiction to obtain such remedy as the court considers appropriate and just in the circumstances."

There are several elements to section 24(1) that may be important in the licensing context. First, the past tense language of the section suggests that a violation of *Charter* rights must have already occurred. The caselaw is unclear on this point. Despite the language of the section, several cases have suggested that an imminent violation is sufficient.[31] Thus, it may be possible for an applicant whose application has been considered and not yet been refused but who has been denied, in his or her view, a fair procedure, to bring a *Charter* application and ask for appropriate relief under section 24(1).

Second, a proceeding brought under section 24(1) must be brought before a "court of competent jurisdiction." The Supreme Court of Canada adopted in *Mills v. The Queen*[32] the Ontario Court of Appeal's definition of those words in *R. v. Morgentaler et al.*,[33] wherein the Ontario Court stated that a "court" is competent "if it has jurisdiction, conferred by statute, over the person and the subject-matter in question and, in addition, has authority to make the order sought."

The Supreme Court of Canada has yet to decide whether a "court" includes administrative tribunals. Several lower courts have determined that various tribunals constitute "courts" for purposes of section 24(1).[34] It is arguable that the licensing body, which has jurisdiction over the applicant and the power to grant or refuse licensure, is a court of competent jurisdiction when the jurisdictional and remedial authority test is applied.

A second source of remedial power is found in section 52(1) of the *Charter*, which provides that any "law" which is inconsistent with a provision of the *Charter* is of no force and effect. Not all the actions of a governmental institution attract the remedial powers of section 52(1). The question to be resolved is whether the procedure by which the applicant was refused licensure is "law" within the meaning of section 52(1).

As the Ontario Court of Appeal has stated, where the enabling legislation sets out comprehensive procedures, as does, for example, the *Health Disciplines Act*, the applicant challenges "law." If, however, the procedures reflect merely the internal policy of the decision maker and not a statute or regulation, it is more difficult to label the procedure as "law."

However, the British Columbia Court of Appeal has suggested that "law" in section 52(1) includes all actions of government and other bodies, whether as a result of following rules or exercising discretion.[35] If this interpretation is correct, then those registration committees considered to be governmental actors and not following an explicit statutory regulatory scheme but having the authority to set the licensing procedure, may still enact "laws." It may be that, for *Charter* purposes, the rules or policies of the body do not necessarily have to be adopted as regulations to have the force of "law."[36]

THE CHARTER AND FAIR PROCEDURE

If one assumes that the actions of a licensing tribunal constitute governmental laws, then the applicant who has been refused licensure may allege that he or she has been deprived of the "right to life, liberty and security of the person" in a manner that is not in accordance with "the principles of fundamental justice," as stated in section 7 of the *Charter*. It may be that the right to obtain a licence to practise one's calling or profession is an interest encompassed in the notion of "liberty."

Should the right to obtain licensure be a protected *Charter* right, the applicant might argue that to be denied licensure without an oral hearing and without the right to counsel or to cross-examine witnesses constitutes a deprivation of his or her right to security of the person, which is not in accordance with fundamental justice. Alternatively, the applicant might suggest that the imposition of onerous qualification standards that are not rationally connected to the practice of the profession leads to a similar denial of fundamental justice.

The section 7 analysis requires a determination of whether the interest claimed deserves constitutional protection and, then, whether the individual was deprived of that interest in a way that is fundamentally just. As a preliminary matter, it should be noted that a licensing requirement might be considered simply regulative and not prohibitive. Thus, there would be no "deprivation" but only a "restriction,"[37] and therefore the protections of section 7 would be unavailable.

Is the "Right" to Licensure a Protected Right?

In the United States, the right to practise one's profession is a constitutionally protected right because the 14th Amendment protects life, liberty, and, specifically, property. A licence is considered "property." However, the right to practise is not an unqualified or absolute right. The "right" to practise is subject to the power of the government to regulate in the public interest for health and safety reasons.[38]

The issue has not yet been directly addressed by the Supreme Court of Canada, although several cases suggest that the right to pursue one's occupation may be included in the liberty component of section 7.

In *Reference Re Public Service Employee Relations Act* (Alta.),[39] Chief Justice Dickson considered whether associational activity for the pursuit of economic ends should receive constitutional protection. He stated, in a dissenting opinion, that he could not agree that something as fundamental as a person's livelihood or dignity in the workplace was beyond constitutional protection. However, he suggested that exclusively pecuniary concerns may be excluded from such protection.[40]

In *Law Society of Alberta v. Black*,[41] the Supreme Court considered whether Law Society rules prohibiting national law firms infringed mobility rights as guaranteed by section 6(2)(a)(b) of the *Charter*, which provides that every Canadian citizen and permanent resident has the right to move and take up residence in any province and to pursue the gaining of a livelihood in any province. Mr. Justice La Forest stated that section 6(2)(a) specifically protects "the right to pursue the livelihood of choice and subject to the same conditions as residents." The broad right, however, would be subject to local laws concerning qualifications unless those laws discriminate on the basis of province of residence.[42]

Although the *Charter* section at issue in both the *Public Service* case and in *Black* was not section 7, the comments of the Supreme Court may be indicative of an eventual finding of the fundamental constitutional importance of being able to pursue one's occupation.

Obiter comments in *R. v. Wigglesworth*[43] indicate that proceedings to determine fitness to obtain or maintain licensure are caught by the protections of section 7. In that case the Supreme Court was asked to consider whether section 11 of the *Charter* applied to private, domestic, or disciplinary matters intended to maintain discipline or professional standards. The Court concluded that only matters of public welfare required the procedural protections of section 11. The majority stated, however, that such proceedings might be subject to the constitutionally guaranteed procedural protections available under section 7. The Court expressed no further opinion because the appellant had elected to base his case on section 11 alone.[44]

In *R. v. Morgentaler*,[45] Madam Justice Wilson dealt with the content of "liberty," although she was the sole member of the Court to do so. She stated that:

> Individuals are afforded the right to choose their own religion and their own philosophy of life, the right to choose with whom they will associate and how they will live and *what occupation they will pursue*. These are all examples of the basic theory underlying the Charter . . . [emphasis added][46]

Several Courts have expressed opinions on the constitutional protections guaranteed in the granting and revocation of licences. The cases deal with three types of licences: driving licences, licences to practise a profession, and business licences.

The driving cases illustrate the divergence of opinion on the definition of "liberty." The British Columbia Court of Appeal in *R. v. Robson*[47] determined that once a driver's licence is granted, a general liberty to employ one's skill and ability to drive then attaches. Liberty is not confined to mere freedom from bodily restraint.[48]

Conversely, the Alberta Court of Appeal has interpreted the ambit of section 7 more narrowly. In the Court's view, "liberty" is directed solely at protection of persons from physical restraint.[49] The operation of vehicles is not a fundamental liberty, but a mere regulated activity.

The interpretation of the right to practise a profession as an incident of liberty has, similarly, not been uniform. In *Branigan v. Yukon Medical Council*,[50] the Yukon Territory Supreme Court considered the question of whether the withdrawal of a licence through disciplinary proceedings affected a protected right under section 7. The Court concluded that "liberty" should encompass the right to continue practising a profession after full licensure and years of practice, given the fundamental importance of the economic interests and the question of reputation.[51]

Conversely, the Ontario Divisional Court has concluded that the weight of authority suggests that the right to engage in a particular professional calling is a mere economic right. Hence, the disciplinary proceedings of the Law Society of Upper Canada were not subject to the protections of section 7.[52]

A 1988 decision of the British Columbia Court of Appeal considered whether the provisions of the *Medical Services Act*[53] denied or infringed a "liberty" interest.[54] The *Act* required a doctor to obtain a practitioner number in order to participate in the Medical Services Plan and to be reimbursed for services rendered. The Medical Services Commission was empowered to issue billing numbers to practitioners, depending upon the need for medical services in particular areas of the province. The provisions of the *Act* had the net effect of restraining a doctor's liberty to practise wherever he or she chose within the province. The issues before the Court of Appeal were whether the right to "liberty" under section 7 was broad enough to include the opportunity of a qualified doctor to practise medicine without restraint as to place, and whether the *Act* procedurally or substantively violated the principles of fundamental justice.

The Court concluded that the *Act* denied the appellants the right to practise their profession. Although there was an economic component to the practice of a profession, the asserted *Charter* interest could not be characterized as a purely business interest and was therefore deserving of

Charter protection. However, the Court in *obiter* remarked that the mere regulation of standards of admission, practice, and behaviour would likely not constitute an infringement of section 7.

The decision of the British Columbia Court of Appeal was followed by the Nova Scotia Court of Appeal in *Re Khaliq-Kareemi*.[55] The Court was satisfied that the order of the Nova Scotia Health Services and Insurance Commission, which prohibited Dr. Khaliq-Kareemi from practising under the insurance plan for one year, affected the doctor's right to liberty under section 7.[56]

The third group of cases involves business licences. The majority of the cases indicate that the right to operate a business or to earn a livelihood cannot be characterized as a "liberty" right.[57] For example, certain municipal bylaws have been considered to be merely regulatory, not prohibitive.[58] Operation of a public service carrier was held to be a privilege and not a right.[59] The right to a business licence is thought to relate to a purely economic interest.

The Content of Fundamental Justice

Even if the right to pursue one's calling is a protected *Charter* right, this does not automatically mean that applicants who have been refused registration have been denied their right not to be deprived of liberty except in accordance with the principles of fundamental justice. The key questions for our purposes are whether the registration requirements fairly test competence to practise one's profession, and whether an application process that limits procedural rights is fundamentally just. Those determinations depend on the interpretation by the Courts of the content of "fundamental justice."

At an early stage of the *Charter's* history, it was thought that "fundamental justice" meant nothing more than the traditional concepts of natural justice and fairness. This theory was put to rest in *Reference Re Section 94(2)* of the *Motor Vehicle Act* R.S.B.C. 1979 c. 228.[60] The Supreme Court of Canada concluded that "it would be wrong to interpret the term 'fundamental justice' as being synonymous with natural justice."[61] Further, fundamental justice includes the notion of "substantive fairness" in addition to procedural fairness. Substantive fairness allows a litigant to challenge the fairness of the legislation itself.

The content of fundamental justice was considered in *Singh v. Minister of Employment and Immigration*.[62] An applicant for refugee status sought judicial review of the procedure that denied him both the right to an oral hearing and the right to know what evidence the decision maker had considered.

Madam Justice Wilson concluded that this procedure was not fundamentally just. An oral hearing would not be required in every case but, where a serious issue of credibility was involved, it was a necessity.[63]

The content of fundamental justice also was considered in the professional discipline context in the *Branigan* case. Complaints of incompetence were made to the Yukon Medical Council, which subsequently held an inquiry wherein Dr. Branigan's licence was suspended on an interim basis. One of the complainants was the chairman of the council, who also took part in the discussion and voted on the resolution to strike the committee of inquiry. Dr. Branigan alleged that the provisions of the *Medical Professions Ordinance*[64] were inoperative under the *Charter* on the basis of the tribunal's bias.

In considering the components of fundamental justice, the Court looked at the statutory discipline procedures and noted the medical council's general duty to act fairly. The rules of natural justice would apply to such adjudications because they were an exercising of a judicial power. Although the *Act* allowed the council to appoint judges in their own cause, this was constitutionally permissible.[65]

In the *Wilson* case, the Court concluded that the statutory billing number scheme was administered by one man, appointed by the Government, who was not obliged by statute to hold hearings or give reasons for his decision. There were no means by which an applicant could ascertain if his or her application was under consideration, or on what evidence it was being considered. Vague criteria combined with unfettered discretion offended the requirements of fundamental justice.[66] Notably, the Court rejected the argument that, despite the procedural deficiencies of the *Act*, fundamental justice was preserved by the fact that an applicant could apply for judicial review.[67]

In *Khaliq-Kareemi*, the Nova Scotia Court of Appeal considered whether the order of the Health Services and Insurance Commission deprived the doctor of his right to liberty contrary to the principles of fundamental justice. The doctor had appeared before the Medical Review

Committee to discuss a computer analysis of his claims for services rendered after allegations were made that he had submitted fraudulent claims and claims for services not medically required. Minutes of the meeting were kept by the secretary of the committee, who later swore a statutory declaration in support of the allegations against the doctor when a hearing was held before the commission. The minutes of the committee meeting were attached to the statutory declaration.

The Court held that the commission was not strictly bound by all the rules of evidence, and it found that the allegations in the minutes had been substantiated by the evidence. In coming to those conclusions, the Court approved previous cases which had held that the procedural intent of fundamental justice is not immutable and depends on the circumstances of each case.[68] Therefore, the denial of the right to practise had been in accordance with the principles of fundamental justice.

Another aspect of fairness in the licensing context involves a consideration of whether the registration criteria ensure in a fair way the competence of the applicant. It may be that an applicant believes that the qualification standards which must be met before registration is granted are unduly onerous and not rationally connected to his or her ability to practise. As yet, there have been no Canadian cases that discuss the issue, although there is a wealth of jurisprudence in the United States.

The U.S. Supreme Court has recognized the legitimacy of the government's interest in regulating admission standards but, conversely, has warned that the standards must bear some relationship to the actual practice of the profession. In *Dent v. West Virginia*,[69] Mr. Justice Field stated that:

> . . . it has been the practice of different states from time immemorial, to exact in many pursuits a certain degree of skill and learning upon which the community may confidently rely, their possession being generally ascertained upon an examination of parties by competent persons, or inferred from a certificate to them in the form of a diploma or licence from an institution established for instruction on the subjects, scientific or otherwise, with which such pursuits have to deal. The nature and extent of the qualifications required, must depend primarily upon the judgment of the state as to their necessity. If they are appropriate to the calling or profession, and obtainable by reasonable study or application, no objection to their validity can be raised because of their stringency or difficulty. It is only when they have no relationship to such calling or profession or are unobtainable by such reasonable study or application,

that they can operate to deprive one of his right to pursue a lawful vocation.

U.S. courts have considered several admission requirements in the light of the *Dent* case.

Citizenship

The requirement of citizenship has been challenged successfully in the United States under the equal protection clause of the 14th Amendment on the basis that classifications which restrict the right to work solely on the fact of alienage are discriminatory. For example, *In re Griffiths*[70] involved a challenge to the Connecticut requirement that applicants to the state bar be U.S. citizens. The Court concluded that the right to work for a living in a common occupation is the essence of the personal freedom at the heart of the 14th Amendment. The state could not demonstrate to the satisfaction of the Court that the citizenship classification was necessary to accomplish a state purpose, and it was declared unconstitutional.

Exceptions to the general rule have, however, been made by the Court where the individual holds a legislative, judicial, or executive position or participates in the formulation, execution, or review of public policy. For example, the Court determined that citizenship requirements are valid for police officers because they are employed to enforce the law for the benefit of the public and participate directly in the execution of broad public policy.[71]

Similarly, the Court decided that legislation which requires public school teachers to be U.S. citizens is valid, because teachers influence attitudes towards government, the political process, and social responsibility.[72]

The Good Character Requirement

One standard which has been the subject of much litigation in the United States is the requirement that applicants be of "good moral character." This requirement has been challenged as violative of due process. The Supreme Court has dismissed the notion that the requirement of "moral character" is too vague,[73] stating that there are "well defined contours" to moral character.

Two leading cases, *Konigsberg v. State Bar of California*,[74] and *Schware v. Board of Bar Examiners of New Mexico*,[75] suggest that admission to a profession cannot be denied on the basis of acts which the profession contends demonstrate a lack of moral character but are simply acts of which it does not approve or which are politically unpopular. The profession must demonstrate that the acts which it contends illustrate a lack of good character have an adverse impact on the applicant's ability to practise. For example, where the applicant has been convicted of a criminal offence that is related to his or her ability to practise, that record may be evidence of a lack of good character.[76]

Educational Requirements

Most professions require that applicants demonstrate that they possess appropriate educational credentials. The *Dent* case confirms that government has the authority to determine what credentials are necessary before licensure is granted.

Many court challenges centre on accreditation. Various state licensure statutes of the legal profession require that the applicant graduate from an American Bar Association accredited school. The courts have uniformly upheld that requirement in the face of challenges under the due process and equal protection clauses.[77] The courts recognize that the association's accreditation system is sophisticated and that it would be too time-consuming for courts to perform this function on a case-by-case basis. The accreditation requirement is rationally related to the government's interest in a competent bar.[78] Accreditation has been considered and upheld by the courts in the health profession context as well.[79]

In some cases, the professional association may have the discretion to grant waivers of the accreditation requirement. Applicants have challenged this exercising of discretion. In *Application of Anderson*,[80] a duly qualified British solicitor was refused admission to the state bar of Louisiana because she had not graduated from an American Bar Association accredited school. The Court acknowledged that although the applicant's education did not satisfy the requirement, the educational differences were not significant, and it granted an exemption from the accreditation requirement.[81]

Conversely, other courts have refused to grant such a waiver. In *Florida Board of Examiners In re Hale*,[82] and *Re Application of Adams*,[83]

Canadian graduates were refused admission to the state bars of Florida and New Mexico, respectively.

The problem of the equivalency of education of foreign graduates has also been considered by the courts. In *Pascual v. State Board of Law*,[84] a Philippine-educated applicant contended that his right to equal protection had been violated by the state board's decision that he lacked an equivalent education. Two particular Philippine schools were thought to provide equivalent degrees, but the applicant had not attended either. The Court was of the opinion that the classification of Philippine applicants based on the school attended was reasonable and rational.[85]

DISCRIMINATION AND THE CHARTER

Section 15(1) of the *Charter* provides that:

> Every individual is equal before and under the law and has the right to the equal protection and equal benefit of the law without discrimination and, in particular, without discrimination based on race, national or ethnic origin, colour, religion, sex, age or mental or physical disability.

The key words of the section are "without discrimination." In the *Andrews* case, the Supreme Court of Canada held that the mere fact that a law makes a distinction between people does not in itself amount to "discrimination" within the meaning of section 15. Indeed, the Court held that even an unreasonable or unjustifiable distinction would not offend section 15.

The Court held that the only kind of distinction that would amount to "discrimination" within the meaning of section 15 is one based on the grounds listed in section 15 or on grounds analogous to those listed therein.

In the licensure context, an applicant may argue that certain statutory licensing criteria relied upon by the professional body to deny registration to a foreign-trained applicant unfairly discriminates against him or her. For example, as we have noted in other chapters, foreign-trained applicants may be required to undergo additional training not required of Canadian graduates, or to pass more onerous examinations. Further, the professional body may refuse to recognize the academic or experiential requirements of the foreign jurisdiction as equivalent to Ontario standards. The applicant may feel that these determinations are based simply on the fact of his or her place of training. The applicant may also feel that such a determination is linked to his or her national origin.

"National origin" is an enumerated ground in section 15. If a licensing requirement is based on national origin and has a disproportionate impact on immigrants, then such a requirement may be discriminatory. "Place of training" is not an enumerated ground. It may, however, be considered as an analogous ground to which the same principles apply. Distinctions made by licensing groups on the basis of place of training do apply equally to immigrants and Canadian citizens who elect to train in a foreign country. This fact alone, however, does not lessen the disproportionate impact upon foreign-trained applicants of decisions to refuse recognition of foreign qualifications or to impose extra examinations or training.

As discussed above with respect to section 7, there is a wealth of U.S. caselaw that discusses educational qualifications, citizenship, and good character in the context of equal protection and due process under the 14th Amendment. In Canada, a similar overlap between sections 7 and 15 may exist. For example, a process that denies registration because an applicant fails to satisfy onerous additional training or to pass examinations not required of domestically trained graduates may both discriminate against a foreign-trained professional and deny him or her a fundamentally just admissions procedure.

The citizenship requirement of the British Columbia Law Society has already been challenged successfully under section 15. In the *Andrews* case, the Supreme Court of Canada rejected arguments that members of the Law Society should be citizens or undertake to become so to ensure they are familiar with Canadian institutions and customs and to demonstrate a commitment to society and the administration of justice as an officer of the court.[86]

The *Law Society Act* in Ontario was amended in 1989 so that membership in the Law Society of Upper Canada is now open to permanent residents of Canada.[87]

Educational requirements that differentiate between foreign and domestic medical graduates have been challenged under section 15. In *Re Jamorski et al. and The Attorney General for the Province of Ontario*,[88] several Polish-trained physicians challenged the constitutionality of amendments to regulations passed pursuant to the *Health Disciplines Act* which provide that only graduates of Canadian or U.S. accredited medical schools are entitled to an educational licence upon acceptance into an approved medical internship. Graduates of other medical schools must first complete a pre-internship program (PIP), which ostensibly provides a means for assessing and upgrading the skills of graduates of unaccredited programs.

Additionally, the introduction of the PIP licensing requirement was accompanied by changes to public funding of internships pursuant to the *Ministry of Health Act,* which limits funding for the PIP program to 24 positions annually. The net result has been that foreign-trained graduates of unaccredited medical schools cannot obtain an internship unless they have first been accepted into and successfully completed the PIP.

The complainants alleged that the regulations discriminated against all graduates of unaccredited schools without taking into account any factor other than medical school attended to determine competence to apply to intern. The Court of Appeal disagreed, however, stating that the mere distinguishing between graduates of accredited and unaccredited schools does not amount to discrimination.

The basis for the Court's decision is two-fold. First, the Court stated that the appellants are not "similarly situated" to graduates of accredited medical schools.[89] They are graduates of a system of medical education about which the Ontario authorities know very little and do not monitor. Second, the system of medical accreditation was seen as nothing more than an ongoing, sophisticated, and *bona fide* system of assessment.[90] The classification, while it might distinguish between two groups, was not pejorative. The reasoning, which is based on the similarly situated test, must be viewed with some doubt in the light of the recent Supreme Court of Canada's rejection of that test in *Andrews.*[91]

Section 1 and the Charter

If a Court should find that a particular registration requirement or application process offends either section 7 or 15, then the registration body must be prepared to justify the requirement or the process under section 1, which states that:

> The *Canadian Charter of Rights and Freedoms* guarantees the rights and freedoms set out in it subject to such reasonable limits prescribed by law as can be demonstrably justified in a free and democratic society.

In justifying a limitation on a right or freedom, the registration body must satisfy two criteria. First, it must be demonstrated that the governmental objective in enacting the legislation is "pressing and substantial." Second, the means adopted to achieve that objective must meet a proportionality test. Factors considered in assessing proportionality include: (1) whether the means are carefully designed and rationally connected to the objective to be achieved; (2) whether the means impair as little as possible the right or freedom in question; (3) whether the means have the effect of trenching on rights so that the objective is outweighed by the abridgment of rights.[92]

For example, in the *Andrews* case, a majority of the Supreme Court of Canada was not persuaded that the objective of the legislation requiring citizenship for admission to the B.C. bar was not so pressing or substantial to warrant the trenching on individual rights, nor was it carefully tailored or rationally connected to the objective of ensuring familiarity with Canadian institutions and commitment to Canadian society.[93]

Finally, it should be noted that the state cannot justify its actions under section 1 by simply relying on arguments of administrative convenience. Mr. Justice Lamer in the *Reference re s. 94(2)* case stated that:

> Section 1 may, for reasons of administrative expediency, successfully come to the rescue of an otherwise violation of section 7, but only in cases arising out of exceptional conditions such as natural disasters, the outbreak of war, epidemics and the like.[94]

In the *Branigan* case, however, the Court appeared to accept the administrative expediency argument. The Court noted that administrative law had long recognized the need for tribunals; without them, the caseload of the courts would be awesome. In view of the fact that the complainant had a right of appeal, the discipline procedures were held to be proportionate and rational.[95]

SUMMARY

Many of the professional groups that the Task Force studied not only are created by statute but to some degree are statutorily controlled by government, and thus they may constitute "government" within the meaning of section 32 of the *Charter*. Similarly, if those bodies exercise statutory powers, they are covered by the word "legislature" in section 32 and thus are likely caught by the *Charter*, whether or not they are directly controlled by government, so long as the actions of the body can be characterized as "public" actions. Because the registration process involves public interests of health and safety, the exercising of licensing powers should attract constitutional scrutiny.

It is arguable that the "right" to obtain a licence to practise the calling one has been trained for is not a "liberty" within section 7 because it is a mere economic right unprotected by the *Charter*. Another point of view, however, suggests that the practice of a profession is a "liberty" because it involves more than mere pecuniary interests and is also tied to an individual's concept of self-worth and community. The weight of opinion in Ontario currently favours the former interpretation.

If the right to practise a profession is a liberty interest within section 7, then an applicant has a corresponding right not to be deprived of that right, except in accordance with the principles of fundamental justice. Clearly those principles incorporate, at a minimum, existing notions of natural justice and fairness, but they may include additional safeguards not available previously at common law.

Arguably, then, an applicant who has been refused registration without, for example, an oral hearing, knowledge of the evidence relied upon by the tribunal, reasons for the denial of the licence, or a right of appeal may have been denied principles of fundamental justice.

Similarly, where the legislation or the professional body which has the authority to set admission standards demands that the applicant satisfy unduly onerous requirements, the admission procedure may also be challenged on the basis that the criteria do not fairly test competence to practise, which is a breach of the principles of fundamental justice.

Admissions criteria that distinguish the foreign-trained applicant from the domestically trained applicant may be found to be discriminatory if challenged under section 15 of the *Charter*. The Supreme Court of Canada has stated in *Andrews* that a rule which bars an entire class of persons from certain forms of employment solely on the enumerated or analogous grounds of section 15, and without consideration of educational and professional qualifications or other individual merits or attributes, infringes equality rights. Although "place of education or training" is not a specifically enumerated ground of discrimination, it is closely tied to place of origin and may be considered as an analogous ground of discrimination.

In attempting to justify either limitations on procedural rights or its own discriminatory actions, the registration body will have to prove that its actions are justified under section 1. The registration body will have to prove that the licensing objectives are pressing and substantial and that the licensing criteria are proportionate to the objective sought. The *Charter* has influenced and will continue to influence reform of administrative law procedures. The Task Force has made its recommendations for reform of the admissions procedure with this in mind.

Conclusions

In view of the fact that current *Charter* jurisprudence suggests an oral hearing may not be necessary in all cases, legislation governing the professions should be amended to incorporate both the right to a review of the written documentation and the right to an oral hearing (particularly important where issues of credibility are involved), which rights may be waived by the applicant. This is reflected in our recommendations on this subject in Chapter 11, "Review of Registration Decisions."

Requiring additional examinations of foreign-trained individuals imposes a burden or disadvantage not imposed upon domestically trained individuals and may in some situations be in contravention of section 15 of the *Charter*. Therefore, the Task Force concludes that licensure examinations for foreign-trained professionals should be reassessed in accordance with the recommendations seen in this Report's chapters on "Prior Learning Assessment" (Chapter 5) and "Licensure Testing" (Chapter 6).

RECOMMENDATION

13.1   *The Task Force is of the view and recommends that legislation and regulations governing entry to a profession or providing for a reserved title, with a "good character" stipulation, be worded to provide that registration is denied only where the evidence relied upon as demonstrating a lack of good character is rationally related to the applicant's competence or ability to practise.*

APPENDICES

Appendix A   Orders in Council

Appendix B   Terms of Reference

Appendix C   Submissions to the Task Force

Appendix D   Meetings and Contributors

Appendix E   Commissioners and Task Force Staff

Appendix F   Consultants

Appendix G   List of Background Studies

Appendix H   Professional Summaries

Notes

Bibliography

APPENDIX A

Orders in Council

Ontario

Executive Council

WHEREAS the Cabinet Committee on Race Relations has received and considered a report outlining the difficulties encountered in obtaining professional or trade certification in Ontario by persons whose training or experience comes from outside of Canada;

AND WHEREAS the Cabinet Committee on Race Relations has determined that a thorough review of all rules and practices governing access to professions and selected trades is desirable in order to determine whether entry standards disadvantage persons with training or experience from outside of Canada, and if so to determine whether those standards are required to protect the public.

NOW THEREFORE, on the recommendation of the Minister of Citizenship and Minister Responsible for Race Relations, the Lieutenant Governor by and with the advice and concurrence of the Executive Council, orders that Professor Peter Cumming be appointed chairperson of the Task Force on Access to Professions and Trades in Ontario, and that Enid Lee and Dr. Dimitrios Oreopoulos be appointed members of the Task Force, and that the Task Force be authorized to enquire into and report to the Minister of Citizenship and Minister Responsible for Race Relations by the 1st of November, 1988 on the impact on foreign qualified individuals, and in particular, members of racial minority and ethnic groups, of the rules and practices governing entrance to professions and selected trades in Ontario, and, in particular, to:

(i) Review all rules and practices affecting entry to professions and those trades selected by the Task Force for review to determine whether they have an actual or potential discriminatory effect on persons with training or experience from outside of Canada, and in particular, members of racial and ethnic minorities.

(ii) Determine whether the identified rules or practices can be justified as necessary to maintain professional or trade standards.

(iii) Investigate actual or potential barriers beyond the control of the professions and trades, such as lack of support services during re-training periods.

(iv) Conduct a survey of foreign trained professionals and tradespersons to verify the effects of the requirements and to obtain data on race, ethnicity and gender.

(v) Consider and comment on practices and requirements in other jurisdictions, such as the assessment of academic equivalencies, granting credit for work experience, and testing language proficiency.

(vi) Conduct further research and studies as deemed appropriate by the Task Force.

(vii) Recommend changes to rules and practices which cannot be justified as necessary for the maintenance of professional or trade standards, and recommend how foreign qualified persons can be assisted to meet those rules which can be justified.

AND THAT all government ministries, boards, agencies and commissions, shall assist the Task Force to the fullest extent in order that it may carry out its duties and functions, and that the Task Force shall have authority to engage such counsel, expert technical advisors, researchers, other staff and consultants as it deems proper at rates of remuneration to be approved by the Management Board of Cabinet.

AND THAT the Ministry of the Attorney General shall be responsible for providing administrative support to the enquiry.

Recommended _____   Concurred _____
Minister of Citizenship   Chairman
and Minister Responsible
for Race Relations

Approved and Ordered October 22, 1987   _____
                    Date   Lieutenant Governor

Ontario
Executive Council

Order in Council

On the recommendation of the undersigned, the Lieutenant Governor, by and with the advice and concurrence of the Executive Council, orders that

WHEREAS by Order-in-Council numbered 2359/87 and dated the 22nd day of October, 1987, the Task Force on Access to Professions and Trades in Ontario was established and ordered to report to the Minister of Citizenship and Minister Responsible for Race Relations by the 1st of November, 1988;

AND WHEREAS the above-mentioned Task Force has been unable to complete its enquiries by the date specified in the aforesaid Order-in-Council;

NOW THEREFORE it is ordered that the 30th day of September, 1989 be substituted for the 1st of November, 1988 in the aforesaid Order-in-Council;

AND FURTHER it is ordered that this change be effective as of the 2nd day of November, 1988.

Recommended _____ Concurred _____
             Minister of Citizenship   Chairman

Approved and
Ordered   February 22, 1989   _____
             Date   Lieutenant Governor

APPENDIX B

Terms of Reference

Ontario

TERMS OF REFERENCE

This Task Force was appointed by the Minister of Citizenship, the Minister Responsible for Race Relations, and the Lieutenant Governor by and with the advice and concurrence of the Executive Council on October 22, 1987 to enquire into the impact on foreign qualified individuals, and in particular, members of racial minority and ethnic groups, of the rules and practices governing entrance to professions and selected trades in Ontario.

The Task Force shall:

1) Review all rules and practices affecting entry to professions and trades to determine whether they have an actual or potential discriminatory effect on persons with training or experience from outside of Canada.

2) Determine whether the identified rules or practices can be justified as necessary to maintain professional or trade standards.

3) Investigate actual or potential barriers beyond the control of the professions and trades, such as lack of support services during re-training periods; and

4) Recommend changes to rules and practices which cannot be justified as necessary for the maintenance of professional or trade standards, and recommend how foreign qualified persons can be assisted to meet those rules which can be justified.

Written Submissions are invited and must be received by February 15, 1988.

APPENDIX C

Submissions to the Task Force

Individuals

Abraham, Dr. G.
Ahmad, Dr. N.
Ahmed, Mrs. T.M.
Albin-Cook, Dr. K.
Ansari, Dr. Z.

Bertlik, Dr. M.
Bouma, Mr. B.

Calderon, Dr. E.
Camargo, Mr. V.H
Chauhan, Mr. J.
Chernin, Dr. D.A.
Chicaiza, Ms L.
Codina, Ms A.
Cvercko, Mr. M.

Daniel, Mr. S.
Davis, Lt. Col. H.A.
Dcunha, Dr.
De Jager, Capt. P.
De Santis, Mr. G.
Dey, Mr. H.
Doshi, Ms S.

Ferguson, Mr. D.C.
Fernandes, Dr. N.
Fernando, Mr. T.
Fleet, Mr. D., M.P.P.
Footman, Dr. J.
Francis, Mrs. T.

Gajaria, Mr. C.
Garcia, Mr. A.
Gelman, Mr. S.
Gnanambikai, Mr. P.
Gopinath, Ms R.
Grabowski, Dr. M.

Hipsz, Mr. R.
Holness, Mr. W.A.
Hore, Dr. K.
Hossein-Doost, Dr. M.
Hoosein-Doost, Mrs. F.
Hunter, Ms J.

Jack, Mr. K.
Joyce, Ms A.

Kandiah, Mr. K.
Kanevsky, Mr. E.
Katz, Mr. G.
Khawja, Mr. B.
Kleiman, Dr. A.
Kletter, Mr. T.
Klonowski, Dr. W.
Kondor, Dr. G.A.
Kovács, Dr. I.
Kraljevic, Dr. M.
Krishna, Prof. V.
Kuganesan, Mrs. R.
Kuganesan, Mr. T.
Kun, Mr. G.I.

Larsen, Mr. H.
Leuteritz, Mr. H.

Machon, Mr. M.A.G.
Manapul, Mr. E.
Mandal, Mr. N.J.
Mateja, Mr. S.
Mew, Mr. G.
Mighty, Mr. J.H.
Mukhojee, Mr. A.

Najarian, Dr. S.
Nazroo, Mr. R.C.
Nishio, Ms M.
Nordemann, Mr. A.

Odisho, Mr. S.I.
O'Malley, Dr. B.P.
Osuch, Dr. J.
Osuch, Dr. M.
Oyelese, Dr. O.O.
Oyston, Dr. J.

Papathanassiou, Mr. N.
Patel, Mr. C.
Powley, Mr. J.
Prosmushkin, Mr. B.
Pucaj, Dr. K.
Piotrowski, Dr. P.
Puddu, Dr. S.
Pudlowska, Mrs. G.
Pulido, Dr. O.M.

Ray, Dr. A.K.
Rivera, Mr. E.
Romero V., Mr. J.A.
Rose, Dr. C.
Roy, Mr. L.

Sangha, Mr. A.
Sarpong, Mr. J.
Satolo, Dr. E.
Sawadi, Mr. S.G.
Schneider, Ms L.
Seevaratnam, P.
Sehdev, Mr. S.
Shaba, Mr. K.
Sharp, Mr. D.J.
Shek, Mr. E.
Shivakumar, P.
Shivarattan, Mr. S.
Singaraja, Dr. C.
Srikanthan, Mrs. S.
Stoisor, Dr. I.P.
Sukhinder, Mr.
Syed, Mr. H.A.
Szotyori, Ms E.

Thiyagendran, Dr. T.

Vaiman, Mrs. M.
Venczel, Ms I.
Vikhman, Mr. V.
Vikhman, Mrs. Y.
Villavarayan, Mr. S.C.
Visoi, Mr. D.

Willis, Mr. A.H.
Wojcicki, Dr. A.
Wong, Mr. S.

Yadav, V.

Zakaria, Mr. M.B.
Zofia, Dr. P.
Zonis, Mrs. R.V.

1 Submitter requested that
name be withheld

11 Anonymous submissions

Associations

Access Alliance-Multicultural, Community Health Centre
- I. Furtado

Accurate Appraisals Consultant Services
- H. Killian, Senior Appraiser

Affected Sri Lankan Professional Group
- J. Balakrishnan, Co-ordinator

African Newcomer Aid Centre of Toronto (C.A.N.A.C.T.)
- B. Riddel, Executive Director

Aish Hatorah Learning Centre

Algonquin College of Applied Arts and Technology
- P. Killeen, President

Association of Central-American Health Professionals in Canada
- Dr. C. Rubio-Reyes, President

Association of Chinese Community Service Workers
- K. Fung, President

Association of Former Czechoslovak Political Prisoners in Exile
- K. Kalenda, Chairman

Association of Hispanic Canadian Professionals
- J.A. Libaque-Esaine, Organizing Committee

Association of Ontario Land Surveyors
- L. Petzold, Executive Director

Association of Polish Engineers in Canada
- M.J. Zaremba, President

Association of Professional Engineers of the Province of Ontario
- A.C. Cagney, Executive Director

Association of Registered Dental Technicians
- B. Huybrechts, Secretary

Association of Vietnamese Physicians in Canada, Ontario Chapter
- Dr. S.D. Nguyen, President

Assyrian Community of Canada Welfare Committee
- M. Shmoil, Chairman

Board of Directors of Drugless Therapy, Naturopathy,
Province of Ontario
- E.F. Shrubb, Chairman of the Board

Board of Funeral Services
- A.M. Reynolds, Registrar

Board of Ophthalmic Dispensers, Ontario
- C. Beaulieu, Chairman, Competency Committee

Board of Regents, Chiropody Act, Province of Ontario
- Dr. D.M. Schatz, Chairman

Brock University
- K. Rae, Associate Registrar, Admissions and Graduate Studies

Cambridge Multicultural Centre
- I. Sousa-Batista, Coordinator

Canada-Pakistan Association
- S.M. Khan, President

Canadian Association of Occupational Therapists
- M. Brockett, Executive Director

Canadian Association of Orthodontists
- Dr. M. Yasny, Public Relations Chairman

Canadian Ethnic Journalists' and Writers' Club Inc.
- Mr. H.A. Syed, Chairman, Special Committee

Canadian Ethnocultural Council
- E. Sanchez de Malicki, Chairperson

Canadian Latin American Professional Association
- M. Hernandez, President
- R. Hernandez

Career Preparation for Immigrants
- V. Danyliu

Certified General Accountants' Association of Canada
- E.J. Boudreau, President

Certified General Accountants Association of Ontario
- G.W. Fuller, Executive Director

Chinese Canadian National Council

Chinese Interpreter and Information Services
- H. Lau, Chairperson

College of Nurses of Ontario
- M. Risk, Executive Director

College of Optometrists of Ontario
- I. Baker, Registrar

Filipino Association for Academic Accreditation
- M. Catre, President

Governing Board of Denture Therapists
- P.A. Clark, Registrar

Government of Newfoundland and Labrador
Department of Career Development and Advanced Studies
- C.J. Carter, Director Industrial Training

Government of Quebec, Department of Manpower and
Income Security
- J. Beaunoyer, Director

Guelph and District Multicultural Centre Inc.
- L. Scott, Executive Director

Hamilton and District Electrical Contractors Association
- D.L. Thornton

Humber College of Applied Arts and Technology
- D.H. Foster, Coordinator, Funeral Service Education Program

Insurance Brokers Association of Ontario
- K.W. Martin, General Manager

International Brotherhood of Electrical Workers, Local Union 105
- P.J. Dillon, Business Manager,

Jamaican Canadian Association
- J.G. Cummings, Caribbean Immigrant Services Coordinator

Japanese Canadian Cultural Centre
- K. Suyama, Chairperson

Joint Committee on Accreditation
- Professor V. Krishna, Executive Secretary

Kingston Committee for Racial Harmony
- B. Dev Batchelor, President

Kingston and District Immigrant Services
- R.E. Kennedy, Acting Executive Director

Kitchener/Waterloo Central American Cultural Association
- M. Villalta, President

Kitchener-Waterloo Refugee Co-ordinating Committee
- M. Hennig

McMaster University
- A.L. Darling, Registrar and Director of Institutional Analysis
  Office of the Registrar

Multicultural Health Coalition
- Dr. R. Masi, President

National Organization of Immigrant and Visible Minority Women
of Canada (N.O.I.V.M.W.C.)
- S. Damiani

Northwestern Ontario Cross-Cultural Conference
- P. Monks, Chairperson

Ontario Council of Agencies Servicing Immigrants (O.C.A.S.I.)
- P. Chud, Executive Director

Ontario Association of Architects
- B. Parks, Executive Director and Registrar

Ontario Association of Certified Engineering Technicians
and Technologists
- J.R. Fisher, Registrar

Ontario Cloakmakers, Dress and Sportswear District Council
of International Ladies Garment Workers' Union,
Locals 14, 83 and 92
- H. Stewart, Business Manager

Ontario Dental Nurses and Assistants Association
- J. Miller, Executive Director

Ontario Human Rights Commission
- R. Anand, Chief Commissioner

Ontario Ministry of Education
- M. Rogers, Co-ordinator, Regional Schools for Nursing
  Assistants Special Education and Provincial Schools Branch

Ontario Pharmacists' Association
- R.B. Franceschini, Executive Director

Ontario Professional Foresters Association
- J.W. Ebbs, Executive Director

Ontario Psychological Association
- Dr. E.A. Stasiak, Executive Director

Ontario Separate School Trustees' Association
- E.F. Nyitrai, Executive Director

Ontario Teachers' Federation
- M. Wilson, Secretary-Treasurer

Ontario Veterinary Association
- H.H. Grenn, Registrar

Organization of South Asian Canadians
- S. Edwards

Pharmacy Examining Board of Canada
- J. Creasy, Registrar-Treasurer

Prabasi Bengali Cultural Association
- Dr. K. Hore, Coordinator, Subcommittee: Special Tasks
- U.K. Mandal
- H. Dey
- A. Mukhojee
- L. Roy
- 10 Anonymous

Refugee Women's Workshop
- F. Pérez

Rexdale Women's Centre
- B. Shore

Seneca College of Applied Arts and Technology
- W.R. McCutcheon, President

South Asian Women's Group (SAWG)
- Q. Alam
- J. Khaki
- D. Kassan

South East Asian Project (Y.E.C.C.)
Woodgreen Community Centre
- P. Goyette, Chairperson

St. Lawrence College
- B. Cruden, President

Steven Shaw Management Consultants Inc.
- S. Shaw, President

Swedish Women's Educational Association of Canada
- K. Camenietzki

Teachers of English as a Second Language Association
of Ontario (TESL)
- S. Firth, President

Terrace Bay/Lake Superior Multicultural Association

The Board of Directors of Physiotherapy,
Province of Ontario
- R. Wolpert, Registrar

The Cabinet Office, Office of Francophone Affairs
- R.M. Beauregard, Executive Director

The College of Physicians and Surgeons of Ontario
- D. McLaren, Administrative Coordinator, Registrars' Office

The Federation of Chinese Canadian Professionals

The Hospital for Sick Children
- M.S. MacDonald, Vice-President, Medical

The Institute of Chartered Accountants of Ontario
- D.A. Wilson, Executive Director

The Nova Scotia Dental Hygienists Association
- T. Mitchell, President

The Ombudsman/Ontario
- G. Morrison, Director, Investigations

The Ontario Dental Association
- J.C. Gillies, Executive Director

The Ontario Society of Periodontists
- Dr. F.H. Compton, President

The Organization of Ontario Auto Repairers
- W. Killins, President

The Polish Institute of Arts and Sciences in Canada
Polski Instytut Naukowy W Kanadzie
- L. Kos-Rabcewicz-Zubkowski, Vice-Chairman

The Romanian Canadian Society 'CARPATI' of Toronto
- C. Chisu, Sr. Vice-President

The Sir Mortimer B. Davis - Jewish General Hospital
- Dr. M.J. Palayew, Professor, Department of Radiology,
  McGill University

The Society of Management Accountants of Ontario
- R.W. Dye, Executive Director

The University of Western Ontario
- D. Radcliffe, Associate Dean, Faculty of Education

The University of Western Ontario
- G.J. Smiley (Student Affairs) and Registrar

The Urban Alliance on Race Relations
- Dr. W. Head, President

The Workers' Educational Association of Canada
- J.P. Langdon, President

Thunder Bay Chamber of Commerce
- J. Colosimo, President

Thunder Bay Multicultural Association
- J. Potestio, President

Toronto General Hospital
- Dr. J.B. Cullen, Deputy Pathologist-in-Chief

Toronto Western Hospital
- Dr. G. Abraham, Division of Nephrology

University of Alberta, Faculty of Pharmacy and Pharmaceutical Sciences
- Dr. J.A. Bachynsky, Dean

University of Ottawa
- G.J. Marcotte, Director of Admissions and Associate Registrar

University of the Philippines Alumni Association (Toronto Chapter)
- Dr. V. Santiago-Liu, President

University of Toronto, Faculty of Dentistry
- Dr. A.R. Ten Cate, Dean

Wilfrid Laurier University
- B.G. Granger, Associate Registrar, Admissions

Windsor-Essex County Family YMCA
- E. Barsky, Co-ordinator, New Canadian Program

Women Immigrants of London
- A. Taylor, Manager, Counselling Services

Women of Many Cultures (W.O.M.C.)
- L. Kosowan, Chairperson, Planning Committee

Working Skills Centre
- A. Menozzi, Executive Director

APPENDIX D

Meetings and Contributors

PROFESSIONAL ASSOCIATIONS

Accounting - Certified General Accountants

- G. W. Fuller, Executive Director, Certified General
  Accountants Association
- M. Masters, Registrar and Director Student Services,
  Certified General Accountants Association

Accounting - Certified Management Accountants

- W. Wilson, Director, Professional Standards, Society
  of Management Accountants of Ontario

Accounting - Chartered Accountants

- D. Beech, President, Institute of Chartered Accountants
- R. McNeil, First Vice-President, Institute of Chartered
  Accountants
- R. Peck, General Counsel, Institute of Chartered Accountants
- T. Warner, Associate Registrar, Institute of Chartered
  Accountants

Agrology

- L. McLean, Administrative Secretary, Ontario Institute
  of Agrologists

Architecture

- J. Arnold, Deputy Registrar, Ontario Architecture Association
- L. Gates, Chairman, Canadian Architectural Certification
  Board
- B. Parks, Director, Ontario Architecture Association
- M. Tawadrof, Claims Consultant, Ontario Architecture
  Association
- P. Wright, Acting Dean, Faculty of Architecture and
  Landscape Architecture

Chiropody

- D. Schatz, Chair, Board of Regents, Chiropody Act, and President, Toronto Institute of Medical Technology
- P. Wilson, Secretary Treasurer, Board of Regents, Chiropody Act

Chiropractic

- D. Dainty, Academic Dean, Canadian Memorial Chiropractic College
- S. Stolarski, Registrar, Board of Directors of Chiropractic Ontario
- J. Watkins, Executive Vice-President, Canadian Chiropractic Association

Dental Hygiene

- L. Stevens, Executive Assistant, Royal College of Dental Surgeons of Ontario

Dental Technology

- W.J. Arnsby, Registrar, Governing Board of Technicians
- B. Huybrechts, Secretary, Association of Registered Technicians

Dentistry

- J. Gillies, Executive Director, Ontario Dental Association
- B. Henderson, Director, Education and Accreditation, Canadian Dental Association
- G. Kravis, Director, National Dental Examining Board
- G. Nikiforuk, President, Royal College of Dental Surgeons for Ontario
- K. Pownall, Registrar, Royal College of Dental Surgeons for Ontario
- R. Ten Cate, Dean, University of Toronto, Faculty of Dentistry

Denture Therapy

- P. Clark, Registrar, Governing Board of Denture Therapists
- P. McCabe, Member, Board of Denture Therapists

- M. Shuhendler, Chairman, Board of Denture Therapists
- R. Steinecke, Counsel, Board of Denture Therapists

Dietetics

- M. Hedley, President, Ontario Dietetic Association
- M. Law, Chairman, Professional Standards, Ontario
  Dietetic Association
- M. Rangam, Executive Director, Ontario Dietetic
  Association
- M. Telford, Director, Membership and Standards,
  Ontario Dietetic Association

Early Childhood Education

- A. Parle, Ontario Ministry of Community and Social Services
- M. Hamilton, Past President, The Association for Early
  Childhood Education

Education

- S. Hibbitt, Manager, Registrar Services,
  Ontario Ministry of Education
- C. Lundy, Registrar, Faculty of Education,
  University of Toronto
- M. Stager, Assistant to the Dean, Faculty of Education,
  University of Toronto
- J. Westcott, Federation of Women Teachers Association
  of Ontario
- M. Wilson, Ontario Teachers' Federation

Engineering

- A. Cagney, Executive Director, Association of Professional
  Engineers of Ontario
- J.O. Harold, Administrator, Association of Professional
  Engineers of Ontario
- P. Osmond, Registrar, Association of Professional
  Engineers of Ontario

Engineering Technicians and Technologists

- J. Fisher, Past Registrar, Ontario Association of
  Certified Engineering Technicians and Technologists

- D. Holmes, Registrar, Ontario Association of Certified Engineering and Technologists

Forestry

- J. W. Ebbs, Executive Director, Ontario Professional Foresters Association

Funeral Services

- S. Brodie, Executive Secretary, Funeral Services Association
- D. Foster, Coordinator, Funeral Services Program, Humber College
- A. Reynolds, Registrar, Board of Funeral Services

Insurance Brokerage

- R. G. Cooper, General Manager, Registered Insurance Brokers of Ontario

Land Surveying

- G. Gracie, Professor, Survey Science, University of Toronto
- L. Petzold, Executive Director, Association of Ontario Land Surveyors

Law

- K. Jarvis, Secretary-Treasurer, Law Society of Upper Canada
- V. Krishna, Secretary, Joint Committee on Accreditation
- T. Kerzner
- G. Thomson, Director, Legal Education Committee

Massage Therapy

- M. Rangaswami, Chair, Board of Directors of Masseurs
- H. Barber, Secretary-Treasurer, Board of Directors of Masseurs

Medical Laboratory Technology

- V. Booth, Executive Director, Canadian Society of Laboratory Technologists

- A. Browner, Registrar, Canadian Society of Medical Technologists
- K. Fuller, President, Ontario Society of Medical Technologists

Medicine

- G.A. Barker, Director, Critical Care, and Chairman, Medical, Advisory Committee, Hospital for Sick Children
- S. Barret, Counsel, Professional Association of Interns and Residents in Ontario
- T. Boadway, Director, Health Policy, Ontario Medical Association
- K. Bregija, Manager, Medical Research, Ontario Medical Association
- D. Chiro, Vice President, Human Resources, Hospital for Sick Children
- J. Connon, Director of Graduate Medical Education, University of Toronto
- J.P. DesGroseillier, Director, Royal College of Physicians and Surgeons, Ottawa
- M. Dixon, Registrar, College of Physicians and Surgeons of Ontario
- P. Gardner, Ontario Ministry of Health
- A. Goldbloom, Director of Medical Education, Hospital for Sick Children
- S.J. Hanmer, Director, Administrative Services, Department of Paediatrics
- R.H.A. Haslam, Professor and Chairman, Department of Paediatrics
- A.E. LeBlanc, Executive Coordinator, Ontario Ministry of Health
- M. Levine, Hon. Past President, Professional Association of Interns and Residents in Ontario
- M.S. MacDonald, Vice President, Medical, Hospital for Sick Children
- R. Masi, President, Multicultural Health Council
- J.L. Provan, University of Toronto
- L. Ross, Executive Director, Professional Association of Interns and Residents in Ontario
- A.A. Shardt, Associate Registrar, College of Physicians and Surgeons of Ontario
- B. Sheppard, Associate Dean, Medical Education, University of Toronto
- L. Truax, Ontario Ministry of Health

- B. Winston, Vice-President, Professional Association of Interns and Residents in Ontario

Naturopathy

- K. Dunk, Vice-Chair, Board of Directors of Naturopathy, Drugless Therapy
- E. Shrubb, Chair, Board of Directors of Naturopathy, Drugless Therapy

Nursing and Nursing Assistancy

- G. Donner, Registered Nurses Association of Ontario
- J. Monaghan, Assistant Professor, Faculty of Nursing, University of Toronto
- M. Raspor, Regional School for Nursing Assistants (Toronto)
- B. Secord, College of Nurses of Ontario
- M. Wheeler, Registered Nurses Association of Ontario

Occupational Therapy

- M. Brockett, Executive Director, Canadian Association of Occupational Therapists
- B. Graff, Executive Director, Ontario Society of Occupational Therapists
- R. Schaffer, Director, Occupational Therapy, University of Toronto
- E. Yack, Registrar, Ontario College of Occupational Therapists

Ophthalmic Dispensing

- D. Bowen, Executive Secretary, Board of Ophthalmic Dispensers, Ontario
- M. Bloom, Registrar, Board of Ophthalmic Dispensers, Ontario

Optometry

- I. Baker, Registrar, College of Optometrists
- A.P. Cullen, School of Optometry, University of Waterloo
- M. Samek, Vision Institute of Canada

Osteopathy

- V. Dejardine, Board of Directors of Osteopathy

Pharmacy

- J. Creasey, Registrar, Pharmacy Examining Board of Canada
- I. Feldman. Assistant Director, Licensing, Ontario
  College of Pharmacy
- S. Kassam, Secretary, Ontario College of Pharmacy
- D. Perrier, Dean Faculty of Pharmacy, University
  of Toronto
- B. Wensley, Registrar, Ontario College of Pharmacy

Physiotherapy

- J. Cornwell, Coordinator, Clinical Component, University
  of Toronto
- A. Scott, Education Director, Canadian Physiotherapy
  Association
- S. Stuart, Chair, Toronto Re-entry Programme,
  Canadian Physiotherapy Association
- R. Wolpert, Registrar, Board of Directors of Physiotherapy

Psychology

- E. Stasiak, Executive Director, Ontario Psychological
  Association
- B. Wand, Registrar, The Ontario Board of Examiners
- H.P. Edwards, former member of Ontario Board of Examiners
  in Psychology

Radiological Technology

- D. Alton, Chairman, Board of Radiological Technicians
- C. Cowling, Toronto Institute of Medical Technology
- R. Hesler, Executive Director, Ontario Association
  of Medical Radiation Technologists
- A. Kind, Director, Ontario Association of Medical Radiation
  Technologists
- R. Scott, Vice-Chair, Board of Radiological Technicians

Real Estate and Business Brokerage

- A. Coleclough, Registrar, Real Estate and Business Brokers Act

- C.K. Wen, Administrative Officer, Ontario Ministry of Consumer and Commercial Relations

Social Work

- V. Munns, Registrar, Ontario College of Certified Social Workers
- M.J. Stewart, Executive Director, Ontario Association of Professional Social Workers

Veterinary Medicine

- H. Grenn, Registrar, Ontario Veterinary Association
- R. Downey, Assistant Dean, Academic Affairs, University of Guelph

TRADES

Ontario Ministry of Skills Development

- B. Butterworth, Senior Manager, Community and Workplace, Literacy Unit
- G. Carr, Deputy Minister
- H. Demeris, Manager, Program Standards
- C. Fairclough, Assistant Director, Apprenticeship
- G. Fell, Program Coordinator
- J. Lanthier, Director, Apprenticeship
- J. Rush, Assistant Deputy Minister
- A. Shepperd, Policy Advisor
- W. Tuohy, Manager of Access Policy Unit
- H. Zisser, General Manager, Federal/Provincial Relations Group

Labour Organizations

- J. Block, Labourers International Union, Local 183
- C. Brown, Training Coordinator, United Brotherhood of Carpenters and Joiners of America
- B. O'Donnel, Electrical Contractors Association
- H. Stewart, Ladies Garment Workers Union
- E. Thornton, Labourers International Union, Local 183

- J. Veecock, Ontario Federation of Labour

COMMUNITY AND ETHNO-CULTURAL COMMITTEES

Access Action Committee
- A. Ogale

Advisory Committee on Visible Minorities
- C. Dabydeen

Association of former Czechoslovak Political
Prisoners in Exile
- K. Kaleada, Chair

Canadian Ethnic Journalists Club
- H. Syed

Canadian Ethnocultural Association
- E. Sanchez de Malicki

Chinese Information and Community Services
- K. Fung, Program Director

Coalition of Visible Minority Women, Equal
Opportunity Division
- A. Benjamin

COSTI-ILAS Immigrant Services
- D. Szado

Cross Cultural Communication Centre
- M. Williams, Employment Equity
  Project Coordinator

Downtown Employment Services
- P. Kwok

Jewish Vocational Services
- P. Chud

Kingston Committee for Racial Harmony
- B. Dev Batchelor

Kitchener-Waterloo Refugee
Coordinating Committee
- M. Hennig

Macauliffe Institute of Sikh Studies
- T. Sher Singh

Multicultural Council of Saskatchewan
- T. Mountjoy, General Manager

Multicultural Health Coalition,
- R. Masi, President

National Coalition of Jamaican Canadians
- B. Armstrong

National Congress of Filipino Canadian Association
in Canada
- R. Falco

North York Immigrants Services Network
- A. Wirsig

Ontario Council of Agencies Servicing Immigrants (O.C.A.S.I.)
- P. Chud

Ontario Congress of Black Women
- A. Benjamin

Ontario Coalition of Black Trade Unionists
- C. Moore

Prabasi Bengali Cultural Association
- K. Hore, Chairperson

Rexdale Women's Centre
- B. Shore

South Asian Women's Network
- Q. Alam, Board Member

The Pickering Carib Canadian Cultural Association
- C. Christian, Chair

Thunder Bay Chamber of Commerce
- J. Colosimo, President

Thunder Bay Multicultural Association
- J.V. Boeckner, Executive Director

Toronto Mayor's Committee on Community and Race Relations
- T. Hitner, Vice-Chair

University Settlement House
- J. Wah

Windsor Community Briefing - Windsor-Essex County
Family YMCA
- E. Barsky, Coordinator

Winnipeg Immigration and Settlement Services
- G. Thompson

Women's Law Association
- S. Chapnik

Women of Many Cultures, Scarborough Centre
- L. Kosewan, Chair

PRIOR LEARNING ASSESSMENT AND RETRAINING

- E. Allmen, Project Analyst Multiculturalism,
  Ontario Ministry of Community and Social Services
- J. Berry, Director, International Division, Association
  of Universities and Colleges of Canada, Ottawa
- K. Clements, Association of Registrars of the Universities
  and Colleges of Canada, Ottawa
- G. Collins, Executive Director, Association of Colleges of
  Applied Arts and Technology of Ontario
- R. Conlon, Social Service Worker, Loyalist College
- D. Cooke, Director, E.S.L. Program, Glendon College
- B. Cruden, President, St. Lawrence College
- D. Daigneault, Ordre des Technologues des Sciences
  Appliquées
- O. Kindiakoff, Comparative Education Service, University of
  Toronto
- C. La Plante, Informations Officer, Communications
  Division, Association of Universities and Colleges
  of Canada, Ottawa
- P. Luening, Senior Program Coordinator, Employment Unit,
  Ontario Ministry of Community and Social Services
- C. Lundy, Registrar, Faculty of Education,
  University of Toronto
- M. Orris, Dean, Continuing Education, Ryerson
  Polytechnical Institute

- C. Pascal, Chairman, Ontario Council of Regents for Colleges of Applied Arts and Technology
- R. Patry, Director, Government Relations, Association of Universities and Colleges of Canada, Ottawa
- J. Salmona, Coordinator, Continuing Education, George Brown College of Applied Arts and Technology
- W. Sayers, Director of Communications, Council of Universities
- B. Stedman-Smith, Industrial Training, Durham College of Applied Arts and Technology
- A. Thomas, Ontario Institute for Studies in Education, Department of Adult Education
- Mr. Paul Zakos, Coordinator, Loyalist College

Other Models: Alberta

- D. W. Bell, Executive Director, Alberta Career Development and Employment, Edmonton
- D.J. Corbett, Director, Alberta Immigration and Settlement
- D. Gartner, Executive Director, Professions and Occupations Bureau, Alberta
- L. Henderson, Secretary, Universities Coordinating Council, Edmonton
- L. Richardson, Director, Alberta Legislative Services
- A. J. Schuld, Alberta Professional Engineers, Geologists, Geophysists of Alberta (APEGGA)

Other Models: British Columbia

- G. Biggs, Manager, Trades and Technical Programs, Ministry of Advanced Education and Job Training
- C. Moss, Assistant Registrar, Open Learning Institute, Richmond, British Columbia
- R. Scales, Dean, Open Learning Institute, Richmond, British Columbia

Other Models: Quebec

- R. Gropper, Coordinator, Academic Programs, Vanier College, St-Laurent, Québec
- R. Isabelle, Director, Technical Assistance Services, Federation of College d'enseignment general et professionnelle (CEGEP)

- J-C. Létourneau, Conseiller, Service de l'Evaluation et
  de Référence scolaire et professionnelle, Ministère
  des Communautés culturelles et de l'Immigration
- E. Zinman-Madoff, Chef de la division des Equivalences,
  Service de l'Evaluation et de Référence scolaire et
  professionnelle, Ministère des Communautés culturelles
  et de l'Immigration

Other Models: U.S.

- College Level Examination Program College Board,
  New York, N.Y.
- H. Fernandez, Deputy Commissioner, Office of the
  Professions, Albany, N.Y.
- M. Keeton, President, Council for Adult and
  Experiential Learning (CAEL), Columbia, Maryland
- B. Sargent, Office of External Programs, Waterbury,
  Vermont

LANGUAGE

- M. Belfiore, TESL Ontario Group
- M. Canale, Associate Professor, Centre for Franco
  Ontario Studies (OISE)
- R. Colter, Chairman, ESL, Seneca College Representative
- D. Hall, Coordinator, ESL Humber College
- J. Jones, Chairman, English Language Studies,
  Mohawk College
- S. Jones, Department of Linguistics, Carlton University
- A. Maoyedi
- I. Martin, Chairman, English Language Studies,
  Glendon College
- B. Wall, Project Director, Metro Labour Education
  and Skills Training Centre

OTHERS WHO PROVIDED ASSISTANCE

- R. Anand, Chief Commissioner, Ontario Human Rights
  Commission
- C. Assaly, Adjointe administrative Service,
  Corporation professionnelle des médecins du Québec
- A. Bayefsky, University of Ottawa Faculty of Law

- R. Beauregard, Executive Director, Office of Francophone Affairs
- L. Bigford, Manager, Ontario Welcome House
- J. Breithaupt, Q.C., Chair, Commercial Registration Appeal Tribunal
- M. Cocks, Internal European Policy Division, Department of Trade and Industry, United Kingdom
- J. Colson, Analyst, Policy Analysis and Planning Unit, Ontario Ministry of Colleges and Universities
- The Hon. Mr. Justice E.C. Ewaschuk
- D. Fleet, M.P.P.
- R. Friedman, Secretary of State, Multiculturalism Branch, Ottawa
- A. Gilles, Coordinator of Special Employment Projects, Human Resources, Ottawa
- J. Gray, Programme Manager, Centre for Advancement in Work in Living (CAWL)
- P.J. Hector, Assistant Secretary, British National Council for the Fédération Européene des Associations Nationales d'Ingénieurs (FEANI)
- A. Juneau, Director General, Immigration Policy Branch, Employment and Immigration Canada
- C. Kilmartin
- Y. Lazor, Senior Counsel, Legal Branch, Ministry of the Solicitor General
- B.J. Leblanc, Director, Office of Equal Opportunity Ottawa
- K. McDade, Research Assistant, Studies in Social Policy, Institute for Research on Public Policy
- B.S. Phillips, Member of the Council of the Ontario College of Pharmacy
- Z. Poona, Executive Director, Council of Race Relations and Policing
- A. Quaile, Protect Apprenticeship Training and Quality, Ontario Public Services Employment Union (OPSEU)
- The Hon. Mr. Justice R.F. Reid
- N. Spencer-Nimmons, Executive Director, Refugee Documentation Project, York University
- L. Svegzda, Office of Reconsideration, Ontario Human Rights Commission

Commissioners and Task Force Staff

Chair

Peter A. Cumming

Commissioners

Enid L.D. Lee
Dimitrios G. Oreopoulos

Executive Coordinators

Ann E. Wilson
Project Coordinator

Patricia S. Bregman
Project Director

Katherine E. Laird
Assistant Project Director

Administration

Inge Sardy
Administrator

Editorial

Dan Liebman
Editor

Duncan McKenzie
Assistant Editor

Research

Shona Bradley
Martha Campbell
Susan Charendoff
Lisa Douglas
Carlota Ferrier
Catherine Frid
Wenona Giles
Shireen Jeejeebhoy
Winnie Lem
Winston Mattis
Odida Quamina
Philip Schalm
Kaan Yigit

Secretarial and Clerical

Linda McClenaghan
Senior Secretary

Carol Brown
Kay Coghlan
Marilyn Harris
Peak-Choo Hew
Peter Melnychuk
Sharon Miller
Cherilyn Roosen-Runge
Samer Tabar
Helen Warburton

Consultants

Hugh Ashford	- Canadian Charter of Rights and Freedoms - Federal and Ontario Human Rights Legislation
Dr. Barbara Burnaby	- Language Testing and Language Training
Dr. Betty Chan	- Accreditation and Certification in New York State
Graham Debling	- Cumulative Certificates in Vocational Education in England and Scotland
Nancy Goodman	- Immigration Law
Dr. Frances Henry	- Survey of the Literature on Immigration Certification
Dr. Peter Hogg	- Canadian Charter of Rights and Freedoms
Bjorn Johansson	- Immigrants in Sweden
Azmina Karim	- Mobility of Professionals in the European Community
Kenneth Marley	- Impact of the Canada-U.S. Free Trade Agreement
Dr. Les McLean	- Licensure Testing and Language Testing
Christopher Reed	- Labour Relations
Philip Schalm	- Training, Retraining, and Prior Learning Assessment
Dr. Alan Thomas	- Prior Learning Assessment
Dr. Sharon Williams	- The European Community

APPENDIX G

List of Background Studies

The following background studies, prepared by the Task Force and issued in conjunction with its Final Report, are available through:

Ontario Ministry of Citizenship
Library/Resource Centre
9th Floor
77 Bloor Street West
Toronto, Ontario
M7A 2R9

Telephone: (416) 965-6763

Accounting:
  Certified General Accounting
  Certified Management
    Accounting
  Chartered Accounting
Agrology
Architecture
Chiropody
Chiropractic
Dental Hygiene
Dental Technology
Dentistry
Denture Therapy
Dietetics
Early Childhood Education
Education
Engineering
Engineering Technology
Forestry
Funeral Services

Registered Insurance Brokerage
Land Surveying
Law
Massage Therapy
Medical Laboratory Technology
Medicine
Naturopathy
Nursing
Occupational Therapy
Ophthalmic Dispensing
Optometry
Osteopathy
Pharmacy
Physiotherapy
Psychology
Radiological Technology
Real Estate and Business
  Brokerage
Social Work
Veterinary Medicine

APPENDIX H

Professional Summaries

For a further discussion of practices and procedures in each of the professions described briefly here, reference should be made to the relevant background studies (see Appendix G). Please note that although efforts have been made to provide up-to-date figures for the cost of licensure examinations where they are cited, some recent variations may not be reflected here.

ACCOUNTING (CERTIFIED GENERAL ACCOUNTANTS)

Regulatory Status: Private legislation; reserved title

Governing Statute: *Certified General Accountants Association of Ontario Act, 1983*, S.O. 1983, c. Pr6

Responsible Body: Board of Governors of the Certified General Accountants Association of Ontario (CGAAO)

ASSESSMENT PROCEDURE

Educational Requirements

Ontario and
Other Provinces   Minimum of Ontario Secondary School graduation or its equivalent and the completion of the CGA 16-course academic program. The CGA program is offered at 17 community colleges and universities throughout Ontario or by correspondence.

Elsewhere   Equivalent course work completed at a foreign institution. Advanced standing in the form of up to 12 exemptions from examinations and/or courses may be granted. Assessment of foreign credentials is performed by the Director of Student Services on a case-by-case, course-by-course basis, although an exemption policy exists for many foreign institutions. There are no exemptions based on work experience.

| Comments | The Director of Student Services works closely with individual applicants to be sure that they receive the appropriate exemptions. Challenge examinations are permitted if there is doubt about equivalency. |

Experience Requirements

Prior to certification, candidates must acquire a minimum of 2 years' practical experience at a sufficiently senior level to be compatible with Levels 4 and 5 of the study program. The experience must be through full-time employment and may be gained in the public or private sector. The work-experience requirement may be completed at any time prior to certification. One year of the required 2 years of experience must be completed in Canada. The student's employment experience profile is reviewed by the Undergraduate Qualifications Review Committee.

LICENSURE TESTING

Subject to the exemption policy outlined above, all applicants must complete examinations for individual courses, and successful completion of course assignments is a prerequisite to writing the examinations. All candidates must complete the 4 mandatory components of the universally required examination program.

LANGUAGE TESTING

No formal testing. Applicants must complete an approved business communications course prior to second academic year or sit a challenge examination. The course contains a language component which must be satisfied or the applicant will be required to attend a separate course to improve his or her language skills.

RETRAINING

Retraining is delivered through universities and the profession itself.

REVIEW OF DECISIONS

No formal internal appeal process. Applicants refused membership, enrolment in the program, or advanced standing may petition the Student Petitions Committee. There is a statutory right of appeal to Divisional Court on refusal of membership.

ACCOUNTING

(CERTIFIED MANAGEMENT ACCOUNTANTS)

Regulatory Status: Private legislation; reserved title

Governing Statute: *Society of Management Accountants of Ontario Act,* S.O. 1981, c. 100

Responsible Body: Council of the Society of Management Accountants of Ontario

ASSESSMENT PROCEDURE:

Educational Requirements

Ontario and
Other Provinces

Secondary school graduation is not mandatory but is considered necessary. An 18-course professional program is offered at post-secondary institutions and by correspondence.

Elsewhere

Education equivalent to that offered in Ontario.

Comments

Most transcripts for foreign degrees are evaluated by the National Curriculum Committee of the National Society. The final decision regarding exemptions from the courses rests with the provincial society.

Individuals trained outside Canada are assessed on the basis of transcripts and course descriptions. Up to 18 course exemptions and 15 examination exemptions may be granted, but it is unlikely that a foreign-trained candidate would receive exemption from all 18 courses, since some include substantial Canadian content. Advanced standing is not granted on the basis of work experience, although some credit may be given for such experience in the data-processing field.

Experience Requirements

Two years of work experience in financial and management accounting is required. Such experience may be obtained at any time before, during, or after completion of academic requirements, and in any place. The experience requirement is assessed by the admissions committee. Foreign experience is considered for credit against the requirement.

REGISTRATION EXAMINATIONS

Subject to the exemption policy, applicants are required to sit an examination following each of the 15 courses in the first 4 levels of the program. The 3 Level-5 Final Accreditation Examinations (FAEs) are mandatory for all candidates.

A description of the FAEs is provided in the syllabus. Examination booklets with past examination solutions are available, as are preparation packages. The examinations may be taken in English or French and a minimum of 60 per cent is the required pass mark. Three attempts at examinations are generally permitted.

LANGUAGE TESTING

No formal testing. Students may take time off from the program to study English if necessary. The examinations act as language screens.

RETRAINING

The Society is not involved in any retraining programs. The advanced standing structure is the only available route in this case.

REVIEW OF DECISIONS

Appeal to an internal review committee for reconsideration of a refusal of enrolment or exemption is available. An appeal to the Divisional Court for a refusal of membership is possible.

ACCOUNTING (CHARTERED ACCOUNTANTS)

Regulatory Status: Private legislation; reserved title. Also licensing function under public legislation.

Governing Statute: *The Chartered Accountants Act, 1956*, S.O. 1956, c. 7

Responsible Body: Council of the Institute of Chartered Accountants of
                         Ontario (ICAO)

ASSESSMENT PROCEDURE

Educational Requirements

Ontario and   Student admission requires a university degree, mature
Other Provinces   student status, or qualification as a Certified
                       Management Accountant or Certified General
                       Accountant. The program consists of 45 hours of
                       prescribed university courses; a one-week staff training
                       program; and a 4-week School of Accountancy.

Elsewhere   Members of designated accounting bodies in other
                       jurisdictions are eligible for registration upon successful
                       completion of examinations in Canadian taxation and
                       business law, the CICA Handbook, and rules of
                       professional conduct. Members of certain non-
                       designated accounting bodies in other jurisdictions are
                       exempt from degree requirement but must complete the
                       prescribed university credit courses. Other foreign-
                       trained accountants must register as students and
                       complete all educational and experience requirements.

Comments   Foreign accounting bodies thought to merit
                       consideration are assessed by the International
                       Qualifications Appraisal Board of the Canadian Institute
                       of Chartered Accountants (CICA). Case-by-case
                       assessment of individual credentials is not available
                       except to qualify for advanced standing towards
                       prescribed university course work. Challenge
                       examinations are available only to members of
                       designated accounting bodies.

Experience Requirements

For candidates from Ontario and other provinces, 3 years of post-registration
prescribed practical experience are required, reduced to 2 years if a mark of 280
is obtained on Uniform Final Examination. Mature students, CMAs, and CGAs
must have, in addition, 3 more years of accounting, business or other relevant
experience prior to student registration.

For foreign applicants accounting experience may be recognized in one of two
ways: (1) if a person is a member of a designated accounting body outside
Canada, completion of 3 years of acceptable public accounting experience in the
jurisdiction of the designated body will qualify him or her for full membership

in the ICAO upon establishing residency in Ontario; (2) if a person is a member of certain non-designated accounting bodies outside of Canada, 3 or more years of acceptable accounting experience in any country will qualify him or her for student registration with the ICAO without meeting the standard requirement of a university degree.

Experience is assessed on a case-by-case basis by the applications committee of the ICAO. The foreign accounting experience of accountants who are not members of designated bodies cannot be credited against the student requirement of 2 or 3 years practical experience in Ontario.

LICENSURE TESTING

All applicants must take the comprehensive Uniform Final Examinations (UFE). Exemption is available to members of designated accounting bodies outside Canada and members of CA institutes in other provinces. UFE is a 4-part examination and it can be retried 4 times. Examination syllabus and past examinations are available to help candidates prepare. Members of designated accounting bodies must pass prescribed examinations in Canadian taxation and business law, and on the CICA Handbook and rules of professional conduct.

LANGUAGE TESTING

No formal testing requirement. Fluency is necessary to complete the program.

RETRAINING

ICAO does not provide any form of retraining for foreign-trained persons; however, courses can be taken through university programs.

REVIEW OF DECISIONS

Applicants may appeal to the Divisional Court in case of refusal to grant a licence.

AGROLOGY

Regulatory Status: Private legislation; reserved title

Governing Statute:	*The Ontario Professional Agrologists Act, 1960*, S.O. 1960, c. 158
Responsible Body:	Ontario Institute of Professional Agrologists

ASSESSMENT PROCEDURE

Educational Requirements

Ontario and Other Provinces	B.Sc. in agriculture from a recognized Canadian university or non-agricultural bachelor's degree and M.Sc. and/or Ph.D. in an agricultural specialty. Non-agricultural bachelor's degrees are considered acceptable if the candidates also successfully complete an examination requirement.
Elsewhere	Minimum of a bachelor's degree in agriculture from a university outside Canada.
Comments	Non-Canadian degrees are assessed by the Comparative Education Service (CES) of the University of Toronto. The assessment of the CES is accepted by the Institute. If academic requirements are considered incomplete or inadequate, candidates must complete acceptable degrees. Experience outside Canada is not a consideration.

Experience Requirements

Although there is no specific reference in the bylaws to an experience requirement, the guidelines for membership indicate a significant experience component. To be registered as a Professional Agrologist, the applicant must have:

- 4 or more years' relevant experience plus a bachelor's degree;
- 3 or more years' relevant experience plus a master's degree;
- 2 or more years' relevant experience plus a Ph.D.

Work prior to a postgraduate degree, but after an undergraduate degree, is taken into consideration. Non-Canadian experience is not considered relevant.

Candidates with limited professional experience participate in the Associate Professional Agrologist (APAg) program prior to the granting of Professional Agrologist status. The program is one to 2 years in length, depending on the experience and the education of the applicant.

REGISTRATION EXAMINATIONS

The professional examination testing the general knowledge of Ontario and Canadian agriculture is generally required only of Ontario candidates with non-agricultural degrees and of foreign-trained candidates. The examination may be waived at the discretion of the Board of Examiners. The examination consists of both oral and written components and is one to 2 hours in length. Examination questions are supplied to the applicants in advance of the examination so that they can prepare.

LANGUAGE TESTING

No formal testing. However, written and oral examinations are in English, and fluency is necessary for successful completion.

RETRAINING

Limited opportunities. Candidates with inadequate academic training must complete an acceptable degree. The experience requirement can be met only by finding employment in Canada, but as employment without certification is permitted, there are opportunities to meet this requirement.

REVIEW OF DECISIONS

No formal procedure for review of a decision to refuse membership.

ARCHITECTURE

Regulatory Status:	Licensure
Governing Statute:	*Architects Act, 1984*, S.O. 1984, c. 12, as amended 1987, c. 13
Responsible Body:	Council of the Ontario Association of Architects (OAA)

ASSESSMENT PROCEDURE

Educational Requirements

Ontario and Other Provinces	Graduation with a degree in architecture or the equivalent.

| Elsewhere | Degree in architecture or the equivalent. |

| Comments | All applicants, including Ontario graduates, must have their academic credentials assessed. An assessment fee of $400 applies to non-Canadian graduates. Candidates whose credentials are considered adequate will receive a "certificate of certification" from the Canadian Architectural Certification Board (CACB), a national organization. |

The assessment committee requires a description of each architecture course passed, plus certified English copies of transcripts. These are compared against the outline of an accepted academic program provided by the Royal Architectural Institute of Canada (RAIC). If the assessment committee is not satisfied with the applicant's qualifications, or if it cannot ascertain the equivalency of a degree, then the applicant is sent to the Committee of Examiners. This committee evaluates the applicant's portfolio and conducts an interview. If the committee finds the candidate's qualifications inadequate, he or she may be directed to additional course work. If the candidate's academic qualifications are adequate, he or she may proceed to professional examinations.

Experience Requirements

The same experience requirements apply to all candidates. The assessment is conducted by the Experience Requirements Committee of the OAA. Three years of Canadian experience under a supervising architect are required, 6 months of which must be in Ontario. All applicants must complete 4 Canadian experience record books, each of which covers 9 months of work experience. The Experience Requirements Committee reviews the books. If the committee's opinion is that an applicant is lacking in experience, he or she may be asked to attend an interview. A maximum foreign experience credit of 18 months can be applied against the Canadian experience requirements, although this cannot total more than $\frac{1}{3}$ of the candidate's non-Canadian experience. In Ontario, then, this could total only 12 months.

LICENSURE TESTING

All candidates for licensure must pass the professional examinations, referred to as the "Admissions Course," consisting of a 6-day lecture series followed by examinations.

LANGUAGE TESTING

A candidate from a country where English is not the official language must complete the MTB. An average mark of 90 is required, although the OAA may accept scores as low as 85. French-speaking candidates are exempted from English language testing by the Attorney General of Ontario; however, the OAA thinks this practice jeopardizes the public interest.

RETRAINING

Possible through the RAIC home study and apprenticeship program, or through universities and Ryerson Polytechnic Institute.

REVIEW OF DECISIONS

An applicant may appeal a refusal of licence, on grounds other than academic or experiential qualifications, to the Registration Committee. There is a right of appeal to the Divisional Court from the committee.

CHIROPODY

Regulatory Status: Licensure

Governing Statute: *Chiropody Act*, R.S.O. 1980, c. 72

Responsible Body: Board of Regents of Chiropody

ASSESSMENT PROCEDURE

Educational Requirements

Ontario   Completion of an Ontario diploma program in chiropody that is approved by the Ministry of Colleges and Universities. There is only one training program in Canada, a 3-year program offered jointly by George Brown College, Toronto General Hospital, and Toronto Institute of Medical Technology.

United Kingdom	Any U.K.-trained chiropodist who is eligible to be registered in the U.K. is also eligible for registration in Ontario. Approximately 15 U.K. schools produce graduates who are eligible for registration.
Elsewhere	Graduation from an approved program in chiropody. The regulations specify that such a program must be 4 years in length, although the Ontario program is 3. Applicants' academic backgrounds are assessed individually. The board considers 4-year American podiatry programs to be equivalent to the 3-year Ontario program, so that such applicants may currently proceed to the licensing examinations. (This may not continue to be the case.) Australian and New Zealand programs are also recognized. If a candidate's education is considered inadequate, further training is required before he or she attempts the examinations.

Experience Requirements

Three months of clinical experience required, which is typical of any approved programs, including approved foreign programs.

LICENSURE TESTING

Ontario- and U.K.-trained candidates are exempt from registration examinations. Candidates from elsewhere must satisfactorily complete the 3-part (written, oral, practice/clinical) registration examinations.

The examination lasts 3 to 4 days and is offered once a year. The fee is $400. Candidates must score 60 per cent or higher on each part in order to proceed on to the next part of the examination. Supplementary examinations may be offered.

LANGUAGE TESTING

For candidates whose training was in another language, the board has discussed the use of the TOEFL and TSE assessments. However, no specific language testing has been instituted.

RETRAINING

None. Unqualified applicants must repeat the whole program, subject to credits that may be received from the educational institution. The board hopes to have a retraining program in place in 2 years.

REVIEW OF DECISIONS

There is no mechanism for external review of a decision to refuse registration.

CHIROPRACTIC

Regulatory Status: Licensure

Governing Statute: *Drugless Practitioners Act*, R.S.O. 1980, c. 127; R.R.O. 1980, Reg. 248, as amended

Responsible Body: Board of Directors of Chiropractic

ASSESSMENT PROCEDURE

Educational Requirements

Ontario, Other Provinces, U.S., and Australia
Graduation from a designated institution offering a 4-year program with at least 4,200 hours of instruction, covering a number of specific subject areas. The Canadian Memorial Chiropractic College (CMCC) is the only accredited institution in Canada. There are 14 colleges accredited in the U.S. and one in Australia.

Elsewhere
Candidates from unaccredited schools are required by the board to have their educational qualifications assessed by an accredited college. The college may assign retraining courses to applicants.

Comments
Chiropractic programs are accredited by the Accreditation Commission of the Council on Chiropractic Education (CCE) or one of the reciprocal bodies in the U.S.A. or Australia.

Experience Requirements

Clinical training is included in the required academic program of accredited institutions.

LICENSURE TESTING

All candidates for certification from CCE-approved institutions write the national Canadian Chiropractic Examining Board (CCEB) examinations and the provincial examinations.

The national examinations are primarily in English, but specifically marked questions may be answered in French. The CCEB examinations are offered in 4 locations (2 in Canada, one in the U.S. and one in the U.K.) and held over a 5-day period, in which candidates complete 9 evaluations. The passing score for each subject is 50 per cent. An overall average of 60 per cent in 9 subjects must be attained. The failure rate ranges between 8 and 12 per cent. Supplemental examinations are available to some candidates. Examination results may be appealed internally. The Ontario board substitutes its own Principles of Practice examination and also requires its own written, oral, and clinical examinations.

LANGUAGE TESTING

A working knowledge of English is required by the board. All CCE-approved institutions use English as the language of instruction.

RETRAINING

Retraining is through the CMCC in Ontario.

REVIEW OF DECISIONS

There is no external appeal mechanism for candidates refused registration.

DENTAL HYGIENE

Regulatory Status: Licensure

Governing Statute: *Health Disciplines Act*, R.S.O. 1980, c. 196, as amended 1983, c. 59; 1986, c. 28; 1986, c. 34

Responsible Body: Council of the Royal College of Dental Surgeons of Ontario

ASSESSMENT PROCEDURE

Educational Requirements

Ontario and
Other Provinces

The applicant must have completed a course in dental hygiene conducted by the faculty of dentistry of an Ontario university or a college of applied arts and technology (CAAT). At present, 10 CAATs offer such programs in Ontario. To be admitted to a CAAT program in dental hygiene, a candidate must be a certified or certifiable dental assistant.

Elsewhere

Graduation from a program in dental hygiene equivalent to those offered in Ontario.

Comments

Assessment of all prior education is conducted by the Dental Hygiene Matters Committee of the Council of the Royal College of Dental Surgeons of Ontario. Essentially all North American programs are accredited, and candidates from these jurisdictions are permitted to proceed to the licensing examination. If the applicant is from a jurisdiction from which there have been no previous applications, a detailed review of the applicant's program is undertaken. The committee considers the hours spent by the candidate in training and the functions which were learned during that training. Programs are accredited by the Canadian Dental Association (CDA) and the American Dental Association (ADA) in the United States.

Experience Requirements

Not applicable.

LICENSURE TESTING

A qualifying $1/2$-day written and $1/2$-day clinical examination is required although Ontario graduates are exempted from written segments. Licensing examinations are offered 3 times per year. The cost is $200; they can be retried twice.

LANGUAGE TESTING

No formal testing. However, the ability to complete the licensing examination is considered to be an adequate demonstration of fluency.

RETRAINING

Limited places are available at the community college for retraining. There is no formal program offered through the college. An upgrading course is offered at George Brown College for those who have failed the licensing examination.

REVIEW OF DECISIONS

There is no formal external appeal process from a refusal of registration.

DENTAL TECHNOLOGY

Regulatory Status: Reserved title

Governing Statute: *Dental Technicians Act*, R.S.O. 1980, c. 114

Responsible Body: Governing Board of Dental Technicians

ASSESSMENT PROCEDURE

Educational Requirements

Ontario

Completion of an approved program in dental technology plus one year of apprenticeship (the only program in Ontario is offered at George Brown College); or completion of a 4-year apprenticeship to a Registered Dental Technologist or a dentist in Ontario.

Elsewhere

No assessment of training is undertaken beyond high school level.

Comments

An applicant from outside Ontario, regardless of his or her qualifications, must either obtain admission to the George Brown program and complete it along with one year of apprenticeship, or have his or her credentials assessed by the Ministry of Education as equivalent to Ontario Grade 12, and complete the 4-year apprenticeship requirement.

Experience Requirements

One-year apprenticeship in Ontario for Ontario graduates. No credit is given for work experience or training in the field elsewhere. Apprenticeship must be completed under the supervision of a dentist or a registered dental technician.

REGISTRATION EXAMINATIONS

All applicants must complete the registration examinations. The examinations are held once a year in Toronto and cover 4½ days. They consist of 6 subject portions and oral and written sections. The cost was $465 in 1988. Pass rate has been in the range of 18 per cent to 54 per cent over the past 5 years. Candidates may be given an opportunity to repeat one or two subject areas or the entire examination.

LANGUAGE TESTING

The certifying examinations act as a language screen. No other testing is undertaken.

RETRAINING

Candidates who are not fully trained in Ontario must complete the George Brown program or complete 4 years of apprenticeship.

REVIEW OF DECISIONS

There is no right of appeal from a refusal of registration.

DENTISTRY

Regulatory Status: Licensure

Governing Statute: *Health Disciplines Act*, R.S.O. 1980, c. 196, as amended 1983, c. 59; 1986, c. 28; 1986, c. 34

Responsible Body: Council of the Royal College of Dental Surgeons of Ontario

ASSESSMENT PROCEDURE

Educational Requirements

Ontario, Other
Provinces and U.S.

Degree in dentistry from an accredited university in Canada or the United States.

Elsewhere

Degree from an unaccredited institution outside Ontario listed by the World Health Organization (WHO). Such candidates may apply to complete the National Dental Examining Board (NDEB) examinations. Although the regulations specify that equivalency of training is required, no assessment of equivalency is done.

Comments

Canadian and American programs are accredited by the Canadian Dental Association (CDA), and virtually all Canadian and U.S. schools are considered to meet the standard.

Experience Requirements

Not applicable.

LICENSURE TESTING

For candidates trained in:

Ontario and
Other Provinces

None.

U.S.

One written and 2 clinical examinations (NDEB examinations).

Elsewhere

One written and 3 clinical examinations (NDEB examinations).

Comments

The cost is $3,300 for the clinical examinations and $860 for the written examination. The applicants are also responsible for the travel and living expenses for themselves and for one to 3 patients who must be provided by them. There is no limit to the number of retries. The applicant must complete the clinical examinations successfully within 6 years of the written examinations. The examinations are developed by the NDEB. Examiners for the clinical examinations are dental academics and practitioners.

LANGUAGE TESTING

No formal testing. Under the regulations, candidates for licensure must be reasonably fluent in English or French. It is thought that the examinations ensure this.

RETRAINING

No formal retraining is available. The University of Western Ontario offers a brief course for preparation for the NDEB examinations. The University of Toronto offers an advanced-standing program permitting entrance into second year for qualified applicants, but vacancies are rare.

REVIEW OF DECISIONS

Under the bylaws of the NDEB, an applicant who fails any portion of the examination has the right to appeal that decision in writing and to receive a written response. There is no right to a hearing. A refusal of registration may be appealed to the Health Disciplines Board, and from there to the Divisional Court.

DENTURE THERAPY

Regulatory Status: Licensure

Governing Statute: *Denture Therapists Act*, R.S.O. 1980, c. 115

Responsible Body: Governing Board of Denture Therapists

ASSESSMENT PROCEDURE

Educational Requirements

Ontario	Program in denture therapy at an Ontario college of applied arts and technology. The only program in Ontario is at George Brown College.
Other Provinces	The programs in Quebec and Alberta have been approved by the Board as being equivalent; those in British Columbia and Nova Scotia are currently under review.

Elsewhere	Program in denture therapy equivalent to that at George Brown College. Applications from foreign-trained candidates are assessed on a case-by-case basis by the registrar of the Governing Board of Denture Therapists. Canadian programs are also approved as equivalent by the board.

Experience Requirements

Not applicable.

LICENSURE TESTING

All applicants are required to sit the George Brown College final examination. The examination is offered once a year.

LANGUAGE TESTING

If an applicant has not received training in either English or French, he or she is required to demonstrate reasonable fluency in one or the other. All applicants to date have been trained in English or French.

RETRAINING

Limited retraining is available through non-credit courses at George Brown College.

REVIEW OF DECISIONS

If the registration committee of the Governing Board of Denture Therapy intends to refuse a licence, notice with reasons is served upon the applicant and the Denture Therapists appeal board. The applicant is entitled to a hearing by the Appeal Board and may appeal from there to the Divisional Court.

DICTETICS

Regulatory Status:	Private legislation; reserved title
Governing Statute:	*Ontario Dietetic Association Act*, S.O. 1958, c. 147

Responsible Body: Board of Directors of the Ontario Dietetic Association

ASSESSMENT PROCEDURE

Educational Requirements

Ontario and Other Provinces	Bachelor's, master's or Ph.D. degree from an educational institution which is acceptable to the Canadian Dietetic Association (CDA). Canadian programs are accredited by the CDA.
Elsewhere	Equivalent education. U.S. candidates who are members of the American Dietetic Association are entitled to immediate registration.
Comments	Applicants who trained outside Canada and the U.S. are directed by the CDA to the Comparative Education Service (CES) of the University of Toronto for an assessment of their degrees. If a degree is evaluated as equivalent, CDA further reviews the candidates course work to see if it meets the requirements of specified set competencies. If some elements are missing, the admissions committee refers the applicant to a contact person at the local university.

Experience Requirements

A dietetic internship consists of one year's experience in a hospital accredited by the CDA. A master's or a doctoral degree in food nutrition administration or an allied discipline also satisfies this requirement, as does a 2-year internship program at a non-hospital institution. Foreign experience is recognized for credit. Although the internship or master's degree technically need not be completed in Ontario, it must be equivalent to Ontario training. Experience requirements are assessed by the CDA.

REGISTRATION EXAMINATION

Canadian graduates who have not completed their internships in a hospital environment (i.e., 2-year TYP program), and applicants who completed their experience requirement in jurisdictions outside Canada and the U.S. are generally required to write the qualifying examinations. An applicant can choose to write the examination in one of 4 areas of specialization. A study guide is available to all applicants. An applicant can take the examination up to 3 times, but academic upgrading specified by the CDA is required after the first failure.

LANGUAGE TESTING

No formal testing. The qualifying examination is offered in English or French.

RETRAINING

Retraining requirements either for academic credit or to prepare for the examination after a failure are specified by the Admissions Committee. A contact person at the educational institution sets up a program for the candidate, who is admitted as a special student.

REVIEW OF DECISIONS

Any applicant to the CDA can request a remarking of the CDA qualifying examination. Also, the decision of the Admissions Committee may be appealed to the CDA or ODA Board of Directors, whichever is applicable. There is no external appeal.

EARLY CHILDHOOD EDUCATION

Regulatory Status:
1) approval procedure through Director, Ministry of Community and Social Services
2) credentialing procedure, Association of Early Childhood Education, Ontario (AECEO)

Governing Statute: *Day Nurseries Act*, R.S.O. 1980, c. 111, as amended

Responsible Body:
1) Ministry of Community and Social Services
2) AECEO

ASSESSMENT PROCEDURE

Educational Requirements

Ontario

Diploma in early childhood education (ECE) from an Ontario college of applied arts and technology or a degree in ECE from a recognized university meet both Ministry and AECEO guidelines.

Elsewhere

The Ministry requires equivalent training or training that is "otherwise approved" by the director.

Presentation of a certificate of equivalent status issued by the AECEO is the most commonly employed method of meeting the requirement.

The assessment of previous training by the AECEO is conducted on a case-by-case basis and consists of evaluation of transcripts and official course outlines. The AECEO considers studies in a related profession to an equivalent level, including specific child- and family-related studies and supervised practice, or a letter from the coordinator of a course in ECE stating status equivalent to the college's diploma program in ECE to constitute equivalent training. For those assessed as having adequate training, an examination is also required.

The Ministry standard for "approval" appears to be somewhat broader. Guidelines are currently being developed.

Experience Requirement

There is no formal experience requirement to qualify to work in day care, but most training programs have a significant fieldwork requirement.

LANGUAGE TESTING

No formal testing by the Ministry or the AECEO. The AECEO equivalency assessment involves an examination in which fluency is important for successful completion.

RETRAINING

Available through colleges and universities offering ECE programs. Candidates may apply for credit on the basis of training completed.

REVIEW OF DECISIONS

There are no appeal mechanisms on a refusal of membership in the AECEO or refusal of approval by the Ministry.

EDUCATION

Regulatory Status: Licensure

Governing Statute: *Education Act*, R.S.O. 1980, c. 129, as amended

Responsible Body: Ministry of Education

ASSESSMENT PROCEDURE

Educational Requirements

For General Studies

Ontario

Acceptable university degree or equivalent, and successful completion of one year of professional training in an approved teacher education course offered by the faculty or college of teacher education of an Ontario university.

Other Canadian Jurisdictions and Outside Canada

Evidence of completion of 16 years of education ("scholarity") including an acceptable university degree, and one year of acceptable teacher education. Fewer than 16 years may be considered adequate if the candidate can show a pattern of acceptance at Ontario educational institutions.

In Ontario there are 10 universities which offer teacher education programs approved by the Ministry. Non-Ontario applicants make their applications directly through the Ministry of Education. The documents are evaluated by the Information and Teacher Evaluation Unit of Registrar Services at the Ministry of Education. If the degree is granted by an institution and falls within one of several specified acceptable categories, the evaluation unit then looks at the length of the degree program. The one-year teacher education program, which makes up the 16th required year of scholarity, must be taken at an acceptable institution and must meet certain content requirements.

For Technological Studies

Ontario

Ontario Grade 12 or equivalent plus one year of acceptable teacher education.

Elsewhere	Equivalent education equivalent to Ontario Grade 12, and acceptable teacher training.
Comments	Assessment is conducted by the evaluation unit of the Ministry of Education and is similar to the process for General Studies.

Experience Requirements

For General Studies

Ten months of employment with a school board under the authority of a temporary letter of standing for foreign-trained candidates. After the term is complete, the candidate is eligible to receive an Ontario Teacher's Certificate (OTC).

For Technological Studies

Five years of wage-earning business or industrial experience in the area(s) of technological studies for which the candidate's teacher education prepared him or her. A maximum of 3 years of postsecondary education in that trade may be substituted for up to 3 of those 5 years (no less than 16 months of which must be continuous employment). Teaching experience may not be substituted for the required trade experience.

LICENSURE TESTING

Not applicable.

LANGUAGE TESTING

No formal testing. The Ministry relinquished the responsibility of assessing fluency to the Boards of Education in 1978. The local boards, upon hiring the holder of a letter of eligibility to a permanent position, attest to fluency by signing that letter. The fluency assessment process varies from board to board.

RETRAINING

Candidates who are deficient in terms of numbers of years of scholarity may upgrade to meet Ministry standards by completing a specified number of university courses. Candidates whose teacher education is considered inadequate are also given direction by the Ministry as to what further course work is required.

REVIEW OF DECISIONS

There is no right of appeal from a decision of the Ministry of Education to deny an applicant an Ontario Teacher's Certificate, a letter of eligibility, or a temporary letter of standing.

ENGINEERING

Regulatory Status: Licensure

Governing Statute: *Professional Engineers Act, 1984*, S.O. 1984, c. 13

Responsible Body: Council of the Association of Professional Engineers of Ontario (APEO)

ASSESSMENT PROCEDURE

Educational Requirements

Ontario and Other Provinces

Graduation from an accredited university program, or CAAT diploma. Canadian universities are accredited by the Canadian Engineering Accreditation Board (CEAB) which is a standing committee of the Canadian Council of Professional Engineers (CCPE).

U.S.

Graduation from a program accredited by the Accreditation Board for Engineering and Technology (ABET). All ABET-accredited degrees, like all other foreign degrees, are generally assessed individually in Ontario.

Elsewhere

Training equivalent to the Ontario standard. Education equivalent to at least a 3-year college diploma is necessary to be considered for registration.

Comments

The Academic Requirements Committee (ARC) of the APEO assesses the candidate's documentation of previous education and compares it to the CCPE syllabus for equivalency. Candidates with extensive experience who have been assigned examinations by the ARC are referred to the Experience Requirements Committee (ERC). This committee may recommend that examinations be waived, or exemptions granted; however, the final decision rests with the ARC. A graduate from an unaccredited engineering school assessed as equivalent may be required to write the "confirmatory" examinations set by the APEO. These examinations confirm that the applicant's academic qualifications are equivalent to those of any accredited Canadian university graduate. Failed applicants are considered not to have the equivalency of knowledge of Canadian graduates, and must successfully complete an "examination program" along with candidates otherwise assessed as less than equivalent in training. The examination program is tailored by the ARC to meet the specific needs of individual applicants. A maximum of 21 examinations may be assigned, although this is seldom done. A thesis may also be required.

Experience Requirements

All candidates for licensure must have 24 months of postgraduate experience. One year of this experience must be obtained in Canada, under the supervision of a person legally authorized to practise engineering in the jurisdiction where the experience is gained. The work experience is monitored through 4 referees, 2 of whom should be Canadian professional engineers; one of the latter should be the applicant's direct technical supervisor. Credit for foreign experience is assessed by the ERC.

LICENSURE TESTING

All applicants, except those who have been registered for 5 years or more in another province, must write the Professional Practice Examination (PPE). The PPE can be written twice yearly; the fee is $85 for each attempt, and 4 retries are allowed. The examination consists of 2 parts and all applicants for licensure must pass the PPE within 2 years of becoming eligible to write it. Pass rate is 88 per cent. Of those who fail, 60 per cent pass the PPE on their second attempt.

LANGUAGE TESTING

No formal testing. The PPE is used informally to ensure basic comprehension and communication in English. If the referees suggest language may be a problem, the candidate may be interviewed by the ERC.

RETRAINING

Available through the universities, in regular undergraduate courses, correspondence courses, and night courses. Completion may result in exemptions from parts of the examination program. There is a right of appeal to the Divisional Court from the committee.

REVIEW OF DECISIONS

An applicant may appeal a refusal of licence, on grounds other than academic or experiential qualifications, to the Registration Committee. There is a right of appeal to the Divisional Court from the committee.

ENGINEERING TECHNOLOGY

Regulatory Status: Private legislation; reserved title

Governing Statute: *The Ontario Association of Certified Engineering Technicians and Technologists Act, 1984*, S.O. 1984, c. Pr14

Responsible Body: Council of the Ontario Association of Certified Engineering Technicians and Technologists (OACETT)

ASSESSMENT PROCEDURE

Educational Requirements

Ontario
Graduation from an institution accredited or otherwise approved by the OACETT. Such training is available through 22 colleges of applied arts and technology as well as at Ryerson Polytechnical Institute, Lakehead University, through some corporations in technical industries, and through some private educational institutions.

Other Provinces
Graduates from programs evaluated against the Canadian Technology Accreditation Board (CTAB) guidelines are considered to have met the educational requirements.

Elsewhere	Comparable educational background to that currently accepted in Ontario.
Comments	Assessment of previous education is conducted by the OACETT. Files of information collected on foreign institutions and documentation received from foreign trained candidates are used to evaluate foreign qualifications. Foreign-trained candidates are requested to provide copies of their transcripts, diplomas, and course calendars, if possible, to the board of examiners of the OACETT. Experience may gain candidates some credit against academic requirements.

Experience Requirements

All candidates are required to have completed a minimum of 2 years' experience at a level commensurate with their standing. A detailed work experience description, provided by the candidate and initialled on each page by his or her supervisor, is the primary document relied upon in experience assessment. Experience outside Canada is taken into account in assessing a candidate's ability to meet this requirement.

REGISTRATION EXAMINATIONS

Technicians complete 12 and technologists complete 20 examinations and a thesis. These examinations are associated with individual courses in the curriculum, and are not technically registration examinations. The Professional Practice and Ethics Examination is not currently a mandatory requirement of all candidates but it may become so. Graduates of unaccredited programs, which may include Ontario graduates, are typically assigned 2 "confirmatory examinations"; candidates applying for technologist recognition may also be requested to complete a thesis. If the candidate fails in the confirmatory examinations or if training is clearly deficient, he or she is entered into an examination program of from one to 20 examinations.

LANGUAGE TESTING

No formal language testing. Candidates whose first language is not English may be assigned a thesis, be required to write the Professional Practice and Ethics Examination to assess language abilities, or be required to write the TOEFL. Graduates of Canadian colleges are considered to have adequate language skills.

RETRAINING

Some retraining is available through community colleges, universities, and correspondence courses.

REVIEW OF DECISIONS

Any person refused registration by the registrar may appeal the decision to the Registration Committee and from there to the Council. There is no restriction on the grounds of refusal that can be appealed. A further appeal to the Divisional Court is available from a refusal of admission at any stage of the internal process.

FORESTRY

Regulatory Status: Private legislation; reserved title

Governing Statute: *The Ontario Professional Foresters Association Act, 1957*, S.O. 1957, c. 149

Responsible Body: Council of the Ontario Professional Foresters Association (OPFA)

ASSESSMENT PROCEDURE

Educational Requirements

Ontario and Other Provinces

Graduation from a degree course in forestry in a university accredited by the council of the OPFA. An applicant from an accredited program in another province automatically satisfies these requirements. Degrees from non-forestry programs or unaccredited forestry programs or other forms of limited training are assessed on a subject-by-subject basis against a core program. Candidates are assigned examinations in areas of deficiency.

Elsewhere

Education equivalent to that of an Ontario graduate. The program and transcript of each applicant is reviewed to ensure that all core subjects have been covered. As with Ontario candidates, applicants for membership who have graduated from programs that do not include all the core subject areas or applicants without a degree or diploma are required to write examinations on core subject areas. An applicant may be required to write up to 20 examinations.

Comments	The accreditation of programs and the assessment of educational background are conducted by the OPFA. Relevant work experience is considered in the assessment.

Experience Requirements

Ontario graduates of an OPFA-accredited forestry program wishing to register must have at least 18 months' postgraduate forestry experience within a period of 5 years immediately preceding their application for membership. The work must be directly related to one or more of the core subjects.

The work-experience requirement for candidates trained in forestry in other provinces is the same as for Ontario graduates. The OPFA may accept forestry experience from outside Ontario if it is deemed to be relevant to the practice of forestry in Ontario.

Graduates of Ontario non-university programs in forestry or of university programs in disciplines other than forestry or of non-Canadian programs, must be employed in Ontario in work directly related to one or more of the core subjects at the time of application. Individuals must have been so employed continuously for 5 years prior to application for registration.

Registration Examinations

Applicants who are required to write examinations must complete at least one of them within 18 months of being informed of the requirement. All examination requirements must be completed within 8 years of being informed. The cost of sitting each examination is $50. Candidates' requests as to time and place of examination are accommodated.

A candidate must obtain 60 per cent in each core subject. The examination may be attempted only once more if the first attempt is not successful. The application for registration is terminated after 2 unsuccessful attempts.

LANGUAGE TESTING

No specific language policy or requirement. Fluency is necessary for successful completion of the examinations.

RETRAINING

There are no specific retraining programs offered by the association or in the universities. Applicants who require further academic training must enrol in the forestry program in an educational institution. Both full- and part-time studies are offered at Lakehead University and at the University of Toronto.

REVIEW OF DECISIONS

A rejected candidate may apply again to the council of the OPFA for reconsideration. There is, however, no further right of appeal.

FUNERAL SERVICES

Regulatory Status: Licensure

Governing Statute: *Funeral Services Act*, R.S.O. 1980, c. 180, as amended

Responsible Body: Board of Funeral Services

ASSESSMENT PROCEDURE

Educational Requirements

Ontario

Graduate of a program in funeral services education, currently offered in Ontario at Humber College of Applied Arts and Technology.

Elsewhere

Graduate of a program in funeral services education. This requirement may be waived by the board under appropriate circumstances.

Comments

A preliminary assessment of a foreign-trained applicant's prior education is conducted through an interview. The applicant's training and experience are reviewed, as are the functions of a funeral director in the applicant's home jurisdiction. The board may direct the applicant to write a challenge examination if the initial assessment is satisfactory. After the challenge examination, the applicant may be directed to write the licensing examination, to do additional training at Humber College, and/or to apprentice. All assessments are conducted by Humber College on behalf of the Board of Funeral Services.

Experience Requirements

Ontario-trained applicants meet the 12-month in-service training requirement upon graduation. Foreign-trained applicants may be required to complete the experience requirement by apprenticing for up to one year. The assessment of experience for credit is conducted by the board.

LICENSURE TESTING

The licensing examination is required of all candidates. The examination consists of 3 parts and is offered annually. It can be retried, provided the candidate remains in-service training. The pass rate in 1986 was 87 per cent.

LANGUAGE TESTING

The board does not impose any formal language requirement, but successful completion of the examination requires a good command of English. A French examination has also been offered in the past.

RETRAINING

Available at Humber College as required to fulfil requirements.

REVIEW OF DECISIONS

An applicant who is refused licensure is entitled to a hearing before the Funeral Services Review Board. The appeal may be taken from there to the Divisional Court.

REGISTERED INSURANCE BROKERAGE

Regulatory Status: Licensure

Governing Statute: *Registered Insurance Brokers Act*, R.S.O. 1980, c. 444

Responsible Body: Council of the Registered Insurance Brokers of Ontario

ASSESSMENT PROCEDURE

Educational Requirements

Courses in insurance brokerage are offered by the Insurance Brokers Association of Ontario (IBAO) and by several Ontario community colleges. The usual entry requirements to community colleges apply. As an alternative to the program, a self-study text is available for candidates preparing for the licensure examination. None of these courses is compulsory.

Experience Requirements

Not applicable.

LICENSURE TESTING

All applicants must sit a basic qualifying examination and an advanced-level examination. A pass mark in the basic qualifying examination (75 per cent) entitles the applicant to receive a restricted "Registration under Supervision" licence. To remove the restriction and to function as a fully-licensed broker, the candidate must achieve 75 per cent in the advanced-level examination, with a minimum of 60 per cent in each section. Both examinations may be rewritten within a 12-month period. An applicant who fails either of the examinations 3 times must wait 12 months before the next attempt.

LANGUAGE TESTING

No formal testing is done. The licensure examinations function as a language screen.

RETRAINING

Access to the training programs is open to anyone and the programs are relatively brief.

REVIEW OF DECISIONS

Applicants who are refused certification are given written reasons for refusal. The applicant is entitled to a hearing by the Qualifications and Registration Committee, the original decision-making body. A decision of the committee may be further appealed to the Divisional Court.

LAND SURVEYING

Regulatory Status: Licensure

Governing Statute:	*Surveyors Act 1987*, S.O. 1987, c. 6
Responsible Body:	Council of the Association of Ontario Land Surveyors (AOLS)

ASSESSMENT PROCEDURE

Educational Requirements

Ontario and Other Provinces	Graduation from an approved survey science course (Erindale College, University of Toronto) or a Canadian university offering a B.Sc. in surveying. There are 3 such programs outside Ontario; they are offered at the University of New Brunswick, and the Université de Laval, both of which are accredited by the Canadian Council of Land Surveyors (CCLS); and at the University of Calgary, which is not accredited.
Elsewhere	Education or experience equivalent to Erindale College survey science degree.
Comments	Assessment of academic credentials is conducted by the AOLS with assistance from the Comparative Education Service at the University of Toronto. The assessment is conducted on a subject-by-subject basis. If the AOLS encounters difficulty in establishing equivalency, he or she may be directed to write a challenge examination. If the degree is assessed as equivalent, the candidate may proceed to articling. Previous experience may be credited towards academic requirements.

If training is assessed as less than equivalent, the candidate may be assigned a number of courses and examinations in order to obtain additional credits. Typically, 15 to 16 AOLS examinations are assigned to foreign-trained candidates. Land surveyors from other jurisdictions are generally evaluated by the AOLS according to the number of years of experience they have. Those applicants with 15 or more years of experience in cadastral land surveying are required to complete 6 examinations and to article one year in Ontario. Surveyors with 5 to 15 years experience outside Ontario must complete the requirements assigned to their more experienced colleagues, and will have additional technical and planning courses required of them. Applicants with less than 5 years' experience are not given any credit and are assessed similarly to

recent out-of-country graduates. Such candidates must
have postsecondary training to qualify.

Experience Requirements

The experience requirement is 2 years of articling or its equivalent. For an
individual who has obtained experience in professional land surveying elsewhere
in Canada, the duration of articling may be reduced by either the period of the
experience gained or one year, whichever is the lesser. All foreign-trained
candidates must complete at least 12 months of their experience (articling) in
Ontario. Assessment of experience is conducted by the board of examiners of
the AOLS.

LICENSURE TESTING

All applicants who have successfully completed the required professional
education and who have received certificates of experience are eligible to attempt
the Professional Examination. The examination must be completed within 12
months of receipt of the certificate of experience. There are oral and written
components. In the event of failure, the examination must be rewritten after one
year and before 2 years following the date of failure. Candidates are not
permitted to take the examinations more than 3 times.

LANGUAGE TESTING

No formal testing. The AOLS considers fluency to be essential, and ability is
assessed through the oral and written licensure examinations.

RETRAINING

Retraining courses that review the information tested on the AOLS examinations
are available for auditing at Erindale College in Mississauga.

REVIEW OF DECISIONS

An applicant who is refused membership in the AOLS may appeal the refusal
to the Registration Committee. It is not clear from the legislation whether
questions involving academic or experience requirements can be reviewed by the
committee. There is a right of appeal to the Divisional Court from the
committee.

LAW

Regulatory Status: Public legislation; licensure

Governing Statute: *Law Society Act*, R.S.O. 1980, c. 233, as amended 1982, c. 60; 1986, c. 64; 1989, c. 14

Responsible Body: Benchers of the Law Society of Upper Canada

ASSESSMENT PROCEDURE

Educational Requirements

Ontario

LL.B. degree and the completion of the 18-month Bar Admission Course (BAC) consisting of 12 months of articling and 6 months of academic studies plus examinations.

Other Provinces

Graduation from an approved law school (all 16 law schools in Canada are approved).

Elsewhere

The Joint Committee on Accreditation (JCA) evaluates the legal training and professional experience of persons with foreign law credentials. The JCA develops a profile of each applicant's legal education to determine if advanced standing should be granted towards a Canadian law degree. The JCA makes a recommendation with respect to additional educational requirements and, upon completion of such requirements at a Canadian law school, will issue a certificate of qualification. Professional qualifications and legal experience are considered. If the candidate requires less than one year's attendance at a Canadian law school, the JCA may allow him or her to attempt the challenge examinations. The JCA does not make recommendations to the Law Society about exemptions from BAC requirements.

The JCA considers the applicant's prior experience in its assessment; candidates categorized as "experienced" (more than 3 years in practice) are more likely to be eligible to write challenge examinations.

Experience Requirements

Twelve-month articling term required of all Ontario-trained and foreign-trained candidates and of lawyers from other provinces who have not been in active practice for 3 of the last 5 years. Articling abridgments may be granted to candidates with relevant experience but foreign-trained candidates are unlikely to receive an exemption solely on the basis of experience obtained in another jurisdiction.

LICENSURE TESTING

Ontario	Six-month BAC term of studies with examinations.
Other Provinces	Candidates with 3 years of active practice must pass 2-part transfer examination on Ontario statutes and procedure. Other candidates must complete the BAC including articling.
Quebec	Pass 2-part transfer examination and pass a comprehensive common law examination. Applicants with less than 3 years of experience must complete the BAC including articling and a one-year course in common law.
Elsewhere	If the applicant receives a certificate of qualification from the JCA, a 6-month teaching term and examinations must be completed.

LANGUAGE TESTING

No formal requirement; however, the LSUC may require a candidate to take the TOEFL test if his or her correspondence indicates a lack of language proficiency.

RETRAINING

Canadian law schools will admit foreign-trained lawyers on an advanced-standing basis, often on the recommendation of the JCA. A part-time program was introduced recently at the University of Toronto and might be attractive to foreign-trained lawyers seeking to obtain retraining while supporting dependants.

REVIEW OF DECISIONS

There is no appeal from a decision of the JCA as to the equivalency of prior legal training and experience. In addition, applicants transferring from other provinces or countries who are refused admission to the Ontario Bar by the Admissions Committee of the Law Society of Upper Canada have no right of appeal to an independent tribunal or to the courts.

MASSAGE THERAPY

Regulatory Status: Licensure

Governing Statute: *Drugless Practitioners Act*, R.S.O. 1980, c. 127; R.R.O. 1980, Reg. 250, as amended

Responsible Body: Board of Directors of Masseurs

ASSESSMENT PROCEDURE

Educational Requirements

Ontario

Applicants must have attained a minimum of Grade 12 secondary school and completed a 2-year massage therapy course at one of 4 Ontario institutions registered under the *Private Vocational Schools Act*.

Elsewhere

Equivalent to currently accepted education and training in Ontario.

Comments

Assessment of foreign training is conducted by the Committee to Assess Offshore Applicants of the Board of Directors of Masseurs. First, candidates are requested to provide information about the scope and number of hours in their training, and the diploma received. Details of particular and general massage therapy experience must also be supplied to the Committee. Following this, the candidate is interviewed by 2 examiners. Responses to technical questions are assessed against a standard questionnaire and a clinical test is performed. Candidates assessed as equivalent may proceed to the registration examinations; others must complete the 2-year training program in Ontario.

The board is indirectly involved in the accreditation process. It recommends a course syllabus to the provincial Government and the Government uses this in registering massage schools under the *Private Vocational Schools Act.*

Experience Requirements

Not applicable.

LICENSURE TESTING

All applicants must complete oral, practical, and written examinations. The examinations are offered once annually over a period of 2 days. Supplementary examinations are available, and they must be taken within 4 months of the registration examination.

LANGUAGE TESTING

Candidates who have not received their professional education in English are required to achieve a score on TSE that is equivalent to 500 on the TOEFL.

RETRAINING

Foreign-trained candidates seeking registration within the board may work alongside practising Ontario massage therapists to upgrade their skills, but this is not a formal program of retraining. The board is currently involved in developing retraining courses to be run by the 4 Ontario massage therapy schools.

REVIEW OF DECISIONS

There is no right of appeal from a board decision.

MEDICAL LABORATORY TECHNOLOGY

Regulatory Status:
1) Approval procedure through Ministry of Health (private laboratories only)

2) Credentialing procedure through Canadian Society of Laboratory Technologists (CSLT)

Governing Statute:	*Laboratory and Specimen Collection Centre Licensing Act*, R.S.O. 1980, c. 409, as amended 1981, c. 66; 1983, c. 10; 1984, c. 409; Canadian Society of Laboratory Technologists (CSLT) Bylaws
Responsible Body:	Ontario Society of Medical Technologists (OSMT)

ASSESSMENT PROCEDURE

Educational Requirements

Ontario and Other Provinces	Two- or 3-year program in medical laboratory technology. Such programs are offered through 10 community colleges in Ontario, and all but 2 of them are 3 years in length. Both the Ministry and the CSLT requirements are met through these programs.
Elsewhere	Proof of education equivalent to an accredited program in Canada is the basic requirement.
Comments	Assessment of credentials is done on an individual basis by the CSLT in conjunction with the Comparative Education Service at the University of Toronto. Where university-level credentials are involved, transcripts are reviewed. If a program is assessed as not equivalent to the standard of an Ontario program, the applicant's training may be considered equivalent upon proof of adequate working experience. Certification by CSLT automatically entitles the applicant to be a member of OSMT.

Ministry requirements are met by certification by the CSLT. However, other, broader, grounds of approval appear to exist, including a satisfactory record of employment with the current employer.

All Canadian programs are accredited, with the exception of some programs in Quebec. Graduates of unaccredited Quebec programs are subject to the same requirements as candidates trained outside Canada.

Experience Requirements

The Ministry has no specified experience requirements. In the case of the CSLT, applicants trained outside Canada must have 6 months of acceptable full-time work experience in Canada. Credit is given for clinical experience gained outside Canada within the previous 5 years, the assessment of such experience being based on the scope and relevance of the work to the certification being attempted. The applicant must supply detailed documentation of work experience for assessment by the CSLT.

CERTIFICATION EXAMINATIONS

The Ministry does not require licensure testing. The CSLT requires all applicants to complete the General Registered Technologist examinations. The certification process must be completed within 14 months of the initial attempt at the examinations. The General Certification examinations are offered twice a year at a fee of $210. The specialist area or subject examinations are offered once a year. The format is the same as for the general certification examination. Sample questions are provided to facilitate preparation. If the examinations cannot be completed within the stipulated 14-month period, evidence of additional training is required before trying again.

LANGUAGE TESTING

No formal testing required by the Ministry or the CSLT. Successful completion of the qualifying examination is considered evidence of an acceptable level of fluency.

RETRAINING

There are limited opportunities. Although there are no formal retraining programs, an applicant may, if there is space available, be accommodated in a particular specialty course in the programs offered by the Toronto Institute for Medical Technology or at Mohawk College.

REVIEW OF DECISIONS

There is no appeal mechanism for either a failure during the examinations or a refusal to grant certification by the CSLT. There are no appeals available within the Ministry of Health approval procedure.

MEDICINE

Regulatory Status: Licensure

Governing Statute: *Health Disciplines Act,* R.S.O. 1980, c. 196, as amended 1983, c. 59; 1986, c. 28; 1986, c. 34

Responsible Body: Council of the College of Physicians and Surgeons of Ontario

ASSESSMENT PROCEDURE

Educational Requirements

Ontario, Other Provinces and U.S.	Degree from an accredited medical school. Canadian schools are accredited by the Council on Accreditation of Canadian Medical Schools (CACMS) and American schools are accredited by the Liaison Committee on Medical Education (LCME).
Elsewhere	Degree from an acceptable unaccredited medical school. To be eligible, the school in question must be listed in the World Health Organization (WHO) directory, offer a 4-year medical program, and have been in existence for 10 years.
Comments	Assessment of educational credentials is conducted by the College.

Experience Requirements

Graduates of accredited schools in Canada and the U.S.	Completion of a one-year rotating medical/surgical internship in an accredited medical school in Canada or the United States.
Graduates of unaccredited schools	Completion of 2 approved internships, or an approved internship and an acceptable residency. One of the internships must be a rotating internship, and one of the internships or the residency must be taken in Canada.
Comments	To complete an internship, a graduate of an unaccredited foreign medical school must complete a pre-internship program (PIP). Only 24 candidates per year are admitted to the program. The candidates who apply for the PIP must first pass the Medical Council of Canada Evaluating Examination (MCCEE). Successful candidates then take a written medical problem-solving examination. Seventy-two candidates proceed to the next stage and take a specially structured clinical examination. Of these, 24 are

selected for the PIP.

The MCCEE is available in English and French, and is intended to test the candidate's knowledge of the principal fields of medicine. The exam is 7 hours long and written in 2 $3^1/_2$-hour sessions. The MCCEE costs $350 for the first time and $300 for each subsequent attempt. There is no limit to the number of times a candidate can attempt it.

LICENSURE TESTING

Graduates of accredited schools in Canada or the U.S. must write a qualifying examination offered by the Medical Council of Canada (the MCCQE). Graduates of American schools may substitute the examination given by the National Board of Medical Examiners of the United States.

The MCCQE is designed to evaluate the candidate's medical knowledge and understanding and his or her ability to apply this to clinical situations.

LANGUAGE TESTING

Examinations for non-Ontario graduates are held in English or French, and fluency is considered critical for successful completion. Graduates of non-English/French programs are required to achieve a score of 580 in the TOEFL and 200 in the TSE or a comparable French fluency test.

RETRAINING

All graduates of non-accredited schools must complete the PIP. For those candidates who do not qualify for the PIP, the only available retraining is through a return to medical school.

REVIEW OF DECISIONS

There is no right to a hearing. A refusal of registration may be appealed to the Health Disciplines Board, and from there to the Divisional Court.

———

NATUROPATHY

Regulatory Status: Licensure

Governing Statute: *Drugless Practitioners Act*, R.S.O. 1980, c. 127; R.R.O. 1980, Reg. 250, as amended

Responsible Body: Board of Directors of Drugless Therapy

ASSESSMENT PROCEDURE

Educational Requirements

Ontario

Graduation from a naturopathy course at an approved school or college. The only naturopathy program in Canada is offered at the Ontario College of Naturopathic Medicine (OCNM), in Etobicoke, Ontario. Three years of full-time university education are required prior to enrolment in the college.

Other Provinces

For candidates registered in other provinces, the board may exercise its discretion in requiring them to write some or all of the registration examination, as there is no formal reciprocity between naturopathy licensing bodies in the Canadian provinces. In practice, a waiver of the examination requirement is not common.

Elsewhere

Academic qualifications are assessed by the OCNM, as retraining is generally required. The clinical background of the candidate is also assessed. People with specific naturopathy qualifications beyond their basic university training may be eligible to bypass the college and be assessed by the board. Almost all foreign-trained candidates are directed to complete an upgrading program, with the exception of graduates from 2 American programs that have been accredited in the U.S. and approved by the Ontario board.

Comments

The accreditation process is conducted by the Board of Directors of Drugless Therapy and the Council of Naturopathic Medical Education (U.S.).

Experience Requirements

Not applicable.

LICENSURE TESTING

All applicants must complete the registration examinations. They consist of 17 sections, including written clinical, oral, and practical components. Pass standard is 50 per cent on individual subjects and a minimum 60 per cent overall. The examinations are held over a 4-day period, once a year. Candidates who fail part of the examinations may be permitted to write up to 3 supplemental examinations.

LANGUAGE TESTING

English ability is assessed through an interview by the OCNM or the board. The candidate may be directed to ESL/FSL courses for upgrading before entering the OCNM retraining program, which must be completed before the registration examination is written.

RETRAINING

Retraining opportunities are offered by the OCNM in Etobicoke. After the college has assessed the candidate, he or she is placed into regular courses or an individual program.

REVIEW OF DECISIONS

Although it is not required under the *Drugless Practitioners Act*, any candidate who is refused registration as a naturopath has a right of appeal to the board. Applicants who are required by the OCNM to complete courses are also entitled to appeal this decision to the naturopathy board. There is no provision for external review.

NURSING

Regulatory Status: Registration

Governing Statute: *Health Disciplines Act*, R.S.O. 1980, c. 196, as amended 1983, c. 59; 1986, c. 28; 1986, c. 34

Responsible Body: Council of the College of Nurses of Ontario (CNO)

ASSESSMENT PROCEDURE

Educational Requirements

Ontario	Nurses: degree or diploma in nursing from a college or university. Nursing assistants: completion of a nursing assistant program.
Other Provinces	Education equivalent to Ontario and successful completion of Canada-wide registration examinations. In addition, if a candidate has valid registration in another Canadian jurisdiction, and has practised in the past 5 years, there will be immediate licensure. Otherwise, retraining courses may be required.
Elsewhere	Education equivalent to Ontario plus current registration in home jurisdiction or eligibility for such registration.
Comments	Nursing programs are offered in 35 institutions in the province. Thirty-three institutions offer nursing assistant programs. Assessment of foreign credentials is conducted by the CNO. The candidate's program is assessed on a course-by-course basis against the CNO requirements. Those with extensive experience may be exempted from retraining in areas of academic deficiency. Foreign-trained nurses whose qualifications do not meet the CNO minimum criteria are given the choice of retraining and then writing the nursing licensing examination, or of immediately writing the nursing assistant examination. The nursing and nursing assistant programs are accredited by: Ministry of Colleges and Universities (community colleges); the Association of University Schools of Nursing (universities); Academic Council of Ryerson Polytechnical Institute (Ryerson).

Experience Requirements

Nurses and nursing assistants trained in Ontario automatically complete the practical experience requirement upon graduation (1,200 and 600 hours, respectively). For foreign-trained candidates, the assessment of their training will take into consideration these requirements.

A foreign-trained candidate for licensure must have practised as a registered nurse in another jurisdiction, or as a non-registered graduate nurse in Ontario, within the past 5 years. Applicants who have not practised in the last 5 years must complete an upgrading program.

LICENSURE TESTING

All applicants must write the registration examinations. These examinations are offered over a 2-day period for nurses, and a one-day period for nursing assistants. The examinations are developed by the Canadian Nurses Association Testing Service. The failure rate is 8 per cent for Ontario graduates and 41 per cent for out-of-province applicants. The CNO is preparing an information kit to enable better preparation for the examinations. Both English and French examinations are available for nursing, with English only for nursing assistants.

LANGUAGE TESTING

All candidates must be reasonably fluent in English or French. An overall score of 500 on the TOEFL, with a minimum of 50 in each of the component parts, is required as a demonstration of proficiency. Candidates also must achieve a score of 200 on the TSE, although they may be exempted if they provide proof of fluency through employment or postgraduate study.

RETRAINING

Retraining opportunities may be pursued through 6 community colleges in Ontario. George Brown College provides a full-time refresher program. There are also 8 refresher courses offered for nursing assistants.

REVIEW OF DECISIONS

A refusal of registration may be appealed to the Health Disciplines Board and from there to the Divisional Court.

OCCUPATIONAL THERAPY

Regulatory Status: Voluntary certification

Governing Statute: Not applicable

Responsible Body: Ontario College of Occupational Therapists (OCOT)

ASSESSMENT PROCEDURE

Educational Requirements

Ontario and Other Provinces	Graduation from a CAOT-accredited program in Canada. Twelve programs in Canada are accredited.
Elsewhere	Graduation from a program of study in occupational therapy approved by the World Federation of Occupational Therapists (WFOT). WFOT guidelines state that programs must be at least 3 years in length, and meet other specified criteria.
Comments	The CAOT does not assess academic credentials; instead, the association relies completely on the WFOT approval process. If an applicant's program is not recognized by the WFOT, its approval must be obtained before a candidate may attempt Canadian licensing evaluation.

Experience Requirements

Ontario and Other Provinces	Applicants trained in Canada must complete 1,200 hours of clinical practice within one year of graduation. This is included in the curricula of all accredited programs.
Elsewhere	Completion of a minimum of 1,000 hours of clinical fieldwork in the country of training within one year of graduation is required. This will be included as part of any WFOT-approved program.

CERTIFICATION EXAMINATIONS

All applicants must write the CAOT National Certification Examination. It consists of 2 3-hour papers. The cost is $150. The examination may be retried as often as necessary. It is offered once per year in 18 testing centres across Canada, 6 of them in Ontario.

LANGUAGE TESTING

No formal testing. The certification examination is given in English or French and is presumed to demonstrate language proficiency.

RETRAINING

Limited retraining opportunities are available through Woodsworth College at the University of Toronto. Also, the OCOT offers a refresher education package. Graduation from a WFOT-approved program is a prerequisite to entry to retraining programs.

REVIEW OF DECISIONS

Bylaws of the CAOT create an appeal board and empower it to hear appeals from refusals for individual membership. There is no external appeal.

OPHTHALMIC DISPENSING

Regulatory Status: Licensure

Governing Statute: *Ophthalmic Dispensers Act*, R.S.O. 1980, c. 364, as amended 1986, c. 64

Responsible Body: Board of Ophthalmic Dispensers

ASSESSMENT PROCEDURE

Educational Requirements

Ontario

Must be a graduate of an approved course of study in ophthalmic dispensing. Two such programs are offered, at Seneca College and Georgian College.

Elsewhere

Current dispensing licence from home jurisdiction with good standing. If the candidate is from a jurisdiction where ophthalmic dispensing is not a regulated profession, he or she may be required to complete the Ontario training program.

Comments

Assessment of a candidate's prior education is conducted by the board. After his or her documentation is verified, the candidate is invited to write an assessment examination and then be interviewed by the board's competency committee. Assessment is done on a case-by-case basis; no precedents are set or observed. If the candidate is assessed to be deficient in training, he or she is directed to Georgian or Seneca College for an assessment of their training needs. If assessed as equivalent to an Ontario graduate, he or she is directed to write the examinations and work under supervision with "special status" in the meantime.

Experience Requirements

To become registered as an ophthalmic dispenser in Ontario, an applicant must have one year of "in-service training" in Canada. This must be done under the supervision of a qualified ophthalmic dispenser. During fieldwork training, the applicant must maintain a log book of the number of fittings done, and the number of hours worked under supervision. One year's fieldwork amounts to 250 fittings (1,750 hours). The fieldwork requirement is never waived. Credit is given for experience in other provinces.

LICENSURE TESTING

All applicants must write the licensure examination. It consists of 10 parts at a cost of $35 per part. If the applicant fails one or more sections of the examination, he or she may retry those sections in a supplementary examination. If an applicant fails a second time, he or she is required to complete additional upgrading.

LANGUAGE TESTING

No formal testing. Informal language assessment is made by the competency committee of the board, and a recommendation that the candidate take ESL courses may be made.

RETRAINING

Georgian or Seneca College may assess retraining needs of candidates. Retraining is available at both these colleges.

REVIEW OF DECISIONS

There is no mechanism for an external review of a decision to refuse registration.

OPTOMETRY

Regulatory Status: Licensure

Governing Statute: *Health Disciplines Act*, R.S.O. 1980, c. 196, as amended 1983, c. 59; 1986, c. 28; 1986, c. 34

Responsible Body: Council of the College of Optometrists of Ontario

ASSESSMENT PROCEDURE

Educational Requirements

Ontario and Other Provinces	Degree in optometry is required from one of the 2 universities in Canada which offer the program.
U.S.	Degree in optometry from an accredited institution.
U.K., Australia, New Zealand, South Africa, Nigeria	Graduates from these jurisdictions must obtain an accredited degree but may be eligible to obtain advanced standing to complete additional training in an accredited Canadian or U.S. institution. Advanced standing is determined by the educational institution, but a minimum of 2 years' training is required.
Elsewhere	Applications from these unaccredited institutions are eligible to be assessed on a case-by-case basis by the registrar of the College of Optometrists; however, in practice, full retraining is necessary for such candidates. A degree in optometry may be obtained in Ontario at the University of Waterloo.
Comments	Council of Education of the American Optometric Association accredits the U.S. programs. The Ontario college has elected to adopt the U.S. accreditation procedure.

Experience Requirements

Not applicable.

LICENSURE TESTING

Candidates from Ontario must write the University of Waterloo final year comprehensive examination. Candidates from other provinces and the U.S. must sit board qualifying examinations. Candidates from elsewhere are required to do additional training before attempting the examination.

The qualifying examination is substantially the same as the University of Waterloo comprehensive examination written by Ontario graduates. The examination consists of 6 written, 6 oral, and 5 clinical parts, and costs $1,425. The college prepares a syllabus for its candidates outlining the material to be covered in the examination. If 2 parts are failed, supplementary examinations may be tried, provided the applicant has obtained a 60 per cent average. If more than 2 parts are failed, or if the overall average is less than 60 per cent, the examination is failed. The candidate may be permitted to retry the entire examination on application to the board. The examinations are developed by the registration committee of the College of Optometrists of Ontario, and are held once per year.

LANGUAGE TESTING

No formal testing. The regulations require that all applicants for licensure be fluent in English or French. The entry requirements to this profession are such that fluency is not an issue.

RETRAINING

No retraining program. Applicants with less than the required academic training must complete a degree at an accredited institution. The amount of credit then granted is determined by the institution.

REVIEW OF DECISIONS

A rejected candidate may appeal a refusal by the committee to the Health Disciplines Board; from there, he or she may appeal to the Divisional Court.

OSTEOPATHY

Regulatory Status: Licensure

Governing Statute: *Drugless Practitioners Act*, R.S.O. 1980, c. 127; R.R.O. 1980, Reg. 252, as amended

Responsible Body: Board of Directors of Osteopathy

ASSESSMENT PROCEDURE

Educational Requirements

Ontario, Other Provinces and U.S.	A 4-year acceptable course in osteopathy with a minimum of 5,000 hours of instruction.
Comments	The Ontario Board of Directors of Osteopathy is responsible for the assessment of academic credentials. The Board recognizes only those programs accredited by the American Osteopathic Association (AOA). There are only 15 such colleges, all in the U.S.; therefore, in practice, all applicants are trained in the U.S.
Elsewhere	Essentially, if the candidate is not a graduate of a program accredited by AOA, his or her credentials will not be accepted.

Experience Requirements

No formal requirements; however, registration in another jurisdiction usually requires 2 years of internship.

LANGUAGE TESTING

No formal testing. However, the only osteopathic training institutions acceptable to the board are in the U.S., where the medium of instruction is English.

RETRAINING

No training or retraining opportunities in Ontario.

REVIEW OF DECISIONS

Very low demand for licensure, so there are no appeal procedures in place.

PHARMACY

Regulatory Status: Licensure

Governing Statute:	*Health Disciplines Act*, R.S.O. 1980, c. 196, as amended 1983, c. 59; 1986, c. 28; 1986, c. 34
Responsible Body:	Council of the Ontario College of Pharmacists (OCP)

ASSESSMENT PROCEDURE

Educational Requirements

Ontario	B.Sc. in Pharmacy from the University of Toronto or equivalent.
Other Provinces and U.S.	B.Sc. in Pharmacy from any accredited program.
Elsewhere	A 3- or 4-year degree from a foreign university with an acceptable standard of admission.
Comments	Assessment of foreign-trained degrees to determine "acceptability" is conducted by the Pharmacy Examining Board of Canada (PEBC). Candidates with acceptable training may attempt an evaluating examination. Candidates who pass (see below, under "Licensure Testing") may write the qualifying examination.
	Canadian and U.S. programs are accredited by the PEBC and the American Council of Pharmacy Education, respectively. Most currently have accredited status.

Experience Requirements

Forty-eight weeks of in-service training is required of all candidates. A maximum of 24 weeks' credit is given for experience obtained in other provinces, the United States, the United Kingdom, Australia, or Ireland. Graduates of Canadian programs may be given up to 11 months of credit. The registrar of the OCP reviews applications for credit on an individual basis.

LICENSURE TESTING

Ontario Applicants	Qualifying examination.
Other Provinces and accredited U.S. programs	Qualifying examination (PEBC) and jurisprudence examination required by the Ontario College of Pharmacists.

Applicants from elsewhere (with acceptable degrees)	Evaluating and qualifying examinations and jurisprudence examination.
Comments	The evaluating examination tests knowledge of current pharmaceutical practice. It costs $265 and may be retried with no upgrading requirement. It is offered twice each year, with a pass rate of about 60 per cent. The qualifying examination is also a written examination but has a more clinical emphasis. It costs $200, is also offered twice a year, and may be tried 3 times. After the third failure, the applicant must complete upgrading course work. The pass rate is about 70 per cent, and a triple failure is extremely rare. Jurisprudence examinations are offered by the OCP.

LANGUAGE TESTING

The regulations require that an applicant's English or French be tested if he or she studied pharmacy in another language, or if fluency is in doubt. A minimum score of 500 on the TOEFL, or a score of 80 in the Michigan tests must be achieved to qualify for registration as a pharmacy student. The required score for licensure is 550 on the TOEFL or 88 in the Michigan tests. An oral test is also administered by the college, with a score of 60 per cent necessary. Three attempts are allowed. The TSE is accepted as an alternative to the oral test. French fluency tests may also be administered.

RETRAINING

No formal retraining, although attempts have been made in the past to offer retraining programs. "Continuing education" program is offered on a voluntary basis. Candidates with "unacceptable" degrees must complete an acceptable degree. Advanced standing may be available. Places are very limited.

REVIEW OF DECISIONS

A refusal of registration may be appealed to the Health Disciplines Board and from there, to the Divisional Court.

PHYSIOTHERAPY

Regulatory Status: Licensure

Governing Statute: *Drugless Practitioners Act*, R.S.O. 1980, c. 127; R.R.O. 1980, Reg. 253, as amended

Responsible Body: Board of Directors of Physiotherapy

ASSESSMENT PROCEDURE

Educational Requirements

Ontario

Degree in physiotherapy from any university in Ontario or a diploma in physiotherapy from Mohawk College of Applied Arts and Technology.

Other Provinces

Degree in physiotherapy plus completion of clinical requirements for registration in their home jurisdiction.

Accredited Programs in U.K.

Treated in the same manner as Ontario graduates.

Elsewhere

Equivalent educational qualifications to those required in Canada, or sufficient qualifications to be recognized by the governing body in their home jurisdiction.

Foreign qualifications are subjected to limited assessment by the Canadian Physiotherapy Association (CPA) using the World Confederation of Physical Therapy (WCPT) directory and its own sources of information. The Canadian physiotherapy programs are accredited by the CPA every 7 years.

Experience Required

Clinical experience is an integral part of physiotherapy education in Ontario. The clinical component of programs ranges in length from 1,000 to 1,500 hours; the average is 1,264 hours, the equivalent of about 7 months. Foreign-trained candidates are required to complete a minimum of 4 consecutive months of full-time clinical practice. No credit is given for clinical practice outside Canada.

LICENSURE TESTING

The CPA Registration Examination is required of foreign-trained candidates to achieve CPA membership. The cost is $800 and the examination is offered in 3 2-hour sessions twice per year. The pass mark is 50 per cent. As an aid to preparation, the CPA provides a "Recommended Core Curriculum for Physiotherapy Education Programs" that details the content of physiotherapy education programs in Canada. Candidates are permitted to attempt the written examination 3 times over a 2-year period.

LANGUAGE TESTING

To be eligible to write the CPA examination in English or French, and to complete clinical residency, applicants who do not speak English or French must show that one of these languages was the language of instruction in their program, or pass the TOEFL with a minimum score of 500.

RETRAINING

There is no specific retraining available for foreign-trained candidates; however, the CPA Toronto Re-entry Program is open to some examination candidates.

REVIEW OF DECISIONS

There is no formal right of appeal from a registration decision.

PSYCHOLOGY

Regulatory Status: Reserved title

Governing Statute: *Psychologists Registration Act*, R.S.O. 1980, c. 404

Responsible Body: Ontario Board of Examiners in Psychology

ASSESSMENT PROCEDURE

Educational Requirements

Ontario   Ph.D. in psychology from an accredited Ontario university.

Elsewhere	Ph.D. in psychology from accredited institution in or outside Canada.
Comments	For candidates who are graduates of institutions not accredited by the Canadian Psychological Association, the Ontario Board of Examiners in Psychology conducts a comprehensive assessment. Among the assessment criteria are these: training in psychology must be at the doctoral level; the program must be publicly labelled and identified as a psychology program; the curriculum must encompass a minimum of 3 years' full-time graduate study. The board conducts a detailed review to see whether the degree earned is a "pure" psychology degree and the quality of the degree and/or institution is also assessed. The Comparative Education Service of the University of Toronto assists with general assessment of unfamiliar degrees, in particular those from institutions outside North America. Candidates with unacceptable degrees must do sufficient training to obtain acceptable degrees. The amount is determined by the educational institution.

Experience Requirements

To practise as a Registered Psychologist in Ontario, applicants must have at least one year of supervised post-doctoral experience to be completed prior to completing the examinations. Such experience is evaluated by means of a work appraisal form which includes an assessment of the applicant's level of competence in an area of specialty, among other things. Non-Ontario experience is recognized in the case of experienced psychologists licensed in jurisdictions whose standards are similar to those in Ontario. In some cases, experience requirements may be waived for previously licensed applicants who have graduated from an accredited North American doctoral program. The requirement may be shortened for applicants who studied outside North America.

REGISTRATION EXAMINATIONS

All applicants must complete the Examination for Professional Practice in Psychology (EPPP) developed by the American Association of State Psychology Boards, and an oral examination. The cost of the written examination is $350, it is held twice a year, and there are no limits to the number of retries. However, if an applicant fails twice, the board may make recommendations for further study. Content outlines and past examinations are available for preparation. An acceptable pass grade in Ontario is 65 per cent. The oral examination is conducted by a panel of 3 psychologists. Unsuccessful candidates may retry any number of times, but must retrain after a failure.

LANGUAGE TESTING

No formal testing. A passing mark on the EPPP is considered an adequate indicator of the candidate's fluency in French or English. Candidates for whom English or French is a second language are allowed extra time on the examination.

RETRAINING

Candidates with inadequate credentials effectively have no option but returning to school to complete an acceptable doctorate.

REVIEW OF DECISIONS

A refused applicant may have his or her case reviewed by the board and may appeal from there to the Divisional Court.

RADIOLOGICAL TECHNOLOGY

Regulatory Status: Licensure; reserved title

Governing Statute: *Radiological Technicians Act*, R.S.O. 1980, c. 430

Responsible Body: Board of Radiological Technicians, Ontario Association for Medical Radiation Technologists (OAMRT)

ASSESSMENT PROCEDURE

Educational Requirements

(1) For registration with the Board of Radiological Technicians

Ontario   A program of training offered by community colleges and the Toronto Institute of Medical Technology must be completed. It must last at least 24 months, but length varies according to specialty.

Elsewhere	Applicants from other provinces, and from countries with which Canada has reciprocity, are automatically granted registration. Reciprocity is based on the CAMRT (Canadian Association of Medical Radiation Technologists) definition and is determined by the other country's membership in an international association. The CAMRT accredits Canadian programs.

The board also grants immediate registration to technologists who are graduates of other specified programs, if it is satisfied that these are equivalent to the Ontario program.

Other applicants must first undergo screening by the board to determine whether they have sufficient training. The type and length of program from which they graduated is considered. Qualified candidates are permitted to move on to the board examination. The candidates must also complete a clinical evaluation conducted through one of the affiliated hospitals or central schools.

(2) For certification by the Canadian Association of Medical Radiation Technologists (CAMRT)

Ontario	Approved program of training in Ontario. The criteria for approval are the same as those set out in the *Radiological Technicians Act*.

Elsewhere	Graduates of programs in countries with which Canada has reciprocity are advised that they have met all the necessary criteria and are certified and admitted for membership.

Applicants from all other jurisdictions should have completed equivalent academic requirements to those offered in Ontario.

Experience Requirements

(1) For registration with the Board of Radiological Technicians

Recognition is given to clinical experience obtained elsewhere, although some Canadian experience will always be required.

(2) For certification by CAMRT

Applicants from jurisdictions with which there are no reciprocity agreements must have "acceptable clinical experience and competence." The assessments are performed by instructors at one of the central schools and at one of the participating hospitals. In practice, it appears that all candidates must complete a minimum of one year of clinical training in Canada, regardless of any other experience.

LICENSURE TESTING

(1) Board of Radiological Technicians

Board examination upon completion of training. A pass is 70 per cent and one rewrite is allowed. However, the board accepts certification by the CAMRT as evidence of satisfactory completion of its requirements. Therefore, relatively few candidates write the board examinations: namely, candidates from non-reciprocal countries.

(2) CAMRT

The CAMRT examinations are multiple-choice, and are offered twice yearly in English and French. Required of all candidates except those from reciprocal countries.

LANGUAGE TESTING

The Board of Radiological Technicians requires candidates whose first language is not English to pass the TOEFL with a score of at least 470. The CAMRT does not administer language tests.

RETRAINING

Opportunities are very limited and available only to small numbers of candidates.

REVIEW OF DECISIONS

Although the *Radiological Technicians Act* contains a right of appeal for suspension of registration, there is no right of appeal specified in the *Act* for refusal to register.

REAL ESTATE AND BUSINESS BROKERAGE

Regulatory Status: Licensure

Governing Statute: *Real Estate and Business Brokers Act*, R.S.O. 1980,
c. 431

Responsible Body: Ministry of Consumer and Commercial Relations,
Registrar of Real Estate and Business Brokers

ASSESSMENT PROCEDURE

Educational Requirements

Ontario

All applicants for registration as brokers are required
to complete courses of study approved by the registrar.
The real estate educational program is administered by
the Ontario Real Estate Association (OREA). Most
OREA courses are taught in community colleges.
Sellers must complete a 150-hour introductory course
entitled "An Introduction to Real Estate." Brokers
must complete the same course, plus 4 additional
courses to conclude a "certificate program," and a
"real estate administration" course.

Elsewhere

Real estate and business brokers registered in a
jurisdiction outside Ontario may be exempted from
examinations by the registrar.

Experience Requirements

No experience requirements for sellers. Candidates for registration as brokers are
required to have been registered and actively employed as sellers for 2 years
within the immediately preceding 3 years.

LICENSURE TESTING

For all applicants, certification examinations are a part of the required training
courses. Those registered in other jurisdictions may be fully or partially
exempted by the registrar.

LANGUAGE TESTING

There are no formal language requirements, but adequate fluency is necessary
to be successful in the courses.

RETRAINING

Since the courses are modular and offered frequently, retraining does not pose a potential barrier.

REVIEW OF DECISIONS

If a candidate is refused registration, he or she may appeal to the Commercial Registration Appeal Tribunal (CRAT). Its decision may further be appealed to the Divisional Court.

SOCIAL WORK

Regulatory Status: Voluntary association

Governing Statute: Not applicable

Responsible Body: Ontario Association of Professional Social Workers (OAPSW), Ontario College of Certified Social Workers (OCCSW)

ASSESSMENT PROCEDURE

Educational Requirements

Ontario and Other Provinces	Graduation from a program that is accredited by the Canadian Association of Schools of Social Work (CASSW).
U.S.	Graduation from a program accredited by the Council on Social Work Education (CSWE).
Elsewhere (candidates from unaccredited programs)	Degree in social work equivalent to an Ontario degree.
Comments	Non-accredited degrees are assessed by the Canadian Association of Social Workers (CASW). Required documents include transcripts, degrees or diplomas, course descriptions, social work field practice evaluation (where applicable), and proof of membership in professional social work association(s) from another

country. The World Guide to Social Work Education and the International Association of Schools of Social Work (IASSW) directory are used as references.

In evaluating the applicant's degree, the requirements of Canadian bachelor's and master's degrees are considered. Field practice and research experience are also considered.

Experience Requirements

All candidates must have 2 years of paid social work experience (a minimum of 3,000 hours within 6 years) after graduation, plus the equivalent of 6 months' full-time paid social work experience within the 2 years prior to the date of their application for membership in the college. Under its guidelines, at least one of the 2 years of experience must be supervised either by a member of the college and/or the association or by a social worker eligible for such membership. Association guidelines require the experience to be in Canada; the college guidelines differ on this point. If candidates have 10 or more years of paid social work experience (Canadian or foreign), then the supervision requirement may be waived.

CERTIFICATION EXAMINATIONS

All candidates must complete both written and oral examinations. These test practical knowledge rather than "academic knowledge," and are available in English or French. Two retries are permitted. Examinations were developed by the National Association in the U.S. in conjunction with the Educational Testing Service (ETS). The College adopted them and worked with ETS to make them reflect the Canadian system.

LANGUAGE TESTING

Neither the association nor the college has any formal testing programs but the examinations require fluency. Any further assessment of language competency is left to the employer.

RETRAINING

Graduates of unaccredited social work programs or those with unacceptable foreign degrees have no access to specific retraining. Their only option is to take an entire accredited social work program against which the university may give credits for past work done.

REVIEW OF DECISIONS

An applicant who is refused eligibility for membership in the association can appeal this decision to the registration committee. Similarly, an individual whose application is refused by the college or who has had limitations imposed upon his or her registration can appeal to the appeals committee of the college. There are, however, no external review mechanisms.

VETERINARY MEDICINE

Regulatory Status: Licensure

Governing Statute: *The Veterinarians Act*, R.S.O. 1980, c. 522

Responsible Body: Council of the Ontario Veterinary Association (OVA)

ASSESSMENT PROCEDURE

Educational Requirements

Ontario,
Other Provinces,
and U.S.

Veterinary medical degree from an accredited school. There is also an accredited program in Utrecht which is given equal status with domestic programs.

Elsewhere

Graduation from a veterinary medical school listed in the World Health Organization (WHO) directory. Candidates from unaccredited schools must undergo an admission process that is more rigorous than that required of other applicants. For applicants from schools listed in the WHO directory, the review of academic credentials and the authenticating of documents is conducted by the OVA.

The accreditation process is conducted by the Canadian Veterinary Medical Association (CVMA) in conjunction with the American Veterinary Medical Association (AVMA).

Experience Requirements

Not applicable.

LICENSURE TESTING

Ontario-trained applicants

Exempt from all examinations, including the provincial jurisprudence examination, if the candidate applies to the OVA within one year of graduation.

Graduates of accredited schools elsewhere

Parts I and II of the certification examination — the National Board Examination (NBE) plus the Clinical Competency Test (CCT) — although graduates of Canadian schools are regularly exempted from these examinations. Provincial jurisprudence examinations are required of these candidates.

Graduates of unaccredited schools

All 3 parts of the certification examinations: the NBE, the CCT, and the Clinical Proficiency Examination (CPE), plus the provincial jurisprudence examination.

Comments

The cost is $220 for the NBE, $150 for the CCT, and $2,500 for the CPE. The jurisprudence examination was developed by the OVA. The NBE and CCT have been developed under the direction of the National Board Examination Committee of the AVMA in collaboration with the Public Examining Service, subject to some input by the CVMA.

LANGUAGE TESTING

The NBE and CCT examinations are offered in both English and French. CPE is English only. These examinations, along with the provincial jurisprudence examination, function as language screens.

RETRAINING

The OVA is in the process of establishing a standard preparatory program with the Ontario Veterinary College for candidates taking the examinations for the first time and those who have failed and want more training before they retry.

REVIEW OF DECISIONS

No formal review process of a negative decision as to registration.

Notes

CHAPTER 2

1. *Report of the Royal Commission on the Economic Union and Development Prospects for Canada*, Vol. 2 (Ottawa: Supply and Services Canada, 1985), p. 663.
2. The 1976 *Immigration Act* took effect in 1978 (*Immigration Act 1976*, S.C. 1976-7, c. 52, proclaimed in force April 10, 1978).
3. From a speech by Bud Cullen, Minister of Employment and Immigration, to the National Inter-Faith Immigration Committee, Toronto, April 21, 1978. Quoted in Warren E. Kalbach, "Guess Who's Coming to Canada Now," *TESL Talk* 10(3) (Immigration and Multiculturalism — *A Decade To Remember*, Summer 1979), p. 17.
4. Employment and Immigration Canada, *Annual Report*, 1987-88, p. 45
5. *Report of Royal Commission on the Economic Union and Development Prospects for Canada*, Vol. 2, p. 662.
6. *The Relative Economic Situation of Immigrants in Canada*, October 1986 (prepared for "Review of Demography and Its Implications for Economic and Social Policy," Health and Welfare Canada, by Roderic Beaujot), p. 2.
7. *Annual Report to Parliament on Future Immigration Levels*, pp. 25, 26.
8. *Ibid.*, p. 32.
9. EIC *Annual Report*, 1987-88, pp. 45-46.
10. *New Directions* (an interministerial bulletin on multicultural issues) (Toronto: Ontario Ministry of Citizenship, Winter 1989), p. 3.
11. Ontario Ministry of Citizenship, Ethnocultural Data Base Materials, Immigration Statistics, June 1987 and June 1988 compilations (for 1985 and 1986 data).
12. *Immigration Act* s. 2(1).
13. Immigrant Category — Definitions; excerpted from materials published by EIC.
14. EIC *Annual Report*, 1987-88, p. 45.
15. Kalbach, "Guess Who's Coming to Canada," pp. 17, 22.
16. S.C. 1988, c. 31.
17. Jean Burnet, draft paper, "Living in a Multicultural Society," prepared for the International Symposium at Oxford University: "The Refugee Crisis: British and Canadian Responses," January 1989.

CHAPTER 3

1. In Canada, the number of trades for which an apprenticeship training program has been established varies from province to province. For example, Ontario regulates 70, Newfoundland regulates 29, Alberta regulates 52, and British Columbia regulates 82 trades. (Reported in *The Ellis Chart of Apprentice Training Programs*, which is issued by the Interprovincial Standards Program Co-ordinating Committee in cooperation with the federal, provincial, and territorial governments and published by the training branch, Employment and Immigration Canada, 1985. Branches of trades are counted separately.)
2. *Apprenticeship and Tradesmen's Qualification Act*, R.S.O. 1980, c. 24, as amended.
3. Labour Market Research Group, *Adjusting to Change: An Overview of Labour Market Issues in Ontario, 1988* (Toronto: Ontario Ministry of Skills Development, 1988), p. 9.

4. Ontario Manpower Commission, *Labour Market Outlook for Ontario, 1984-88* (Toronto: Ontario Ministry of Labour, August 1984), p. 28.
5. Labour Market Research Group, p. 27.
6. The growing importance of training and retraining has been emphasized in the Report of the Premier's Council, *Competing in the New Global Economy*, Vol. 1, Chap. 10 ("Investing in People") (Toronto: Queen's Printer, 1988).
7. *The Apprenticeship Act, 1928*, S.O. 1928, c. 25.
8. *Training for Ontario's Future* — Report of the Task Force on Industrial Training (the Dymond Report) (Toronto: Ontario Ministry of Colleges and Universities, 1973), p. 29.
9. The term "licensure" is used here and throughout this Report to indicate a legal prerequisite to practice (see discussion in Chapter 6). It is noted, however, that the Ministry of Skills Development describes those trades in which journeyman's status is a precondition of practice as "compulsory" certified trades. There is no legislative definition as such. See ss. 9, 10, and 11 of the *ATQA* and s. 5 of the General Regulations.
10. Dymond Report, p. 32.
11. Ontario Ministry of Colleges and Universities, *Apprenticeship Programs in Ontario: Regulated and Non-Regulated Administration Methods and Selection Criteria* (Toronto: Queen's Printer, 1983), pp. 4-5.
12. Throughout this chapter and generally in literature on apprenticeship, the term "journeyman," which is not defined in legislation, is used to describe a fully qualified practitioner of a regulated trade. We use the term, of course, to include female as well as male practitioners.
13. S. 11(1) of the *ATQA* provides that the provincial Cabinet "may designate any trade as a certified trade for the purposes of this *Act*."
14. General Regulations under *Apprenticeship and Tradesmen's Qualification Act*, Regulation 36, R.R.O. 1980, as amended by O. Regs. 246/81, 75/83, 52/84, and 717/86, s. 3(b). Grade 12 is required for motor vehicle mechanic. Grade 9 is required for barbers, hairdressers, and hairstylists. Grade 8 is required for masons, plasterers, autobody repairers and painters, service station attendants, and bakers.
15. There is a lack of clarity on this point; the Task Force was advised that the test was administered only to applicants not educated in English or French.
16. Regulation 36, s. 10(1). If the employer is the only journeyman, wages are calculated based on the average rate of pay for journeymen in the area.
17. *Unemployment Insurance Act*, R.S.C. 1985, c. U-1.
18. *National Training Act*, R.S.C. 1985, c. N-19.
19. Regulation 36, s. 9.
20. General Regulations, s. 20. Although s. 20 clearly requires the prior experience considered be experience *as a journeyman*, MSD advised us that, in practice, experience *as an apprentice* is also considered in meeting the requirement of equivalent experience.
21. General Regulations, s. 17. Although this section refers to "approved" training programs, we understand that in practice programs are not approved.
22. Employment and Immigration Canada. *Job Entry: Cooperative Education Guide to Applicants* (Ottawa: Supply and Services Canada, 1985).
23. Premier's Council. *Competing in the New Global Economy*, Vol. 1, p. 228.
24. *Occupational Health and Safety Act*, R.S.O. 1980, c. 321, as amended; and Regulations for Mines and Mining Plants, R.R.O. 1980, Reg. 694, as amended.
25. Premier's Council. *Competing in the Global Economy*, Vol. 1, p. 232.
26. This section is based on research carried out for the Task Force by Susan Simosco Associates, Regency House, Sheffield, England, and reported in an unpublished manuscript, "Cumulative Certificates in Vocational Education in England and Scotland" (June 1988).

27. As discussed above, employers in the apprenticeship system include union hiring halls, local apprenticeship committees, the Ontario Industrial Training Institute in rare instances, and private businesses, such as construction contractors or automobile service stations.

28. During the period prior to 1985, when the Ministry of Colleges and Universities was responsible for apprenticeship training, it prepared a policy manual for use by its operations branch. This manual has not been revised since 1982 and apparently is no longer used by the Ministry.

29. *ATQA*, ss. 8, 24.

30. *Report of the Select Committee on Manpower Training* (the Simonett Report) (Toronto: Ontario Legislative Assembly, 1963).

31. Ontario Ministry of Skills Development, *Breaking New Ground: Ontario's Training Strategy* (Toronto: Government of Ontario, 1986).

32. *Unemployment Insurance Act*, R.S.C. 1985, c. U-1.

33. *National Training Act*, R.S.C. 1985, c. N-19.

34. This discussion is based on "Proposal To Create a Canada Training Allowance," MSD, November 1987.

35. *Ibid.*, p. 12.

36. *Ibid.*, p. 6.

37. The inadequacy of federal training allowances was noted in the *Report of the Commission on Equality in Employment* (the Abella Report) (Ottawa: Supply and Services Canada, 1984), p. 172.

38. *National Training Regulations*, S.O.R./82-776, as amended.

39. Premier's Council. *Competing in the New Global Economy*, Vol. 1, pp. 228-30.

40. MSD, *Overview of the Findings of the Survey, "Participation of Visible Minorities in Employer-Based Training,"* 1989.

CHAPTER 4

1. *Report of the Royal Commission of Inquiry into Civil Rights*, Report No. 1, Vol. 3, Part III, s. 4 (Toronto: Queen's Printer, 1968), pp. 1163, 1166.

2. *Report of the Professional Organizations Committee* (Toronto: Ontario Ministry of the Attorney General, April 1980).

3. *Ibid.*, p. 9.

4. Report of the Committee on the Healing Arts, Vol. 3 (Toronto: Queen's Printer, 1970), p. 51.

5. *Ibid.*, p. 56.

6. S.O. 1981, c. 53, as amended.

7. *Constitution Act, 1982*, ss. 1-34 en. by the *Canada Act, 1982* (U.K.) c. 11, Schedule B.

8. The *Veterinarians Act*, R.S.O. 1980, c. 522, s. 4.

9. *Striking a New Balance: A Blueprint for the Regulation of Ontario's Health Professions* (Toronto: The Health Professions Legislation Review, 1989).

10. Other occupational groups established by private statute include, among others, the Registered Music Teachers Association, the Institute of Professional Librarians, the Institute of Chartered Secretaries and Administrators, the Association of Municipal Clerks and Treasurers, the Association of Chartered Industrial Designers, the Association of Clerical Professions, and the Registered Interior Designers.

11. The chartered accountants have both regulations and bylaws, but there is little distinction between the two in terms of accountability. The regulations are not subject to review or approval by the government (see *Chartered Accountants Act*, ss. 8, 9).

12. In many cases, a "reserved title" as such is not granted, but the relevant credential is simple membership in a voluntary organization that controls entry through certification procedures. Membership in and of itself becomes significant for employment. Throughout our discussion, all such certification regimes are referred to.
13. *Radiological Technicians Act*, R.S.O. 1980, c. 430.
14. *Healing Arts Radiation Protection Act*, R.S.O. 1980, c. 195, as amended.
15. *Public Accountancy Act*, R.S.O. 1980.
16. S. 14 of the *Public Accountancy Act* permits two exceptions for individuals registered under some specified previous accounting legislation, but these grandfathering provisions become increasingly less relevant with time.
17. Partly in response to these concerns, the Professional Organizations Committee, in its report, recommended that the three certifying bodies in the profession — the Institute of Chartered Accountants of Ontario, the Certified General Accountants Association of Ontario, and the Society of Management Accountants of Ontario — be given the power to grant public accounting licences to qualified members and as such "be constituted in accordance with the structures and processes of professional self-government" (p. 142). The Public Accountants Council would thus relinquish its licensing function in favour of the bodies actually setting and administering the entry criteria, and these bodies would, through the mechanism of public regulation, become publicly accountable. *Report of the Professional Organizations Committee.*
18. *Crown Timber Act*, R.S.O. 1980, c. 109, as amended.
19. *Public Health Act*, R.S.O. 1980, c. 409.
20. *Day Nurseries Act*, R.S.O. 1980, c. 111, as amended.
21. *Human Rights Code, 1981*, S.O. 1981, c. 53, as amended.
22. Correspondence from E. M. Todres, Management Board of Cabinet, Human Resources Secretariat, Government of Ontario.
23. *Report of the Professional Organizations Committee*, pp. 221-34.
24. Statistics provided by the College of Physicians and Surgeons of Ontario.
25. A brief review of appeal procedures as they apply to insurance agents licensed under the *Insurance Act*, R.S.O. 1980, c. 218, s. 11, was also undertaken to ensure consistency of treatment with insurance brokers in this respect.

CHAPTER 5

1. Submission to the Task Force by the Ontario Human Rights Commission, May 24, 1988, p. 15.
2. Interview with Sherron Hibbitt, manager, Registrar Services Unit, Ministry of Education, April 7, 1988; and correspondence, August 8, 1989.
3. Interviews with O. Kindiakoff, Administrative Offices, Comparative Education Service, University of Toronto, February 1, 1988; July 28, 1989.
4. Nell P. Eurich, *Corporate Classrooms: The Learning Business* (Lawrenceville, N.J.: Princeton University Press, 1985), p. 8.
5. Kim Lillemor, "Widened Admission to Higher Education in Sweden (the 25/5 scheme)," *European Journal of Education* 14(2) (1979), p. 183.
6. It should also be noted that some postsecondary education faculties waive admission requirements on the basis of individual appeals, reviewed by institutional staff, that are relatively unstructured (there is no provision for a challenge examination and the format is less intensive than portfolio development). Such appeals do not appear to be the instruments of institutional policy or even faculty policy, but seem to be used on a case-by-case basis.
7. Henry Spille, et al., "Assuring High Standards, Quality Control, and Consistency," *New Directions for Experiential Learning*, no. 7 (1980), p. 9.

8. Henry Spille, "Credit for Learning Gained in Military Service of Employment," *New Directions for Experiential Learning*, no. 7 (1980), p. 26.

9. American Council on Education, *Guide to Evaluation of Educational Experiences in the Armed Forces* (Washington, D.C.: 1976).

10. Program on Noncollegiate Sponsored Instruction, *Guide to Educational Programs in Noncollegiate Organizations* (Albany, N.Y.: 1978).

11. Jeanette Baker, "Credit for Prior Learning from a Canadian Perspective" (Toronto: York University Educational Development Office, May 1984).

12. Alan M. Thomas, "Educational Equivalents: New Politics for Learning," unpublished manuscript prepared for the Canadian Association for the Study of Adult Education (Calgary: May 1988).

13. Michele Clarke, associate registrar of Humber College, North Campus, telephone interview, December 15, 1987.

14. General Regulation R.R.O. 1980, Reg. 399, s. 1, as amended under the *Funeral Services Act*, R.S.O. 1980, c. 180.

15. The *Funeral Services Act*, R.S.O. 1980, c. 180, s. 6(2)(b).

16. Recent developments in Australia relating to significant steps being taken in the assessment of prior learning through the Council on Overseas Professional Qualifications came to our attention as well. See National Population Council, *Recognition of Overseas Qualifications and Skills* (Canberra, A.C.T., Australia: December 1988).

17. See for example Michael J. Trebilcock, Gordon Kaiser, and J. Robert S. Prichard, "Interprovincial Restrictions on the Mobility of Resources: Goods, Capital and Labour," in *Intergovernmental Relations: Issues and Alternatives* (Toronto: Ontario Economic Council, 1977), pp. 101-22.

18. See for example *Law Society of Alberta v. Black*, S.C.C. [1989] 1 S.C.R. 591 (S.C.C.).

19. This section draws upon an interview at and correspondence with the State Education Department, University of the State of New York, Office of the Professions, March 17, 1988; and the Office of the Profession's *Annual Report*, 1986-87.

20. Correspondence and documentation from R. Buchanan, director, California Office, International Consultants of Delaware, Inc., April 29, 1988; J. Frey, executive director, Educational Credential Evaluators, Inc., May 26, 1988; and E. Popovych, director of evaluations, World Education Services, Inc., May 16, 1988.

21. Council for Adult and Experiential Learning, *Opportunities for College Credit: A CAEL Guide to Colleges and Universities* (Columbia, Md.: CAEL, 1986).

22. Lois Lamdin, "CLEO: A Regional Consortial Assessment Model," *New Directions for Experiential Learning*, no. 19 (1983), p. 46.

23. Larraine R. Matusak, "What Next?" *New Directions for Experiential Learning*, no. 14 (1981), p. 135.

24. Correspondence from Brent Sargent, director, Office of External Programs, Vermont State Colleges (Waterbury, Vermont), February 25, 1988.

25. Norman Evans, *Assessing Experiential Learning: A Review of Progress and Practice* (London: Longman, 1987), p. 10.

26. *Regulations for Students Registered Centrally with the CAT Scheme* (London: Council for National Academic Awards, 1987), p. 3.

27. Interview with L. Richardson, director, Alberta Legislative Services, October 25, 1988.

28. Interview with L. Henderson, secretary, UCC, and director, Professional Examinations Office, October 24, 1988.

29. Interview with D.J. Corbett, director, Alberta Immigration and Settlement, and G.F. Denhart and A. Smith of Equity Initiatives, Apprenticeship and Certification, October 25, 1988.

30. Interview with D. Gartner, executive director, and D. Charlton, research officer, Professions and Occupations Bureau, October 25, 1988; see also the bureau's "Organization and Mandate," October 24, 1988 (draft).

31. Interview with E. Zinman-Madoff, chef, Division des équivalences, Quebec, January 18-19, 1988; and correspondence, June 13, 1989.

32. Correspondence from E. Egron-Polak, assistant director, International Division, AUCC, May 25, 1988; July 17, 1989.

33. Correspondence and discussions with C. Moss, associate registrar, Open Learning Agency, Richmond, B.C., June 1988.

34. Open Learning Agency, "B.C. Credit Bank Statement of Principles — Assessment of Non-Formal Learning" (Richmond, B.C.: Open Learning Agency, 1988), p. 2.

35. Correspondence and discussion with R. Isabelle, executive director, Technical Assistance Service, Federation of CEGEPs, Montreal.

36. Much of the commentary in this section is based upon interviews with P.J. Hector, assistant secretary, British National Council for the Fédération Européene d'Associations Nationales d'Ingénieurs (FEANI), and with Matthew Cocks, Internal European Policy Division, Department of Trade and Industry, United Kingdom; London, U.K., January 1989.

37. *Single European Act*, February 17, 1986, 29 O.J. Eur. Comm. (no. L 169) 1 (1987).

38. See *The Single Market: Europe Open for Business* (2nd edition), prepared by the Department of Trade and Industry and the Central Office of Information (London: September 1988).

39. Article 52 does not specifically refer to professionals. It states: "Freedom of establishment shall include the right to engage in and carry on non-wage earning activities . . ." This phrase has been interpreted to mean any independent activity aimed at the production of income. See for example *Jean Reyners v. Belgium*, Case 2/74, [1974] E.C.R. 631.

40. See for example *Jean Reyners v. Belgium*, ibid.; *Van Binsbergen v. Besturer Von de Bedrijtsvereniging voor de Metaalnijverheid*, Case 33/74, [1974] E.C.R. 1299.

41. *Brekmeulen v. Huisarts Registratie Commissie*, Case 246/80, [1982] 1 C.M.L.R. 91; see also *Thieffry v. Conseil de l'Ordre des à la Cour de Paris*, Case 71/76, [1974] E.C.R. 767 in which the Court held that the Paris bar must accept a Belgian's law degree as equivalent.

42. See *The Single Market: Europe Open for Business (The Facts)*, p. 42.

43. In *Claude Gullerng v. Conseil de l'Ordre des Avocats du Barreau de Colmar and Conseil de l'Ordre des Avocats du Barreau de Saverne*, Case 292/86, January 19, 1988, the Court of Justice considered Article 52 and held that the establishment of a lawyer in the territory of another member state was conditional upon registration with the law society in the host state where such registration was a statutory requirement for domestic lawyers of that state. The applicant, a member of a bar in the Federal Republic of Germany, was denied admission to the bar of France because he was considered to not fulfil the necessary good character conditions. Thus, in the absence of specific community rules, the Court held that the particular member state remained free in principle to regulate the exercise of the legal profession in its territory.

44. Professionals move only to where their services are in demand. The practical limitation of gaining employment or in establishing a self-employed professional practice in a new country limits the number of professionals who move within the European Community, even for those professions where there now exist specific directives. Fewer than 2,000 of the Community's 600,000 doctors cross borders each year. *The Economist*, June 11, 1988, p. 54.

45. Directive 7533/88.

46. An exception is made in respect of the legal profession, the choice of an aptitude test or a period of supervised practice resting with the host member state rather than with the professional. Thus, the host member state, if it chooses to, will be able to demand that a lawyer trained in another member state undergo a transition period for up to three years under the supervision of a local lawyer. See "Europe's Legal Revolution," Brigid Phillips, in *Canadian Lawyer*, April 1989, p. 26.

47. J.C. Levy, "Europe 1992: Engineers and Engineering," report prepared for the Engineering Council (London: December 1988), p. 5.

48. See the British National Committee for FEANI "Fact Sheet," July 1989.

49. Trans Regional Academic Mobility and Credential Evaluation, "Statement of the Interim Steering Committee" (Washington, D.C.: TRACE, April 1988).

50. Canada, *Canada-U.S. Free Trade Agreement (FTA)*, Article 105 (Ottawa: Supply and Services Canada, 1988).

51. *FTA*, Article 1402.

52. See Murray G. Smith, "Services," in John Crispo, ed., *Free Trade: The Real Story* (Toronto: Gage, 1988), pp. 34-53.

53. *FTA*, Articles 1401 and 1408 and Annex 1408.

54. It seems likely that, for example, bricklayers, chemists, heavy machine operators, industrial designers, interior designers, landscape architects, purchasing managers, secretaries, and wood energy technicians are brought within the enumerated categories of services in Annex 1408. As well, although only the mentioned professions are expressly listed, "professional services" are listed in Annex 1408 as a general category. However, "covered service" is defined in Article 1408 to mean "a service listed in the schedule to Annex 1408 *and described for purposes of reference in that Annex*" (emphasis added).

55. *FTA*, Article 1402.3(a). The conditions set forth in Article 1402.3(b) and (c) must be met before the discriminatory treatment can be justified.

56. *FTA*, Annex 1404, Part A.

57. *FTA*, Annex 1404, Part A, Article 3.

58. Defined in Article 1506 as meaning entry without the intent to establish permanent residence.

59. Note that the category of "business visitors" relates to occupations and professions of those business activities listed in Schedule 1 to Annex 1502.1. One business activity, "General Service," speaks of professionals' generally receiving entry, provided no salary remuneration is being paid within the host jurisdiction.

60. *FTA*, Annex 1502.1(c)6.

CHAPTER 6

1. M.T. Kane, "The Validity of Licensure Examinations," *American Psychologist* 37(8) (1982), pp. 911-18. G.R. Norman, "Defining Competence: A Methodological Review," in V.R. Neufeld and G.R. Norman (editors), *Assessing Clinical Competence* (N.Y.: Springer, 1985), p. 15. B. Shimberg, "Testing for Licensure and Certification," *American Psychologist* 36(10) (1981), pp. 1138-46.

2. American Educational Research Association, American Psychological Association, and National Council on Measurement in Education, *Standards for Educational and Psychological Testing* (Washington, D.C.: American Psychological Association, 1985), p. 75.

3. *Ibid.*, p. 84.

4. B. Preston and J. Conklin, *Physician Quality of Care Methodologies: Review of the Literature* (Washington, D.C.: Systemetrics/McGraw-Hill), 1987. P. Liu, et al., "Videotape Reliability: A Method of Evaluation of a Clinical Performance Examination," *Journal of Medical Education* 55(8) (1980), pp. 713-15.

5. V.R. Neufeld, "Written Examinations," in V.R. Neufeld and G.R. Norman (editors), *Assessing Clinical Competence*, p. 112.

6. L.J. Muzzin and L. Hart, "Oral Examinations," in V.R. Neufeld and G.R. Norman (editors). *Assessing Clinical Competence*, p. 71. V.R. Neufeld, "Written Examinations," p. 102.

7. J.R. Feightner, "Patient Management Problems," in V.R. Neufeld and G.R. Norman (editors), *Assessing Clinical Competence*, p. 183.

8. D.S. Hill, et al., *Oral Examinations for Licensing or Certification: A Manual for Psychology Boards*, American Association of State Psychology Boards, 1986, p. 2.

9. L.J. Muzzin and L. Hart, "Oral Examinations," p. 71.

10. D.S. Hill, et al., *Oral Examinations for Licensing or Certification*, p. 4.

11. B. Shimberg, "Testing for Licensure and Certification," pp. 1138-46.

12. Ronald A. Berk (editor), *Performance Assessment Methods and Applications* (Baltimore: Johns Hopkins University Press, 1986).

13. I.R. Hart, "The 5Ms Approach to Assessing Clinical Competence," in I.R. Hart and R.M. Harden (editors), *International Conference Proceedings: Further Developments in Assessing Clinical Competence* (Montreal: Can-Heal Publications, 1987), p. 114.

14. Meeting with G. Rosen of the Professional Examination Service, March 22, 1988.

15. American Educational Research Association, *Standards for Educational and Psychological Testing*, p. 84.

16. Meeting with Dr. L. MacLean, Ontario Institute for Studies in Education, April 7, 1989.

17. Meeting with H.P. Edwards, American Association of State Psychology Boards, May 30, 1988. Also, Shimberg, "Testing for Licensure and Certification," pp. 1138-46.

18. See for example American Association of State Psychology Boards, "Information for Candidates: Examination for Professional Practice in Psychology," 1988.

19. P. Liu, et al., "Videotape Reliability," p. 713.

20. American Psychological Association, *Standards for Educational and Psychological Testing*. (Standards reprinted, with permission, from *Standards for Educational and Psychological Testing*. Copyright 1985 by the American Psychological Association. Further reproduction without the express written permission of the APA is prohibited.)

21. *Ibid.*

CHAPTER 7

1. For a discussion of language assessment requirements particular to the trades, and relevant recommendations, see Chapter 3, "Issues Facing the Trades."

2. We use the term "standardized test" to refer to a test that is of general application and has been normed over a large population. Tests geared to a particular discipline fall outside this definition.

3. J.A. Cardoza (editor), *ETS Today* (Princeton, N.J.: Educational Testing Service, 1985).

4. *Ibid.*

5. H.F. Dizney, "Concurrent Validity of the Test of English as a Foreign Language for a Group of Foreign Students at an American University," *Educational and Psychological Measurement* 25(4) (1965), pp. 1129-31.

6. W.H. Angoff and A.T. Sharon, "A Comparison of Scores Earned on the Test of English as a Foreign Language by Native American College Students and Foreign Applicants to U.S. Colleges," *TESOL Quarterly* 5(1971), pp. 129-36. J.B. Ayers and R.M. Peters, "Predictive Validity of the Test of English as a Foreign Language for Asian Graduate Students in Engineering, Chemistry, or Mathematics," *Educational and Psychological Measurement* 37(1977), pp. 461-63. D. Hosley, "Performance Differences of Foreign Students on the TOEFL," *TESOL Quarterly* 12(1978), pp. 99-100. D.C. Johnson, "The TOEFL and Domestic Students: Conclusively Inappropriate," *TESOL Quarterly* 11(1977), pp. 79-86.

7. Gordon A. Hale, et al., *Summaries of Studies Involving the Test of English as a Foreign Language, 1963-1982*, TOEFL Research Report no. 16 (1984), ETS.

8. See *Re Registration Hearing* under s. 211 of the *Health Disciplines Act*, X, and the Registration Committee of the College of Nurses of Ontario, January 21, 1988.

9. T.J. Homburg, "TOEFL and GPA: An Analysis of Correlations," Proceedings of the Third International Conference on Frontiers in Language Proficiency and Domestic Testing (1979), pp. 29-35. K-Y Hwang and H.F. Dizney, "Predictive Validity of the Test of English as a Foreign Language for Chinese Graduate Students at an American University," *Educational and Psychological Measurement* 30(1970), pp. 475-77. D.C. Johnson, "The TOEFL and Domestic Students," pp. 79-86.

10. Interview with Barbara Burnaby, Ontario Institute for Studies in Education, March 1989.

11. See M. Wesche, et al., *The Ontario Test of English as a Second Language (OTESL): A Report on the Research* (Toronto: Ontario Ministry of Education, 1987). See also M. Wesche, "Second Language Testing Performance: The Ontario Test of ESL as an Example," *Language Testing* 4(1) (1987), pp. 28-47.

12. M. Wesche, et al., *Ontario Test of English as a Second Language*.

13. *Ibid*.

CHAPTER 8

1. *National Training Act*, R.S.C., 1985, c. N-19.

2. CEIC employment manual (unpublished), para. 23.19.

3. CEIC operational procedures manual (unpublished), para. 8.15(1).

4. *Immigration Act*, R.S.C. 1985, c. I-2. The definitions of the various classes of immigrants are outlined in Chapter 2 of this Report, "Foreign-Trained Individuals in Ontario."

5. Ontario Ministry of Skills Development, *Building a Training System for the 1990s: A Shared Responsibility* (Toronto: Queen's Printer, February 1989).

6. Monica Boyd, "Migrant Women in Canada: Profiles and Policies" (prepared for Immigration Canada and Status of Women, March 1987), p. 29.

7. Citizenship and language instruction agreement (unpublished), para. 5.1.

8. The information on NLOC and on the following four programs or services is from Ontario Ministry of Citizenship, *Annual Report*, 1986-87 (Toronto: Queen's Printer, 1987).

9. Ontario Federation of Labour, "Basic Education for Skills Training (BEST) Project Description" (Toronto: OFL, 1988).

10. See Table 2.1 in Chapter 2, "Foreign-Trained Individuals in Ontario."

11. The information in this section was received from the Quebec Ministry of Cultural Communities and Immigration in a package entitled "L'enseignement du français aux immigrants."
12. Interview with D.J. Corbett, director, Alberta Immigration and Settlement, October 25, 1988.
13. From a summary of federal and provincial language programs prepared by Status of Women Canada, June 1987. Much of the description in this section is based on information from the coordinators of the assessment and referral centres in Edmonton and Calgary.
14. From a speech by Norm Kinsella, representative of the Government of the Province of Alberta, at the Symposium on Adult ESL/FSL, Quebec City, June 13-15, 1988, as quoted in *TESL Canada Policy and Action Newsletter*, p. 7.
15. This section is based largely on the written notes for a speech by D'Arcy Phillips of the Adult and Continuing Education Branch and the Immigration and Settlement Branch of the Manitoba Government; TESL Canada Symposium on Adult ESL, June 1988.
16. *Ibid.*
17. The Task Force reviewed the following reports, and draws upon their findings and conclusions as its source for the criticisms listed in this section:

   a. Association of Teachers of English as a Second Language of Canada (TESL Canada), "The Provision of English as a Second Language Training to Adult Newcomers: Six Principles Toward a National Policy" (position paper prepared by the TESL Canada Action Committee, December 1981).
   b. Association of Teachers of English as a Second Language of Ontario (TESL Ontario), "The Teaching of English as a Second Language in Ontario: Current Issues and Problems" (undated).
   c. Monica Boyd, "Migrant Women in Canada, Profiles and Policies."
   d. Canada Employment and Immigration Commission, "A Discussion Paper on a New Framework for Immigrant Language Training" (Ottawa: Supply and Services Canada, 1983).
   e. Canada Employment and Immigration Commission, Settlement Branch, "Presentation to Standing Committee on Labour, Employment and Immigration" (1988).
   f. Canada, *Report of the Commission on Equality in Employment* (Judge Rosalie S. Abella, Commissioner) (Ottawa: Supply and Services Canada, 1984).
   g. Canadian Human Rights Commission, *Annual Report*, 1986 (Ottawa: Supply and Services Canada).
   h. Alma Estable, "Immigrant Women in Canada — Current Issues" (prepared for the Canadian Advisory Council on the Status of Women, March 1986).
   i. Wenona Giles, "Language Rights are Human Rights" (prepared for Equality in Language and Literacy Training: A Colloquium on Immigrant and Visible Minority Women, November 1987).
   j. National Organization of Immigrant and Visible Minority Women of Canada, "Status Report and Action Plan" (March 1988).
   k. Ontario Ministry of Skills Development, *Building a Training System for the 1990s*.
   l. Settlement Program and Planning Committee, Subcommittee on Language Training, "Consultation Paper on the Delivery of English as a Second Language in Metropolitan Toronto" (Toronto: 1981).

18. Canada, *Report of the Commission on Equality in Employment* (Judge Rosalie S. Abella, Commissioner) (Ottawa: Supply and Services Canada, 1984).

19. Canada, Employment and Immigration Commission Settlement Branch, "Presentation to Standing Committee."
20. Ontario Ministry of Skills Development, *Building a Training System.*

CHAPTER 9

1. P. Hawken, *The Next Economy* (New York: Holt, Rinehart and Winston, 1983).
2. Max Goldens, "Towards Fuller Employment: We Have Been Here Before," *The Economist*, July 28, 1984, pp. 19, 21.
3. Employment and Immigration Canada, *Canadian Jobs Strategy* (Ottawa: Employment and Immigration Canada, 1985), p. 3.
4. This information was provided in a plenary session of the National Retail Merchants Association Fall Conference, New York, September 11, 1986.
5. Nell P. Eurich, *Corporate Classrooms: The Learning Business* (Lawrenceville, N.J.: Princeton University Press, 1985), pp. 7-8.
6. Ontario Ministry of Skills Development, *Breaking New Ground: Ontario's Training Strategy* (Toronto: Queen's Printer, 1986).
7. Labour Market Research Group, *Adjusting to Change: An Overview of Labour Market Issues in Ontario, 1988* (Ontario Ministry of Skills Development, 1988), p. 9.
8. *Ibid.*, pp. 36-37.
9. *Ibid.*, p. 32.
10. *Ibid.*, p. 33.
11. *The Canadian Jobs Strategy: How It Benefits Employers* (Ottawa: Employment and Immigration Canada, 1985), p. 6.
12. Council of Ministers of Education, Canada, *The Financing of Elementary and Secondary Education in Canada* (Toronto: CMEC, 1986), p. 16.
13. Ontario Ministry of Colleges and Universities, *Horizons: A Guide to Postsecondary Education in Ontario, 1988-89* (Toronto: Queen's Printer, 1989).
14. Discussions with: H. Zimmer (April 20, 1988) and S. Holloway (April 25, 1988), George Brown College, Toronto; and O. Moran and B. Steadman-Smith (April 26, 1988), Durham College, Oshawa.
15. W.M. Brooke and J.F. Morris, *Continuing Education in Canadian Universities: A Summary Report of Policies and Practices — 1985* (Ottawa: Canadian Association for University Continuing Education, 1987), p. 15.
16. *Ibid.*, p. 25. Information is based on Canada-wide responses to a survey; Ontario-specific information was not treated separately.
17. Ryerson Polytechnic Institute, "Action Access Transitional Education Pilot Program in Human Services," unpublished proposal, December, 1988, p. 10.
18. From notes taken during a meeting with A. Quaile and A. Thornton, Protect Apprenticeship Training and Quality, Ontario Public Service Employees Union Office, April 26, 1988.
19. Interview with Diane Schatz, director, Toronto Institute of Medical Technology, January 5, 1988.
20. Manitoba Employment Services and Economic Security, *Recognition: Manitoba Work Experience for Professional and Technically Trained Newcomers* (Winnipeg: no date).
21. This framework was used in P.K. Cross, *Adults as Learners* (San Francisco: Jossey Bass, 1981); Advisory Council for Adult and Continuing Education, *Continuing Education: From Policies to Practice* (Leicester, England: ACACE, 1982); and Continuing Education Review Project, *Project Report: For Adults Only* (Toronto: Ontario Ministry of Colleges and Universities, 1986).

22. Meetings with: J. Scott, education officer, Ontario Ministry of Education (May 31, 1988); H. Zimmer, program head, Women in Trades and Technologies, George Brown College, Toronto (April 20, 1988); and J. Gray, program manager, Centre for Advancement in Work and Living, Toronto (May 5, 1988).
23. Submission to the Task Force by the Workers' Educational Association of Canada, Toronto, March 30, 1988.
24. Meeting with S. Holloway, dean of technology, George Brown College (April 25, 1988).
25. *Ibid.*
26. Meeting with J. Scott.
27. Submission to the Task Force by W.R. McCutcheon, president, Seneca College of Applied Arts and Technology, February 15, 1988.
28. Attachment to submission to the Task Force by the Rexdale Women's Centre, May 9, 1988.
29. Ontario Ministry of Colleges and Universities, *Horizons.*

CHAPTER 10

1. Note for example the Task Force on the Use and Provision of Medical Services; the Pharmaceutical Inquiry of Ontario; and the Premier's Council on Health Strategy.
2. Note for example *Physician Manpower in Canada, 1980-2000: A Report of the Federal/Provincial Advisory Committee on Health Manpower*, October 1984.
3. *Health Disciplines Act*, R.S.O. 1980, c. 196, as amended.
4. For a discussion of mechanisms for review of registration decisions in general and in professions governed by the *Health Disciplines Act* in particular, see Chapter 11, "Review of Registration Decisions."
5. O. Reg. 448, s.16(1).
6. From the pamphlet on requirements for entry to the profession, prepared by the Ontario College of Physicians and Surgeons: "Requirements of Licensure for Graduates of Accredited Medical Schools" (p. 21).
7. O. Reg 448, s.16(1).
8. O. Reg 448, s.16(2).
9. O. Reg 448, s.14(1)(b).
10. For a detailed discussion of issues relating to fluency testing, see Chapter 7, "Language Testing."
11. Interviews with foreign-trained physicians who submitted briefs to the Task Force.
12. O. Reg. 448, s. 17(1)(b)(iii)A.
13. Meeting with members of PAIRO (Professional Association of Interns and Residents of Ontario), June 21, 1988.
14. Statistics provided by the College of Physicians and Surgeons of Ontario.
15. Task Force meeting with representatives of PAIRO. Evidence, *Jamorski et al. and The Attorney General for the Province of Ontario* (1988), 64 O.R. (2d) 161 (C.A.). This case challenged the constitutionality of the introduction of the PIP under section 15 of the *Canadian Charter of Rights and Freedoms*; for a discussion of the case, see Chapter 13, "Application of the Canadian Charter of Rights and Freedoms."
16. We have been advised that physicians admitted to the PIP thus far have performed generally on a par with Canadian students and in some cases were much more advanced. (Correspondence, Dr. J. R. Ross, Ontario Pre-Internship Program, December 12, 1988.)

17. This summary is an amalgam of many sources, among them: representatives of the Ministry of Health and academic consultants, including those whose views were presented in the case of *Jamorski et al. and The Attorney General for the Province of Ontario* (1988). Reference has also been made to the numerous magazine and newspaper articles that have focused on this issue. See for example: Orland French, "How Many MDs Do We Need?" *Globe and Mail* (November 5, 1988), p. D5; Caroline Gray, "North in Dire Need of Psychiatrists," *Ontario Medicine* (June 19, 1989), p. 5; and Elaine Carey and Marilyn Dunlop, "Our Ailing Health Care System Needs Cure," *Toronto Star* (March 27, 1988), p. A1.

18. Evidence, *Jamorski et al. and The Attorney General for the Province of Ontario* (1988).

19. *Health Disciplines Act*, R.S.O. 1980, c. 196, as amended.

CHAPTER 11

1. This is in accordance with the philosophy of the Royal Commission Inquiry into Civil Rights. *Report of the Royal Commission Inquiry into Civil Rights* (the McRuer Report) (Toronto: Queen's Printer, 1968), Vol. 3, pp. 1162-63.

2. *Statutory Powers Procedure Act*, R.S.O. 1980, c. 484.

3. *Judicial Review Procedure Act*, R.S.O. 1980, c. 224, as amended.

4. See for example *Re Hughes Boat Works Inc. and International Union, United Automobile, Aerospace, Agricultural and Implement Workers of America (UAW) Local 1620 et al.* (1979), 26 O.R. (2d) 420 at 428 (Div. Ct.).

5. *JRPA*, s. 2(1), but see *Re Woodglen & Co. Ltd. and City of North York, et al.* (1983), 42 O.R. (2d) 385 (Div. Ct.).

6. The Courts have had difficulty interpreting s. 2(1). Declarations and injunctions are available only in relation to the exercise of a statutory power (or the refusal to exercise it). Although there is no explicit reference to "statutory power" in the *JRPA* with respect to the remedies of *certiorari* or *mandamus*, it is not clear from the case law whether the Court will take jurisdiction over a matter absent the exercise of a statutory power (or the refusal to exercise it). This ambiguity becomes relevant for our purposes because those professions that are not established by and do not act pursuant to legislation do not exercise a statutory power. The Courts may therefore refuse to take jurisdiction over registration matters of these groups.

7. In some cases, the Courts have applied the doctrine of fairness to expectancy interests such as licensure. See for example *T.E. Quinn Truck Lines Limited v. Snow*, [1981] 2 S.C.R. 657; *Re Collins et al. and Pension Commission of Ontario et al.* (1986), 56 O.R. (2d) 274 at 289 (Div. Ct.).

8. *SPPA*, R.S.O. 1980, c. 484.

9. *Ibid.*, ss. 6(1), 10, 17.

10. *Health Disciplines Act*, R.S.O. 1980, c. 196, as amended.

11. *Denture Therapists Act*, R.S.O. 1980, c. 115, s. 7(1); *Funeral Services Act*, R.S.O. 1980, c. 180, ss. 2(2)(b), 9(1).

12. *Health Disciplines Act*, ss. 32(2)(3)(4), 56(2)(3)(4), 79(2)(3)(5), 101(2)(3)(4), 125(2)(3)(4).

13. *Professional Engineers Act, 1984*, S.O. 1984, c. 13.

14. *Architects Act, 1984*, S.O. 1984, c. 12, as amended.

15. *Surveyors Act, 1987*, S.O. 1987, c. 6.

16. *Denture Therapists Act*, R.S.O. 1980, c. 115.

17. *Funeral Services Act*, R.S.O. 1980, c. 180, as amended.

18. *Registered Insurance Brokers Act*, R.S.O. 1980, c. 444.

19. *Health Disciplines Act*, s. 11.

20. *Ibid.*, ss. 11(6) and 12(2).
21. *Ibid.*, ss. 11(6), 12(5).
22. *Ibid.*, ss. 11(6), 12(7).
23. *Ibid.*, ss. 11(6), 12(4).
24. See for example the requirement for public hearings under the *SPPA* but, conversely, the requirement for *in camera* hearings under the *Health Disciplines Act.*
25. *Ministry of Consumer and Commercial Relations Act*, R.S.O. 1980, c. 274, as amended.
26. *Real Estate and Business Brokers Act*, R.S.O. 1980, c. 431.
27. *Ibid.*, s. 9(1)(2).
28. *Ministry of Consumer and Commercial Relations Act*, s. 10(3)(b).
29. *Ibid.*, s. 10(4).
30. *Registered Insurance Brokers Act*, R.S.O. 1980, c. 444, ss. 13(1)(2), 14(1)(3)(7).
31. ICAO bylaw 53.
32. ICAO bylaws 57, 87, 88, 90.
33. The *Surveyors Act, 1987,* provides for a similar scheme. The registrar may refer applications to the ARC or the ERC, whose determination is "final and binding on the Registrar and on the applicant." The ARC/ERC is not required to provide the applicant with an oral hearing (section 12(5) (6)). The legislation, however, allows an applicant denied a licence to request a hearing before the registration committee, except those applicants denied a licence because of previous revocations by the discipline committee (section 17(2)). No explicit exemption is made for decisions of ARC or ERC as provided for in the legislation for architects and engineers. The legislation in our view is equivocal as to whether the phrase final and binding on the applicant in section 12(5) precludes review by the registration committee.
34. *Professional Engineers Act, 1984,* s. 19(11); *Architects Act, 1984,* s. 25(12); *Surveyors Act, 1987,* s. 17(15).
35. *Ibid.*, s. 19(12)(14).
36. See for example in the disciplinary context the decisions of *Re Reddall and the College of Nurses of Ontario* (1983), 42 O.R. (2d) 412 (Ont. C.A.) and *Re Del Core and Ontario College of Pharmacists* (1985), 51 O.R. (2d) 1 (Ont. C.A.).
37. The Report of the Health Professions Legislation Review has recommended minor changes to the current appeal provisions to clarify the nature and extent of the powers of the Court under the *Health Disciplines Act.* The intention of the proposed amendments is to give the Divisional Court the powers of both the committee and the board. *Striking a New Balance: A Blueprint for the Regulation of Ontario's Health Professions* (Toronto: Queen's Printer, 1989).
38. *Health Disciplines Act,* s. 13(2).
39. *Ministry of Consumer and Commercial Relations Act,* s. 11(1)(2)(5) and *Registered Insurance Brokers Act,* s. 21(1)(2).
40. *Professional Engineers Act, 1984,* s. 19(2)(3); *Architects Act,* s. 25(2)(3); *Surveyors Act, 1987,* s. 17(2)(4).
41. *Psychologists Registration Act*, R.S.O. 1980, c. 404, as amended.
42. *Ibid.*, ss. 2(1), 5, 7, 8.
43. *Licences of Insurance Agents*, R.R.O. 1980, O. Reg. 528, s. 4(1).
44. *Insurance Act*, R.S.O. 1980, c. 218, s. 11.
45. *Public Accountancy Act*, R.S.O. 1980, c. 405, s. 21.
46. *Society of Management Accountants of Ontario Act*, 1941, as amended, s. 11a(3).
47. *Certified General Accountants Association of Ontario Act*, S.O. 1983 c. Pr6, s. 8(4).

CHAPTER 12

1. S.O. 1981, c. 53, as amended 1984, c. 58, s. 39; and 1986, c. 64, s. 18.
2. *Code*, s. 26(1).
3. *Ibid.*, s. 28(a).
4. See Ontario Human Rights Commission, *Annual Report* 1986-87, p. 3.
5. *Ibid.*, p. 9.
6. *Ibid.*
7. *Ibid.*, pp. 10-11.
8. S.O. 1986, c. 64, s. 18.
9. The protected subject areas have some variation in respect of the prohibited grounds applicable to each. For example, harassment in accommodation or employment is unlawful in respect of 12 prohibited grounds. However, harassment in accommodation does not include "record of offences" as a prohibited ground, whereas harassment in employment does not include "the receipt of public assistance" as a prohibited ground.
10. *Constitution Act, 1982*, ss. 1-34, en. by the *Canada Act, 1982* (U.K.), c. 11, Sched. B.
11. S.C. 1976-77, c. 33, as amended.
12. *Code*, s. 46.
13. *Ibid.*, s. 31(1).
14. *Ibid.*, s. 31(2).
15. *Ibid.*, ss. 32,33.
16. OHRC, "Human Rights in Employment," May 1977, para. 10.
17. *Ibid.*
18. *Code*, s. 38.
19. *Ibid.*, s. 36.
20. *Ibid.*, s. 37.
21. "Human Rights in Employment," para. 10; *Code*, s. 40.
22. *Code*, s. 41.
23. S.B.C. 1984, c. 22.
24. (1983) 4 C.H.R.R. D/1432.
25. *Ibid.*, paras. 12330-31.
26. *Ishar Singh v. Security and Investigation Services Ltd.*, May 31, 1977 (Ontario Board of Inquiry), unreported; and *Re Ontario Human Rights Commission et al. and Simpsons-Sears Ltd.*, [1985] 2 S.C.R. 536, 23 D.L.R. (4th) 321, at 326, 332 (S.C.C.).
27. Even where the occupational requirement itself is seen to be unreasonable, as discussed above, it may be difficult to find that discrimination occurred because of a prohibited ground. A recent decision, *Victor Romano v. Board of Education for the City of North York and G.L. Zumpano* (1987), 8 C.H.R.R. D/4347 (Ontario Board of Inquiry), appeal dismissed, Divisional Court, November 24, 1988, is illustrative. The complainant, an Italian-Canadian, applied for a job as a schoolbus driver. He was refused on the grounds that his proficiency in English was not good enough. The Commission argued that the requirement for English proficiency was not a *bona fide* occupational requirement for the position of bus driver and had a discriminatory impact on a person of Italian origin; it therefore constituted a violation of s. 10 of the *Code*. The board found that while the requirement for English proficiency was unreasonable and not demonstrably related to the requirements for being a schoolbus driver, the Commission had not proven that this requirement had a discriminatory impact on a group defined by their ethnicity. The requirement also had an adverse impact on persons born in Canada who are functionally illiterate, and therefore no discrimination as prohibited by the *Code* was found to have occurred (at paras. 34100-12).

28. *Code*, s. 10(2).
29. Submission to the Task Force by the Ontario Human Rights Commission, May 24, 1988, p. 14.
30. OHRC, *Annual Report* 1987-88, p. 7.
31. *Code*, s. 10(2).
32. *Ibid.*
33. See *Cindy Cameron v. Nel-Gor Castle Nursing Home et al.* (1984), 5 C.H.R.R., D/2170, at paras. 18371-87; appeal dismissed, Divisional Court, September 1985; leave to appeal to Court of Appeal denied, November 1985; and *Re Ontario Human Rights Commission et al. and Simpsons-Sears Ltd., supra* note 26, at pp. 334-39 (S.C.C. per McIntyre, J.).
34. Submission by Ontario Human Rights Commission, pp. 16-17.
35. *Ibid.*, pp. 17-18.
36. See for example the *Victor Romano* case, *supra* note 27.
37. The defence seen in s. 23(1)(b) of the *Code* would be extended to the new prohibited ground of "place of training or education."
38. S. 23(2) of the *Code* would apply, as at present, to a defence asserted under s. 23(1)(b).
39. *Code*, s. 40(1)(b).
40. *Ibid.*, s. 40(1)(a).

CHAPTER 13

1. [1987] 3 W.W.R. 577, at 618 (S.C.C.).
2. *Constitution Act, 1982*, ss. 1-34 en. by the *Canada Act, 1982* (U.K.), c. 11, Sched. B.
3. *Andrews v. Law Society of British Columbia*, [1989] 1 S.C.R. 143 (S.C.C.).
4. *Ibid.*, at 174.
5. [1986] 2 S.C.R. 573.
6. (1986), 54 O.R. (2d) 513 (C.A.).
7. Notably, Justine Blainey was not without a remedy. The Court acknowledged that s. 19(2) of the *Ontario Human Rights Code*, which excepted gender discrimination in respect of membership in an athletic organization or participation in an athletic activity, was in itself discriminatory and in contravention of s. 15 of the *Charter*. The Court struck down the offending section, rendering the remaining provisions operative to afford Blainey her remedy.
8. The Supreme Court has granted leave to appeal the following decisions: *Harrison v. University of British Columbia*, [1988] 2 W.W.R. 688 (B.C.C.A.); *Stoffman v. Vancouver General Hospital*, [1988] 2 W.W.R. 708 (B.C.C.A.); *Douglas/Kwantlen Faculty Association v. Douglas College*, [1988] 2 W.W.R. 718 (B.C.C.A.); and *Re McKinney and Board of Governors of Guelph* (1986), 57 O.R. (2d) 1 (H.C.) affd. (1987), 63 O.R. (2d) 1 (C.A.).
9. See *Harrison v. UBC, supra* note 8, at 694; *Stoffman v. Vancouver General Hospital, supra* note 8, at 711; and *Douglas/Kwantlen Faculty Association v. Douglas College, supra* note 8, at 722.
10. See *Harrison v. UBC, supra* note 8.
11. *Supra* note 8.
12. *Ibid.*, at 14.
13. See for example *Re Ontario English Catholic Teachers Association and Essex County Roman Catholic School Board* (1987), 58 O.R. (2d) 545 (Div. Ct.); *Re Lavigne and Ontario Public Service Employees Union* (1989), 69 O.R. (2d) 536 (Ont. C.A.), leave to appeal to the Supreme Court of Canada granted June 8, 1989; and *Re Klein and the Law Society of Upper Canada* (1985), 16 D.L.R. (4th) 489 (Ont. Div. Ct.).

14. *Re Klein, supra* note 13.
15. *Law Society Act*, R.S.O. 1980, c. 233, as amended.
16. *Supra* note 13, at 528-29.
17. *Re Lavigne, supra* note 13.
18. *Re McKinney, supra* note 8, at 23-24.
19. *Colleges Collective Bargaining Act*, R.S.O. 1980, c. 74.
20. *Re Lavigne, supra* note 13, at 552 and 556-57.
21. See *Re Ontario English Catholic Teachers Association and Essex County Roman Catholic School Board, supra* note 13.
22. *Re Tomen et al. and Federation of Women Teachers' Association of Ontario et al.* (1987), 61 O.R. (2d) 489 at 506 (H.C.).
23. *Health Disciplines Act*, R.S.O. 1980, c. 196.
24. *Architects Act, 1984*, S.O. 1984, c. 12.
25. *Professional Engineers Act, 1984*, S.O. 1984, c. 13
26. *Surveyors Act, 1987*, S.O. 1987, c. 6.
27. See for example the *Insurance Act* and the reserved-title professions included under the *Drugless Practitioners Act*.
28. *Statutory Powers Procedure Act*, R.S.O. 1980, c. 484.
29. See P. Hogg, *Constitutional Law of Canada* (2d ed.) (Toronto: Carswell, 1985), p. 671.
30. *Supra* note 8.
31. See for example *Attorney General Quebec v. Quebec Association of Protestant School Boards et al.*, [1984] 2 S.C.R. 66.
32. *Mills v. The Queen*, [1986] S.C.R. 863.
33. *R. v. Morgentaler et al.* (1984), 41 C.R. (3d) 262 at 272.
34. See for example *Law v. Solicitor General of Canada* (1984), 57 N.R. 45 at 47-48 (Immigration Appeal Board); *Moore v. B.C. Government*, [1988] 3 W.W.R. 289 at 298-300 (Labour Arbitration Board); and *Cuddy Chicks Ltd. v. Ontario Labour Relations Board and United Food and Commercial Workers International Union* (1988), 66 O.R. (2d) 284 at 289 (Div. Ct).
35. *Douglas College, supra* note 8, at 726.
36. *Re Klein, supra* note 13, at 528.
37. See for example *Francen v. City of Winnipeg*, [1986] 4 W.W.R. 193 (Man. C.A.).
38. See for example *Dent v. West Virginia* 129 U.S. 114 (1889).
39. Supra note 1.
40. *Ibid.*, at 618.
41. S.C.C. April 20, 1989 (unreported).
42. *Ibid.*, at 26.
43. *R. v. Wigglesworth*, [1987] 2 S.C.R. 541.
44. *Ibid.*, at 560-62.
45. *R. v. Morgentaler*, [1988] 1 S.C.R. 30.
46. *Ibid.*, at 166.
47. *R. v. Robson* (1985), 45 C.R. (3d) 68.
48. See also *Hundal v. Superintendent of Motor Vehicles* (1985), 64 B.C.L.R. 273.
49. *R. v. Neale* (1986), 46 Alta. L. R. (2d) 225, at 232.
50. *Branigan v. Yukon Medical Council* (1986), 1 B.C.L.R. (2d) 350 (Y.T.S.C.).
51. *Ibid.*, at 360-61.
52. *Re Feldman and the Law Society of Upper Canada*, Ont. Div. Ct. December 9, 1987 (unreported).
53. *Medical Services Act*, R.S.B.C. 1979, c. 255.
54. *Wilson et al. v. The Medical Services Commission of British Columbia* (1988), 30 B.C.L.R. (2d) 1 (C.A.). Leave to appeal to the S.C.C. denied November 3, 1988.
55. N.S.C.A., March 22, 1989 (unreported).
56. *Ibid.*, at 26.

57. See for example *Francen v. City of Winnipeg, supra* note 37; *Gershman Produce Company v. Motor Transport Board* (1986), 17 C.R.R. 132; *Re Abbotsford Taxi* (1986), 23 D.L.R.(4th) 365; and *The Queen v. Miles of Music Ltd. and Roch*, Ontario Court of Appeal, March 16, 1989, at p. 15 (unreported).
58. *Francen v. City of Winnipeg, ibid.*, at 203.
59. *Gershman Produce Co, v. Motor Transport Board, supra* note 57.
60. [1985] 2 S.C.R. 486.
61. *Ibid.*, at 494.
62. [1985] 1 S.C.R. 177.
63. *Ibid.*, at 213-14.
64. S.Y.T. 1979 (2d), c. 12.
65. *Branigan v. Yukon Medical Council, supra* note 50, at 362.
66. *Wilson v. The Medical Services Commission of British Columbia, supra* note 54, at 34-35.
67. *Ibid.*, at 36.
68. *Re Khaliq-Kareemi, supra* note 55, at 26-42.
69. *Dent v. West Virginia, supra* note 38, at 122.
70. 413 U.S. 717 (1973).
71. *Foley v. Connelie*, 435 U.S. 291 (1978).
72. *Ambach v. Norwick*, 441 U.S. 68 (1979).
73. *Law Students Civil Rights Research Council v. Wamond*, 401 U.S. 154 (1971).
74. *Konigsberg v. State Bar of California*, 353 U.S. 252 (1957).
75. *Schware v. Board of Bar Examiners of New Mexico*, 353 U.S. 232. (1957).
76. See for example "Criminal Record as Affecting Applicant's Moral Character for Purposes of Admission to the Bar," 88 A.L.R.3d.
77. See "Validity, Construction and Application of Enactment, Implementation, or Repeal of Formal Educational Requirements for Admission to the Bar," 44 A.L.R.4th 910.
78. See for example: *Application of Urie*, 617 P.2d 505 (1980); *Re Application of Hansen*, 275 N.W.2d 790 (1978); *Lombardi v. Tauro*, 470 F.2d 798 (1972 1st Cir.); *Graves v. Minnesota*, 272 U.S. 425 (1926); *Hacklin v. Lockwood*, 361 F.2d 499 app. dism. 389 U.S. 143 (1967).
79. See for example: *Draganosky v. Minnesota Board of Psychology*, 367 N.W.2d 521 (1985); *Szabo v. Board of Osteopathic Examiners*, 181 Cal. Rptr. 473 (1982); *Mann v. Board of Medical Examiners*, 187 P.2d 1 (1947); *Lay v. State Board of Osteopathic Examiners*, 3 Cal. Rptr. 727 (1960); and *Savelli v. Board of Medical Examiners*, 40 Cal. Rptr. 171 (1964).
80. *Application of Anderson*, 377 So.2d 1185 (1980).
81. See also *Application of Faylona*, 381 So.2d 1203 (1980) wherein a Philippine applicant was also granted an exemption.
82. 433 So.2d 969 (1983).
83. *Re Application of Adams*, 700 P.2d 194 (1985).
84. *Pascual v. State Board of Law*, 435 N.Y.S.2d 387 (1981).
85. See also *Sodha v. New York State Board of Law Examiners*, 431 N.Y.S.2d 885 (1980).
86. *Andrews v. Law Society of British Columbia, supra* note 3, at 156.
87. *Law Society Amendment Act, 1989*, S.O. 1989, c. 14.
88. *Re Jamorski et al. and The Attorney General for the Province of Ontario* (1988), 64 O.R. (2d) 161 (C.A.).
89. *Ibid.*, at 167.
90. *Ibid.*, at 168.
91. *Supra* note 3, at 168.
92. *R. v. Oakes*, [1986] 1 S.C.R. 103; *Edwards Books & Arts Ltd. et al. v. The Queen*, [1986] 2 S.C.R. 713.

93. *Andrews v. Law Society of B.C.*, supra note 3, at 153-57.
94. *Reference re s. 94(2) supra* note 60, at 518.
95. *Branigan v. Yukon Medical Council, supra* note 50, at 363-64.

Selected Bibliography

Advisory Council of Adult and Continuing Education. *Continuing Education: From Policies to Practice.* Leicester, England: ACACE, 1982.

American Association of State Psychology Boards. "Information for Candidates: Examination for Professional Practice in Psychology." Montgomery, Al.: the Association, 1988.

American Council on Education. *Guide to Evaluation of Educational Experiences in the Armed Forces.* Washington, D.C.: the Council, 1976.

American Educational Research Association, American Psychological Association, and National Council on Measurement in Education. *Standards for Educational and Psychological Testing.* Washington, D.C.: American Psychological Association, 1985.

Association of Teachers of English as a Second Language of Canada. "The Provision of English as a Second Language Training to Adult Newcomers: Six Principles Toward a National Policy." Position paper. Toronto: TESL Canada Action Committee, December 1981.

Association of Teachers of English as a Second Language of Ontario. "The Teaching of English as a Second Language in Ontario: Current Issues and Problems." Toronto: TESL Ontario, undated.

Augoff, W.H., and A.T. Sharon. "A Comparison of Scores Earned on the Test of English as a Second Language by Native American College Students and Foreign Applicants to U.S. Colleges. *TESOL Quarterly* 5 (1971): 129-36.

Australia. National Population Council. *Recognition of Overseas Qualifications and Skills.* Canberra, A.C.T., Australia: the Council, December 1988.

Ayers, J.B., and R.M. Peters. "Predictive Validity of the Test of English as a Foreign Language for Asian Graduate Students in Engineering, Chemistry, or Mathematics." *Educational and Psychological Measurement* 37 (1977): 461-63.

Baker, Jeanette. "Credit for Prior Learning from a Canadian Perspective." Toronto: York University Educational Development Office, May 1984.

Berk, Ronald A., editor. *Performance Assessment Methods and Applications.* Baltimore: Johns Hopkins University Press, 1986.

Boyd, Monica. "Migrant Women in Canada: Profiles and Policies." Paper prepared for Employment and Immigration Canada and Status of Women Canada. Ottawa: March 1987.

British National Committee for FEAN. "Fact Sheet." London: the Committee, July 1989.

Brooke, W.N., and J.F. Morris. *Continuing Education in Canadian Universities: A Summary Report of Policies and Practices — 1985.* Ottawa: Canadian Association for University Continuing Education, 1987.

Burnet, Jean. "Living in a Multicultural Society." Draft paper prepared for "The Refugee Crisis: British and Canadian Responses" (international symposium). Oxford: Oxford University, January 1989.

Canada. Employment and Immigration Canada. *Annual Report*, 1987-88. Ottawa: 1988.

———. Employment and Immigration Canada. *Canadian Jobs Strategy*. Ottawa: Employment and Immigration Canada, 1985.

———. Employment and Immigration Canada. *Job Entry: Cooperative Education Guide to Applicants*. Ottawa: Supply and Services Canada, 1985.

———. Employment and Immigration Canada. *The Ellis Chart of Apprenticeship Training Programs*. Ottawa: Interprovincial Standards Program Co-ordinating Committee, 1985.

———. Employment and Immigration Commission. "A Discussion Paper on a New Framework for Immigrant Language Training." Ottawa: the Commission, 1983.

———. Employment and Immigration Commission, Settlement Branch. "Presentation to Standing Committee on Labour, Employment and Immigration." Ottawa: the Commission, 1988.

———. *Equality and Employment: Report of the Commission on Equality in Employment*. Ottawa: Supply and Services Canada, 1984.

———. Health and Welfare Canada (prepared by Roderic Beaujot). *The Relative Economic Situations of Immigrants in Canada*. Ottawa: October 1986.

———. *Report of the Royal Commission on the Economic Union and Development Prospects of Canada*, Vol. 2. Ottawa: Supply and Services Canada, 1985.

———. *The Canada-U.S. Free Trade Agreement*. Ottawa: Supply and Services Canada, 1988.

Canadian Human Rights Commission. *Annual Report*, 1986. Ottawa: Supply and Services Canada.

Cardoza, J.A., editor. *ETS Today*. Princeton, N.J.: Educational Testing Service, 1985.

Carey, Elaine, and Marilyn Dunlop. "Our Ailing Health Care System Needs Cure." *Toronto Star*, March 27, 1988, A1.

College of Physicians and Surgeons of Ontario. *Practice of Medicine in Ontario*. Pamphlet. Toronto: the College, undated.

Council for Adult and Experiential Learning. *Opportunities for College Credits: A CAEL Guide to Colleges and Universities*. Columbia, Md.: CAEL, 1986.

Council for National Academic Awards. *Regulations for Students Registered Centrally with the CAT Scheme*. London: the Council, 1987.

Council of Ministers of Education, Canada. *The Financing of Elementary and Secondary Education in Canada*. Toronto: the Council, 1986.

Cross, P.K. *Adults as Learners.* San Francisco: Josey Bass, 1981.

Dizney, H.F. "Concurrent Validity of the Test of English as a Foreign Language for a Group of Foreign Students at an American University." *Educational and Psychological Measurement* 25:4 (1965): 1129-31.

Estable, Alma. "Immigrant Women in Canada — Current Issues." Paper prepared for the Canadian Advisory Council on the Status of Women. Ottawa: March 1986.

Eurich, Nell P. *Corporate Classrooms: The Learning Business.* Lawrenceville, N.J.: Princeton University Press, 1985.

Evans, Norman. *Assessing Experiential Learning: A Review of Progress and Practice.* London: Longman, 1987.

Federal/Provincial Advisory Committee on Health Manpower. *Physician Manpower in Canada, 1980-2000: A Report of the Federal/Provincial Advisory Committee on Health Manpower.* October 1984.

Feightner, J.R. "Patient Management Problems." In *Assessing Clinical Competence,* edited by V.R. Neufeld and G.R. Norman. New York: Springer, 1985.

French, Orland. "How Many MDs Do We Need?" *The Globe and Mail,* November 5, 1988, D5.

Giles, Wenona. "Language Rights and Human Rights." Paper prepared for Equality in Language and Literacy Training: A Colloquium on Immigrant and Visible Minority Women. November 1987.

Goldens, Max. "Towards Fuller Employment: We Have Been Here Before." *The Economist,* July 28, 1984, 19, 21.

Gray, Caroline. "North in Dire Need of Psychiatrists." *Ontario Medicine,* June 19, 1989, 5.

Hale, Gordon A., et al. *Summaries of Studies Involving the Test of English as a Foreign Language, 1963-1982.* TOEFL Research Report no. 16. Princeton, N.J.: Educational Testing Service, 1984.

Hart, I.R. "The 5Ms Approach to Assessing Clinical Competence." In International Conference Proceedings: Further Developments in Assessing Clinical Competence, edited by I.R. Hart and R.M. Harden. Montreal: Can-Heal Publications, 1987.

Hawken, P. *The Next Economy.* New York: Holt, Rinehart and Winston, 1983.

Homburg, T.J. "TOEFL and GPA: An Analysis of Correlations." Proceedings of the Third International Conference on Frontiers in Language Proficiency and Domestic Testing (1979).

Hosley, D. "Performance Differences of Foreign Students on the TOEFL." *TESOL Quarterly* 12 (1978): 99-100.

Hwang, K-Y, and H.F. Dizney. "Predictive Validity of the Test of English as a Foreign Language for Chinese Graduate Students at an American University." *Educational and Psychological Measurement* 30 (1970): 475-77.

Johnson, D.C. "The TOEFL and Domestic Students: Conclusively Inappropriate." *TESOL Quarterly* 11 (1970): 79-86.

Kalbach, Warren E. "Guess Who's Coming to Canada Now." *TESL Talk* 10(3) (Summer 1979): 17.

Kane, M.T. "The Validity of Licensure Examinations." *American Psychologist* 37(8) (1982): 911-18.

Labour Market Research Group. *Adjusting to Change: An Overview of Labour Market Issues in Ontario, 1988.* Toronto: Ontario Ministry of Skills Development, 1988.

Lamdin, Lois. "CLEO: A Regional Consortial Assessment Model." *New Directions for Experiential Learning* 14 (1981): 135.

Levy, J.C. "Europe 1992: Engineers and Engineering." Report prepared for the Engineering Council. London: December 1988.

Lillemor, Kim. "Widened Admission to Higher Education in Sweden (the 25/5 scheme)." *European Journal of Education* 14:2 (1979): 1983.

Liu, P., et al. "Videotape Reliability: A Method of Evaluation of a Clinical Performance Examination." *Journal of Medical Education* 1980 55(8): 713-15.

Manitoba Employment Services and Economic Security. *Recognition: Manitoba Work Experience for Professional and Technically Trained Newcomers.* Winnipeg: undated.

Matusak, Larraine, R. "What Next?" *New Directions for Experiential Learning* 19 (1983): 46.

Muzzin, L.J., and L. Hart. "Oral Examinations." In *Assessing Clinical Competence,* edited by V.R. Neufeld and G.R. Norman. New York: Springer, 1985.

National Organization of Immigrant and Visible Minority Women of Canada. "Status Report and Action Plan." March 1988.

Neufeld, V.R. "Written Examinations." In *Assessing Clinical Competence,* edited by V.R. Neufeld and G.R. Norman. New York: Springer, 1985.

Neufeld, V.R., and G.R. Norman, editors. *Assessing Clinical Competence.* New York: Springer, 1985.

Norman, G.R. "Defining Competence: A Methodological Review." In *Assessing Clinical Competence,* edited by V.R. Neufeld and G.R. Norman. New York: Springer, 1985.

Ontario. *Competing in the New Global Economy* (Report of the Premier's Council, Vol. 1). Toronto: Queen's Printer, 1988.

————. Health Professions Legislation Review. *Striking a New Balance: A Blueprint for the Regulation of Ontario's Health Professions.* Toronto: 1989.

————. Ministry of Citizenship. *Annual Report,* 1986-87. Toronto: Queen's Printer, 1987.

─────. Ministry of Citizenship. "Ethnocultural Data Base Materials, Immigration Statistics" (1985, 1986). Toronto: the Ministry, 1987, 1988.

─────. Ministry of Citizenship. *New Directions* (Winter 1989).

─────. Ministry of Colleges and Universities. *Apprenticeship Programs in Ontario: Regulated and Non-Regulated Administration Methods and Selection Criteria.* Toronto: Queen's Printer, 1983.

─────. Ministry of Colleges and Universities. *Horizons: A Guide to Postsecondary Education in Ontario, 1988-89.* Toronto: Queen's Printer, 1989.

─────. Ministry of Colleges and Universities. *Training for Ontario's Future* (Report of the Task Force on Industrial Training). Toronto: 1973.

─────. Ministry of Labour, Manpower Commission. *Labour Market Outlook for Ontario, 1984-88.* Toronto: 1984.

─────. Ministry of Skills Development. *Breaking New Ground: Ontario's Training Strategy.* Toronto: Queen's Printer, 1986.

─────. Ministry of Skills Development. *Building a Training System for the 1990s: A Shared Responsibility.* Toronto: Queen's Printer, 1989.

─────. Ministry of Skills Development, Labour Market Research Group. *Adjusting to Change: An Overview of Labour Market Issues in Ontario, 1988.* Toronto: 1988.

─────. Ministry of Skills Development. "Overview of the Findings of the Survey: Participation of Visible Minorities in Employer-Based Training." Toronto: the Ministry, 1989.

─────. Ministry of Skills Development. "Proposals to Create a Canada Training Allowance." Toronto: the Ministry, 1987.

─────. Ministry of the Attorney General. *Report of the Professional Organizations Committee.* Toronto: the Ministry, 1980.

─────. *Report of the Committee on the Healing Arts.* Toronto: Queen's Printer, 1970.

─────. *Report of the Royal Commission Inquiry into Civil Rights*, Vol. 3. Toronto: Queen's Printer, 1968.

─────. *Report of the Select Committee on Manpower Training.* Toronto: Ontario Legislative Assembly, 1963.

Ontario Federation of Labour. "Basic Education for Skills Training (BEST) Project Description." Toronto: the Federation, 1988.

Ontario Human Rights Commission. *Annual Report,* 1986-87. Toronto: the Commission.

─────. "Human Rights in Employment." Toronto: the Commission, May 1977.

Open Learning Agency. "B.C. Credit Bank Statement of Principles — Assessment of Non-Formal Learning." Richmond, B.C.: the Agency, 1988.

Phillips, Brigid. "Europe's Legal Revolution." *Canadian Lawyer*, April 1989, 26.

Preston, B., and J. Conklin. *Physician Quality of Care Methodologies: Review of the Literature.* Washington, D.C.: Systemetrics/McGraw-Hill, 1987.

Programs on Noncollegiate Sponsored Instruction. *Guide to Educational Programs in Noncollegiate Organizations.* Albany, N.Y.: 1978.

Ryerson Polytechnical Institute. "Action Access Transitional Education Pilot Programs in Human Services" (unpublished proposal). Toronto: Ryerson Polytechnical Institute, December 1988.

Settlement Program and Planning Committee, Subcommittee on Language Training. "Consultation Paper on the Delivery of English as a Second Language in Metropolitan Toronto." Toronto: 1981.

Shimberg, B. "Testing for Licensure and Certification." *American Psychologist* 1981 36(10): 1138-46.

Simosco, Susan (Associates). "Cumulative Certificates in Vocational Education in England and Scotland." Unpublished manuscript. Sheffield, U.K.: 1988.

Smith, Murray G. "Services." In *Free Trade: The Real Story*, edited by John Crispo. Toronto: Gage, 1988.

Spille, Henry. "Credit for Learning Gained in Military Service of Employment." *New Directions for Experiential Learning* 7 (1980): 26.

Spille, Henry, et al. "Assuring High Standards, Quality Control, and Consistency." *New Directions for Experiential Learning* 7 (1980): 9.

Thomas, Alan M. "Educational Equivalents: New Policies for Learning." Unpublished manuscript prepared for the Canadian Association for the Study of Adult Education. Calgary: May 1988.

Trans Regional Academic Mobility and Credential Evaluation. "Statement of the Interim Steering Committee." Washington, D.C.: TRACE, April 1988.

Trebilcock, Michael J., Gordon Kaiser, and J. Robert S. Prichard. "Interprovincial Restrictions on the Mobility of Resources: Goods, Capital and Labour." In *Intergovernmental Relations: Issues and Alternatives*, edited by the Ontario Economic Council. Toronto: the Council, 1977.

U.K. Department of Trade and Industry, and the Central Office of Information. *The Single Market: Europe Open for Business.* London: September 1988 (2d edition).

Wesche, M. "Second Language Testing Performance: The Ontario Test of ESL as an Example." *Language Testing* 4:1 (1987): 28-47.

Wesche, M., et al. *The Ontario Test of English as a Second Language (OTESL): A Report on the Research.* Toronto: Ontario Ministry of Education, 1977.